Inflation

Penguin Modern Economics Readings

General Editor

B. J. McCormick

Advisory Board

K. J. W. Alexander
R. W. Clower
G. R. Fisher
P. Robson
J. Spraos
H. Townsend

Inflation

Selected Readings

Edited by R. J. Ball and Peter Doyle

Penguin Books

Penguin Books Ltd, Harmondsworth,
Middlesex, England
Penguin Books Inc., 7110 Ambassador Road,
Baltimore, Maryland 21207, U.S.A.
Penguin Books Australia Ltd, Ringwood,
Victoria, Australia

First published 1969
This selection © R. J. Ball and Peter Doyle 1969
Introduction and notes © R. J. Ball and Peter Doyle 1969

Made and printed in Great Britain by
Richard Clay (The Chaucer Press) Ltd,
Bungay, Suffolk
Set in Monotype Times

Contents

Introduction

The concept of inflation has undergone considerable modification since it was first treated by the neo-classical economists. To them inflation usually meant what we would today describe as hyper-inflation, or a complete loss of confidence in the currency resulting in astronomical price rises and perhaps complete monetary collapse. It was, of course, recognized that fluctuations in trade would be expected to be accompanied by fluctuations in prices. Indeed rising prices were thought of as a sign of good times and falling prices as signs of poor trade and poor profits. But these reflected movements and adjustments are to be expected in the normal course of business. Inflation, however, was regarded as a destroying disease born out of lack of monetary control whose results undermined the rules of business, creating havoc in markets and the financial ruin of even the prudent.

Since the Second World War, however, the western industrial world has witnessed an almost unbroken rise in prices and money incomes. All this has been achieved without major panics or, to date at least, without the erosion of the rules under which the business game is played. Prices have not shown the signs of galloping away that we associate with hyperinflation but have grown steadily with some interruptions associated with variations in the pressure of demand. Indeed the experience of the period from the beginning of the Second World War to the late forties is nicely described by the title of A. J. Brown's book on the period, *The Great Inflation*. Since that time we have been accustomed to what is now sometimes described as creeping inflation.

It would not be strictly accurate to say that the concept of inflation has changed over the last forty years, but rather that many economists would now argue there are several different strains of the disease. We are no longer confined to the wild feverish strain of hyperinflation, but constantly experience the slow, strength-sapping qualities of the creeping variety. There are, however, those who still maintain a unity of diagnosis in these matters and argue that rising prices can always be traced to a failure to control the monetary bacilli. This is a view held firm by the University of Chicago but not widely shared by professional economists in general.

Principles of Selection

The literature in the field of inflation is, of course, voluminous. In the space available in this volume we have sought to present a selection of papers from that literature which with guiding comments provide a reflection of the major issues as they have developed and are seen today. In selecting such papers we have had perforce to omit a host of valuable and significant papers and books to whose authors we must apologize. Our choices as explained below, however, are constrained not only by space but also by the balance of one paper with another within the structural layout we have chosen.

There are clearly several ways of structuring the literature. The first and most obvious method is to begin with some detailed classification of possible types of inflation, for example, as set out in an early paper by Turvey [79][1] and then to group contributions to our understanding of the theory and policy relating to each type. A second approach would be a methodological one of considering the literature under the three headings of theory, applications, and policy. A third is to build up the development of thought and practice historically with some attempt to reflect the way in which the subject has developed as time has progressed.

Our own preference has been somewhat nearer to the third of the alternatives listed. We have attempted to give some picture of how thought has developed in the field in the years since the Second World War. To this we have added a special section on the econometric analysis of wages and prices. In general, we take the view that econometric analysis is simply a particular branch of applied economics and there is no case for distinguishing in general between economic and econometric papers. However, in the context of the field a considerable literature has grown up over the last ten years which has a particular unity given by the

1. All references in the introductory notes relate to the Further Reading list, pp. 380–84.

structure of the many wage–price models that have been statistically treated. This literature is now so large that we have wished to recognize it by giving some examples in a separate section.

We have started our collection with the Second World War. This choice has been made on the grounds of the opportunity cost of space. There are, of course, many interesting papers that stem from an earlier period, but we have felt that much of what is valuable in the earlier literature is reflected in more recent writings. Moreover, there is something to be said for the view that greater weight should be given to the present state of thought than to that of the very distant past. Thus, we have balanced this against our other objective, which is to trace through the extent to which patterns of thought have been modified over time. This latter objective is always a valuable one in economics since it helps at one level to put into perspective the developments in economic thinking.

We have confined our selections to those papers and books that have appeared in English. This reflects in part the potential readership that we expect the volumes in this series to have, and partly our own incapacity to deal with much of the literature that has appeared in other languages. This is not to say that there is not a valuable literature whose sources we have not adequately mined. However, institutionally we are more specifically interested in the problem of inflation as it has been viewed in Britain and the United States and our selections have been made accordingly.

The Keynesian Revolution

It is worth recalling why Keynes's major work incorporated in its title the expression 'General Theory', by which as a shorthand title it has been known ever since. It was not intended to be general in the sense that it purported to provide a complete framework for the discussion of all major macro-economic problems ranging from the determination of the level of employment to the determinants of economic growth. Indeed, since Keynes much literature has appeared on the question of what the 'Keynesian' theory of growth actually amounts to. It is still inconclusive.

What was general about the General Theory was that it provided a framework for the integration of monetary and value theory. In neo-classical economics value theory was concerned essentially with the relative valuations of goods and services and factors of production which entered into the determination of the allocation of resources. The essential element here was the focus on relative as opposed to absolute prices. Monetary theory, however, was concerned with the determination of the price level, usually starting in neo-classical economics from some version at least of the quantity theory of money. The principal concept in monetary theory was the general price level or what was sometimes referred to as the value of money. Thus, value theory was concerned with the relative values or prices of commodities and monetary theory with the absolute values of all prices or the value of money. In view of the nature of the neo-classical model of the economy, these two elements could be treated separately. At the macro-economic level the so-called real factors were part of the explanation of the level of employment, while the monetary factors simply operated to determine the general price level. Keynes's contribution to a general theory was to argue that these two results, one from value theory and one from monetary theory, were in fact related.

Thus prior to the General Theory it was implicitly assumed that the problem of inflation, as reflected in changes in the value of money, could be adequately discussed independently of the other economic variables that entered into the determination of levels of employment and real output. The particular model of the economy suggested by Keynes denied this, although there were those who argued that the Keynes conclusions only followed from the consideration of underemployment as a special case. Thus it was said that, given the level of employment as full, the neo-classical propositions concerning the relationship between the price level and the quantity of money would be restored.

The General Theory itself contains some considerable discussion of the behaviour of prices in the macro-economy, but the best known starting point for an application of Keynesian principles to the problem of inflation is to be found in a series of articles by Keynes subsequently printed as *How to Pay for the War*. The outbreak of war in 1939 resulted in a rapid reduction in the level of unemployment, as measured then, as labour was absorbed not only into the armed forces but also into wartime production. The upshot was a rapid rise in the level of money incomes accompanied, however, by a volume reduction in the consumer goods on which a large proportion of the incomes would have been spent. Just as Keynes had explained in the General Theory how the equality of income and expenditure could take place at less than full employment such that unemployment was maintained by an excess of savings over investment at the margin, so inflation could result from the fact that under certain circumstances the reverse would be true. Thus, at full employment there would be an excess of planned expenditure over income which would tend to pull prices up. This gap was christened the 'inflationary gap' and was intended after measurement to provide the basis for planning increases in taxation which were intended to remove the gap and so stabilize the general price level. (See the papers by Friedman [22] and Salant [66] for some discussion and criticism of the gap concept.) It was assumed in this analysis that full-employment prices were flexible upwards, that is that they would respond to excess demand in the market for goods. Moreover, it was thought that money wages would be sticky in the face of such rising prices and that the share of profits would rise. Thus, we had a type of demand inflation in which there was price flexibility and profit inflation. The multiplier analysis that had been used as part of the theory of employment now became a tool in the analysis of inflation. As an example of the type of analysis that emerged from this we give the paper by Holzman printed in the text (Reading 2). We also include a statement from Keynes himself (Reading 1).

This analysis of Keynes was extended in a number of ways of which we focus on two. The first is that, as pointed out, the original Keynesian version of what came to be known as demand inflation assumed flexibility in goods prices at full employment. But in industrial economies the widespread existence of oligopoly in such markets makes such prices sticky in relation to demand but highly responsive in relation to costs. Thus, it was argued that pressure of excess demand might work not by raising goods prices directly but via the increase in costs, particularly wage costs that would emerge from excess demand in factor markets. Thus, we would have a kind of derived inflation. Models of this type were extensively examined more generally allowing for both types of excess demand by Hansen [34]. For a discussion of the issue we include the paper by Turvey and Brems (Reading 3).

The second line of thought that has had lasting significance stems from the fact that in the General Theory itself Keynes stressed the relationship between prices, productivity, and costs in the shape of the money wage level. Thus, we have in a sense two approaches to the determination of the general price level arising from the Keynesian literature, the one demand and the other cost oriented. The latter aspect has been most fully urged by Weintraub [81] and the juxtaposition of the views is set out in his paper (Reading 4). The paper by Ball and Bodkin (Reading 5) is an attempt to synthesize these two apparently different approaches in a general formulation of the determination of the general price level following Keynesian principles, which treats them as interacting and giving special cases at each end of the spectrum.

The Monetary Revival

These developments along Keynesian lines did not, however, go unchallenged. Early criticism is exemplified in the paper by Morton (Reading 6). If Keynesian inflation of the first (demand) type was occurring, then it was argued this could only stem from an inappropriate monetary policy that failed to bring aggregate demand into line with aggregate supply. It was after all a monetary problem that could be solved by appropriately neo-classical monetary policies. However, the second or cost oriented analysis had led some to drop even the notion of excess demand in the factor market as an indirect cause of price rise and substitute for this a more or less exogenously determined money wage level that was forced up by the independent power of organized labour. Such a situation resembled what Hicks [36] was later to describe as being on a labour rather than a gold standard. Morton and his fellow critics argued that prices and wages were rising only because the monetary authorities in their utmost desire to maintain full employment were prepared to create the quantity of money that was appropriate to maintain full employment for any money wage level secured by the unions. Thus the authorities' action led to the creation of money in relation to the wage level rather than to the gold stock as under the gold standard.

The Keynesian analysis had relegated the quantity of money to the job of primarily determining the interest rate level. But in the fifties and after, led by Friedman there was a revival of interest in the role of the money stock in the inflationary process. The monetary group have resurrected the importance of the substitution relationship between goods and money rather than the Keynesian substitution margin between money and other assets. This issue has generated much debate and attempts have been made to discriminate between the two views.[2] A balanced view of the debate suggests that the majority of economists have not swallowed the monetary line certainly as far as recent inflation is concerned, but still rest rather uncertain as to how the monetary effect should be taken into account.

There would be more general agreement about the special role of changes in the monetary stock during hyperinflations. Historically most hyperinflations have been characterized by disruptions of a political nature (the U.S. Civil War in the South, the World Wars in Europe) which have usually had two sorts of effect. The first is a basic shock to confidence which has resulted in an exceptional gap between the demand and supply of goods. The second is the enormous creation of money by resort to the printing press in many cases carried out to finance government expenditures. In such cases the velocity of circulation also rises along with the money stock, but historically the proportionate rate of growth of the money stock has been much greater. This subject is dealt with at length by Cagan in the paper we have included (Reading 7).

Demand and Cost Inflation

The twin lines of thought that we noted earlier as springing up from the work of Keynes continued to divide economists and politicians into the present. Many in the world of banking and

2. In particular, see the papers by Friedman and Meiselman [27] and [28], and by Ando and Modigliani [1] and [2]. Also the classic paper by Friedman [24], reprinted in the companion volume on *Monetary Theory,* edited by R. W. Clower, Penguin Books (in press).

business have followed the traditional monetary line. But some of the bitterest battles have been fought among the neo-Keynesians themselves.

The reason why the conflict has been so animated is that on the surface at least the choice does lead to alternative policies which have major political import. In the middle fifties there were those who said that the continuation of inflation in Britain and the United States was due to a failure to manage aggregate demand effectively. High rates of government expenditure plus inappropriate monetary and fiscal policies were said to overheat the economies with the result that money incomes grew faster than productivity and prices rose. Thus the supporters of this view argued that a proper use of traditional instruments for controlling aggregate demand would suffice to allow for economic growth without inflation. Extremists on the other side held that the cause of rising prices was excessive monopoly power on the part of organized labour. If that is the case, they said, then traditional weapons for controlling aggregate demand are useless. Some alternative must be found.

It is of some interest to note that while both these arguments were rife in both the U.K. and the U.S.A., those who lined up behind them were quite different in origin. Thus, in the U.K. it was the 'left' who were to be found on the side of cost inflation and the 'right' in favour of traditional monetary measures. The reason for this relates to the question of central control and interference. In the U.K. the existence of cost inflation was seen as a need for organized labour to be brought more into economic management and consulted as a partner to control inflation. On the other hand the unions in the U.S.A. protested that the rise in wages they were getting simply reflected the proper pull of market forces. Big business on the other hand tended to conclude that the situation provided the grounds for legislation that would restrict union monopoly power.

Reacting to the dispute a number of economists considered the empirical evidence. The focus of the early investigations concerned the relationship between the pressure of demand as measured by unemployment and the rate of change in wage rates. In this context we include the paper by Phillips. Thus it was thought that the associations that emerged for the U.K. were evidence against the cost-push thesis. Others argued that even if wage rates were largely set institutionally plant bargaining would be directly influenced by demand pressure and would result in the phenomenon of wage drift which was common in the U.K. and Sweden [35]. The majority of these studies implicitly or explicitly accepted the phenomenon of administered pricing in the oligopolistic sector so that the effects of demand pressure were primarily related to the wage level rather than the price level directly. Some writers produced eclectic models which allowed for flexible prices in some markets and administered in others.[3] The result was a series of wage–price interaction models as exemplified in the papers of Dicks-Mireaux (Reading 16), Klein and Ball (Reading 17), and Schultz (Reading 12). There are, of course, many others and many variants which are given in the bibliography.

The Present State of Knowledge

Economics is at once the most artistic of the sciences and may hope to become the most scientific of the arts. At present it is a brave man who will define exactly what we know and what we do not know about economic behaviour. Despite this, economists, business men, and politicians must take decisions and offer advice and we cannot escape some appraisal of what our investigations and theoretical constructions lead us to. There is still much empirical work to be done and issues to be resolved. Our summing up must therefore (and will be so interpreted by those with different views) be very subjective.

The critical question initially is whether traditional (or novel) monetary and fiscal weapons alone are sufficient to make the ultimate goals of full employment and growth consistent with stable prices on average. There are still those who believe that this is possible, and that suitable monetary policies can keep the rise in incomes in line with productivity at full employment. On the basis of the empirical evidence such as it is and the general arguments propounded, such a view is not widely accepted either by professional economists or as far as one can judge by governments.

3. See the paper by Duesenberry [20].

It would appear to be accepted in most Western industrialized countries that the avoidance of excess monetary demand is a necessary but not sufficient condition for price stability. Whether this is true only in the short or medium term rather than the longer run is at present still open to question. It is clear that wages and prices can continue to rise even when the pressure of internal demand is reduced to levels that border on a major affront to social values. The monetary expansion that has financed the rising income level has been a combination of increases in the supply of nominal money and increases in the velocity of circulation. The key question in the long term is how far can the velocity of circulation continue to rise if the money supply is stabilized?

Such evidence as there is is consistent with the view that the rate at which inflation takes place in industrial countries is determined by the interaction of the balance between aggregate supply and aggregate demand and the monopoly power of organized labour. The dissenters from this view are those who, like the Chicago School, believe that this is an illusion based on a validation of union monopoly by inadequate monetary control, and those who believe that price stability can be bought at the cost of a small underutilization of resources. The latter hypothesis is usually referred to as the Paish hypothesis and we include Paish's own statement of the case (Reading 13).

It is certainly true that variations in the pressure of demand have in a number of countries, including the U.K., been correlated with the rate of inflation. This suggests that there exists some unique level of pressure as measured by the degree of capacity utilization or unemployment that will just permit money incomes to grow as fast as productivity. Our own view is that it is not possible to infer from these short-run correlations what would happen as a result of attempting to create a permanent pool of unemployment to ensure price stability. This issue is still open for debate.

In so far as it may be true that strict control over the level of demand could result in price stability, such stability may have to be bought at the cost of a socially unacceptable rate of output growth. Thus, countries have sought for alternative policies to attempt to maintain price stability at full employment which take into account the specific nature of the monopoly power of organized labour. Various attempts have been made ranging from direct legislation over short periods to the establishment of public guide lines or targets set by the authorities. At the time of writing no adequate assessment of such policies as long-term devices can be made. There is still strong scepticism as to the capacity of governments to find acceptable solutions in the form of 'incomes policies' which do not require such a control of internal demand as to make them redundant. As yet the theory of incomes policy as opposed to the desperate '*ad hoc*-ery' of practice has not come to grips with resolving some form of wage, dividend, and price control with the resource allocating function that both goods and factor prices are held to play. Inevitably interference with the direct setting of prices and wages implies interference both with the distribution of income and the allocation of resources in a direct way that has hitherto only been accepted during periods of national emergency such as wartime.

The political and theoretical issues of incomes policy as an administrative device have yet to be resolved. In addition the bulk of economists are still uncertain about the real character of the relationship between the monetary and real sectors of the economy. The papers collected in this volume bring us roughly to this point. There remains, however, much empirical and theoretical work to do before our understanding of the phenomenon of inflation can be said to be complete.

Part One The Keynesian Revolution

Whereas previously orthodox economists largely imputed
changes in the price level to changes in the quantity of money,
Keynes in *How to Pay for the War* emphasized the level of
income and expenditure as the main determinant of the price
level. Rising money incomes at full employment would, given a
constant average propensity to save, lead to an imbalance
between demand and supply and a consequent rise in prices,
unless the Government intervened to reduce the level of
disposable income. Post-war developments like that of
Holzman made use of difference equations to recast Keynesian
analysis in dynamic terms. Holzman (Reading 2) emphasizes
the redistribution of income which occurs at full employment
and the resistance of economic groups to such changes which
may cause money incomes and prices to rise to a much greater
extent than can be accounted for by multiplier analysis alone.
Another development, reflected in the work of Turvey and
Brems (Reading 3), was the consideration of the market for
factors of production in addition to the market for goods. It
is pointed out that for a full inflation there must be both a
goods and a factor gap, each involving positive excess
demand.

The major feature of the post-war debate on inflation has
been the distinction between 'demand-pull' and 'cost-push'
explanations. Weintraub (Reading 4) here provides a
theoretical rationale for this dichotomy tracing its origin to
alternative ways of interpreting the Keynesian system: the one
in terms of real output and the familiar 'Keynesian cross', the
other in terms of *ex post* and *ex ante* money demand and
supply functions. In the final paper (Reading 5) Ball and

Bodkin develop a generalized Keynesian approach to the problem of income determination which incorporates price-level effects explicitly in order to demonstrate the impact of particular policies on both real income and the price level.

1 J. M. Keynes

The Inflationary Gap

Excerpt from J. M. Keynes, *How to Pay for the War*, Macmillan and
Harcourt Brace, 1940, pp. 61–70.

[. . .]

There is no difficulty whatever in paying for the cost of the war
out of voluntary savings – provided we put up with the consequences. That is where the danger lies. A government, which has
control of the banking and currency system, can always find the
cash to pay for its purchases of home-produced goods. After
allowing for the yield of taxation and for the use of foreign
reserves to pay for the excess of imports over exports, the balance
of the Government's expenditure necessarily remains in the hands
of the public in the shape of voluntary savings. That is an arithmetical certainty; for the Government having taken the goods,
out of which a proportion of the income of the public has been
earned, there is nothing on which this proportion of income can
be spent. If prices go up, the extra receipts swell someone's
income, so that there is just as much left over as before. This
argument is of such importance and so little understood that it is
worth our while to follow it out in detail.

Let us suppose that the value of the output[1] of the country is
£5500 million at pre-war prices, that individual incomes (including transfer payments) come to £6000 million, that the yield of
taxation is £1400 million, that we supplement our own output by
importing £350 million more than we export paid for out of
foreign reserves or overseas loans, and that the expenditure of the
Government, also reckoned at pre-war prices, is £2750 million,
i.e. £2250 million excluding transfer payments. After deducting
£1400 million which they pay in taxation, individuals are left

1. I am taking round figures in the neighbourhood of the facts. But I
simplify the illustration by ignoring the depletion of capital as a source to
meet government expenditure.

with £4600 million which they are free to spend if they choose. But, since the Government has already purchased £2250 million of the output, there is only £3250 (£5500 — £2250) million of goods (valued at pre-war prices) left for the public to buy with their remaining incomes of £4600 million. Now if the public voluntarily save £1350 million, that is to say the whole of the difference between their incomes of £4600 million and the value of the available goods, namely, £3250, at pre-war prices, obviously the problem is solved. There will be just the right amount of goods available to satisfy the demand without any rise of prices.

But, if in these circumstances, the public do not choose to save so much as £1350 million, does the system of financing the war by voluntary savings break down? Certainly not. For in the last war we used the voluntary system successfully; yet, since prices rose more steeply than wages, it follows that the readiness of the public to save cannot have been sufficient to satisfy the above conditions. What happens then? How is the paradox explained?

Let us suppose that, instead of saving the necessary £1350 million, the voluntary savings of the public are, in the first instance, only £700 million, and that they try to spend the rest of their incomes, namely £3900 million, on goods worth only £3250 million at pre-war prices. Obviously prices will have to rise 20 per cent which will equate supply and demand; for the goods will then be worth £3900 (£3250 + £650) million, which is just equal to the desired expenditure. Moreover, those who have sold for £3900 million goods which only cost them £3250 million will have the balance of £650 million left over as extra unspent income, just the amount the Government requires.

It soon appears, however, that this only solves the problem momentarily. For we have no reason to expect that the whole of the unspent windfall profits of £650 million will represent permanent savings. A certain time will elapse before this sum reaches those who will be entitled to spend it. But in the next innings, so to speak, it will be added to the total of potentially spendable incomes, so that we shall have incomes of £5250 million (£4600 + £650) facing goods which, after allowing for the continuance of the 20 per cent price rise, are only worth £3900 million. Moreover, it will be impossible for the Government to keep down the prices of its own purchases if open market prices have risen 20 per cent. Thus we shall soon find ourselves in much the same position as before with a substantial discrepancy between the amount of money which the public are preparing to spend and the value (at the new price level, 20 per cent higher than before) of the goods available for them to buy. A further rise in prices will be required to provide a temporary respite, and so on.

Fortunately this is not a complete picture of the second chapter of the story. If it were, the voluntary savings system would *not* have been successful, and we should be faced with a progressive inflation of prices without limit. Yet this is not what happened in the last war. And it is not likely to happen this time, even if we pursue the same policy of depending on voluntary savings.

What, then, is the actual course of events? The initial rise in prices will relate to goods which were produced at the lower pre-war price level, and the resulting profits will belong, as we have seen, to the owners of these goods. That is to say, aggregate incomes will indeed rise by £650 million (apart from the effect of any rise in the price of goods bought by the Government), but not everyone's income will rise in the same proportion, if at all. The initial increase of income will mainly belong to a limited class of individuals and of trading and manufacturing companies, whom (without intending any insult, for it is by no fault or intention of theirs) we can call for short 'the profiteers'. Now the profiteers are liable to a very high rate of taxation, both on account of excess profits tax and because many of them will be rich enough to be liable to a high rate of income tax and surtax. Thus the profiteers become, so to speak, tax collectors for the Treasury. More than half (more than three-quarters in some cases)[2] of the £650 million will become payable as taxes. Moreover, it is likely that a considerable proportion of the balance will be voluntarily saved; not so much because the recipients, being relatively rich, will save more readily, but because the profits will largely belong to companies which will be disinclined, for various reasons, to distribute the bulk of them in higher dividends but will prefer in the circumstances to save them on behalf of their shareholders. Thus, in fact, only a small part of the £650 million

2. E.P.T. + Income Tax is 75 per cent, and E.P.T. + Income Tax + Surtax on incomes of £5000 is 83·5 per cent of the increased income.

(or of this figure augmented by such higher prices as the Government may pay for its own purposes) will come on the consumption market in the second innings. Instead of another 20 per cent rise of prices being required to preserve equilibrium, it may be that a rise of 2 or 3 per cent would be sufficient. In this case a modest increase of taxation on the general public will be sufficient to offset the increased consumption of the profiteers, and avoid the necessity (if it were not for what follows in a moment) for any further rise of prices beyond the initial 20 per cent.

Unfortunately this is not yet the complete story; for we have now gone to the other extreme, having slipped in an assumption much less troublesome than the facts. We have assumed that, in spite of the rise of 20 per cent in prices, workers are content with the same money wages as before; so that the profiteers continue to make a profit of £650 million in the second innings and to act as tax collectors for the Treasury on the same scale as before without the aid of any further rise in prices. But in fact the workers will press for higher wages – with at least partial success. For employers will put up much less resistance than usual to a rise in wages. The scarcity of labour will force them to agree if they are to retain their men; and, since the Government is taking away in taxation 75 per cent of their excess profits, it will not cost them much to share their profiteering with their employees and their salaried staff. If, indeed, wages and other money costs were to go up fully in proportion to the cost of living, we should be faced, as before, with an unlimited inflation, proceeding by 20 per cent at each step – the process generally known as the vicious spiral.

But we still have one more card to play. Some costs are fixed by law or by contract, so that the *rentier* and pensioner class who have fixed money incomes cannot escape the sacrifice. Wage adjustments and the like take time. It takes time, and sometimes a considerable time, before adjustments are made even when the pressure is sufficient to make them inevitable sooner or later. It is these time-lags and other impediments which come to the rescue. Wars do not last for ever. Wages and other costs will chase prices upwards, but nevertheless prices will always (on the above assumptions) keep 20 per cent ahead. However much wages are increased, the act of spending these wages will always push prices this much in advance. If at the end of six months wages and other costs have risen by an average of 10 per cent, prices will have risen 32 per cent (120 per cent of 110). If at the end of two years costs have risen 40 per cent, prices will have risen 68 per cent (120 per cent of 140). Thus, after all, the system of voluntary savings will have worked successfully. That is to say, the money will have been raised 'voluntarily' without an unlimited increase of prices. The only condition for its success is that prices should rise relatively to wages to the extent necessary to divert the right amount of working class and other incomes into the hands of the profiteers and thence into the hands of the Treasury, largely in the form of taxes and partly in the form of extra voluntary savings by the profiteers.

The larger the amount of voluntary savings at each stage, the better, of course, it will be for everyone. If the campaign of the National Savings movement increases the volume of voluntary savings, the necessary rise in prices relative to wages will be correspondingly smaller. Let us go back to our arithmetical illustration. We started with an excess of spendable incomes, over the available supply of consumption goods valued at pre-war prices, amounting to £1350 million and we assumed that £700 million of this was voluntarily saved. This left £650 million, or 20 per cent more than the available supply of goods at pre-war prices. But if the National Savings movement were to be successful in increasing the amount of the voluntary savings by (say) another £100 million, making £800 million altogether instead of £700 million, then the excess of spendable incomes is reduced to £550 million or about 17 per cent above the available supply at pre-war prices. In this case we can reach equilibrium with a rise in prices only 17 per cent (instead of 20 per cent) in excess of the rise in wages and other costs.

Thus an increase in voluntary savings is entirely beneficial. There is nothing to be said against it, except its inadequacy. The question for the individual is whether he would prefer to become £2 richer by deferment of pay, and have no inflation of prices or become £1 richer by voluntary savings, and suffer inflation with its evil social consequences. For the individual (unless he belongs to the profit-making class) the answer is surely obvious. He is certain to gain by the system of deferment. It is like asking him whether he would prefer to have a compulsory rule of the road with few accidents and no traffic congestion, or a voluntary rule with many accidents and much traffic congestion.

For the Treasury and for future taxpayers the answer is not so obvious. A system of deferment of pay – and equally, a system of highly successful voluntary savings – will leave us with a larger national debt measured in terms of real value, than if we adopt the method of imperfectly successful voluntary savings supplemented by inflation. For inflation is a mighty tax gatherer. But the Treasury and the taxpayer of the future need only remain in doubt if they expect the price level reached by inflation to continue permanently. For the national debt under the inflationary system is likely to be larger in terms of money than under the system of compulsory savings; so that if prices subsequently fall back, the benefits of inflation will have proved illusory even to the Treasury.

Thus it is quite true that, in the last resort, the amount of saving necessary to balance the expenditure of the Government after allowing for the yield of taxation can always be obtained by 'voluntary' savings. But whether this is a good name for it is a matter of taste. It is a method of *compulsorily* converting the appropriate part of the earnings of the worker which *he* does not save voluntarily into the voluntary savings (and taxation) of the entrepreneur. 'We shall depend on the voluntary system' is another way of saying 'We shall depend on inflation to the extent that is necessary'. Sir Robert Kindersley in his savings campaign could justly argue as follows:

The Government needs the money. But this is a free country. Someone, therefore, must save it voluntarily. If you (and your friends) do not do so, the necessary amount will be taken compulsorily from the real value of your earnings through the action of higher prices and handed to the profiteer; and *he* will save it voluntarily (such part as he does not pay in compulsory taxes). In this way we shall avoid any departure, which would be anathema to the city, from the voluntary system.

Ambiguous though this may be, as a defence of the principles of liberty, it would be a sound and convincing argument to the worker in favour of increased saving if it were not for one flaw. An individual cannot by saving more protect himself from the consequences of inflation if others do not follow his example; just as he cannot protect himself from accidents by obeying the rule of the road if others disregard it. We have here the perfect opportunity for social action, where everyone can be protected by making a certain rule of behaviour universal.

[. . .]

2 F. D. Holzman

Income Determination in Inflation

F. D. Holzman, 'Income determination in open inflation', *Review of Economics and Statistics*, vol. 32 (1950), pp. 150–58.

A new analytical approach is needed in the explanation of the determination of money income and prices in periods of inflation. It will be the thesis of this paper that the multiplier technique, which is useful in the analysis of income determination in periods of underemployment, is not adequate in periods of full employment and inflation. The multiplier technique, as used, abstracts from changes in the distribution of income. In periods of underemployment it may not be too unrealistic to assume that the distribution of income does not change with changes in income: net increases in demand (or investment) lead to greater employment which automatically increases wages; profits increase by virtue of additional output; in other words, it is possible to increase the real income of the workers and owners simultaneously and perhaps, but not necessarily, close to proportionately. In many instances, of course, increments to demand will be expressed in price rises. But with resources not fully utilized, the possibility of increased employment always exists and will usually be realized, at least in part. At full employment the situation is different: *the share of one group in the national output can only be increased at the expense of another.*[1] Resistance by economic groups to loss of real income which comes about through differential cost–price rises, rather than the multiplier process of the Keynesian approach, is the dynamic element in the inflationary process. The importance of this factor is commonly recognized by economists, particularly in its most familiar

1. Aside from increases in productivity. Sectors in which labor bottlenecks occur may be considered areas of full employment under conditions of general underemployment.

manifestation: the wage–profit–price spiral.[2] To my knowledge it has received little systematic or quantitative treatment.[3]

I

At full employment the multiplier approach has serious limitations. If the aggregate demand for the output of the community should be increased or released (in any of the ways mentioned below), the immediate effect would be to raise prices and profits, since all resources are already fully employed. Some increase in wages might occur due to competition by different industries for labor. The increase in wages is not, however, likely to be so great as that in profits.[4] The distribution of income would shift at this point in favor of profits, and real wages would tend to decline. If labor should accept a decrease in real income, the multiplier approach could be used theoretically[5] to predict the successive levels of money income resulting from an initial increase in net investment.[6] If the marginal propensity to consume were constant and equal to one, the level of income resulting from a single increment in investment would be maintained in each succeeding period. If the marginal propensity to consume were less than one,

2. Several clear examples of the wage–price spiral are to be found in contemporary economies. In France, wage and price rises have been closely associated. For example, the decontrol in 1948 of the price of meat, an essential element in the French workers' cost of living, led to a demand for, and rise in, wages which was followed by still higher prices. In the United States, though less spectacularly, price rises also have been followed by pressure for wage increases which have in turn been passed on, in large part, in the form of higher prices. In Great Britain, in February 1948, as an essential part of the anti-inflation program, wages, profits, and prices were frozen (with minor exceptions) in recognition of the danger of spiral inflation.

3. Related articles are: Koopmans (1942), Smithies (1942). See also Turvey (1949). This article appeared after the present article had been accepted for publication. For brilliant analytic description of the process of inflation in Germany after World War I see Robinson (1938).

4. It can be assumed that any substantial increase in wages arising from a shift in demand can be passed on in price rises, for if this were not true, workers would not have been bid away in the first instance.

5. Abstracting from leaks.

6. Although it might be necessary to revise the value of the multiplier periodically to account for the effect of successive changes in the distribution of income.

income would gradually decline until it was at its original level, at which point intended savings and investment would again be equal.

Let us suppose, however, that the workers decide to fight for wage rises to offset rising prices, and owners raise prices again to offset the wage rises. Clearly, considerations will have been introduced affecting the level of money income which are completely exogenous to the multiplier analysis. As will be demonstrated below, money income may be raised to much higher levels without additional increments to demand.[7] The inflationary process which results from the struggle for shares in national output will be designated the 'redistribution-of-income' effect.

The process of wage–price inflation can be analysed by the use of two conceptual devices, viz. the inflationary shock and the reaction of the economy to the shock. An inflationary shock is here defined as anything which will increase some of the prices or costs in the economy more than others and thereby redistribute the real income of the community.[8]

Examples of possible inflationary shocks are: exchange depreciation, budgetary deficit, a rise of net investment above anticipated net savings, discontinuance of subsidies or price controls, large-scale dis-saving, etc. An inflationary shock which changes the distribution of income is not a sufficient condition to set off a *continuing* or *dynamic* process, however. It is also necessary that the power of the various economic groups be such that the new distribution of income be unstable, i.e. that reactions occur. If the new distribution of income should be stable, the

7. Goodwin (1947). Dr Goodwin derives a formula for a full employment multiplier which is larger than the ordinary value of the multiplier because of the inelasticity of supply at full employment. This multiplier theoretically would give the correct value for the increment to income resulting from investment in excess of anticipated savings but would not account for increments to income associated with the 'redistribution-of-income' effect.

8. A shock which would increase all costs and prices proportionately and with the same speed is a special case in which the distribution of income would remain the same, and according to our definition would not be considered inflationary. The mere fact of price rise is insufficient for a shock to be considered inflationary. If all prices and costs should increase in proportion, no one would experience a change in the relationship between the level of prices and his money income. Real consumption and saving would presumably remain unchanged.

level of money income would remain the same or decline (depending on the value of the marginal propensity to consume) in the absence of additional inflationary shocks.[9] If the new distribution of income should be unstable, money income would continue to increase by virtue of the reactions discussed below.

The reactions comprise the economic adjustments which take place following the shock, i.e. the action taken by groups whose real income has fallen with the rise of prices to recoup some part of their loss, and the continuing succession of reactions to re-actions which may follow. Some forms which the reactions might take are the following:

(a) If prices have risen, workers might strike or bargain for higher wages, i.e. indirectly increasing real income by obtaining a larger share of money income. If wages cannot be increased, asset holdings may be liquidated or borrowing may take place.

(b) If industrial prices should rise, interested groups may force a rise in agricultural prices. Under certain circumstances, farmers may withhold output from the market, increasing their own consumption of agricultural commodities, or bartering them for industrial goods. This is a direct method of maintaining a share of real income in contrast to the indirect method of increasing real income by increasing money income.

(c) In the case of exchange rate depreciation, prices of both exports and imports would rise. The rise in export prices would be accompanied by higher profits which might induce the workers in these industries to ask for higher wages. The rise in import prices would tend to raise the domestic cost structure to the extent that imports are used in further production. To offset this increase in cost, entrepreneurs are likely to raise prices; this in turn would stimulate the workers to ask for wage increases and the farmers to raise the price of agricultural goods.

This paper will concentrate on the wage–profit–price spiral as an example of the inflationary pressures generated by changes in the distribution of income *between* and *within* all economic groups.

9. This would be strictly true only in the simplest Keynesian models, of course. The introduction of expectations or of investment as a function of income could cause further increases in money income without additional shocks.

To simplify the analysis, problems of mobility of the factors of production, changes in productivity and output, and expectations, will be abstracted from; the supply of money and credit it assumed to be nonrestrictive.

II

The essence of the wage–profit–price spiral at full employment necessarily lies in the reactions and practices of the workers (the union movement) with respect to their standard of living and to price changes, and of owners with respect to changes in demand, cost, and prices. It will be assumed in the models below that workers react only when their standard of living relative to that of other groups is affected. In other words, if prices other than wages should rise, workers would strive for wage increases.

Initially it will be assumed that prices and profits have risen due to the presence in the economy of excess demand or what we have termed an inflationary shock. After the initial shock, the assumption will be made that the pricing policy of entrepreneurs is based entirely on a cost mark-up system; that demand will function only as a permissive, but not a price-determining, factor. Since output will remain constant, the mark-up or profit equation (see equations 3 and 8 below) will also determine money national income.[10]

10. (a) This description of the pricing mechanism is supported by the results of several studies. See, for example, the N.B.E.R. Committee on Price Determination (1943). On p. 283: '... various versions of the "full cost principle" are used by a large number of firms as a basis for pricing, at least in periods of good business. ...' Hall and Hitch (1939), as a result of their study, conclude: '... there is a strong tendency among business men to fix prices directly at a level which they regard as their "full cost". ... Prices so fixed ... will be changed if there is a significant change in wage or raw material costs, but not in response to moderate or temporary shifts in demand. ...' For criticism of this position, see Machlup (1946).

The case for cost mark-up is strengthened in periods in which wage–price inflation is in process. Entrepreneurs would find it almost impossible to estimate the change in price appropriate to the increase in wages from the demand side, although strong incentive would exist to pass on wage increases by raising prices. The writer recognizes that in the relatively competitive sectors of the economy, such as agriculture, price would continue to be determined by demand and supply. In order to explore the formal properties

More specifically, in the first model it will be assumed that entrepreneurs pass on wage increases in the form of price increases to maintain an *absolute* level of profits. This could be considered a short-run normal-profit rule of thumb under conditions in which prices are not rising too rapidly. In model 2, the case will be examined in which a *percentage* mark-up system is employed. This could be the situation under conditions of more rapidly rising prices, since an absolute level of money profits would in this case represent a declining level of real profits.[11]

Model 1

Let money national income (Y_0) be distributed between wages ($W_0 = \alpha Y_0$), profits and dividends ($Q_0 = \beta Y_0$), and a residual

---

of the redistribution-of-income effect, the models which follow will abstract from this part of the problem.

(b) With regard to demand functioning as a permissive factor, it should be recalled that this paper is concerned with economies suffering from strong inflationary pressures such as experienced by the European belligerents after World War II. Demand is not likely to have a restrictive effect in these countries, with their heavy real backlogs for both investment and consumption goods. With regard to overdemand, it may be reasoned either that the initial shock raises prices and profits to the full extent of the excess demand or, alternatively, that additional increments of excess demand constitute additional shocks.

(c) It should be emphasized that the monetary value of the contribution to the national output of an economic unit can be determined by the impact of demand on price (i.e. multiplier-determined) *or* by the entrepreneur's reaction to changes in his costs – but not by both in the same instance. The absence of the marginal propensity to consume from the models presented below results from our simplifying assumption that all prices are based on a cost mark-up system and that demand is permissive.

A concrete example is that of the automobile industry in post-war United States (or any industry in which queues exist). It is obvious here that price has not been determined by demand or the queues would have disappeared. It would be incorrect therefore to estimate the changes in money income generated in the automobile industry on the basis of the demand for automobiles since demand remains unfulfilled.

11. The controversy between adherents of full-cost and marginal-cost pricing, respectively, is not an issue here. The controversy is concerned with pricing policy under conditions of changing output. As noted above it is assumed here that output remains constant and that only the basic wage rate changes. Hence marginal cost is not involved.

$(R_0 = (1 - \alpha - \beta)Y_0)$ comprising mainly rent, royalties, and interest. Thus:

$$Y_t = W_t + Q_t + R_t. \qquad 1$$

We will denote by η the ratio of money-wage rise to price (income) rise or $\dfrac{W_t/W_0}{Y_t/Y_0}$. This coefficient indicates the ability of labor to recapture income lost by price rise. For example, if $\eta = 1$, labor is able to raise wages proportionally to price rises; if $\eta < 1$, the real income of the workers falls; if $\eta > 1$, their real income rises. It would appear reasonable to expect some time to elapse before the workers are able to force a rise in wages in response to a rise in prices. Therefore it will be assumed that the wage rise occurs in the period following the price (income) rise. Thus:

$$W_t = \alpha\eta Y_{t-1}. \qquad 2$$

We will denote by γ the proportion of the absolute increase in wages which the owners will pass on in the form of price rises. If $\gamma = 1$, all wage increases will be passed on to prices. For example, if wages should increase by 8 per cent, and they constitute one half of costs, prices would be advanced by 4 per cent. It will be assumed that the profits adjustment occurs immediately (in the same period) following the wage rise:

$$Q_t = Q_{t-1} + \gamma - 1(W_t - W_{t-1}). \qquad 3$$

It will be assumed that the recipients of rents, royalties, and interest do not attempt to change their money incomes (consequently, as prices rise, the real income of these distributive shares will decline):

$$R_t = R_0. \qquad 4$$

As mentioned above, no change in output will occur – hence increases in money income will represent increases in prices. Solving the system represented by equations 1, 2, 3, and 4 results in the equation which represents the first model and by which successive changes in money income, hence prices, can be calculated:[12]

$$Y_t = Y_{t-1} + \alpha\eta\gamma(Y_{t-1} - Y_{t-1}).$$ 5

The general solution is:

$$Y_t = \frac{AY_0 - Y_1}{A - 1} + \frac{Y_1 - Y_0}{A - 1}A^t,$$ 6

where $\alpha\eta\gamma$ is designated by A.

For purposes of illustration, the following values can be assigned to the variables mentioned above: $\alpha = 0\cdot6$, $\beta = 0\cdot3$, $(1 - \alpha - \beta) = 0\cdot1$, $\eta = 1$, $\gamma = 1$, $Y_0 = 100$, x (shock) = 10.

These values of our variables mean that national income is distributed as 60 per cent in wages, 30 per cent in profits and dividends, and 10 per cent in rent, royalties, and interest. These values are not far from the actual post-war percentages in the United States. It is assumed also that workers maintain real income ($\eta = 1$) and owners pass on all wage increases as price increases ($\gamma = 1$). The data in Table 1 indicate the changes that occur in money income (and prices) and distributive shares as the result of the initial inflationary shock and the consequent redistribution-of-income effect.

12. From equation 2:

$W_t = W_{t-1} + \alpha\eta(Y_{t-1} - Y_{t-2})$.

Substituting in equation 3:

$Q_t = Q_{t-1} + \alpha\eta\gamma(Y_{t-1} - Y_{t-2}) - \alpha\eta\,(Y_{t-1} - Y_{t-2})$.

From equation 4:

$R_1 = R_{t-1}$.

Adding:

$Y_t = Y_{t-1} + \alpha\eta\gamma(Y_{t-1} - Y_{t-2})$.

It is interesting to note that equation 5 is also the solution of a system in which equations 1 and 4 remain unchanged but where the wage adjustment is assumed to be instantaneous and the profits adjustment to lag by one period as follows:

$W_t = \alpha\eta\,Y_t.$ 2a

$Q_t = Q_{t-1} + \gamma\,(W_{t-1} - W_{t-2}) - (W_t - W_{t-1}).$ 3a

Table 1

t	Y	=	W	+	Q	+	R
Equilibrium	100		60		30		10
Shock	110		60		40		10
Period 1	116		66		40		10
2	119·6		69·6		40		10
3	121·8		71·8		40		10
4	123·1		73·1		40		10
5	123·9		73·9		40		10
,	,		,		,		,
,	,		,		,		,
∞	125		75		40		10

The table indicates that money income rises until it achieves an increase (relative to the previous equilibrium level) two and a half times greater than the increment due to the primary impact of the shock. This is extremely significant. If the shock had been an increase in investment over savings, and if the marginal propensity to consume were as high as unity, income would have risen only to 110. Hence, with a value for $\alpha\eta\gamma$ of 0·6, the redistribution-of-income effect results in a much larger increase in money national income than the multiplier, given a marginal propensity to consume of one.

A second significant result is that in spite of the fact that labor succeeds in maintaining real income, and all wage increases are passed on in price rises, the model is not explosive. Equilibrium is approached[13] after six rounds of wage–price rises (henceforth to be called periods). At equilibrium all the variables are at the values which satisfy the conditions of the model: money wages are still 0·6 of total money income; the absolute level of profits

13. Approaching equilibrium is defined here as the position reached when: ΔY actual $\div \Delta Y$ total = 0·95. Calling this quotient ϕ, the number of periods required to approach equilibrium can be calculated by:
$$t_e = \frac{\log(1-\phi)}{\log\alpha\eta\gamma} \text{ (see Goodwin, 1947, p. 491)}.$$

has been maintained at a level of 40 reached after the shock;[14] the rentiers continue to receive the same level of money income which now represents about a 20 per cent decline in real income.

The proportion that wages and salaries are of national income varies from nation to nation depending on industrial productivity, stock of capital, importance of tertiary industries, and of agricultural population, etc. In the United States and the United Kingdom, wages and salaries constitute between 60 and 70 per cent of income. On the other hand, in Canada the proportion appears to lie between 50 and 60 per cent, in France it is probably closer to 40 per cent. The importance of this factor (α) in the reaction is simple to determine. If we assume that $\eta = 1$, $\gamma = 1$, $Y_0 = 100$, $x = 10$, the results shown in Table 2 are obtained by varying α.

Table 2

α	Y_∞	t_e*
0·7	133·3	9
0·6	125	6
0·5	120	5
0·4	116·7	4
0·3	114·2	3

* See footnote 13.

It is clear that, *ceteris paribus*, the larger the wage share, the higher prices will rise and the greater the number of periods required for the economic system to approach equilibrium. Of course, as the wage share becomes very small, it is reasonable to presume that the structure of the economy will be such that the

14. If we had assumed $\eta \neq 1$, $\gamma \neq 1$, equilibrium values for wages and profits would be derived as follows:

$$W_\infty = W_0 + \alpha\eta x + (\alpha\eta)^2\gamma x + (\alpha\eta)^3\gamma^2 x + \ldots$$
$$= W_0 + \alpha\eta x \left[1 + \alpha\eta\gamma + (\alpha\eta\gamma)^2 + (\alpha\eta\gamma)^3 + \ldots\right]$$
$$= W_0 + \frac{\alpha\eta x}{1 - \alpha\eta\gamma}$$

Similarly:

$$Q_\infty = Q_0 + \frac{(1 - \alpha\eta)x}{1 - \alpha\eta\gamma}$$

reaction will involve not just wages and profits (including agricultural profits) but instead that the main conflict would probably
ensue between the agricultural and industrial sectors with perhaps
a subconflict in the industrial sector between wages and profits.

If we now assume varying values for η, the ability of labor to
recapture its share of real income (i.e. raise money wages), a
more complete picture of the importance of the wage factor in the
inflationary spiral can be ascertained. The results obtained from
varying η, while keeping $\alpha = 0.5$, $\gamma = 1$, $Y_0 = 100$, $x = 10$, are
given in Table 3.

Table 3

η	Y_∞	t_e*
1·4	133·3	9
1·2	125	6
1·0	120	5
0·8	116·7	4
0·6	114·2	3

* See footnote 13.

It is obvious that varying η operates similarly to varying α,
that is the higher the value of η, the higher the equilibrium level of
money income and the more periods required to approach this
level. This is easily seen from the formula from which the equilibrium level of income is calculated:

$$Y_\infty = Y_0 + \frac{x}{1 - \alpha\eta\gamma}.^{15} \qquad 7$$

The importance of labor in the spiral is really measured by the
product $\alpha\eta$, i.e. the size of the wage share multiplied by the ability
of the labor movement to keep wage rates rising with prices.

It is clear from equations 5 and 6 that the key to the size and
length of the spiral process is given by the product $\alpha\eta\gamma$ or A. It

15. From equation 5:
$$Y_\infty - Y_0 = \frac{AY_0 - Y_1}{A - 1} - \left(\frac{AY_0 - Y_1}{A - 1} + \frac{Y_1 - Y_0}{A - 1}\right)$$
$$= \frac{Y_1 - Y_0}{1 - A}$$
where $A = \alpha\eta\gamma$ and $Y_1 - Y_0 = x$.

should be noted that although the economic significance of each of the variables is different, the importance and position of each in the model is identical. The process is explosive if $\alpha\eta\gamma \geqq 1$ and gradually achieves smaller proportions as $\alpha\eta\gamma < 1$ and declines toward 0. Under no conditions would this model oscillate. It is also clear that the size of the shock will not affect the stability of the system. The level of money income and prices at which equilibrium is reached will be proportional to the size of the shock, however.

Since α is unlikely to exceed 0·7 in any country, the importance of labor as a contributing factor to instability will be small unless η is high. Examination of past inflations shows that real wages usually decline as prices rise, or where an increase in real output occurs, labor's proportional share in the national income declines. Therefore, it may be assumed that $\alpha\eta < 0.7$. In this case the model would not be explosive unless the entrepreneurs should increase prices by more than 43 per cent above the amount necessary to pass on wage rises. Of course, in any actual situation $\alpha\eta\gamma$ could be less than one, and the wage–price spiral maintained with undiminished speed if additional shocks occurred before the reactions to the previous shocks had diminished to any great extent.

Model 2

Let us examine the case in which price policy is directed to maintaining profits at a certain percentage relation to the average costs (or price) of the firm. It will be assumed that employers try to maintain profits at the percentage (to be denoted by β'[16]) of total costs which it is immediately after the initial shock. The profits equation is:

$$Q_t = \frac{\beta'}{1 - \beta'} (W_t + R_t). \qquad 8$$

Solving the system represented by equations 1, 2, 4, and 8 results in the formula of the second model:

$$Y_t = Y_{t-1} + \frac{\alpha\eta}{1 - \beta'} (Y_{t-1} - Y_{t-2}).[17] \qquad 9$$

16. $\beta' = \dfrac{Q_0 + x}{P_0 + x}$.

17. Derivation similar to that of equation 5 above.

The general solution is:

$$Y_t = \frac{mY_0 - Y_1}{m - 1} + \frac{Y_1 - Y_0}{m - 1} m_t \qquad 10$$

designating $\frac{\alpha\eta}{1 - \beta'}$ by m.

By substituting in equation 10, the equation for obtaining the new equilibrium level of income is derived:

$$Y_\infty = Y_0 + \frac{x}{1 - \alpha\eta/(1 - \beta')}. \qquad 11$$

For purposes of comparison let us assume the same values for the variables as in the first case under model 1 ($\alpha = 0\cdot6$, $\beta = 0\cdot3$, $\eta = 1$, $Y_0 = 100$, $x = 10$), replacing γ by β' which has a value of 4/11. Substituting, we obtain the changes in money income and the distributive shares that are given in Table 4.

Table 4

t	Y	$=$	W	$+$	Q	$+$	R
Equilibrium	100		60		30		10
Shock	110		60		40		10
Period 1	119·3		66		43·3		10
2	128·2		71·6		46·6		10
3	137·0		77·2		49·8		10
4	144·9		82·2		52·7		10
'	'		'		'		'
'	'		'		'		'
∞	275		165		100		10

In this case, the increase in income is seventeen and a half times the increase due to the initial shock, and equilibrium is approached only after forty periods have elapsed. In the analogous case in model 1, money income rose two and a half times, and six periods were needed to approach equilibrium. The critical importance of the pricing policy of the entrepreneurs is apparent from this comparison. If owners employ percentage mark-up, thereby keeping the index of profits rising with the index of costs, the model becomes considerably less stable. It is clear from the equations that the model is explosive when $\frac{\alpha\eta}{1 - \beta'} \geqq 1$ or $\alpha\eta + \beta' \geqq 1$. In other words, if the sum of the shares of real income which labor and ownership are implicitly trying to obtain is greater than the actual level of real income, prices and money income will be driven up indefinitely in the struggle. When $\alpha\eta + \beta' < 1$, the level of income at which equilibrium will be reached will be finite, and will decline as $\alpha\eta + \beta'$ declines. Under no circumstances will the system oscillate.

The importance of the passive sector of the population is very apparent here. If R is a large percentage of the national income or if a large percentage of the workers or owners do not participate in the wage–profit–price struggle, a stable system ($\alpha\eta + \beta' < 1$) is much more likely to result. In fact, the system reaches equilibrium only when the real income of the passive sector has declined sufficiently to allow the postulated increases in real income of the active sectors to occur. This factor is very important in operating for stability in model 1 also.

The principal remaining difference between models 1 and 2 is that in the former the size of the shock had no effect on stability, whereas in the latter it does affect stability since it is one of the factors determining the size of β'. In the above case, if the shock were of the magnitude $\frac{Y_0}{6}$, β' would be equal to 0·4 and the model would be explosive.

III

Complications could be introduced into the above models *ad infinitum*. For example, it would be simple to demonstrate the effect of the upward pressure of wages at full employment, a problem which concerned Joan Robinson in connection with the question of stability at full employment.[18] The initial rise in price would result from labor's demand for a wage increase due to its

18. Robinson (1937), p. 5: 'When employment stands above the upper critical level, then, if conditions are such that a general rise in money wages sets up no reaction to reduce effective demand, there will be a progressive rise in wages with a constant level of employment, for prices and profits will rise with money wages and all the circumstances which led to a first rise in wages will remain in force and lead to a second.'

increased bargaining strength at full employment. It could be demonstrated that the model is not necessarily explosive as Mrs Robinson seems to assume.[19]

The effect of the practice in some industries of tying wages to a cost of living index could also be demonstrated by use of the foregoing models although refinements would be necessary for realistic results.[20] In the later stages of hyperinflation (e.g. in Germany and the U.S.S.R. after World War I), wages have frequently been tied to price indices in those instances in which payments were not already being made in kind, although in most cases wage payments lagged behind anyway.

In addition, some of the restrictive assumptions used in this paper should and can be relaxed: for example, adjustments should be made for changes in productivity and output;[21] the effect of expectations of further price rises on actions of the workers and owners should be taken into account;[22] etc.

The redistribution-of-income effect throws light on current economic questions and should be used more frequently and systematically in economic analysis. For example, the debate as to whether nations should leave their inflations 'open' or 'repress' them is principally concerned with a comparison of the economic waste which is likely to occur under each set of conditions viewed rather statically. An important and sometimes decisive question for nations faced with such a decision, but a question rarely raised in theoretical discussions is: can a nation with repressed inflation remove controls without becoming involved in hyperinflation? (no one, to my knowledge, has ever defended hyperinflation). To answer this question would require among other things a knowledge of factors discussed in this paper.

Frequently, of course, the above question is not posed, but the direction of action is determined by politico-economic forces. In

19. Ibid. This is later qualified by consideration of the inelasticity of credit, the rate of interest, and factors related to foreign trade accounts. However, these variables need not be introduced for stability.

20. In Denmark wages are tied to the cost of living (1948).

21. When prices are rising rapidly, the quantity of goods on markets may decline due to speculative hoarding and higher consumption by producers, thereby offsetting increases in productivity and output.

22. In a hyperinflation, expectations may exert a predominant influence on price changes.

those countries which have labor governments (e.g. Great Britain), repressed inflation will be preferred because labor appears to suffer most from open inflation; conversely, where industry holds the balance of power, a degree of open inflation will usually be preferred. Run-away inflation is most likely to occur, *ceteris paribus*, in countries in which either labor or the farmers are economically and numerically strong enough to put up a struggle for their share of real income should there be open inflation, but not strong enough politically to legislate the proper controls to repress it.

Another problem which the mechanism under discussion throws light on, as has already been recognized,[23] is whether or not large profits have a stabilizing effect in periods of full employment and inflation. Thinking in Keynesian terms has led some economists to contend that large profits are a stabilizing factor since they tend to raise the propensity to save.[24] It should be clear, however, from the models discussed above that it is necessary to consider the impact of rising profits not only on the saving function but on the redistribution-of-income effect as well. Changes in the values of η and γ in periods of inflation are apt to be much greater than the corresponding changes in the marginal propensity to consume. Furthermore, as was demonstrated above, the redistribution-of-income effect leads to a greater change in money income than the multiplier under similar conditions (viz, the same amount of shock and identical changes in the marginal propensity to consume and $\alpha\eta\gamma$). For these reasons, large profits may play a strongly destabilizing role in inflation.

IV

In conclusion, the purpose of this paper was to call attention to the importance of the redistribution-of-income effect in the deter-

23. For example, see Harris (1948): 'If profits are too high, their excess becomes a voluble excuse on the part of the trade-union officials, who are always under pressure to obtain wage concessions, to demand further increases . . .'

24. For example, see Haberler (1948), p. 12: '. . . using an argument advanced by Keynes in his *How to Pay for the War*, it must be concluded that the emergence of higher profits is a consequence of inflation which is likely to dampen the inflationary surge, because a comparatively large percentage of profits is saved . . .'

mination of money income and prices in inflation,[25] of the need for its use in economic analysis, and to attempt a preliminary study of its formal properties. The models, simple[26] as they are, and the accompanying analysis, appear to warrant some tentative conclusions:

(1) In periods of full employment and inflation, the redistribution-of-income effect may cause money income and prices to rise to a much greater extent than can be accounted for by multiplier analysis alone. In the absence of periodic shocks, however, it does not appear too probable that the redistribution-of-income effect, of itself, would cause a hyperinflation. To get instability it would probably be necessary to introduce the effect of the price rises on expectations.

(2) If an economy should be exposed to periodic shocks, however, as well as a redistribution-of-income effect, it may experience hyperinflation in the absence of controls. Therefore, if its farmers or workers are very strong economically, a nation which has a large backlog of necessary investment (for example) may not be able to afford the luxury of open inflation without running a serious risk of inducing hyperinflation.

(3) The type of mark-up system employed by entrepreneurs is significant for the wage–price spiral. Under similar conditions, the percentage mark-up of the second model resulted in a much greater increase in money income than the absolute mark-up of the first model.

(4) The larger the passive sector of the population, the less the price and income rise from a shock of given magnitude. In fact, in the case of a single shock, instability would occur only when the active participants in the wage–price spiral attempt to secure real income in excess of total national income, i.e. when by their efforts to increase money income, they implicitly attempt to expropriate the rentiers and other passive elements of a greater share of real income than the latter possess.

25. For example, in a recent symposium on inflation ('Ten Economists on the Inflation', *Review of Economics and Statistics*, February 1948, pp. 1–29), only two of the ten economists contributing mentioned the phenomenon under discussion.

26. In addition to the restrictive assumptions used, no consideration was taken of possible leaks.

(5) Large profits will be inflationary rather than deflationary at full employment if, as appears probable in many countries, the dampening effect of a higher savings function is more than offset by the redistribution-of-income effect which may result.

References

GOODWIN, R. M. (1947), 'The multiplier' in S. E. Harris (ed.), *The New Economics*, New York; Knopf, pp. 495–8.

HABERLER, G. (1948), 'Causes and cures of Inflation', *Review of Economies and Statistics*, vol. 30, pp. 10–14.

HALL, R. L., and HITCH, C. J. (1939), 'Price theory and business behaviour', *Oxford Economic Papers*, vol. 2, pp. 12–45.

HARRIS, S. E. (1948), *Statement Before the Joint Congressional Committee on the Economic Report*, 6 December.

KOOPMANS, T. (1942), 'The dynamics of inflation', *Review of Economics and Statistics*, vol. 24, pp. 53–65.

MACHLUP, F. (1946), 'Marginal analysis and empirical research', *American Economic Review*, vol. 36, no. 4, pp. 519–54.

N.B.E.R. Committee on Price Determination (1943), *Cost Behaviour and Price Policy*, National Bureau of Economic Research, Columbia.

ROBINSON, J. (1937), *Essays in the Theory of Employment*, Blackwell.

ROBINSON, J. (1938), 'Review of *The Economics of Inflation* by Bresciani-Turroni', *Economic Journal*, vol. 48, pp. 507–13.

SMITHIES, A. (1942), 'The behaviour of money national income under inflationary conditions', *Quarterly Journal of Economics*, vol. 56, pp. 113–29.

TURVEY, R. (1949), 'Period analysis and inflation', *Economica*, vol. 16, pp. 218–28.

3 R. Turvey and H. Brems

Factor and Goods Markets

R. Turvey and H. Brems, 'The factor and goods markets', *Economica*, vol. 18 (1951), pp. 57–68.

In recent years a number of connected aspects of income theory have been discussed separately. Professor Goodwin (1949) has shown how the Keynesian multiplier can be generalized to what he calls a matrix multiplier. Professor Metzler (1948) has explained how the different ways in which *ex post* equality of Saving and Investment is brought about are related to the different lags in the circular flow of income. A Danish writer, Grünbaum (1945), has pointed out some important inadequacies of analysis in terms of saving and investment. The present paper endeavours to show how all these contributions fit together.[1]

I

In macroeconomic analysis we consolidate groups of producers, income-recipients and so on into sectors which we treat as units. The transactions internal to sectors are ignored, and only those between sectors are taken into account. The fewer the sectors the simpler will the analysis be, and the simplest macroeconomic model possible is one consisting of two sectors only. Here we shall aim at the maximum simplicity.

The most obvious division to make is then that between producers and consumers. We shall therefore consider a closed economy where there is neither government revenue nor expenditure, consisting of a 'business' sector and a 'factor' or 'household' sector. In this system, apart from financial transactions which we shall not consider, two kinds of transactions take place. Firstly, households buy goods from business (consumption) and secondly business makes payments to households (personal

1. We are indebted to Professor Meade, Mr Day and Mr Graaf for helpful discussion on a number of points.

income) in the form of wages, salaries, rent, interest, and dividends. Since there is but one household sector we lump all these payments together and for convenience call them 'purchase' of factors from households. Thus, ignoring the capital market, there are two markets: a goods market and a factor market.[2]

The relation of factor sales and goods sales to national income is shown by the following definitional equations:

Personal income = sale of factors = purchase of factors.

Consumption = purchase of goods = sale of goods.

Gross national product = Gross investment + consumption
= personal income + gross business saving.

Using the symbols we shall employ these can be rewritten:

Personal income = $S_f = P_f$.   1

Consumption = $P_g = S_g$.   2

$$Y = I + P_g = S_f + \text{gross business saving. } 3$$

In order to explain the determination of income we need a factor purchase function and a goods purchase (consumption) function. We shall assume that both are linear in order to be able to present our model algebraically as well as geometrically. For the consumption function we write:

$$P_g = H + hS_f \qquad 4$$

where H and h are constants, the latter being households' marginal propensity to consume with respect to personal income.

For the factor purchase function we write:

$$P_f = B + bY \qquad 5$$

where B and b are constants, the latter being the marginal propensity of business to purchase factors with respect to value of output. Its meaning may be best explained by an imaginary example: suppose that when Y rises by £100 an extra £50 has to

2. In terms of Leontief's system we are considering a two-row two-column matrix. Much of what follows is a special case of Professor Goodwin's matrix where $n = 2$ and we have tried to make the presentation intelligible to non-mathematicians.

be spent on labour to provide the necessary increase in output and that the increase in profit (fall in loss) of £50 is reflected in an increase in dividend payments of £30, then b is 0.8.[3]

b is *not* the marginal cost of production of consumption goods to the business sector as a whole (or to the final producer) since it refers to money value of output, not to a physical unit of product. Furthermore, even for a given price and output, $£b$ is not the marginal cost of that quantity of goods which is priced at £1 for two reasons. Firstly it includes marginal dividend payments. Secondly if advertising expenditure is related to sales[4] b will include the factor purchase corresponding to marginal advertising expenditure.

B includes all those purchases of factors which do not vary with output. It thus consists of the payment by business to households of rent, interest, and overhead wages and salaries. Since the analysis is short-run, B is constant.

Three problems arise at this point, concerning the purchase functions. The first is that it is extremely unlikely that they can be represented by straight lines, b, for example, will probably vary with output. For example, if output is very low so that business is incurring losses, a rise in output may, since it reduces losses rather than increases profits, lead to no increase in dividends, while at a high level of output dividends may be considerably increased. It remains true, however, that any stretch can be approximated by a linear function, and in any case we have assumed linearity only to aid in exposition.[5]

Secondly we have the aggregation problem. In order to derive a determinate consumption function for households as a whole we must assume either that the distribution of income between them is constant or is a function of the level of personal income or that all households have the same marginal propensity to con-

3. In other words $(1 - b)$ is the marginal propensity of the business sector to save with respect to gross national income. Its magnitude depends upon the marginal relation of profits to value of output and the marginal relation of dividend payments to profits.

4. Recent surveys reveal a strong tendency for advertising expenditure to bear a fixed relation to sales in many industries. Compare Jastram (1949).

5. Straight-line functions may be kinked. It is reasonable, for example, to assume that dividends equal half profits but unreasonable to assume that when losses are being made shareholders pay money to their firm!

sume, h. Analogous assumptions have to be made with regard to the purchase functions of businesses.[6]

Thirdly the values of b and h will depend on the proportions in which an increment of national income is composed of price increase and quantity increase. We shall assume unchanging prices, so that our model describes a Kalecki-like world where marginal costs and gross profit margins are alike constant and our multiplier is a 'quantity multiplier' with constant prices.[7]

Having made these reservations we now turn to the static solution of our model. Starting from:

$$Y = I + P_g \qquad\qquad 3$$

we substitute for P_g according to equation 4, getting:

$$Y = I + H + hS_f.$$

Since, from equation 1, $S_f = P_f$ we can substitute equation 5 into this, giving

$$Y = I + H + hB + hbY$$

so
$$Y = \frac{I + H + hB}{1 - hb}. \qquad\qquad 6$$

This tells us that the level of gross national product depends on two sets of factors: the 'injections' of the two sectors (I, B, and

6. In this case the problem is more complicated, since businesses not only buy factors from households but also buy one-another's products. Two simple solutions may be mentioned here:

(a) The marginal propensity to save of all businesses is assumed to be zero so that if Y increases by x factor purchases increase by x whatever its composition as between different products. If we understand Goodwin rightly he has shown (1949, pp. 541–3) that this is implicitly done in the Keynesian system. It has the disadvantage of ignoring 'the phenomena of internal financing, of the failure to disburse earnings, of heavy fixed charges and of the payment of dividends above current earnings' (p. 543).

(b) The marginal propensity of any business to purchase factors or any raw material is assumed to be the same as that of any other business. It is difficult to conceive of a system fulfilling this condition as consisting of anything other than a number of exactly similar firms all producing the same good. Thus this 'solution' of the problem amounts to assuming it away by postulating a one-commodity world.

7. The theory of open inflation is largely the study of 'price multipliers' with constant quantities.

H) and the marginal propensities to spend of the two sectors (b and h).

It will help in understanding this system if we contrast it with the customary Keynesian-type formula:

$$Y = \frac{I + K}{1 - c} \qquad\qquad 7$$

where Y and I are, as before, gross national product and gross investment respectively, while:

$$\text{Consumption} = K + cY$$

so that K is the constant term in the Keynesian consumption function and c is the marginal propensity to consume with respect to gross national product. Because:

$$K = H + hB \qquad\qquad 8$$

and

$$c = hb \qquad\qquad 9$$

equations 6 and 7 give the same result. Equation 8 shows that the constant term in the Keynesian consumption function is composed of two parts: the constant term in our goods purchase function and the constant term in the factor purchase function multiplied by the marginal propensity to consume with respect to personal income. Equation 9 shows that the latter marginal propensity is only the same as the marginal propensity to consume with respect to gross national income when the marginal propensity to save of the business sector is zero.

Both of these differences derive from our distinction between the factor and goods markets from which follows our separation of the two purchase functions and the corresponding separation of household and business saving. We believe that all this makes income theory along the lines of our model more understandable since the connexion between the macroeconomic functions and the theory of the firm is made much more evident than it is in the Keynesian approach. Furthermore, we believe that our two-sector model is of definite analytical value as we shall proceed to show by considering three problems.

II

Firstly, consider the direct part[8] in income generation played by rent, interest payments and other overheads. This comes out clearly in equation 6, since they all enter into B. Let us suppose that the level of rents is revised upwards against business. Unless the effect is to cause some firms to cease activity, B will rise correspondingly. For any given gross national product this will mean an equal fall in the profits of business and consequently a reduction in dividends (a fall in b).[9] It may well be, however, that the dividends corresponding to that level are reduced by a smaller amount so that there is a net expansionary effect: the fall in b does not quite offset the rise in B, and consequently the equilibrium level of national income is increased.

This sort of consideration has some relevance to problems of growth. If gross investment exceeds maintenance and replacement, B will expand over time even if gross investment is constant, for rents will rise and the new capacity will have overhead labour costs and may have to bear some interest charges. Whether or not b will fall sufficiently to compensate is an open question, depending upon several factors such as the capital intensity of the new investment, the debenture–equity ratio and the rate of interest.

III

Equation 8 shows that even if consumption be a constant proportion of personal income ($H = 0$) the Keynesian consumption function relating consumption to gross national income must necessarily have a constant term equal to hB. Consideration of the items composing B indicates that this constant term is of very considerable magnitude. Its existence is important in the analysis of the effects of a general wage change as we shall now briefly demonstrate.

Let us suppose that all wage rates and the prices of all goods currently produced fall by 10 per cent. Gross investment will then

8. i.e. as distinct from their effect on the inducement to invest.

9. b may fall not only because of a decrease in the profits-output function but also because the dividend-profit function will probably fall; the rise in overhead costs may lead firms to accumulate more reserves than they would otherwise have done.

fall by 10 per cent but B will fall by a much smaller percentage since only a minor part of it consists of wage payments and in the short run interest charges and rents can be assumed constant. Consequently the multiplicand, $I + hB$[10] will fall by less than 10 per cent. With a constant multiplier national income will also fall by less than 10 per cent in monetary terms and thus rise in real terms. We conclude that even when there is no money illusion on the part of households, when real investment remains unchanged and h does not alter, a general wage cut will expand employment in a closed economy.[11]

IV

In the third application of our model we turn to dynamic analysis and show that the separation of the factor and goods markets throws some light upon the saving–investment problem and the time sequence of a multiplier effect. We shall use the period approach, so that all magnitudes must be interpreted *ex ante* and *ex post*,[12] and we shall assume the plan revision periods of business and households to be coterminous and coincident.

The factor purchase function now gives the factor purchases planned for a period as a function of the value of the output planned for that period. This is equal to the sum of the planned investment and the expected consumption sales for that period. The goods purchase function relates planned consumption to expected personal income. There are two equilibrium conditions, one for each market. Planned factor purchase must equal expected factor sales and planned purchase of goods must equal expected sale of goods.

10. H is assumed to be zero. This means that it is indifferent whether we take h to refer to real or money income and therefore that the value of h will not be affected by the price fall. It is possible that b will fall however.

11. Tobin (1947) and Witteveen (1947, pp. 43–5) have shown that a constant money term in the Keynesian consumption function will produce an increase in employment when wages fall, but both authors seem to attribute this possibility only to money illusion on the part of households.

12. That we talk of magnitudes and not schedules as regards, for example, *ex ante* purchases means that we are using what Lindahl calls the 'disequilibrium method' (1939, p. 60). For a diagrammatic exposition of the equilibrium and disequilibrium methods with reference to the goods market see Turvey (1949). For a discussion of the length of the period see section I of Brems (1944).

Now the requirement for equilibrium is usually stated as the single condition that *ex ante* investment must equal *ex ante* saving. What is the connexion between this and our two conditions? To answer this we must define the difference between (gross) investment and (gross) saving in terms of our system:

Investment = that part of gross national product not sold to households

$$= Y - S_g$$

Saving = household saving + business saving

$$= S_f - P_g + Y - P_f$$

so:

Investment − saving

$$= Y - S_g - S_f + P_g - Y + P_f$$
$$= (P_f - S_f) + (P_g - S_g) \qquad\qquad 10$$

which is true both *ex ante* and *ex post*.[13] Using the terminology suggested by Bent Hansen[14] we can rewrite this as:

$$\text{Investment} - \text{saving} = \text{factor gap} + \text{goods gap.} \qquad 11$$

Now our equilibrium conditions mean that both gaps must be zero *ex ante*. If they are so then *ex ante* investment will equal *ex ante* saving. On the other hand, *ex ante* equality of investment and saving only means that the *sum* of the gaps is zero. It is thus evident that the customary condition is necessary, but not sufficient. Period analysis can only be carried on in terms of investment and saving if it is assumed either that the factor gap is always zero or that the goods gap is always zero.[15]

This point is, of course, only one aspect of the general problem

13. Equation 10 and much of the argument immediately following it is taken from Grünbaum's excellent article (1945).

14. In a work on the theory of inflation which is not yet published. In the first few chapters Hansen has developed and applied Grünbaum's ideas to the analysis of suppressed inflation. The present paper is therefore confined to the case where both factor and goods markets are buyers' markets and we thus assume throughout that purchase plans are realized, i.e. that P_f and P_g are the same *ex post* as *ex ante*. This obviously excludes suppressed inflation from our analysis.

15. The reader will observe that some of the points in the following analysis have also been made by Professor Hansen (1950).

of aggregation for, to take an example, a goods gap of zero is quite consistent with the existence of an excess supply of trombones and an equal excess demand for ear plugs. If there are n sectors there will be n markets and n equilibrium conditions, and to concentrate on only two of them is a gross simplification. It is nevertheless true, however, that a macroeconomic model must contain *at least* two sectors[16] and therefore at least two equilibrium conditions, and it seems reasonable to take the division of the economy into producers and consumers as being the most important of the many possible divisions, at least for short-run analysis.

Returning to the relation between *ex ante* investment minus saving and the two gaps, we must point out that if *both* the expected sale of goods and the expected sale of factors are above (below) their equilibrium level saving *ex ante* will exceed (be less than) *ex ante* investment.[17] In spite of this, however, as some simple examples will show, analysis in terms of saving and investment is inadequate. Besides our assumption that purchase plans are always realized, we shall postulate 'Robertsonian' sales expectations (i.e. the sales expected for any period equal the *ex post* sales of the preceding period) and assume that production

16. Since transactions internal to a sector are ignored, there would be nothing to analyse in a one-sector model.

17. We can show this as follows:

Let:
ΔS_f = expected S_f minus equilibrium S_f.
ΔP_f = planned P_f minus equilibrium P_f.
ΔS_g = expected S_g minus equilibrium S_g.
ΔP_g = planned P_g minus equilibrium P_g.

Since in equilibrium both gaps are zero, we can rewrite equation 10 as:

$$\text{Investment} - \text{saving} = (\Delta P_f - \Delta S_f) + (\Delta P_g - \Delta S_g). \qquad 12$$

From equations 4 and 5 we get:

$$\Delta P_g = h\Delta S_f$$
$$\Delta P_f = b\Delta S_g \qquad \text{(Investment being given),}$$

and substitution into equation 12 gives:

$$\text{Investment} - \text{Saving} = (b\Delta S_g - \Delta S_f) + (h\Delta S_f - \Delta S_g)$$
$$= (b-1)\Delta S_g + (h-1)\Delta S_f.$$

Since b and h will normally both be less than unity, this shows that if both ΔS_g and ΔS_f are negative investment must exceed saving *ex ante* and vice versa.

equals expected sales of goods thus ignoring the effects of inventory changes.[18]

Suppose that investment and saving are equal *ex ante*, but that there is a positive goods gap and an (equal) negative factor gap. Then *ex post*, business will have sold more than expected, while personal income will be less than expected. In the following period, therefore, planned purchase of goods will fall while sales expected will rise so that a negative goods gap may appear. Similarly the factor gap may become positive, though it need not necessarily be equal in absolute value to the goods gap. Thus the initial equality of investment and saving means very little.[19]

Again, suppose that expected sales of both goods and factors are above their equilibrium levels so that saving exceeds investment *ex ante*. This situation is quite compatible with the presence of a positive goods gap (smaller in absolute terms than the negative factor gap). This means that sales of goods *ex post* must exceed the expectations of business so that their sales expectations and production planned for the following period will be revised upwards. Thus production will increase, although it should be reduced in order to reach equilibrium.[20]

The connexion between the factor and goods gaps on the one hand and saving and investment on the other hand can be further examined by discussing a multiplier process, and to do this we shall use a diagram. In order to explain the diagram let us temporarily ignore the dashed lines and consider an initial equilibrium position where $Y = OZ$ and the diagram gives the geometric solution of equations 1 to 5.

Let us start with the SW quadrant. Planned production being OZ the factor purchase function shows that planned factor purchase is OX. Since we are assuming full equilibrium, expected

18. On this matter see Metzler's (1941) article on inventory cycles where, however, only the goods market is considered.

19. For other reasons why *ex ante* equality may not mean stability see *inter alia* pp. 141–2 of Lutz (1962), Grünbaum (1945, section V), and the last part of Schneider (1942).

20. Equilibrium will be reached in a series of oscillations of a length of two periods. This can be seen by carrying on the analysis verbally, by using the diagrammatic technique shown below, or by constructing a difference equation. Goodwin has shown that with many sectors, each with a one-period lag, many different patterns of movement can occur.

factor sales will also equal OX. With an expected personal income of OX the consumption function in the NE quadrant shows that planned purchase of goods is OV. Adding planned investment, I, we get a total of OZ which is equal to planned production.

Now suppose that in period 1 planned investment increases from I to I' so that the curve in the NW quadrant (showing planned production as equal to expected sales to households plus

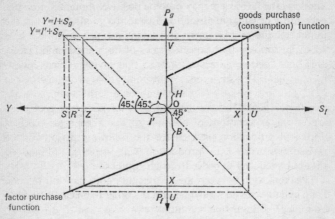

Figure 1

planned investment) shifts to the left by $(I' - I)$. Assuming that the businesses which wish to increase investment are not the same as the businesses which produce the necessary capital goods so that the rise in investment demand is unexpected, a goods gap will arise of SZ and this is equal to the excess of *ex ante* investment over saving since planned factor purchase and expected factor sales are both OX. *Ex post* the goods gap will be closed and investment made equal to saving by unintended disinvestment (unexpected sales to investing businesses) of SZ.

In period 2 planned production will be OS, since we are assuming Robertsonian expectations and neglecting stock replacement. Planned factor purchase will therefore be OU. Expected factor sales, however, is only OX (equal to the personal income received in period 1) so there will be a factor gap of XU. Since expected personal income is unchanged at OX, planned consumption will be unchanged at OV and adding to this the same planned investment of I gives a total of OS equal to planned production. Thus in period 2 the goods gap is zero and there is a factor gap of XU equal to the *ex ante* excess of investment over saving. *Ex post* the factor gap will be closed and saving made equal to investment by an unexpected personal income increase (unintended household saving) of XU.

The argument continues along the same lines [21] for succeeding periods until full equilibrium is reached – theoretically after an infinite number of periods.

Since period 3 is qualitatively the same as period 1 it appears that the 'income generation period' equals two of our periods. The former, however, is customarily subdivided into three lags: [22]

(i) The income–spending lag
(ii) The spending–production lag
(iii) The production–income lag.

Metzler has shown [23] that (i) is the Robertsonian lag and that (ii) is the Lundbergian lag. But (i) is also equivalent to the plan revision period of households and (ii) to the plan revision period of business, while in our system the lag (iii) is zero because we have assumed that the factor purchase corresponding to the production of any period is made during that period.

Now the assumption of correct expectations gives the same result as the assumption of a zero lag. Thus we can say that our multiplier is Robertsonian under the special assumption that business anticipates goods sales correctly, in which case the goods gap is always zero and the excess of investment over saving *ex ante* equals the factor gap. *Ex post* equality is then brought about by unintended saving. [24] Alternatively, our multiplier is Lundbergian [25] under the special assumption that households always anticipate their income correctly so that the factor gap is always

21. Thus in period 3 there will be a goods gap of RS.
22. cf. Metzler (1948) and Turvey (1948) where the relationship of the income-generation period to the income velocity of active cash balances is discussed.
23. op. cit., section III.
24. cf. Metzler: op. cit., p. 18.
25. We have, however, not brought in stock replacement as Lundberg does. Cf. Metzler: op. cit., p. 19.

zero and the excess of investment over saving *ex ante* equals the goods gap. *Ex post* equality is then brought about by unintended disinvestment.

V

What we have done in this paper is to follow a suggestion made by Professor Ohlin in his review of Professor Lindahl's *Studies in the Theory of Money and Capital* (Ohlin, 1941). It has been shown by Professor Lindahl (1939, p. 127) and by Professor Palander[26] that a difference between *ex ante* investment and *ex ante* saving can only exist if buyers' and sellers' expectations with regard to the purchase both of goods and factors of production are divergent. This led Professor Ohlin to say:

The method of regarding a difference between total planned saving and total planned new investment as the factor generating processes of expansion and contraction is thus for several reasons not particularly practical. It is simpler and better to ask: How do purchases for consumption purposes and purchases for business purposes develop from one period to another? (op. cit., p. 181).

We have constructed a simple model along the lines suggested by Ohlin as an alternative to the usual saving–investment approach. In doing so we have endeavoured to build upon the contributions of Grünbaum, Goodwin, Metzler, Hansen, and others, as cited above, applying the analysis to three problems.

26. In his review of Myrdal (*Ekonomisk Tidskrift*, 1941, fn. pp. 124–6). Neither he nor Lindahl, however, went on to draw Grünbaum's conclusions.

References

BREMS, H. (1944), 'Om Stockholmskolen Begreber og Metoder', *Ekonomisk Tidskrift*, vol. 46, no. 1, pp. 40–55.

GOODWIN, R. M. (1949), 'The multiplier as matrix', *Economic Journal*, vol. 59, pp. 537–55.

GRÜNBAUM, I. (1945), 'Inkongruente Forvetninger og Begnebet Monetaer Ligevaegt', *Nationaløkonomisk Tidsskrift*, vol. 47, no. 1, pp. 46–51.

HANSEN, A. H. (1950), 'The Robertsonian and Swedish systems of period analysis', *Review of Economics and Statistics*, 32, no. 1, pp. 24–9.

JASTRAM, R. W. (1949), 'Advertising outlays under oligopoly', *Review of Economics and Statistics*, vol. 31, no. 2, pp. 106–9.

LINDAHL, E. R. (1939), *Studies in the Theory of Money Capital*, Allen & Unwin.

LUTZ, F. A. (1962), 'The Outcome of the Saving Investment Discussion' in F. A. Lutz and L. W. Mints (eds.), *Readings in Business Cycle Theory*, Allen & Unwin, pp. 267–76.

METZLER, L. A. (1941), *Review of Economic Statistics*.

METZLER, L. A. (1948), 'Three lags in the circular flow of income' in L. A. Metzler (ed.), *Income, Employment and Public Policy*, New York; Norton, pp. 171–89.

OHLIN, B. (1941), 'Professor Lindahl om Dynamisk Teori', *Ekonomisk Tidskrift*, vol. 43, no. 2, pp. 171–81.

SCHNEIDER, L. (1942), 'Opsparing og Investering i et Lukket Samfund', *Nationaløkonomisk Tidsskrift*, vol. 44, no. 2, pp. 81–92.

TOBIN, J. (1947), 'Money wage rates and employment' in S. E. Harris (ed.), *The New Economics*, New York; Knopf, pp. 583–5.

TURVEY, R. (1948), 'The multiplier', *Economica*, vol. 15, no. 3, pp. 81–92.

TURVEY, R. (1949), 'A further note on the inflationary gap', *Ekonomisk Tidskrift*, vol. 51, no. 2, pp. 92–7.

WITTEEVEN, H. J. (1947), *Loonshoogte en Werkgelegenheid*, Haarlem; Bohn.

4 S. Weintraub

Two Views on Inflation

S. Weintraub, 'The Keynesian theory of inflation: the two faces of Janus?' *International Economic Review*, vol. I (1960), pp. 143–55.

Considering the high unanimity with which writers of the Keynesian stamp approach problems of total employment and aggregate output, it is somewhat odd and baffling that on the great practical problem of the decade now closing, specifically, the inflation issue, their views have split them into separate camps of 'demand pull' and 'cost push', or some uneasy amalgam of the two, as with varying intensity they have examined the always partial and inconclusive empirical evidence. On the inflationary subject, I think that differences have tended to submerge likenesses, so that we have an unaccustomed array of opponents in the intellectual arena.

A 'school' in dispute is obviously an interesting spectacle and must expect to draw attention to its plight. At the same time, the split intellectual personality that I think I detect on this one great issue is undoubtedly capable of generating new contradictions over time on other problems of greater or lesser importance.

In this paper I am not mainly concerned with the question of which of the two major inflation doctrines best fits the facts, or whether both should not be scrapped in favor of renewed emphasis on monetary factors and a Fisher-type equation of exchange. I have expressed myself elsewhere on this general subject (Weintraub, 1959) and have little more to add to it at this time. What concerns me is a more fascinating theoretical, or methodological and philosophical matter, to wit, why economists who agree that the cure for unemployment is to use remedies stemming from the theory of the consumption function, the investment function, and the rate of interest, should find themselves at loggerheads and arrive at an impasse when it comes to an analysis of inflation and the price level. It is the origin of this Janus-head on inflation, the two voices from one source, that I should like to unravel in the following pages. Perhaps greater clarity on the theoretical plane will help sharpen the important issues with which the present generation of economists must learn to cope.

At the outset I should like to state firmly that I believe this 'muddle in the middle' is more of the making of Keynesians than of Keynes himself; I think I 'know' what Keynes would have emphasized, but I refrain from any attempt at documentation, for it is equally possible for those who hold alternative views to find appropriate supporting passages in Keynes's *General Theory* or his later discussion in *How to Pay for the War* to sanction their doctrinal interpretation. If nothing else, this demonstration of different brands of Keynesianism, which have often been thought of as fully substitutable wares, discloses that there may be new rifts brewing under the quiet façade which may establish divergences in directions currently unsuspected.

One further prefatory remark is in order. I have refrained from identifying proponents of the conflicting views and from identifying them with analytic error for several reasons. In the first place, some parts of the very imposing theoretical edifice have now become common property at the elementary and teaching level, so that, if I am right, the error is widespread. Second, much of this apparatus was constructed without this special problem in view, so that some interpretation is necessary; it is a hard matter to disentangle the price level analyses embodied in even the most rigorous versions of the theory. Third, it has happened that with what I regard as the natural apparatus of 'excess demand' and 'demand pull' – using these terms synonymously – some of the technicians may, and do, adopt a 'cost-push' posture in approaching public policy, and *vice versa*. None of us are entirely free of such contradictions within our theoretical structures, and so more than the usual pains would have been required to make sure that the personifications were not unfair. In any event, it is the split personality in ideas among the school, not the 'error' of individuals, that I want to explore.[1]

1. Originally, as I began to document this paper, I found that the footnote discussion was far outrunning the textual material, and to little or no purpose. On reconsideration and in asking constantly whether the minor thumbnail analyses were fair to the authors I decided to present merely the major ideas.

1. The 45° Line and the Keynesian Equilibrium Cross

The dominant brand of Keynesian analysis, it can be said without fear of contradiction, runs in terms of the 45-degree line bisecting the coordinate field containing the familiar and assorted paraphernalia of consumption function and investment magnitude. I shall examine this diagram in a moment and, as it can be found in practically every modern-day textbook, the examination can be brief. It is this apparatus, with its associated real income equilibrium determination, which has been compared in importance with the demand and supply curves of price theory, and the equilibrium 'cross' of the one identified as equivalent in principle to the equilibrium intersection of the other.

Used somewhat less frequently, and emanating from Professor Hicks' masterly exposition many years ago, are the pair of *IS* and *LM* curves which are supposed to give more generality to the argument by showing the simultaneous macroeconomic adjustment of aggregate output and the rate of interest.[2] Both approaches – and both are really the same for my present purposes, for each rests on the same real output basis – represent the main wing of neo-Keynesian analysis and are equally regarded as Keynesian economics, pure and simple or profound and unadulterated. They have come to occupy a complete teaching tradition, at least in this country, and perhaps through the world, in view of the world-wide dissemination of American textbooks. The ideas may well constitute a fairly universal version of Keynesian economics.

In Figure 1 there is drawn the diagram of the 45° cross which typifies this tradition. The 45° bisector represents the potential equilibrium relationships in a diagram in which real income or real output, measured horizontally and denoted by Y, is associated with real outlay in the form of consumption expenditures C and investment outlay I, also in real terms, and measured vertically. Note that all quantities are in real terms; that is, C, I, and Y are money sums measured in constant dollars. Changing price level phenomena are thus completely eliminated from the picture; real magnitudes alone provide the focus of attention.

2. Professor Hansen (1949) has probably taught us most about this approach which still remains above the elementary textbook level.

The diagram, as drawn, contains the now commonplace figure of the consumption function, lettered C^*, and has superimposed on it a constant sum of real investment (as in the more typical expositions) to comprise the real outlay function $C^* + I^*$. The equilibrium intersection is at a volume of real output equal to Y^*. Here $Y^* = C^* + I^*$, so that macroequilibrium prevails.

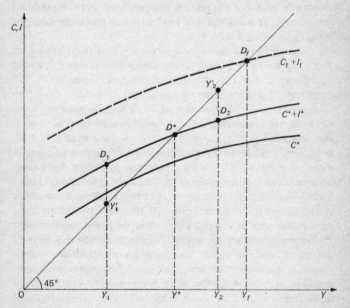

Figure 1

Suppose that full employment output is located at position Y_f. Clearly, an aggregate demand $C^* + I^*$ is inadequate and real output at Y^* is too low, carrying unemployment with it. Usually, the familiar gamut of measures of fiscal policy and monetary maneuvers are recommended to snap the economy out of the unemployment doldrums unless exogenous factors are believed to be in the offing to accomplish the same objective without deeper government intervention. In general, an equilibrium output level to the left of Y_f is described as a deflationary situation of unemployment, ripe for government intervention and compensatory public policy of weak or strong degree in order to lift aggregate demand to $C_f + I_f$.

It is well that we follow the reasoning of the 'stability analysis' by which Y^* is described as the 'equilibrium position'. Suppose that somehow actual output settled at Y_1. Aggregate demand in real terms, it would be explained, would amount to D_1Y_1, an amount in excess of the real output produced $Y_1Y'_1$ by the real difference D_1Y_1 *minus* $Y_1Y'_1$. Would this mean that there would be some incipient 'inflation'?

I think the usual answer would be *yes*, that the D_1Y_1 minus $Y_1Y'_1$ gap would constitute 'excess demand' and that this would be inflationary, so that the system would be driven to the Y^* output level. The peculiar nature of this 'inflation' should be observed. *It is an inflation that does not have, or need not have, any price rise, inasmuch as all of the analysis is cast in real terms so that, presumably, the price level at Y_1 is the same as at Y^*, at Y_2, at Y_f, etc. Price levels are excluded from the analysis*, as being in some way incidental, so that only through some back-door approach can they be brought in. The only valid interpretation of the disequilibrium position at Y_1 is that if output temporarily settled here in some 'round' of production, there would be 'inflation' in the sense of inventory decumulation at the constant price level, equal in amount to the $D_1Y'_1$ discrepancy. The run-down of inventory holdings would constitute an expansionary phenomenon, and a production advance toward the equilibrium 'cross' would be in order.[3] Likewise, at an output level of Y_2 there would be an 'unwarranted' or 'unintended' inventory accumulation of Y'_2D_2, so that pressures would be apparent to drive real output back to Y^*. Deflationary forces would thus start the output cutback and unemployment train.

Other than the minor 'inflation' analysed as part of the stability analysis, the interesting question is how a truly inflationary process would be analysed by Keynesians using this approach. I think that the majority of Keynesians would argue that in inflation what must be happening is a parametric rise in the $C + I$

3. It is surprising to learn that often there is no discussion of the 'stability conditions'. The stronger versions do run in the terms indicated, and properly so, of inventory accumulation and decumulation at nonequilibrium positions.

curve to a position well above the 'full employment equilibrium' function $C_f + I_f$, drawn as a dashed line in Figure 1, so that true 'excess demand' and 'demand pull' materializes in the system, with demands for real output outrunning the capacity of the system to satisfy it. As output cannot be expanded once full employment is reached, they would argue that prices would have to give way. From an analysis of this nature the Keynesians would conclude that the necessary policy steps to avoid a more alarming price level outbreak would be to choke off 'excess demand' or the 'demand pull' by monetary and fiscal means, or some combination of the two. (Those who take a less serious view of the durability and buoyancy of the demand forces would probably countenance learning to live with 'creeping inflation', as a minor price of full employment.)

Where do money wage rates enter the picture? Unfortunately, these have often gone undiscussed. Money wages are assumed constant in the basic argument, and the aggregate demand forces, in real terms, have been accorded the center of the stage. Where money wages are brought in *it is often merely to aver that these will not rise unless there is full employment and excess demand.* If they do rise, the argument seems to lean to the view that their upswing merely supports the price level that has already jumped up because of 'excess demand'. Schematically, because it fits so badly into the formal apparatus which runs in real terms, when this group is pressed on the subject, some rather gratuitous remarks on the effect of money wage changes on the distribution of income and hence on the level of aggregate demand are often tendered. But such effects are generally accorded rather meager attention.

In sum, as inflation is a creature of excess demand, there is no serious price level distortion until full employment is reached. Similarly, the money wage level may be disregarded or accepted as a datum. Typically, exogenous wage movements through union pressure and business acquiescence are ignored until full employment. And then, it is the demand level that is stressed and creates the illusion of the 'cost push', as this school sees it.

The more sophisticated version of Keynesianism of this same stamp, with claims to more generality and insight, seeks to show the simultaneous determination of interest rate and real income level through the interdependence of the self-same functions. Thus in Figure 2 there is the well-known *IS* curve, which is built out of the real investment response to interest rate changes, the consumption function, and the $C + I$ identity, and is associated with various levels of real income or real output measured along the horizontal axis. In deriving *IS* it is the interest rate which is

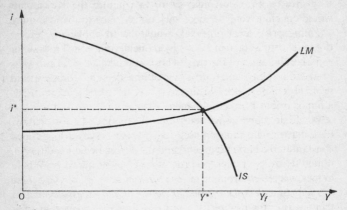

Figure 2

assumed to be the parametric constant, variations in which affect investment and thus the *IS* path. The *LM* curve is erected out of the remaining equations of Keynesianism, namely, the liquidity function and the money supply, regarded ordinarily as a datum. In deriving the *LM* path it is the income level – *real* income[4] – which is temporarily viewed as the parameter. The diagrammatic apparatus thus permits the disclosure of the mutual income–interest rate values that are simultaneously equilibrating. In Figure 2 the equilibrium values are i^* and Y^*. Once again, if full employment real income is at Y_f, achievement of this zenith will

4. I have criticized the inclusion of the interest rate and the *real* – not money – income as the strategic variables in the liquidity function, and have suggested that the price level must also be included as a major parameter. See my *Price Level*, op. cit., p. 72. I have been surprised at certain protests to the effect that the price level has *always* been included in the money-demand equation. I submit that an examination of the literature does *not* bear this out though in common discussion economists will invariably acknowledge its importance.

require parametric movements of the two functions, through consumption, investment, or interest rate developments.

Until 'full employment', in neither of these versions of Keynesianism – which are regarded as equivalent for my purposes – is there any substantial concern with inflation, *for all its concepts are cast in real terms*. The income levels being talked about have no explosive price levels, nor even changing price levels, for all this is assumed away. Surely, there is no concern with money wage changes – the 'cost push' – for the very application of the technique precludes this discussion: it is competent to handle variations in real phenomena, not in monetary phenomena. There is no way in which it can fit in, say, added monopoly power in the sense of discussions of advancing levels of administered prices where these are deemed important. For both changing monopoly power and changing money wages at full employment or less have their impact on price levels rather than on real output. But these are the very problems which have been exorcized by this technique which runs in real terms.

As one reflects on it, it becomes ever more astonishing that diagrams such as those examined have been regarded as useful in illuminating inflation when their very essence consists of conceptions running in real terms, thereby eliminating the very problem of changing price levels, whether due to new issues of money, or velocity changes, or money wage changes, or changes in productivity, or monopoly power – or anything else. This wing of Keynesianism, whose hallmark is either the analysis surrounding Figures 1 or 2, or other similar versions running in real terms, has justifiably been charged as devoid of a basic explanation of inflation.[5] I think this criticism is merited, for in the last two decades, since 1940, the economy can be viewed as operating under conditions of strong aggregate demand, so that levels of real demand have not been in issue, and yet the *numéraire* phenomenon of changing money wage levels which fit uncomfortably in a 'real' scheme has been barging upwards. It is little wonder that analyses springing from the equation of exchange have become more acceptable today than in the immediate heyday of Keynesianism.

Lest it be thought that I am dealing only with straw men

5. Selden (1957), p. 5 n.

picked only from the softer geometrical treatments presented to the neophyte students of economics, an examination of some mathematical models of the same stripe and in the recognized sources discloses exactly the same arguments; there is no inconsistency between mathematical and geometrical versions on this score, although I do not rule out the possibility that more elaborate Keynesian models may deal more adequately with price level phenomena. In those systems that take enough pains to include price level analyses rather than working with real phenomena right from the start, the most common hypothesis is that the money wage level is constant, with the usual reservation that this holds only until 'full employment' obtains. What happens to the price level along the course of the associated C, I, or savings functions until full employment is reached is literally never discussed in these accounts, according to my experience in examining the standard works. The typical assumption seems to be that prices hold constant, or variations are so small that they may be neglected, until full employment is reached. Unless this proviso is mentally inserted, there is no simple way of interpreting the geometrical figures like Figures 1 and 2 that usually accompany the equational statements. One less frequently quoted equational system makes the money wage a function of the level of employment. Apart from the problems (undiscussed in the original) with respect to 'money illusion', this simple function makes the point better than I would expect, for it leads inevitably to the argument that the high levels of money wages occur only in the vicinity of full employment: it would have no way of explaining why, in recent years, with little or no change in employment levels the money wage keeps mounting.

Thus I think I have presented fairly the dominant ideas of 'demand-pull' Keynesian analysis on the inflation issue by way of the formal, and now not so formidable, diagrammatic and mathematical apparatus.

2. Aggregate Money Demand and Aggregate Money Supply Functions

Let us now turn to the other face of Janus, to look instead at an alternate diagrammatic approach which, although not as commonly employed as the 45° line, still has a literature of its own. As I have used this apparatus in several writings over the past few years, the exposition of the main points can be made briefly.[6] The 'cost-push' argument comes out of it quickly, effortlessly, and directly.

In Figure 3 *uncorrected* money levels of actual and expected expenditure are measured vertically, and amounts of labor are measured horizontally. All labor is assumed to be homogeneous,

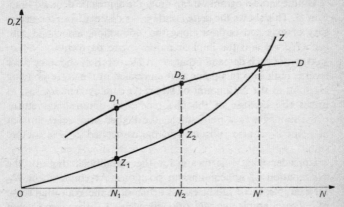

Figure 3

initially at least; this is a simplification not worse (more acceptable in my view) than the use of homogeneous units of real output (Y) in the dominant Keynesian approach. The curve Z, as drawn, represents an aggregate supply function, and it is premised on the short-period (Keynesian) assumption of a given stock of capital equipment, and it also assumes all along its course that the money wage level is held constant: this last hypothesis is tantamount to Keynes's analysis in terms of a given wage unit or money wage structure. As the curve is drawn, rising at an increasing rate to the right, it reflects some implicit diminishing returns phenomena and thus some necessary rising prices (of moderate proportions) as employment advances. Each point on the Z-function is to be

6. See Weintraub (1958), chapter 2. For references to the earlier literature on the Z-function, see p. 24.

interpreted as signifying the volume of outlays expected by firms in the economy in the form of consumer expenditures and investment outlays, which will lead the enterprises to give the associated level of employment.[7] Thus at an expected outlay level of Z_1 the employment that firms will create is N_1, etc. Manifestly, by writing the concomitant production function we can tether each employment level to a particular real output level, as N_1 to Y_1, etc.

On the same diagram we can draw the aggregate demand function D. This shows the *actual* outlays, as distinct from the necessary or expected outlays along the Z-function, associated with each N-level and the implicit money wage payments to labor. Further, at each demand point, as at D_1, precisely the same price level is built into this point as is embodied in the corresponding Z_1 point at the N_1 amount of labor. At employment N_2, say, as prices rise because of the phenomena of diminishing returns while money wages hold stable, the higher price level implicit at point Z_2 is also subsumed in the associated D_2 expenditure sum.

Consider what this means for the stability analysis or the examination of nonequilibrium positions. At employment N_1, for example, there will be excess demand, in the Walrasian sense of microeconomic markets, of goods wanted at the given level of prices outrunning the quantities being offered for sale at the same price scale. To the right of N_1, as we get closer to equilibrium and as prices rise, the level of excess demand dwindles until it disappears entirely at the equilibrium employment level N^*. To the right of N^*, at the still higher price levels implicit at these points, excess supply rather than excess demand obtrudes.

Price level assumptions, and changing price level phenomena, are thus always integral parts of this analysis: whereas Figures 1 and 2 have exorcized price level concepts, Figure 3 keeps them always in mind and in the forefront of the discussion. In general, apart from technological change and/or a change in the volume of capital equipment, changes in money wages will be the primary

7. This would suggest that the Z-function should be decomposed into these components. But exactly the same observation may be made with respect to the 45° line approach. For an early recognition of this, see Dillard (1948), p. 35 n.

reason for parametric shifts in both the Z and D functions. Thus whenever the money wage changes, and whatever the reason for the change, from this diagrammatic apparatus it becomes instantly clear that: (a) the price level *must* change, and (b) the money income or gross national product Z in money terms must change, while (c) employment and real output *may* change only if the new intersection of D and Z functions occurs at a point other than above N^*. If the employment level is affected by the money wage change – and Keynes himself was largely a skeptic on this point – then it should be possible to derive a theory of money wages by aid of this apparatus.[8]

I think this very brief exposition will suffice for my purpose. From the analysis surrounding Figure 3 it can immediately be argued that even if money wages were held constant there would still be price level movements of greater or lesser degree, due to the laws of returns (and changing degrees of monopoly power). More important for the great controversies of the last decade or so, the argument leads inexorably to the conclusion that the prime mover in price level fluctuations, or the factor of overriding importance in discussions of inflation, is the wage level and incipient changes in it. This is the heart of the 'cost-push' thesis: it devolves naturally and inevitably from this diagrammatic approach in contrast to its submersion into utter obscurity in the 45° line story. Excess demand, or a rise in the D-function in Figure 3, when unaccompanied by a money wage change, is seen to have a much less significant impact on the price level, which then merely responds to the laws of return. Conversely, a rise in the money wage level either as a result of changing employment levels or because of sheer exogenous factors, such as the need of labor union leaders to meet the desires of their membership, is shown always to have a clear and direct price level incidence.

3. The Basis and Policy Consequences of the Divergence in Views

It is well to reflect for a moment on how it is that the two Keynesian wings have come up with such divergent views on the

8. I originally adopted this apparatus for just this purpose, a theory of *money* wage determination. See Weintraub (1956).

inflation problem, with one stressing the 'demand pull' and the other the money wage level and the 'cost push'.

For myself, I think that at the bottom of the difference in views there lies the choice of working units by the separate groupings, with the one thinking largely in terms of real output or money amounts *corrected* for price level changes, while the other has regarded the money wage as the appropriate *numéraire* and the employment unit as the bed-rock of analysis. On this interpretation it is the difference in the choice of deflators that seems to have been responsible for the mischief. While we may agree with Professor Hansen in principle when he wrote that 'fundamentally the matter [of the choice of units, of real output or money wage] is of no great consequence',[9] it seems to me that this very matter has led to a great practical cleavage with vast policy implications. For when one thinks of real output as basic, it is an easy step to envisage inflation as ensuing when real output can no longer be increased. On the other hand, when wage units are recognized as the *numéraire*, the value of the money wage is recognized as crucial in deciding the level of prices.

One approach thus leans inevitably to policy recommendations designed to hold wage requests in check. The other school, the dominant Keynesian branch, argues in terms of containing the level of demand to rein in prices, and thereby money wages. But here is the crucial anomaly which must sometimes rend this school, and the conflicting groups, even further: how far must real demand be cut back to control inflation? Must actual unemployment be created? If so, how much? If unemployment is not undertaken to discipline labor, can destabilizing wage movements be prevented?

If unemployment is the answer to the inflation problem, then Keynesianism as a social philosophy is dead, literally interred by Keynesians and, curiously, all in the name of the mentor. For to restrain inflation its ideas must be used – perverted, I think – to *create*, not abolish, unemployment. My own belief is that Lord Keynes's spirit must somewhere be stirring with more than a little discomfiture at the ultimate irony of this strange twist to his ideas.

9. Hansen (1953), p. 44. In this point, as in so many others, Professor Hansen has written with a refreshing breadth and candor on a matter which most other writers since Keynes's day have not even bothered to discuss.

I think that this great antithesis has been recognized, though not in this form, by several who approach Keynesianism in terms of aggregate demand and 'demand pull', and are chary about wage controls because they do not fit readily into their philosophical and analytical systems of thought. I refer to the great emphasis of this group on the role of economic growth as the answer to inflation, and their willingness to tolerate what is now fashionable to call 'creeping inflation'. But growth, if it brings with it exorbitant push-ups in wages, will disappoint their hopes for merely 'creeping inflation', and so the issue will ultimately have to be faced. After all, we have had tremendous growth since, say 1940, and yet, more than a doubling of the price level. Growth, thus, is hardly an answer to the inflation problem.

The only alternative to conscious and deliberate creation of unemployment in an economy in which the forces of aggregate demand are running strong, and one which could still preserve the analytical and philosophical system fashioned by Lord Keynes, would be some deliberate design and control of the money wage level, just as we have learned to use fiscal and monetary policy to control aggregate demand. Only this could permit the social philosophy and moderate policy intervention attitude of Keynes to survive in a world of reasonably full employment. Otherwise, Keynesianism would have to be intentionally reversed, with the intellectual framework originally created to eradicate the curse of unemployment deliberately and perilously distorted, to be used as an analytical engine to foster unemployment, so that the other evil, permanent inflation as a way of life, is repressed in favor of more tolerable standards of price level stabilization. How to contain the money wage level while maintaining full employment, and without breeding unacceptable interferences in labor markets, comes close to being the most important policy issue of our day.[10]

10. Among Keynesians who have given what I think to be the appropriate emphasis to the money wage as the dominant element in inflation, I would cite Professor A. P. Lerner who has described 'seller's inflation' in a number of papers, e.g. Lerner (1958) p. 128, Balogh (1958), and Kaldor (1959), especially pp. 292–6.

References

BALOGH, T. (1958), 'Productivity and inflation', Oxford Economic Papers, vol. 10, pp. 220–45.

DILLARD, D. (1948), *The Economics of John Maynard Keynes*, Prentice-Hall.

HANSEN, A. H. (1949), *Monetary Theory and Fiscal Policy*, McGraw-Hill.

HANSEN, A. H. (1953), *A Guide to Keynes*, McGraw-Hill.

KALDOR, N. (1959), 'Economic growth and the problem of inflation', *Economica*, vol. 26, no. 3, pp. 287–98.

LERNER, A. P. (1958), *Hearings*, Joint Economic Committee, May 1958.

SELDEN, R. T. (1959), 'Cost-push versus demand-pull inflation', 1955–7, *Journal of Political Economy*, February 1959, vol. 67, pp. 1–20.

WEINTRAUB, S. (1956), 'A Macroeconomic approach to the theory of wages', *American Economic Review*, vol. 46, no. 5, pp. 837–56.

WEINTRAUB, S. (1958), *An Approach to the Theory of Income Distribution*, Chilton Co., Philadelphia.

WEINTRAUB, S. (1959), *A General Theory of the Price Level, Output, Income Distribution and Economic Growth*, Chilton Co., Philadelphia.

5 R. J. Ball and R. G. Bodkin

A Generalized Keynesian Model

R. J. Ball and R. G. Bodkin, 'Income, the price level, and generalised multipliers in Keynesian economics', *Metroeconomica*, vol. 15 (1963), pp. 59–81.

The theory of income determination originating in Keynes's *The General Theory* [5] has been passed down to a generation of students in the form of a variety of simple standard models. The theory has usually been presented in real terms, paralleling the treatment in *The General Theory* where variables are sometimes expressed in terms of wage units. Although economists have discussed the problem of price determination in a Keynesian context, there emerges a clear lack of integration between the analysis based on the assumptions of excess capacity and of a constant price level and the analysis of an economy at full employment.

Economists in the Keynesian tradition have not neglected the problem of inflation since the publication of *The General Theory*. Keynes himself paid attention to this problem, both in that volume and in his later work *How to Pay for the War* [6]. Don Patinkin's aggregative model (developed in [9]) focuses on a joint determination of real income, the price level, and other relevant macrovariables. Sidney Weintraub ([13], especially Chapter 2) also emphasizes a joint determination of prices, money income, and employment. Although still other references could be cited, it seems fair to state that the Keynesian tradition has divorced the income determination aspects of the model from the determination of the price level.[1] This divorce has been especially pro-

---

1. As an example of this type of analysis, Alford's recent article [1] comes to mind. Alford's multiplier analysis, which in certain respects parallels our treatment, is based on an 'L-shaped' aggregate supply function, i.e. he assumes a constant price level up to full employment and a constant real income with prices flexible upward, after this point. We shall argue below that an important intermediate case has thereby been left out of consideration.

nounced in applications (e.g. international trade theory, public finance) and in classroom teaching.

It is important to discuss, in some detail, the problems faced by the policy maker concerned with the impact of his actions on the general price level. A general approach to the problem of income determination, incorporating price level effects explicitly, is required. This paper is aimed at taking a small step in this direction. Our approach develops price multipliers along with income multipliers, in order to break up the effects of particular policies on real income and the price level. For the purpose, a theory of aggregate price is introduced into the familiar multiplier analysis and generalized multipliers are obtained. A fairly simple model based on essentially Keynesian considerations is employed although no claim is made to have interpreted precisely what Keynes said (or really meant). Suffice it to say that the approach follows more closely *The General Theory* rather than *How to Pay for the War*, even though the latter has been a more direct inspiration to inflation analysis.[2]

Because the technique used is one of comparative statics, dynamic aspects of the inflationary process are given short shrift. Thus we have not taken account of such effects as changing asset preferences due to changing price levels or an increasing total product at each employment level due to an increasing stock of capital and an improving technology. The determination of the money wage is placed in a static context, instead of emphasizing dynamic forces producing a particular change in money wages. Furthermore, it can be argued that the concept of moving equilibrium (or possibly a movement toward equilibrium) is a better background for a discussion of persistent or chronic inflation which occurs over a period of years. While aware of all these limitations, we feel that generalized multiplier analysis is a useful intermediate step toward such a full dynamic system.

1

Our model is fairly conventional in its broad aspects, but contains several features deserving comment. Methodologically, the procedure adopted is the familiar one of examining the responses of

2. See Weintraub [15 and Reading 4] for a discussion of the two aspects of Keynesian price level theory.

the endogenous variables to changes in exogenous parameters. Thus the analysis is essentially static in character.

We have, as an accounting identity,

$$Y = C + I \qquad 1.1$$

where Y is national income, C consumption expenditures, and I net investment expenditures, all of which are measured in constant dollars. Consumption is assumed to depend upon the level of real income, the real stock of money M/P, the rate of interest i, and the degree of monopoly power π (discussed below), which gives

$$C = C\left(Y, i, \frac{M}{P}, \pi\right). \qquad 1.2$$

Net investment is divided into an endogenous component varying with the income level, the interest rate, and the degree of monopoly power and an exogenous or autonomous component (α), so we have

$$I = I(i, Y, \pi) + \alpha. \qquad 1.3$$

We are dealing with a closed economy, so that no distinction need be made between domestic and foreign investment. As this is short-period analysis, the stock of productive equipment is taken as fixed, and consequently the level of real income varies with the level of employment (N). Hence the production function can be written:

$$Y = f(N), \quad f'(N) > 0, \quad f''(N) < 0. \qquad 1.4$$

We add a profits maximizing condition

$$f'(N)(1 - \pi) = \frac{w}{P}, \qquad 1.5$$

where w is the money wage, P is the price level, and π represents the degree of monopoly power existing in the economy. π is equal to $\frac{1}{|\Omega_D|}$, where Ω_D is the elasticity of demand, on an economy-wide basis. Under pure competition, $\Omega_D = \infty$ and $\pi = 0$. In words, equation 1.5 states that the marginal revenue product of labor is equal to the money wage. π is taken as an exogenous parameter, which follows the spirit of Joan Robinson's recent treatment of this factor in an aggregative context. In her *Ac-*

cumulation of Capital, she seems to take this element as invariant with changes in the level of activity and as determined largely by institutional factors.[3] An increase in the degree of monopoly power will, at any level of employment, decrease the share of total output going to wage-earners. Hence we shall assume that the shift to non-wage-earners will decrease real consumption expenditures but raise real investment outlays.

Since equation 1.5 constitutes essentially the relation of labor demand, a supply equation for labor is required. It is at this point that the model breaks away from the neo-classical formulation. As is well known, to assume that the supply of labor is a function of the real wage, together with equations 1.4 and 1.5 and a market-clearing condition, is to place the determination of the levels of real income and employment in the labor market.[4] Some writers have avoided this situation by postulating an exogenous money wage, or by introducing dynamic features into the model, so that the level of money wages is determined by a market adjustment mechanism.[5] Either way, one escapes determining real wages in the labor market, and leaving the absolute price level to be determined absent-mindedly by the cash balance equation. The procedure followed here, however, is neither of these; instead, it

---

3. See Robinson [11], especially pp. 77–80. If the marginal product of labor is always a constant proportion of the average product (this would be true with a Cobb–Douglas production function), then equation 1.5 reduces to the Weintraub wage–cost–mark-up equation. For if

$$f'(N) = k_1 \frac{f(N)}{N},$$

equation 1.5 becomes

$$\frac{f(N)}{N} k_1 (1 - \pi) = \frac{w}{P}.$$

It immediately follows that

$$p = \frac{kw}{f(N)/N}$$

where $k = \dfrac{1}{k_1 (1 - \pi)}$, and this is Weintraub's wage–cost–mark-up equation, in its standard form ([14], p. 9).

No close connexion should be drawn between our elasticity of demand, on an economy-wide basis, and the Marshallian elasticity of a partial equilibrium demand curve. The effects of relative price changes are assumed to be 'washed out', in an aggregative context.

4. See Modigliani [8] especially pp. 188–90 and Klein [7], pp. 199–204.

5. For some discussion of this problem, see Ball [2].

is held that incomplete real wage adjustment characterizes the labor supply function. Individual workers are considered to be aware of changing price levels, but institutional conditions such as powerful trade unions and a working week of conventional length are held to prevent labor supply from being a simple function of the real wage alone. Taking the supply of labor services to rest upon the money wage and the price level (one can argue that the existence of escalator clauses testifies to union awareness of changing price levels), we may write

$$N = N(w, P). \qquad 1.6$$

Because of our assumption that the supply of labor services cannot be made into a simple function of the real wage, we have $N(\lambda w, \lambda P) \neq N(w, P)$ if $\lambda \neq 1$.

With lack of homogeneity of degree zero in the labor market an equilibrium level of real income cannot be determined there. Thus our later results depend, in a crucial way, upon our assumption about the labor supply relation. As will be shown later, the position of full employment can be interpreted as the point at which the labor supply function becomes homogeneous of degree zero in absolute prices. Under certain suitable conditions (principally the non-vanishing of N_w)[6] we may invert equation 1.6 'in the small' and obtain

$$w = G(N, P). \qquad 1.6a$$

Our final form for the labor supply equation, which is the one we shall use throughout this paper, is a further modification of equation 1.6a. We assume that there are institutional forces operative (e.g. trade union pressures, minimum wage laws) that prevent money wages from falling below a minimum level, w_0. w_0 is taken as exogenous; it is further assumed that the endogenous component of the wage determination mechanism $G(N, P)$ is independent of the exogenous component. Thus we may write

$$w = g(N, P) + w_0, \qquad 1.6b$$

where $g(N, P) \geqq 0$ so that $w \geqq w_0$. It is further assumed that the 'within-system' response of a change in money wages to a change

6. This symbol N_w means the partial derivative of the function N with respect to the variable w. Throughout this paper, analogous symbols should be interpreted similarly.

in the price level is less than proportionate, under underemployment conditions. In symbols, we would have

$$0 < \frac{P}{w} \cdot \frac{\partial w}{\partial P} = \frac{P}{w} g_p < 1.^7$$

This assumption may or may not be a suitable description of economic reality. It gains plausibility if one considers the labor markets of the economy as divided into two different types: one type being characterized by escalator-clause type responses, the other reflecting in the short run largely constant money wages, even in the face of changing prices. Hence the case intermediate between $\frac{\partial w}{\partial P} = O$ and $\frac{P}{w} \cdot \frac{\partial w}{\partial P} = 1$ may appear reasonable. For our purposes it will be assumed that this is the case, and it will become apparent that some of our qualitative conclusions depend upon this assumption.

The final equation of the model describes the money market equilibrium. In the neo-classical literature the demand for money essentially determined the absolute price level, whereas Keynesian employment theory only allowed it the role of directly determining the rate of interest. The view of the demand for money adopted here is largely in accord with the latter position. According to the money market equilibrium described below, shifts in the money supply affect the price level indirectly via their effects on the rate of interest, the level of income, the volume of employment, and the money wage. (It must be remembered, however, that changes in the money supply can affect consumption expenditures directly through a real balance effect.) Effects on the money wage are also not direct but are channelled through changes in the level of employment and indirectly induced price level changes.

Some controversy has emerged over the particular form and properties of the demand for money. Patinkin has developed

7. In a neo-classical model, this partial elasticity would be exactly equal to unity. For if $N = N\left(\frac{w}{P}\right)$ is our labor supply function, then the inverted form becomes $\frac{w}{P} = G^*(N)$ or $w = PG^*(N)$. Hence $\frac{\partial w}{\partial P} = G^*(N)$ and so $\frac{P}{w} \cdot \frac{\partial w}{\partial P} = \frac{1}{G^*(N)} \cdot G^*(N) \equiv 1$. Consequently, we shall say that as full employment is approached, $\frac{P}{w} \cdot \frac{\partial w}{\partial P} \to 1$.

assumptions under which prices will rise in proportion to the quantity of money, without necessitating the hypothesis of a constant velocity of circulation.[8] He asserts that the particular form of the demand for money developed by Keynes does not lead to the neo-classical conclusions because the speculative demand for money is made independent of the price level. Hence the Keynesian demand for money is not homogeneous of degree one in the absolute price level. This view would appear to be correct, but none of Patinkin's discussion really settled the issue of which is the appropriate assumption to use, although it did hint at a possible source of confusion that seems to recur from time to time.

We wish to decompose the demand for money into two parts. The transactions demand is taken to depend upon the level of money income and the rate of interest.[9] There is also a speculative component of the demand for money; this is considered to rest upon the rate of interest alone. The money market equilibrium is described by

$$M = L(PY, i). \qquad 1.7$$

Thus, considering the model as a whole, we have seven equations in seven endogenous variables (Y, C, I, i, N, w, and P). Equation-counting conditions are thus satisfied. Our exogenous variables are M, π, α, and w_0. We shall assume that certain general conditions are satisfied, so that a unique solution of economically meaningful variable values exists, and so we are ready to discuss the response of the system to shifts in the exogenous parameters. We may call this type of discussion 'generalized multiplier analysis'.

II

For convenience, the system of seven equations in seven unknowns is reduced to one of three equations in three unknowns. We have, after some manipulation,

8. See Patinkin [9], especially pp. 193–4.

9. In an application of inventory theory [3], Baumol has shown that the interest rate will govern the allocation of working capital between cash and liquid assets of short maturity. Hence even the transactions demand for money will be sensitive to variations in the interest rate. Tobin [12] has extended Baumol's treatment and reached similar conclusions.

$$f(N) - C\{f(N), i, \frac{M}{P}, \pi\} - I\{i, f(N), \pi\} = \alpha \qquad 2.1$$

$$L(Pf(N), i) = M \qquad 2.2$$

$$Pf'(N)(1 - \pi) - g(N, P) = w_0. \qquad 2.3$$

First, we obtain the traditional expenditure multipliers. Total differentiation of the system with respect to α yields, after some manipulation,

$$f'(N)(1 - C_Y - I_Y)\frac{dN}{d\alpha} - (C_i + I_i)\frac{di}{d\alpha} + C_{\frac{M}{P}}\frac{M}{P^2}\frac{dP}{d\alpha} = 1$$

$$2.4$$

$$f'(N)PL_{Y_m}\frac{dN}{d\alpha} + L_i\frac{di}{d\alpha} + L_{Y_m}f(N)\frac{dP}{d\alpha} = 0 \qquad 2.5$$

$$[Pf''(N)(1 - \pi) - g_N]\frac{dN}{d\alpha} + 0 \cdot \frac{di}{d\alpha} +$$

$$[f'(N)(1 - \pi) - g_p]\frac{dP}{d\alpha} = 0. \qquad 2.6$$

As indicated above, C_Y denotes the partial derivative of consumption with respect to real income, and similar symbols have analogous interpretations. Since $Y_m \equiv PY$, L_{Y_m} denotes the partial derivative of L with respect to money income.

Using Cramer's rule, we can solve for $\frac{dN}{d\alpha}$ and $\frac{dP}{d\alpha}$. This gives

$$\frac{dN}{d\alpha} = \frac{L_i[f'(N)(1 - \pi) - g_p]}{D} = \frac{L_i\left(\frac{w}{P} - \frac{\partial w}{\partial P}\right)}{D}, \qquad 2.7$$

where

$$D = \begin{vmatrix} (1 - C_Y - I_Y)f'(N) & -(C_i + I_i) & C_{\frac{M}{P}} \cdot \frac{M}{p^2} \\ f(N)'PL_{Y_m} & L_i & L_{Y_m}f(N) \\ [Pf''(N)(1 - \pi) - g_N] & 0 & \left(\frac{w}{P} - \frac{\partial w}{\partial P}\right) \end{vmatrix} =$$

$$= (1 - C_Y - I_Y)f'(N)L_i\left(\frac{w}{P} - \frac{\partial w}{\partial P}\right) -$$

$$(C_i + I_i)L_{Y_m}f(N)[Pf''(N)(1 - \pi) - g_N] -$$

$$C_{\frac{M}{P}} \cdot \frac{M}{P^2}L_i[Pf''(N)(1 - \pi) - g_N] +$$

$$(C_i + I_i)f'(N)PL_{Y_m}\left(\frac{w}{P} - \frac{\partial w}{\partial P}\right). \qquad 2.8$$

Following standard theory, we shall assume $(1 - C_Y - I_Y) > 0, f'(N) > 0, L_i < 0, L_{Y_m} > 0, f''(N) < 0, g_N > 0$, and $C_{\frac{M}{P}} > 0$. C_i is of uncertain direction but is small in absolute magnitude, while $I_i < 0$. Hence $C_i + I_i < 0$. Our previous assumption that $\frac{P}{w} \frac{\partial w}{\partial P} < 1$ implies that $\left(\frac{w}{P} - \frac{\partial w}{\partial P}\right) > 0$. Hence $D < O$, and thus $\frac{dN}{d\alpha} > 0$. The standard multiplier, which is $\frac{dY}{d\alpha} = f'(N) \frac{dN}{d\alpha}$, is also positive. It should be noted that in this model, full employment is defined in terms of an inability to obtain further increments of output. However, full employment is not defined in terms of a zero marginal product of labor, which under our assumptions entails a zero real wage. Full employment results from the labor supply function 'locking' so that the money wage changes in the same proportion as the price level. It is impossible to obtain further output increases from an equilibrium position of this type, as further output and employment will require a higher real wage from the side of labor supply and a lower real wage from the demand side of the labor market. Thus we may say that as full employment is approached, $\frac{P}{w} \frac{\partial w}{\partial P} \to 1$. Under these conditions, $\frac{dN}{d\alpha} \to 0$ as $\frac{\partial w}{\partial P} \to \frac{w}{P}$.[10]

Solving for $\frac{dP}{d\alpha}$, we obtain

$$\frac{dP}{d\alpha} = \frac{-L_i[Pf''(N)(1 - \pi) - g_N]}{D} = \frac{L_i[g_N - Pf''(N)(1 - \pi)]}{D}$$

2.9

and

$$\frac{dP}{d\alpha} > 0$$

10. $\frac{dN}{d\alpha}$ is also zero if the demand for money is perfectly interest inelastic so that $L_i = 0$. In this case money income is a monotonic increasing function of the stock of money, and neither the price level, real income, nor the employment level will change when autonomous expenditure is changed if the stock of money remains unchanged. Presumably interest rates would adjust in this case so that endogenous expenditure can be displaced by exogenous expenditure, real income remaining unchanged. Thus expenditure must display some interest elasticity if there is to be such an adjustment mechanism making the system solvable. (If both L_i and $C_i + I_i$ are equal to zero, D vanishes and the full system, equations 2.4, 2.5 and 2.6, cannot be solved.)

since $D < 0$, $L_i < 0$, and $[g_N - Pf''(N)(1 - \pi)] > 0$. In severe underemployment equilibrium, $g_N \to 0$ and $f'(N) \to K$ (a constant), so that $f''(N) \to 0$.[11] Under these circumstances, $\frac{dP}{d\alpha} \to 0$, i.e. it is possible for increases in real expenditures to have negligible effects on the aggregate price level, under a special set of circumstances.[12]

We may similarly compute monetary multipliers, allowing M, the quantity of nominal money balances, to vary. We obtain

$$\frac{dN}{dM} = \frac{\left(\frac{w}{P} - \frac{\partial w}{\partial P}\right)\left[L_i \frac{1}{P} C_{\frac{M}{P}} + (C_i + I_i)\right]}{D} \qquad 2.10$$

and $\quad \frac{dP}{dM} = \frac{[g_N - Pf''(N)(1 - \pi)]\left[(C_i + I_i) + L_i \frac{1}{P} C_{\frac{M}{P}}\right]}{D}.$

$$2.11$$

Hence $\frac{dN}{dM} > 0$ and $\frac{dP}{dM} > 0$, as both numerators are negative and D is negative. Thus an expansion of the money supply both stimulates real income and raises prices, in the typical case. Thus, on a broad level of generality, the direction of the effect on the price level is the same for this theoretical framework as for the quantity theory. Three special cases remain to be considered.

1. Suppose that 'severe' underemployment equilibrium exists. Then, $g_N \to 0$ and $f''(N) \to 0$, as was pointed out previously. In his case $\frac{dM}{dP} \to 0$ and the quantity theory breaks down: changes in the money supply have no effect on the price level. This is not because changes in money have no significance, but merely because all expansionary forces, additions to the money stock

11. In order that the second order condition for profit maximization hold when $\pi = 0$, $f''(N)$ must be negative. Consequently, we say that in 'severe' underemployment equilibrium, $f''(N) \to 0^-$, i.e. $f''(N)$, which is always negative, can be made arbitrarily close to zero. Thus the quantitative importance of diminishing returns becomes negligible in 'severe' underemployment equilibrium while the sufficient condition for profit maximization continues to hold. Similarly, the wage unit may be taken to be unresponsive to changes in the level of employment if the employment level is low enough.

12. $\frac{dP}{d\alpha}$ is also negligible if the demand for money is independent of the rate of interest. This is the somewhat unusual case discussed in footnote 10.

included, result in increased output and employment with negligible price level increases. Under these circumstances, a 'quantity theory' of output and employment would be valid, if in addition the demand for money were independent of the rate of interest and were related to money income in a particularly simple manner.[13]

2. Suppose the real balance effect is totally absent (i.e. $C_{\frac{M}{P}} = 0$); it may be argued that this was the view espoused by Keynes. If, in addition, expenditures are perfectly interest inelastic (this implies that $C_i + I_i = 0$), both $\frac{dN}{dM}$ and $\frac{dP}{dM}$ vanish, as an examination of equations 2.10 and 2.11 will immediately verify. In this case, changes in the money supply have no economic significance for this model, except possibly to affect the division of non-wage income between interest and other forms of property income. Alternatively, if liquidity preference becomes absolute (i.e. if $L_i \to -\infty$), the determinant D increases without limit. (We are still assuming a negligible real balance effect.) Consequently, both $\frac{dN}{dM}$ and $\frac{dP}{dM}$ become arbitrarily close to zero.

13. Suppose $L = kPY$ so that $L_i = 0$ and $L_{Y_m} \equiv \frac{\partial L}{\partial(PY)} = k$.

Equation 2.10 then becomes

$$\frac{dN}{dM} = \frac{\left(\frac{w}{P} - \frac{\partial w}{\partial P}\right)(C_i + I_i)}{D} \qquad 2.10a$$

With 'severe' underemployment conditions,

$$\frac{dN}{dM} \to \frac{\left(\frac{w}{P} - \frac{\partial w}{\partial P}\right)(C_i + I_i)}{(C_i + I_i)\ f'(N)PL_{Y_m}\left(\frac{w}{P} - \frac{\partial w}{\partial P}\right)}$$

as an examination of equation 2.8 will substantiate. Therefore,

$$\frac{dN}{dM} \simeq \frac{1}{f'(N)Pk} \text{ so that } f'(N)\frac{dN}{dM} \simeq \frac{1}{Pk}.$$

But $\frac{dY}{dM} = f'(N)\frac{dN}{dM}$ and $Pk = \frac{M}{Y}$ since $M = L$ in equilibrium. Consequently, these assumptions lead to the result that $\frac{dY}{dM} \simeq \frac{Y}{M}$ or $\frac{M}{Y}\frac{dY}{dM} \simeq 1$.

In this pseudo-neo-classical formulation, the change in real income is proportional to change in the money supply. This case suggests the early real bills theorists, who used to argue that the supply of money had to be adequate for the 'needs of trade' and who consequently advocated an 'elastic' money supply.

These cases illustrate the Keynesian view that monetary policy may be subject to 'many a slip 'twixt cup and lip'; even with underemployment present, there are two special cases where an increase in the money supply leads to negligible employment increases. Similarly, even at full employment, a liquidity trap or negligible interest elasticity of expenditures may prevent changes in the money supply from influencing prices, if the real balance effect is absent. These special cases make apparent, also, that an essential feature of the Keynesian system is that the link between the supply of money and the level of real income is through the rate of interest. Both the Keynesian and the neo-classical systems, however, postulated a direct link between the volume of real spending and the rate of interest. The particular Keynesian form of the demand for money, together with the labor market assumptions, destroy the homogeneity properties of the neo-classical system. Hence whereas in the neo-classical system the property of homogeneity of degree zero in absolute prices separated changes in the money supply from changes in the equilibrium level of real income (one must implicitly assume that such an equilibrium does exist), the conditions discussed above give rise to the same result in the world of John Maynard Keynes.

3. Suppose that full employment exists so that $\frac{w}{P} - \frac{\partial w}{\partial P} \to 0$. If one takes account of the terms that become approximately zero in equation 2.8, equation 2.11 becomes

$$\frac{dP}{dM} \simeq \frac{[g_N - Pf''(N)(1-\pi)]\left[(C_i + I_i) + L_i \frac{1}{P} C_{\frac{M}{P}}\right]}{-[Pf''(N)(1-\pi) - g_N]\left[(C_i + I_i) L_{Ym} Y + C_{\frac{M}{P}} L_i \frac{M}{P^2}\right]}$$

or

$$\frac{dP}{dM} \simeq \frac{(C_i + I_i) + L_i \frac{1}{P} C_{\frac{M}{P}}}{Y(C_i + I_i) L_{Ym} + \frac{M}{P^2} L_i C_{\frac{M}{P}}}. \qquad 2.12$$

We shall say that a 'pure' quantity theory of prices is valid if an increase in the nominal money supply leads to a proportionate increase in the aggregate price level. One set of assumptions sufficient to validate a pure quantity theory of prices is full employment and negligible interest elasticity of both the consumption and investment demand functions. Under these circumstances, $C_i + I_i \simeq 0$ and equation 2.12 becomes

$$\frac{dP}{dM} \simeq \frac{\frac{1}{P} L_i C_{\frac{M}{P}}}{\frac{M}{P^2} L_i C_{\frac{M}{P}}} = \frac{P}{M}. \qquad 2.12a$$

This is equivalent to $\frac{dP}{dM} \frac{M}{P} \simeq 1$, which we had earlier agreed to denote as the 'pure' quantity theory case. A second set of assumptions that leads to similar results is that full employment exists and that the demand for money is of the form $L = kPY$. In this case $L_i = 0$ (i.e. the demand for money is independent of the rate of interest) and $L_{Y_m} = \frac{\partial L}{\partial Y_m} = k$ since $Y_m = PY$. Here equation 2.12 becomes

$$\frac{dP}{dM} \simeq \frac{(C_i + I_i)}{Y(C_i + I_i)k} = \frac{1}{kY} \qquad 2.12b$$

Since $\frac{M}{P} = \frac{L}{P} = kY$, $\frac{dP}{dM} \simeq \frac{1}{\frac{M}{P}}$ or $\frac{M}{P} \frac{dP}{dM} \simeq 1$. Thus both full employment conditions and a rather simplified form of the demand for money are sufficient to validate a 'pure' quantity theory of prices, with changes in the price level proportional to changes in the quantity of money. In general, however, the 'classical' propositions will not hold, since neither set of assumptions is applicable most of the time. It follows that Keynes's claim that at full employment the 'classical' propositions come back into their own is too strong, for it requires postulates that Keynes himself would hardly have made.

We may briefly examine π-multipliers. By similar techniques, we obtain

$$\frac{dN}{d\pi} = \frac{(C_\pi + I_\pi) L_i \left(\frac{w}{P} - \frac{\partial w}{\partial P}\right) -}{D}$$

$$\frac{Pf'(N)\left[(C_i + I_i) f(N)L_{Y_m} + L_i C_{\frac{M}{P}} \frac{M}{P^2}\right]}{D}. \qquad 2.13$$

$$\frac{dP}{d\pi} = \frac{-(C_\pi + I_\pi)L_i[Pf''(N)(1-\pi) - g_N] +}{D}$$
$$\frac{P\{f'(N)\}^2[L_i(1 - C_Y - I_Y) + PL_{Y_m}(C_i + I_i)]}{D}. \quad 2.14$$

The evaluation of these multipliers is subject to some uncertainty. As indicated earlier, $C_\pi < 0$ and $I_\pi > 0$, because an income shift toward non-wage earners will depress real consumption but stimulate real investment. The effects on real spending are in doubt, as is the sign of $C_\pi + I_\pi$. If the consumption effects predominate, $C_\pi + I_\pi < 0$; consequently, $\frac{dN}{d\pi} < 0$ but the sign of $\frac{dP}{d\pi}$ is in doubt. If the stimulus to investment is stronger, $\frac{dP}{d\pi} > 0$ but the sign of $\frac{dN}{d\pi}$ is in question. It should be noted that the rise in the degree of monopoly power will also depress employment if the stimulus to investment is just balanced by the decrease in consumption (i.e. if $C_\pi + I_\pi = 0$), or if the net increase in real spending is small. Similarly, this change will still give rise to an increase in the price level if $C_\pi + I_\pi = 0$, or if the net decrease in real expenditure is small. Two special cases exist: in 'severe' underemployment equilibrium a rise in the degree of monopoly power is certain to raise prices, whereas in full employment a rise in π will, in general, reduce employment. In addition, there are several special cases in which $\frac{dN}{d\pi}$ is zero. One set of sufficient conditions is $C_{\frac{M}{P}} = C_i + I_i = C_\pi + I_\pi = 0$. The others involve the assumption of full employment in place of $C_\pi + I_\pi = 0$, or the assumption that liquidity preference becomes absolute as a substitute for $C_i + I_i = 0$.

The underconsumptionist case would entail the assumption that a reduction in monopoly power would stimulate consumption to a greater degree than it would reduce investment. Consequently, $C_\pi + I_\pi < 0$, and a reduction in monopoly power stimulates employment and real output. This occurs because real consumption expenditure increases directly with such a change; in addition, falling prices may induce a real balance effect or may reduce the transactions demand for money, thereby lowering interest rates. A lower rate of interest could, in turn, stimulate real investment.

The effect of an autonomous increase in money wages can be studied also. We shall have,

$$\frac{dN}{dw_0} = \frac{-\left[C_{\frac{M}{P}} \cdot \frac{M}{P^2} L_i + (C_i + I_i)L_{Y_m}f(N) \right]}{D} < 0. \qquad 2.15$$

$$\frac{dP}{dw_0} = \frac{f'(N)\left[L_i(1 - C_Y - I_Y) + PL_{Y_m}(C_i + I_i) \right]}{D} > 0. \qquad 2.16$$

Thus the effect of an autonomous increase in money wages is to raise prices; the direct effect on costs appears to predominate in our simultaneous system, also. But, in the usual case, there are some system effects on the levels of employment and hence output; in general an increase in the exogenous component of money wages will decrease employment. This is so because the rise in money wages raises prices and so reduces consumption through a real balance effect. Also, the rise in prices raises the rate of interest since the transactions demand depends upon the level of money income; some investment and/or consumption expenditure is thereby choked off. (This does not take account of the distributive effects on consumption. This, however, would not seem to be a serious shortcoming, since the distributive effects between wage and non-wage shares, of a rise in *money* wages are not so obvious and probably will not be substantial.)[14]

The employment effects will be negligible if the real balance effect and the interest elasticity of expenditures are negligible. The same result will occur if, instead of perfect interest inelasticity of expenditures, liquidity preference becomes absolute. Equation 1.5 implies that an increase in money wages through an increase in the autonomous component leads to a higher real wage, provided this change reduces the level of employment. No other special cases appear for a change in the exogenous component of money wages. The effects of a change in this component appear

14. Using a somewhat different model, Holzman concludes that a wage push will reduce employment and raise prices because the redistributive effects are outweighed by the direct employment-decreasing effects. (See 4, especially pp. 32–4.) Hence, the two different models, which emphasize different aspects of such a change, give similar conclusions.

to be similar under 'severe' unemployment, full employment, and intermediate conditions.

III

In this section the equations of the model are reduced to two over-all relationships between real income and the aggregate price level. With these two relationships, which are interpreted as 'aggregate supply' and 'aggregate demand' equations, a graphical presentation of the determination of real income and the price level can be given. After the first reduction, it becomes possible to show that the conventional pedagogic multipliers are special cases of a more general formulation. After the second reduction, some aspects of the joint determination of real income and price are discussed further.

The equations which are relevant to the supply aspects of the system are:

$$Y = f(N). \tag{3.1}$$

$$f'(N)(1 - \pi) = \frac{w}{P}. \tag{3.2}$$

$$w = g(N, P) + w_0. \tag{3.3}$$

We have three equations in four variables and two parameters, which we can reduce to a single equation in two variables and two parameters. We choose to eliminate w and N, leaving a single derived relation among Y, P, π, and w_0. Under certain general conditions Y can be made an explicit function of the P variable as well as of the two parameters. This function, which is termed an 'aggregate supply' function by analogy with the supply curve of an individual industry,[15] can be expressed as

$$Y = \diagdown\!\!\!\diagup(P; \pi, w_0). \tag{3.4}$$

We may also define the elasticity of supply as

$$E_s \equiv \frac{\partial Y}{\partial P} \cdot \frac{P}{Y} \equiv \diagdown\!\!\!\diagup_P \cdot \frac{P}{Y}. \tag{3.5}$$

15. As before, the analogy with the concept of microeconomic theory is loose and imprecise. Thus the concept of the supply curve of an imperfectly competitive industry is vague and erroneous. Moreover, the supply curve of a competitive firm rests on a given wage rate, not on a given labor supply function. However, a more appropriate name for the $\diagdown\!\!\!\diagup$ function is not available, and so, desiring to maintain continuity with pre-existing literature, we have settled on the term given above.

In the appendix [not included in this Reading], a mathematical derivation of the aggregate supply function is given. There it is shown that the level of real output is an increasing function of supply price, except in special cases where the elasticity of supply approaches zero or infinity. In 'severe' underemployment equilibrium, the elasticity of supply becomes nearly infinite, indicating that considerable output increases are consistent with negligible price level increases. At full employment the elasticity of supply is close to zero, indicating that merely negligible output increases can be obtained only through enormous price level rises. It is further shown that an increase in either the degree of monopoly power or the exogenous component of money wages will reduce the level of output, aggregate supply price remaining unchanged. Symbolically, we have $\lozenge_P \geqslant 0$, $\varepsilon < \lozenge_P \leqslant \infty$; $\lozenge_\pi < 0$; $\lozenge_{w_0} < 0$.

After this reduction, our system of equations can be written:

$$Y - C\left(Y, i, \frac{M}{P}, \pi\right) - I(i, Y, \pi) = \alpha \qquad 3.6$$

$$L(PY, i) = M$$

$$Y - \lozenge(P; \pi, w_0) = 0.$$

We shall consider only the response of income to a shift in the exogenous component of spending, $\dfrac{dY}{d\alpha}$. (This is the familiar multiplier of income with respect to a shift in real investment.) Following the techniques outlined in the previous section and employing the definition of the elasticity of supply, we obtain:

$$\frac{dY}{d\alpha} = \frac{L_i \dfrac{Y}{P} E_s}{(C_i + I_i)L_{Y_m}Y(1 + E_s) + L_i\left[\dfrac{Y}{P}E_s(1 - C_Y - I_Y) + C_{\frac{M}{P}}\dfrac{M}{P^2}\right]} \geqslant 0.$$

$$3.7$$

Because the elasticity of supply is non-negative, $\dfrac{dY}{d\alpha}$ is also non-negative.

We are now ready to consider some special cases. If the elasticity of supply becomes infinite, $E_s \to \infty$ and equation 3.7 reduces to

$$\frac{dY}{d\alpha} = \frac{L_i}{P(C_i + I_i)L_{Y_m} + L_i(1 - C_Y - I_Y)}. \qquad 3.7a$$

As liquidity preference becomes absolute, $L_i \to -\infty$, and equation 3.7a approaches

$$\frac{dY}{d\alpha} = \frac{1}{1 - C_Y - I_Y}, \qquad 3.7b$$

the familiar form of the Keynesian multiplier with induced investment. This familiar pedagogic multiplier can also be obtained under conditions of infinite elasticity of the aggregate supply curve if expenditure is also perfectly interest inelastic, so that $C_i = I_i = 0$. In this case too equation 3.7a reduces to equation 3.7b. The simple pedagogic multiplier is also obtained if expenditure is perfectly interest inelastic and the real balance effect is negligible (i.e. $C_{\frac{M}{P}} = 0$), for in this case equation 3.7 reduces directly to equation 3.7b.[16] If the elasticity of supply is negligible, $\frac{dY}{d\alpha}$ vanishes. The two cases $E_s = 0$ and $E_s \to \infty$ represent the two extreme cases often dealt with in Keynesian economics. This concentration, which has given rise to the notion of the so-called L-shaped supply curve, is perhaps unwarranted, for intermediate conditions of neither full employment nor 'severe' underemployment are probably the rule over long periods of time.

The remaining relations of the model, which can be interpreted as expressions of its demand aspects, are:

$$C = C\left(Y, i, \frac{M}{P}, \pi\right). \qquad 3.8$$

$$I = I(i, Y, \pi) + \alpha. \qquad 3.9$$

$$Y = C + I. \qquad 3.10$$

$$M = L(PY, i). \qquad 3.11$$

16. This result also holds if a liquidity trap takes the place of perfect interest inelasticity of expenditure.

Here we have four equations in five unknowns (C, Y, i, P, and I) and three parameters (M, α, and π). By use of the identity 3.10 we can eliminate the C and I variables, thus coming down to two equations in three variables and three parameters. Under certain general conditions, discussed in the appendix, we can eliminate the i variable and write Y as an explicit function of P and the parameters M, α, and π. This relation, which we designate the 'aggregate demand' function because the economic actions which underlie it relate primarily to expenditure decisions, is

$$Y = \psi(P; M, \alpha, \pi). \qquad 3.12$$

A rigorous derivation of the aggregate demand function is provided in the appendix [not included in this excerpt]. There it is shown that for this relation, real income is a non-increasing function of the price level, a non-decreasing function of the money supply, a non-decreasing function of level of autonomous spending, and an indeterminate function of the degree of monopoly power. In symbols, we would have

$$\psi_P \leqslant 0, \quad \psi_M \geqslant 0, \quad \psi_\alpha \geqslant 0, \quad \text{and} \quad \psi_\pi \gtrless 0. \qquad 3.13$$

It is further shown that a necessary and sufficient condition that real income display no response to a change in the price level (i.e. $\psi_P = 0$) is that real income display no response to a change in the money supply (i.e. $\psi_M = 0$). It is further shown that ψ_P, ψ_M, and ψ_α are never zero simultaneously.

If all exogenous variables are given, the relations of aggregate supply and aggregate demand reduce to two-dimensional curves. The determination of real income and aggregate price can now be depicted graphically, as in Figure 1.[17] The supply curve is invariant under shifts in the money supply and the level of autonomous expenditure, while the demand curve is unaffected by changes in the money wage floor. This suggests that in the short period monetary and fiscal policy is primarily directed towards

17. After the first draft of this paper was written (in the summer of 1960), Phelps's article [10] came to hand. Using the aggregate supply and demand curves, Phelps presents a graphical determination of real income and the price level which is almost identical with ours. His derivations of these functions would appear, however, to be verbal, not mathematical. The connexion with the underlying aggregative model of the economy is only stated and not rigorously demonstrated.

the demand side of our economic system; on the other hand wage policy (of either a voluntary or compulsory nature) operates on the supply aspects of the system, at least initially. Anti-trust policy, while of a mixed character, would appear to affect primarily the supply side of the system; at least the direction of change is unambiguous in this regard.

This simple apparatus may be utilized to throw some light on the controversy in the recent literature between the demand and the cost inflationists. In this discussion the distinction between demand and supply price has been very much neglected. As pointed out earlier, the aggregate supply curve is invariant to changes in the money supply. In the short period traditional monetary policies will have the effect of controlling prices through the demand side. In the model considered in this paper, the price level can always be reduced, except in certain special cases, since the demand curve can in general be slid down the supply curve. The difficulty is that except in the limiting case $E_s = 0$, this will result in a reduction of real income and hence employment, so that the traditional monetary policies will be quite unable, subject to the above qualifications, to affect supply price; in particular they will have no direct effect on the money wage level.[18]

Although this seems reasonably accurate, the principle remains that demand and supply jointly determine real income and aggregate price. The real issue cannot turn on whether demand or supply (cost) determines price – the issue of which blade of the scissors does the cutting was resolved a long time ago.[19] In part

18. Weintraub makes essentially the same point in [14], chapter 9.

19. An attempt is sometimes made to distinguish between 'demand' and 'cost' inflation on the basis of the effect of reductions in the level of monetary demand on the real income level. (See, for example, Phelps [10], especially pp. 32–3.) If prices can be reduced – (say) by increases in the average tax rate – without reducing the real income level, then we have 'pure demand' inflation. An appropriate reduction in the money supply will have a similar effect. In terms of the analysis pursued above, this case will correspond to a situation in which the aggregate demand curve cuts the aggregate supply curve well above the point at which supply becomes perfectly inelastic. In this case the aggregate demand curve can be 'slid down' the aggregate supply curve reducing the price level but leaving the level of real income and employment unchanged.

much of the controversy can be explained by the failure to distinguish between arguments relating to demand price and those relating to supply price, which, in general, are not mutually exclusive. This is suggestive of the fact that some of the combatants in the debate have in part been at odds since some have dealt with demand price and others with supply price. In general the 'demand-pull' school has seemed more ready to deny the possibility of autonomous shifts in the schedule on which their attention has not been focused. The Keynesian gap analysis of *How to Pay for the War* is largely responsible for this state of affairs. Here the cost side of aggregate price determination is removed by the assumption of fixed supply. The only price worth considering is demand price since supply is given. Some 'cost inflationists' have fallen into the opposite trap of considering only the problem of supply price, assuming (usually implicitly) that demand, being plastic and passive, will follow to validate almost any increase in supply price.[20]

In summary, we have analysed the separate effects of changes in the exogenous economic variables on real income and the aggregate price level. Our technique has been generalized multiplier analysis, based on a fairly simple aggregative model of the economy. In general, expected results held true. Some special cases were examined; for example, it was found that the conditions under which a 'pure' quantity theory holds true are stringent indeed, if one accepts the Keynesian description of the money market and the conditions of labor supply. The system was then reduced to two relations, the aggregate supply and aggregate demand functions. This reduction enabled us to obtain a pedagogic multiplier as a special case of a more general formulation, and to give a graphical determination of real income and the price level. In turn, this latter device suggests that demand price

20. We should not wish to deny under certain circumstances, such as wartime, it may be appropriate to simplify and approach the problem of price level determination from an extreme point of view. Similarly, there may be occasions when the demand curve is relatively fixed and price level inelastic and the entire floor of the aggregate supply curve shifts upward; here the increase in supply price is the most interesting feature of the upward price level movement. Generally, however, the simultaneous determination of aggregate price and real income by supply and demand has to be considered.

and supply price must be considered jointly in most comparative statics discussions of price level movements. This principle has not always been given appropriate emphasis in the debate between the demand and cost inflationists.

Bibliography

1. R. F. G. ALFORD, 'A taxonomic note on the multiplier and income velocity', *Economica*, N. S., vol. 17 (1960), no. 105, pp. 53–62.
2. R. J. BALL, 'Cost inflation and the income velocity of money: a comment', *Journal of Political Economy*, vol. 68 (1960), no. 3, pp. 288–301.
3. W. J. BAUMOL, 'The transactions demand for cash: an inventory theoretic approach', *Quarterly Journal of Economics*, vol. 66 (1952), no. 4, pp. 545–56.
4. F. D. HOLZMAN, 'Inflation: cost-push and demand-pull', *American Economic Review*, vol. 50 (1960), no. 1, pp. 20–42.
5. J. M. KEYNES, *The General Theory of Employment, Interest, and Money*, Harcourt, 1936.
6. J. M. KEYNES, *How to Pay for the War*, Harcourt, 1940.
7. L. R. KLEIN, *The Keynesian Revolution*, Macmillan, 1947.
8. F. MODIGLIANI, 'Liquidity preference and the theory of interest and money', *Econometrica*, vol. 12 (1944), pp. 45–88, Reprinted in A.E.A. *Reading in Monetary Theory*, (1951), pp. 186–239. (Page references are to this latter reference.)
9. D. PATINKIN, *Money, Interest, and Prices*, Row, Peterson & Co., 1956.
10. E. S. PHELPS, 'A test for the presence of cost inflation in the United States, 1955–57', *Yale Economic Essays*, vol. I (1961), no. 1, pp. 28–69.
11. J. ROBINSON, *The Accumulation of Capital*, Richard D. Irwin, Inc., 1956.
12. J. TOBIN, 'The interest-elasticity of transactions demand for cash', *The Review of Economics and Statistics*, vol. 38 (1956), no. 3, pp. 241–7.
13. S. WEINTRAUB, *An Approach to the Theory of Income Distribution*, Chilton Co., Philadelphia, 1958.
14. S. WEINTRAUB, *A General Theory of the Price Level, Output, Income Distribution, and Economic Growth*, Chilton Co., Philadelphia, 1959.
15. S. WEINTRAUB, 'The Keynesian theory of inflation: the two faces of Janus?' *International Economic Review*, vol. I (1960), no. 2, pp. 143–55 [Reading 4].

Part Two **The Monetary Revival**

In Keynes's *General Theory* changes in the money supply directly affected the rate of interest and the level of expenditure determined the price level. With increasing scepticism after the war about the interest elasticity of aggregate spending the role of the money supply in the inflationary process tended to be neglected by Keynesians. This development, however, did not go unchallenged. Morton's paper (Reading 6) constitutes an important step in reviving emphasis on the importance of the money supply on economic activity. Morton argued that both cost and demand inflation stemmed from inappropriate monetary policies and the authorities' willingness to create the money necessary to maintain full employment for any money wage level negotiated by the trades unions.

Further developments took place during the fifties, inspired in particular by Milton Friedman and the 'Chicago School'. The basic postulate of the new quantity theory is that there exists a stable demand function for money which, although not a numerical constant as implied by the classical theory, depends on a limited number of variables, one of which is the expected rate of price change.

Striking evidence in support of this quantity theory approach to inflation and of the relative stability of the demand function despite a sharp rise in the velocity of circulation itself is contained in Cagan's study of six hyperinflations (Reading 7). Nevertheless, it is fair to say that the approach has not proved nearly so fruitful for analysing the 'creeping inflation' which has characterized the post-war advanced economies. The final paper (Reading 8) is an interesting statement of the modern monetarist position where, in contrast to the conventional Keynesian analysis, it is the stock of money rather than the level of income and expenditure which determines the rate of inflation and the level of output.

6 W. A. Morton

Trade Unionism, Full Employment and Inflation

Excerpts from W. A. Morton, 'Trade unionism, full employment and inflation', *American Economic Review*, vol. 40 (1950), pp. 13–39.

As a result of the post-war experience the belief has grown that one of the strongest impediments to the use of monetary and fiscal powers for the maintenance of a high national income is the increased strength of trade unions and their influence over the wage level. It is feared that trade union policy will compel a continued annual increase in wage rates exceeding the rise in physical productivity, thus making price inflation a necessary concomitant of full employment and forcing the unpalatable alternative of underemployment or inflation. We shall, therefore, inquire into the influence of unionism in the past and what it is likely to be in the future.

I

Although not always clearly formulated, the alleged inflationary influence of unionism can be reduced to three propositions.

1. That trade unions in the postwar period have pursued policies that made the rise in prices much greater than it would have been with individual bargaining and competition in the labor market, and that this policy was made possible by the fact that unionism is a form of monopoly power which is inherently inflationary. This view implicitly assumes that except for unionism, prices would have risen much less and that the wage–price spiral would not have existed under the assumed conditions of perfect competition in the labor market. Wage policies are looked upon as the instigator and principal cause rather than the instrument of the wage–price spiral.

2. That if unions had pursued a policy of money wage stabilization instead of trying to keep wages abreast of prices, the degree of inflation would have been less. This view does not contrast

actual policies with the assumed results of perfect competition but rather with a sacrificial wage policy in which the leadership deliberately sacrificed possible wage gains in order to keep prices down. It assumes such policies were possible for the leadership and would have been more beneficial to the community.

3. That the wage–price spiral could have been prevented if unions had exerted their political influence to retain wage and price control in 1946 instead of asking for the discard of the little steel formula and the determination of wages by voluntary collective action. This is a criticism of labor politics and beyond our purview here where we are dealing with labor policy in a free market.

Those who believe that unionism is inherently inflationary propose that we prepare to suffer its consequences or destroy the unions. Some suggest a drastic change in the allocation of economic power by restoration of atomistic competition and liberalism of the purported nineteenth-century type which they fancy will make our system function more effectively. They would apply the traditional American anti-monopoly philosophy to trade unions which have heretofore been exempt from it. A second group assumes that no substantial change will occur in our institutions, but they believe that unions might pursue better policies, putting their faith in reason, exhortation, intimidation, and economic coercion mixed in uncertain proportions. A third group, believing that unionism is here to stay but that the self-interest of unions is and will remain incompatible with stability of prices and full employment, advocate direct governmental control over the general level of wages through national wage policy enforced by law or custom as a substitute for the determination of wage levels by voluntary collective bargaining. We shall examine these proposals after we have considered the causes of the recent price spiral and the part played therein by organized labor.

II

The recent inflation is unique because it has resulted predominantly from an increase in the velocity of money whereas in previous inflations prices, wages, and the quantity of money moved upward together. We might also characterize it as a delayed effect of the war-time increase in the money supply which had been temporarily dammed up by price control. The process of inflation was the wage–price, expenditure–income spiral. The basic causes were the quantity of money and a persistent demand for goods. In this view the spiral is not an independent, alternative explanation of price changes which can be substituted for the monetary theory; it is merely a description of inflationary processes which fits into the framework of traditional theory. By so treating it we can integrate the mechanism of inflation with the quantity theory of money by means of income–expenditure analysis. The recent treatment of the spiral as an independent causal explanation is, moreover, misleading for policy purposes because it mistakes the instrumentality by which inflation occurs for its causes and puts emphasis upon direct legal regulation of wages and prices rather than on monetary and fiscal control of the quantity and velocity of money. There is, however, a simple explanation for this elevation of a process into a first principle. Because we had given up hope of controlling the dammed up inflation after the war by reducing the quantity of money or lowering its velocity by drastic taxation, we tried to stop the spiral by exhorting and threatening labor and business. As a consequence, the erroneous belief grew that the level of prices is determined by the spiral, and primary attention was directed to the wage bargain and to profits rather than to the quantity of money.

At the close of the war the supply of money was ample to sustain a rise in prices and its velocity was low by all past standards. This inflationary monetary potential was able to support the 50 per cent rise in wholesale prices which took place from the end of price control in the spring of 1946 to the summer of 1948 and is still capable of supporting a further inflation. During this period the Treasury paid off bank debts of approximately nine billion dollars but this was offset by an approximately equal expansion of member bank loans which the Federal Reserve System could not prevent because of its policy of supporting the Government bond market. Interpreting the effect of this increase in the money supply according to the strict quantity theory, it could be held responsible for about 10 per cent of the price rise. But the actual effect was most likely greater than 10 per cent, because these funds

101

were placed in strategic hands and probably had a greater velocity than the rest of demand deposits. Bankers, however, contend that these loans were not inflationary because they were used to overcome bottlenecks, to supply deficiencies, and otherwise to augment the supply of goods which, they contend, with considerable merit, was ultimately deflationary. On the whole, however, there is little doubt that the predominant cause of inflation was not treasury policy or bank policy but the release of idle balances to satisfy a pent-up demand for goods, raising prices, creating full employment, and with it an increased demand for labor which enabled workers to win wage increases.

Because of the lag of wages behind the cost of living, labor leaders contend that higher wages did not cause higher prices but were caused by them. This argument is only half correct. The wage effect was twofold: the pushing or cost effect, and the pulling or demand effect. Increased wages raise marginal costs and hence the price at which output can be supplied. The labor leaders are correct in so far as wage increases as costs did not push up prices; prices were pulled up by a market demand great enough to absorb the entire output at prices yielding substantial profits. In industries operating under competition, wage increases were mainly excuses for price increases, not their cause. In these industries, of which agriculture, cotton textiles, and meat packing are striking examples, prices would have been the same even under the supposititious case that wages were paid by the Government and wage costs to the manufacturer had been zero; or to state it less strikingly but more realistically, even if wage costs to the producer had been much less than they actually were. Changes in wage costs cannot therefore account for changes in the prices of competitive goods sold at equilibrium prices during the inflationary period.

They were, however, an important factor in regulated industry such as railroads and electric utilities where increased costs had to be compensated by higher rates; and in industries pursuing 'price policies' based on costs which induced them to 'underprice' their output. Steel is a notable example of the latter. Subject to these modifications, labor's contention that the 'cost effect' did not raise prices is largely correct. Not so, however, the demand effect.

Higher payrolls raised prices because they increased the total demand for goods. Payrolls rose because of both greater employment and higher wages. Professor Sumner H. Slichter (1948a) shows that between 1945 and 1947 increased demand due to higher wages accounts for only about one-half of the increase in prices, the other half being attributable to greater employment, and the expenditures of other groups. Higher payrolls raised the price of farm products and helped sustain the higher price level at which manufactured goods had to be sold. As these prices rose, labor again asked for a second and then a third round which continued to have the same results. The excessive cash holdings were thus translated first into consumer demand, then into higher prices, then into higher wages and incomes, and again into demand, prices, incomes, expenditures, and so on in the manner described. Forces other than labor also contributing to the inflation were the higher incomes and expenditures of farmers, proprietors and other high-income groups, the eagerness to procure goods, dis-hoarding, reduction in the proportion of savings, the growth of consumer credit, expenditures for new plant and equipment, the growth in mortgage debt on urban real estate, and large federal and local expenditures for domestic and international purposes.

The wage–price spiral was, therefore, a cause of inflation but not the sole cause nor even a sufficient cause to bring about the degree of price change that has taken place. More properly the spiral might be designated as an income–expenditure spiral. And finally, as will be shown, the wage–price spiral is not an exclusive product of unionism but has existed in every inflation regardless of the organization of the labor market and would have existed in the contemporary scene even had there been a competitive labor market.

There is no reason to believe that prices would have risen less even if labor unions had been weak or nonexistent. Labor unions were a negligible factor in our previous great inflations – that of the American Revolutionary War, the War of 1812, the Civil War, and World War I. Nor have they been a predominant factor in the European inflations following World War I or those in Hungary, Austria, Germany, Italy, France, China, or Japan after the last war. Past experience shows that even in a competitive labor market wages rise along with prices, subject to lag, in any price spiral.

It might even be contended with considerable justification that the existence of organized labor has been an anti-inflationary force in so far as it created a fear of future wage rigidity and thus caused employers to resist the upward movement in wages and prices. Many administered prices were deliberately kept down below equilibrium market prices. Manufacturers seemed to have been motivated in this by the desire to maintain business stability, to retain consumer good will, to prevent public intervention, and to keep their wage costs and prices at a long-run equilibrium level. The expected rigidity of wage rates in face of a future fall in demand, along with these other factors, operated to keep prices and wages lower than they might have been under competition. In a completely competitive economy with producers and workers both seeking to maximize immediate money gain, the upward spiral would probably have been faster and prices higher than in the present regimen of a mixture of monopoly and competition.

Accordingly, it seems reasonable to offer the following conclusions regarding the effect of unionism on prices. 1. The wage–price spiral has always existed, with or without unionism. 2. Wages as a cost did not markedly influence market prices of goods sold under competition. 3. In so far as the selling prices of many important manufactures were less than equilibrium prices and producers were governed by the notion of a 'reasonable' profit, wage costs had some influence on administered prices of 'monopolists'. 4. Wage costs also affected governmentally regulated prices. 5. Under conditions of 'perfect competition' throughout the economy, prices would probably have risen faster but wages would have lagged. 6. Assuming monopolistic competition among producers but perfect competition among workers (the position of the anti-unionists), prices would have risen but wages would have lagged even more. 7. Fear of wage rigidity in the slump was one of the reasons that 'monopolistic' producers kept prices and wages lower than they might have been in a competitive labor market. 8. The net influence of trade unionism has been to reduce the wage lag somewhat, but its effect on competitive prices has been negligible and its effect on administered prices, though obscure, appears to have been two-fold, to raise these prices as wages rose but to keep them from rising as high as they might have done had producers not feared future effects of wage rigidity.

[. . .]

V

Although trade unionism as a fomenter of inflation does not come off so badly when its results are contrasted with those to be expected in a competitive labor market, that does not end the matter. We must also inquire whether wage policy could have been executed in a manner less conducive to inflation. If popular interest, criticism, and acclaim, and the writings of economists and publicists are any criterion for judging opinion, it is widely believed to have been within the power of labor unions either to create or to undo the price movement. It is implied that if unions had stabilized wage rates, refused to ask for or to accept wage increases, and if manufacturers had refused to take additional profits, the price level would have been lower. Such action, it is clear, would not have inhibited others with large cash balances from bidding for goods and raising prices in grey markets. Price stabilization by voluntary action was impossible. It would have required concerted action by the whole society in the form of price and wage control.

What was wanted by the critics of labor was a sacrificial wage policy for the purpose of keeping down prices. This fanciful policy would have reduced demand for food and clothing, but it would also have created a large wage lag with the effects already described, and lessened inflation wholly at the expense of organized labor. Unions would have disintegrated or the leadership would have lost control over the membership if they had attempted to carry out such a policy. Why anyone would have expected organized labor to follow voluntarily a sacrificial wage policy, in view of the abandonment of price control, is a problem for social psychology, not economics. Indeed, the implementation of such a policy would have been possible only within the framework of the corporative state.

A sacrificial wage policy would, however, have reduced labor's share of the national income. Salaries, wages, and other labor income rose by $17 billion between 1946 and 1948, proprietors and rental income increased by $12 billion in the same period, and corporate profits after taxes rose $10 billion, altogether adding up to $39 billion. If labor had had no wage increases, part of the $17 billion additional payroll would have been diverted to other groups and prices would still have risen from the impetus provided by non-labor expenditures, though perhaps not quite so much.

Although the sacrificial wage proposal may seem foolish, we should not cavil at it nor conclude that criticism of unionism has been entirely footless. Admonitions, threats, and other forms of popular exhortation coupled with homilies on 'boom and bust' contributed to uncertainty in the public mind, tempered optimism with pessimism, and exerted a braking influence upon the whole community. Public opinion, political threats, and economic opinion biased by its class origin, far from being injurious, had the salutary effect of slowing down the wage and price boom in the administered sectors of the economy and making it possible for wages of white collared workers to catch up with the trend.

We conclude, then, that inflation since the end of price control has probably been smaller in this regimen of administered prices and collective bargaining than it would have been in a society modeled after perfect competition; that the price increase has been no greater and perhaps has been smaller because wages were determined by voluntary collective bargaining rather than by individualistic competition; that a voluntary sacrificial policy would not have stopped inflation and that it is, moreover, an anachronism, impossible of achievement, and not to be expected. It is, however, conceded that the criticism of trade unionism and preachments against inflation probably exerted a favorable psychological effect in diminishing optimism, creating fear of a depression, lowering the stock market, and thus slowing up the inflationary trend.

VI

Let us now turn to the contention that union policies are necessarily inconsistent with full employment at a stable price level. The historical origin of this view is found in the recovery ending in 1937 when wages began to rise rapidly even with many million unemployed, but its present re-emphasis and elucidation can be credited to the psychological impact of the war and postwar experience to which we have just alluded. Our examination of this period did not show that union wage policy may not be inflationary in the future, it merely showed that it had not been so. We have, however, rid ourselves of the misleading and mischievous interpretation that labor has been a driving inflationary force, and thus have cleared the path for a consideration of the incidence of wage policy unbiased by this implicit preconception.

The inflationary influence of unionism is predicated on the basic postulate, assumed to be a categorical *judgement* of fact, that union wage demands will tend to exceed increases in physical productivity. This postulate may be designated as Lewis's Law.[1] For a short time, it is conceivable although not very likely, that higher wages might come out of profits, but this source would soon be dried up and higher wage rates, not offset by increased productivity, would result in higher prices. If the producer could not sell at such prices, unemployment would follow. Wage increases in excess of productivity are therefore inflationary, but still consistent with full employment, if they can be recouped by the producer in higher prices; they are deflationary and will result in unemployment when they cannot be passed on to the con-

1. Although a law is usually named after its discoverer, I have taken the liberty, in this instance, of naming it after its most eminent practitioner, Mr John L. Lewis, of the United Mine Workers. It should be noticed that this law applies to the general level of wage rates, not to any particular scale.

Many economists have remarked upon this tendency, but only a few will be quoted here. Professor Sumner H. Slichter has said: 'Unions are far more likely to force up wages faster than the engineers and managers raise output per man-hour – perhaps 2 per cent or 3 per cent a year faster, perhaps even more. The difference between the rise in money wages and the rise in output per man-hour will have to be compensated by an advance in prices. For example, if output rises by 3 per cent a year and money wages by 5 per cent a year, prices will need to rise by about 2 per cent a year. Otherwise, there will be a creeping increase in unemployment.' (Slichter, 1948b, pp. 60–1.) The same argument is made in his *The American Economy* (Slichter, 1948c, pp. 42–5). Professor Gottfried Haberler says: 'The powerful trade unions are now in the habit of demanding wage increases of 10 per cent or more per year. Since labor productivity cannot possibly rise at that rate, it follows that prices must rise or unemployment appear. In the long run, union policy will probably be the main obstacle to maintaining a high level of employment for any length of time without a rapidly rising price level.' (Haberler, 1948, p. 14).

sumer. The first condition existed from 1946 to 1948, the second may result whenever the incessant demand for goods abates without a relaxation of higher wage demands.

We have unionism and we desire full employment and stable prices. If the co-existence of all three is impossible, we must choose any combination of two: 1. unionism and full employment (with inflation); 2. unionism and stable prices (without full employment); 3. full employment and stable prices (without unionism). That is the implication of Lewis's Law. Whether the supposed alternatives are in fact actual depends solely on the validity of this law.

The evidential basis for this generalization is found in the inherent desire of workers for higher wages and the widespread belief in their possibility; the increasing strength of unionism; the internal political structure of organized labor requiring leaders to obtain continually wage increases in order to stay in power; and the impossibility of a non-inflationary policy by any single union so long as each union acts independently to advance wages, costs, and prices in its industry. Economists now exploring these fields are rediscovering that labor unions act like a nation assuming sovereignty over jobs, and function as a political organization with manifold social, political, and organizational aims known to students of labor for half a century. These rediscoveries, though vitiating the naïve assumption that unions operate as the economic man of simplified price theory who was always maximizing something, still need not cause us to doubt that higher wages are and always have been an essential aim of unionism. It follows, accordingly, that if labor could achieve its wishes without opposition from employers or consumers, money wages would rise. If, moreover, a high employment policy is designed to furnish jobs for all at a price set by the union, then it is obvious that the level of wages will be wholly within labor's discretion. This does not, however, end the matter, but rather raises the question whether such a policy is desirable. And if not, whether the aim of full employment necessarily requires that union demands always be acceded to, regardless of price effects. The issue is not whether unions would like higher wages; it is rather whether they will pursue this aim regardless of opposition and whether such opposition must lead to unemployment.

Those who reckon that labor will have its will at all costs are impressed by the growing economic and political power of organized labor, and its determination to use that power to maintain full employment at rising wages.[2] The wage policies growing out of the demands of individual unions, though uncoordinated by design, soon form a national wage pattern and become imbedded in the price system where they remain unless dislodged by some powerful force. Depression is such a force. But it is believed that if depression is avoided, wages will become flexible upward and inflexible downward, and prices likewise will rise during the boom and remain stable in the recession.

The conjectural generalization which we have branded Lewis's Law does not state an inherent propensity of human beings based on physiological psychology or a behavior pattern of social psychology. Union behavior is not tropismatic, intuitive, habitual, or otherwise irrationally invariant heedless of circumstances. High wage demands though deeply ingrained into union custom are modified whenever unions are opposed by forces which are capable of defeating their will. What are these forces?

In a community with a limited money supply, the employer will resist wage increases when they can not be passed on to the consumer and must come out of his profits. While it is true that the abstract danger of inflation will deter no particular union, the concrete fact that the employer can not grant their demands without losing his market and bankrupting himself, will cause unions to take thought. Lewis's Law as a statement of union power is therefore a fiction rather than a fact; a generalization valid only for inflationary periods. We must not think of labor's behavior as following a fixed pattern, but rather as it has already shown itself to be: political in character and adjustable to the hard facts of working, earning, living, and surviving. Labor leaders may act foolishly and at times impetuously, but they will not continually beat their heads against a stone wall. The question remains,

2. The postwar period, however, provides a misleading basis for judging union wage policy. True, the unions continually demanded higher wages, but this action was part of an inflationary movement having more deep-seated causes to which the wage–price spiral was a response. The apparent success of union wage policy was, moreover, deceptive, because of the lag in real wages.

therefore, whether the policy of price stability is strong enough to stand against the threats against it, or merely a house of straw which can be blown over with the first puff.

The process of labor union inflation is envisioned as follows: 1. Labor will demand higher wages and threaten a strike. 2. Employers will be forced to grant these requests or to cease operations. 3. They will prefer to raise both wages and prices. 4. Higher prices will require additional bank borrowing, thus increasing the quantity of money. 5. Member banks will lend additional funds if security is ample and if they have excess reserves regardless of the effect on the level of prices. 6. Since credit can only be restricted by Federal Reserve policy, the Federal Reserve System will be forced to choose between preventing inflation or causing unemployment. 7. Faced with these alternatives, it is believed that central banking authorities will always choose the inflationary path or, if they should refuse to do so, business and labor will have them replaced by officials who will aid and abet the inflationary trend in the name of full employment.

[. . .]

VIII

The belief that organized labor can control the price level derives to a large degree also from the conception of trade unions as monopolists. We should therefore examine the nature and extent of labor monopoly as it bears on credit and price policy.

Labor monopoly is intrinsically different, and also less powerful than monopoly exercised by business firms. According to the theory of monopoly, the producer of any product has monopoly power when he can raise his price without losing all of his market. He can vary production by small increments according to its effect on costs and revenue so as to yield the highest net profit. He does not lose his entire market if he raises his price as he would under perfect competition. Labor, on the other hand, bargains for all members of the union; in striking for a 5 per cent wage increase it must be willing to sacrifice not an increment of employment and income, but all employment and income for the duration of the strike. Even the most powerful union is in the same theoretical position as a seller under perfect competition, who must sell at the market price or not at all. The loss to the worker is the total value of his labor for the period of the strike, plus the possible loss of employment after he wins the strike in so far as he has priced himself out of the market; the loss of the employer is not his total product but only his fixed costs and possible profit. No producer monopolist operates on the all-or-none basis – he need not risk selling no goods at all if he raises his price by a few per cent. Yet this is labor's predicament in a strike. It is, therefore, misleading to think of labor union monopoly power, based as it is on the small resources of its members and the pitifully small power to resist long unemployment without suffering and starvation, as equal to the power of industrial monopoly, backed by huge financial resources and able to sustain losses for a long period of time without impairing its financial health and stability.

But let us grant for the sake of analysis that the unions can overcome the resistance of the employer and that he seeks to obtain additional funds to finance a higher wage bill. Where is he to get them? When his profit margin is seriously impaired, earnings will be low and the stock and the bond markets will be closed to him. If he seeks to borrow from the banks, they will be doubtful about financing him. But supposing that he overcomes these disabilities and is still able to make a financial showing, the banks can loan only if they have excess reserves which under normal conditions are subject to central banking control. To be successful then in their assumed policy, labor unions must also control banking policy.

[. . .]

X

Let us now turn to fiscally induced inflation. Although the Employment Act of 1946 does not promise full employment by means of fiscal policy, we may ask how trade unionism would impinge upon such a policy should it be adopted. If full employment is insured by governmental spending regardless of its effect on costs and prices, we may feel reasonably sure that labor will make little effort to keep its wage rates in line so as not to price itself out of the market. Producers, knowing that government will take whatever goods they produce regardless of price (as in the cost-plus contracts during the war) will have no need to resist wage demands and unions will have no hesitancy in making them. If, for example, building costs rise too high for the incomes of prospective buyers and unemployment ensues in this trade, it would seem that the industry ought to reduce its costs.[3] Should government, however, assure the industry that it will provide orders whenever private business slumps, the incentive to price its product for private demand will disappear. Wages, costs, and prices will rise and never slump. The error in attempting to insure full employment by the simple device of compensatory spending is that it removes all incentives for producers to adjust their costs to the private market; it assures demand for the entire national product without reference to quality and price, and provides a seller's market for goods and services at a price fixed by the sellers. To describe this guaranty is enough to condemn it.

When the Employment Act of 1946 was under consideration, it was suggested that compensatory policies should be followed only in so far as they were consistent with a stable cost of living, but no such provision was included in the act. If, therefore, we should get inflation by the route of compensatory spending under a full-employment policy, it will not be because of trade unionism alone, but because in a seller's market every element in the community would be induced to raise prices and never to lower them. The principles of functional finance sometimes seem to imply that compensatory devices be used regardless of the cause of unemployment. In some circles, compensatory finance has become a dogma of economic policy with the same authority for its votaries as the 'invisible hand' of Adam Smith had for the *laissez-faire* school, Say's Law for the neo-classicists, and surplus value for the Marxians. As a dogma, it overlooks the multiple causes of depression and forgets that the cure of unemployment must depend upon its cause. If the cause be unbalanced price relationships, such as excessive prices for houses, automobiles, etc., then the remedy is to reduce these prices, not to guarantee a market for the products of these industries at inflated levels. If the cause be underconsumption in the Hobsonian sense, then the remedy is to change the distribution of income; if the cause be inadequate investment incentives, these will need to be augmented. We con-

3. This is in fact the position taken by President Truman in his *Report to Congress, January* 1949.

clude, then, that inflation will result from cyclical depression or stagnation only if government guarantees full employment regardless of its effect on costs or prices and pursues an inflationary policy to achieve it. Neither labor nor the central bank can prevent the consequences of such a policy; it can be prevented only by ridding ourselves of the dogmas responsible for it.

If we recognize that compensatory finance is not the sole means of maintaining aggregate demand in a free market-profit economy, we should not encourage the various economic groups in the belief that they will be protected from the consequences of their own folly by government spending. We should rather make them see the necessity of adjusting their own prices and policies so as to create a demand for their own product. It may be necessary to declare quite deliberately that government will refuse to maintain effective demand in those sectors which refuse to adjust their costs and prices to private market demand, and to use compensatory finance only when the fault does not lie in wage–price policies. Compensatory policies which look only to the aggregates of consumption and investment will create expectation for further inflation and hardly any inducement to correct basic causes of underemployment. In so far as the Keynesian revolution has come to this, it is a purely inflationary philosophy which must end in disaster. But it need not be so. We can still take into account aggregate relations between income, consumption, savings, and investment as emphasized by Malthus, Hobson, Keynes, and by the underconsumptionists, without ignoring the fact that equilibrium is also conditioned by the relations between wages, costs, and prices as described by the classical tradition.

Keynes created a false disjunction between classical and aggregate equilibrium which has produced a fateful dichotomy between policies designed to promote balanced price relationships and those aimed at balanced income relationships. We need not reject the classical cost–price balance in order to accept the Keynesian savings–investment equilibrium; we can rather accept the more reasonable conclusion that both the system of individual prices and the aggregates need to be in an optimum relationship in order to bring about full utilization of resources.

The two systems are indeed not contradictory but complementary. The truth in the classical system was its emphasis upon the need for workable relationships between individual prices to facilitate full employment; the error was the view that the rate of interest produced full employment automatically. The truth in the Keynesian system was in its emphasis upon the need for workable relationships between the aggregates of income, consumption, savings, and investment which it showed were not produced automatically by the rate of interest; the error was that it assumed these aggregates could be brought into optimum relationships by manipulating the rate of interest, the quantity of money, the distribution of income, and the fiscal policy of governments. It is not necessary to accept these exclusive alternatives, and if it is not necessary, it is not desirable. To accept without modification the classical view is to ignore the aggregative relations which were emphasized by Malthus, Marx, Hobson, and others before and after Keynes; to accept the compensatory view without modification is to embark upon a policy which neglects the need for incentives to adjust relative prices to market demand.

We conclude, therefore, that governmentally induced inflation must result from fiscal policy only if it is pursued without regard to the cause of underemployment; and that such a monolithic policy should be cast aside for one that is free from dogma, though not from error in comprehension and execution, but more comprehensive and hence likely to be more timely and fruitful.

XI

If the foregoing is essentially correct, we need not worry about the dire forebodings of those who deny the compatibility of trade unionism with the objectives of high employment and stable prices. We need not set out to disorganize our social life by a war on organized labor; nor let inflation rob the creditor class, the fixed-income groups, and those who have saved for old age; nor mournfully consign part of our resources to idleness and condemn our people to the humiliation and despair of large-scale unemployment. The view posing these stark alternatives, though it flows cogently from its postulates and is not without some truth, still is insufficiently factually accurate for purposes of national policy. We can, moreover, continue our efforts to maintain the high standard of living and the opportunity which full employment makes possible, without inaugurating controls over individual prices and wages.

If we do not need to destroy unionism in order to preserve price stability, neither do we need to establish, as has been sometimes suggested, a board to formulate and enforce a national wage policy fixing the general level of wages. In any event, such a board would hardly be effectual, for, if organized labor were powerful enough to force its views upon employers, bankers, and a reluctant Federal Reserve Board, it would most likely also be able to have its way with a national labor board. A Federal Reserve Board seeking to maintain sound economic conditions for the whole community does not aim its measures at any particular group such as a wage board would have to do, and in pursuit of these wider social aims, it could more easily resist the demands of any one group than could a special board set up for their specific control. Quite likely, a national wage board would be heavily weighted with labor members or public members acceptable to labor who would follow the traditional policy of accepting compromise wage increases, and resisting cuts. It is hard to visualize such a board, no matter how cogent its arguments and eloquent its expression, uncompromisingly resisting wage demands which were within its power to grant. Credit policy, on the other hand, being aimed at the control of total monetary demand leaves its allocation to the market which in turn dominates wage negotiations. An employer, resisting wage demands because the market will not stand them, is in a much stronger position to stop an inflationary rise than a wage board, which apparently has no direct financial responsibility for the result. We may, therefore, tentatively conclude that the establishment of a board to set a national wage pattern would probably be more inflationary than otherwise, and if, moreover, wages were subject to control, so would prices have to be, and we would end up in the position envisioned by those who believe that full employment is impossible without complete regimentation.

Under the circumstances, it seems wiser to continue over-all control of effective demand and to leave the rest of the economy free to adjust individual prices and wages to the resulting market. The concept of an unlimited monetary demand is, of course, inconsistent with price stability; it is this concept of which we must rid ourselves, not of trade unionism. If, however, it be found desirable to restrict, regulate, or destroy monopoly, whether of business, agriculture, or labor because of its effect on prices and production, that can still be done for its own sake; it need not be done in order to control the general price level. The same holds true relative to the need of rules to prevent work stoppages which may paralyze the nation or be dangerous to health and safety. The war and postwar experiences which engendered the ideas of direct controls over prices and wages are not typical of a peacetime economy because war demand is unlimited whereas in peace the consumer can withhold purchases until prices are in line with this income. The present mixture of monopoly, unionism, and competition will not operate after the model of perfect competition. We must accordingly learn to live by the more complex rules of a collective bargaining economy, but we need not yet admit that desiderata of stability and prosperity make our ultimate choice one between perfect competition and complete regimentation. These alternatives have a plausible validity so long as we do not examine too closely the reality of the postulates on which they rest, and, like much abstract theory of this type, present us with apparent alternatives true only at the limits. In a dynamic life, social adjustments, though following no fixed pattern, can be made between the extremes according to the strength of conflicting forces. This is the aim of a collective-bargaining economy with individuals who are still exposed to losses and gains as members of their group and therefore provided with strong incentives to act intelligently in their own and in the social interest.

References

HABERLER, G. (1948), 'Causes and cures of inflation', *Review of Economics and Statistics*, vol. 30, no. 1, pp. 10–17.

SLICHTER, S. H. (1948a), 'Higher payrolls raised the price of farm wages and prices', an address before the Academy of Political Science, Columbia University, vol. 23, no. 1, pp. 50–1.

SLICHTER, S. H. (1948b), 'Wages and prices', an address before the Academy of Political Science, Columbia University, vol. 23, no. 2, pp. 47–63.

SLICHTER, S. H. (1948c), *The American Economy*, Knopf.

7 P. Cagan

The Theory of Hyperinflation

Excerpts from P. Cagan, 'The monetary dynamics of hyperinflation', in M. Friedman (ed.), *Studies in the Quantity Theory of Money*, University of Chicago Press, 1956, pp. 25–117.

General Monetary Characteristics of Hyperinflations

Hyperinflations provide a unique opportunity to study monetary phenomena. The astronomical increases in prices and money dwarf the changes in real income and other real factors. Even a substantial fall in real income, which generally has not occurred in hyperinflations, would be small compared with the typical rise in prices. Relations between monetary factors can be studied, therefore, in what almost amounts to isolation from the real sector of the economy.

This study deals with the relation between changes in the quantity of money and the price level during hyperinflations. One characteristic of such periods is that the ratio of an index of prices to an index of the quantity of money (P/M) tends to rise. Row 6 of Table 1 gives one measure of its rise for seven hyperinflations. (These seven are the only ones for which monthly indexes of prices are available.) Another way to illustrate this characteristic is by the decline in the reciprocal of this ratio, which represents an index of the real value of the quality of money – real cash balances (M/P). Row 15 in Table 1 gives the minimum value reached by this index. Figures 1–7 also illustrate its tendency to decline. In ordinary inflations real cash balances, instead of declining, often tend to rise. The term '*hyper*inflation' must be properly defined. I shall define hyperinflations as beginning in the month the rise in prices exceeds 50 per cent[1] and as

1. The definition is purely arbitrary but serves the purposes of this study satisfactorily. Few ordinary inflations produce such a high rate even momentarily. In Figures 1–7 rates of change are given as rates per month, compounded continuously. A rate of 41 per cent per month, compounded continuously, equals a rate of 50 per cent per month, compounded monthly.

Table 1
Monetary Characteristics of Seven Hyperinflations[1]

Country	Austria	Germany	Greece	Hungary	Hungary	Poland	Russia
1. Approximate beginning month of hyperinflation	Oct. 1921	Aug. 1922	Nov. 1943	Mar. 1923	Aug. 1945	Jan. 1923	Dec. 1921
2. Approximate final month of hyperinflation	Aug. 1922	Nov. 1923	Nov. 1944	Feb. 1924	July 1946	Jan. 1924	Jan. 1924
3. Approximate number of months of hyperinflation	11	16	13	10	12	11	26
4. Ratio of prices at end of final month to prices at first of beginning month	69·9	$1·02 \times 10^{10}$	$4·70 \times 10^8$	44·0	$3·81 \times 10^{27}$	699·0	$1·24 \times 10^5$
5. Ratio of quantity of hand-to-hand currency at end of final month to quantity at first of beginning month	19·3	$7·32 \times 10^9$	$3·62 \times 10^6$	17·0	$1·19 \times 10^{25}$ [2]	395·0	$3·38 \times 10^4$
6. Ratio of (4) to (5)	3·62	1·40	130·0	2·59	320·0	1·77	3·67
7. Average rate of rise in prices (percentage per month)[3]	47·1	322·0	365·0	46·0	19,800	81·4	57·0
8. Average rate of rise in quantity of hand-to-hand currency (percentage per month)[4]	30·9	314·0	220·0	32·7	12,200 [2]	72·2	49·3
9. Ratio of (7) to (8)	1·52	1·03	1·66	1·41	1·62	1·13	1·16

10. Month of maximum rise in prices	Aug. 1922	Oct. 1923	July 1923	Nov. 1944	July 1946	Oct. 1923	Jan. 1924
11. Maximum monthly rise in prices (percentage per month)	134·0	32·4 × 10^3 [5]	98·0	85·5 × 10^6 [6]	41·9 × 10^{15}	275·0	213·0
12. Change in quantity of hand-to-hand currency in month of maximum change in prices (percentage per month)	72·0	1·30 × 10^3 [7]	46·0	73·9 × 10^3 [6]	1·03 × 10^{15}	106·0	87·0
13. Ratio of (11) to (12)	1·86	24·9	2·13	1,160	40·7	2·59	2·45
14. Month in which real value of hand-to-hand currency was at a minimum	Aug. 1922	Oct. 1923	Feb. 1924	Nov. 1944	July 1946	Nov. 1923	Jan. 1924
15. Minimum end-of-month ratio of real value of hand-to-hand currency to value at first of beginning month	0·35	0·030 [8]	0·39	0·0069 [9]	0·0031 [2]	0·34	0·27

---

1. All rates and ratios have three significant figures except those in row 15, which have two.
2. Includes bank deposits.
3. The value of x that sets $(1 + [x/100])^t$ equal to the rise in the index of prices (row 4), where t is the number of months of hyperinflation (row 3).
4. The value of x that sets $(1 + [x/100])^t$ equal to the rise in the quantity of hand-to-hand currency (row 5), where t is the number of months of hyperinflation (row 3).
5. 2 October to 30 October 1923, at a percentage rate per 30 days.
6. 31 October to 10 November, 1944, at a percentage rate per 30 days.
7. 29 September to 31 October, 1923, at a percentage rate per 30 days.
8. 23 October, 1923.
9. 10 November, 1944.

ending in the month before the monthly rise in prices drops below that amount and stays below for at least a year. The definition does not rule out a rise in prices at a rate below 50 per cent per month for the intervening months, and many of these months have rates below that figure. (The three average rates of increase below 50 per cent per month shown in row 7 of Table 1 reflect low rates in some of the middle months.)

Although real cash balances fall over the whole period of hyperinflation, they do not fall in every month but fluctuate drastically, as Figures 1–4 show. Furthermore, their behavior differs greatly among the seven hyperinflations. The ratios in rows 6 and 15 have an extremely wide range. Only when we bypass short but violent oscillations in the balances by striking an average, as in row 9, do the seven hyperinflations reveal a close similarity. The similarity of the ratios in row 9 suggests that these hyperinflations reflect the same economic process. To confirm this, we need a theory that accounts for the erratic behaviour of real cash balances from month to month. This study proposes and tests such a theory.

The theory developed in the following pages involves an extension of the Cambridge cash-balances equation. That equation asserts that real cash balances remain proportional to real income X *under given conditions.* ($M/P = kX$; $k = $ a constant.) Numerous writers have discussed what these given conditions are. Indeed, almost any discussion of monetary theory carries implications about the variables that determine the level of real cash balances. In the most general case the balances are a function, not necessarily linear, of real income and many other variables. [. . .]

The Demand for Real Cash Balances

Because money balances serve as a reserve of ready purchasing power for contingencies, the *nominal* amount of money that individuals want to hold at any moment depends primarily on the value of money, or the absolute price level. Their desired *real* cash balances depend in turn on numerous variables. The main variables that affect an individual's desired real cash balances are his wealth in real terms; his current real income; and the

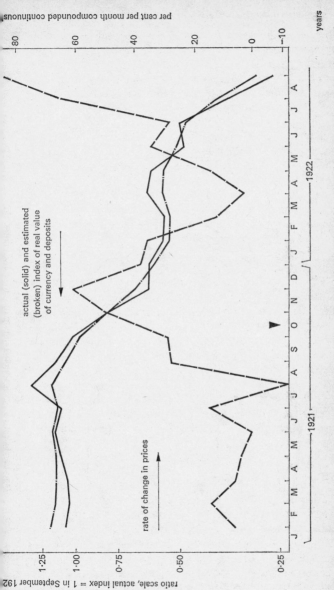

Figure 1 Austria – end-of-month rate of change in prices and index of real value of hand-to-hand currency and bank deposits, January 1921 to August 1922. (▼ indicates beginning month of hyperinflation)

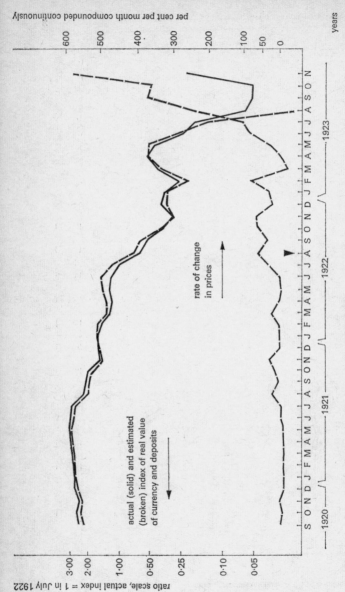

Figure 2 Germany – mid-month rate of change in prices and index of real value of hand-to-hand currency and bank deposits, September 1920 to November 1923. (▼ indicates beginning month of hyperinflation)

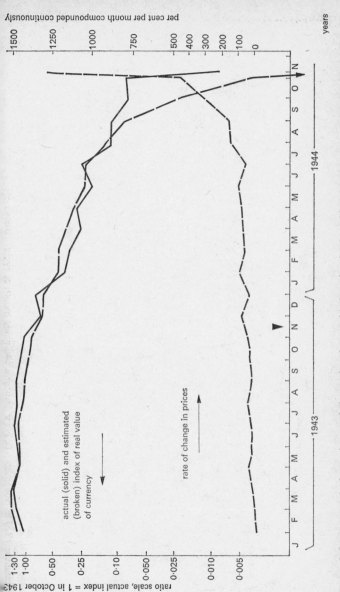

Figure 3 Greece — end-of-month rate of change in prices and index of real value of hand-to-hand currency, January 1943 to October 1944, and including 10 November 1944. (▼ indicates beginning of month of hyperinflation)

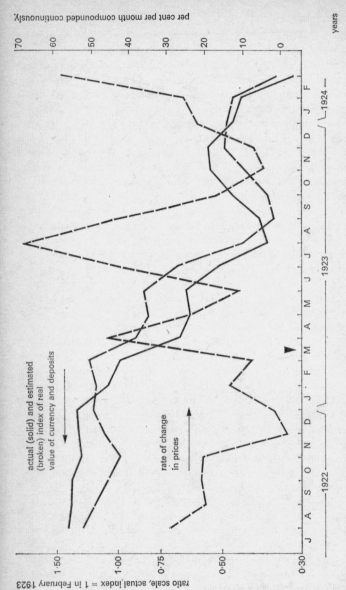

per cent per month compounded continuously.

Figure 4 Hungary – end-of-month rate of change in prices and index of real value of hand-to-hand currency and bank deposits, July 1922 to February 1924. (▼ indicates beginning month of hyperinflation)

expected returns from each form in which wealth can be held, including money.

If an individual's real wealth increases, he will usually desire to hold part of the increase in the form of money, because money is readily accepted in payment for goods and services or debts – it is an asset with a high liquidity.

If his current real income increases, an individual will want to substitute cash balances for part of his illiquid assets, for now he can more readily afford to forego the premium received for holding his assets in an illiquid form, and he may need larger balances to provide conveniently for his expenditures in the periods between income payments.

If the rate of interest on an asset increases, an individual is inclined to substitute this asset for some of his other assets, including his cash balances. His desired real cash balances will decrease. In addition, an increase in the rate of interest reflects a fall in the price of the asset and a decline in the wealth of holders of the asset; this decline in wealth reduces desired real cash balances.

Thus desired real cash balances change in the same direction as real wealth and current real income and in the direction opposite to changes in the return on assets other than money.

A specification of the amount of real cash balances that individuals want to hold for all values of the variables listed above defines a demand function for real cash balances. Other variables usually have only minor effects on desired real cash balances and can be omitted from the demand function. In general, this demand function and the other demand-and-supply functions that characterize the economic system simultaneously determine the equilibrium amount of real cash balances.

A simplified theory of this determination is that the amount of goods and services demanded and supplied and their relative prices are determined independently of the monetary sector of the economy. In one version of this theory – the quantity theory of money – the absolute level of prices is independently determined as the ratio of the quantity of money supplied to a given level of desired real cash balances. Individuals cannot change the nominal amount of money in circulation, but, according to the quantity theory of money, they can influence the real value of their cash balances by attempting to reduce or increase their balances. In this attempt they bid the prices of goods and services up or down, respectively, and thereby alter the real value of cash balances.

During hyperinflation the amount of real cash balances changes drastically (see Table 1). At first sight these changes may appear to reflect changes in individuals' preferences for real cash balances – that is, shifts in the demand function for the balances. But these changes in real cash balances may reflect instead changes in the variables that affect the desired level of the balances. Two of the main variables affecting their desired level, wealth in real terms and real income, seem to be relatively stable during hyperinflation, at least compared with the large fluctuations in an index of real cash balances. Thus to account for these fluctuations as a movement along the demand function for the balances instead of a shift in the function, we must look for large changes in the remaining variables listed above: the expected returns on various forms of holding wealth. Changes in the return on an asset affect real cash balances only if there is a change in the difference between the expected return on the asset and that on money. If this difference rises, individuals will substitute the asset for part of their cash balances. I turn, therefore, to a more detailed consideration of the difference in return on money and on various alternatives to holding money – the cost of holding cash balances.

There is a cost of holding cash balances with respect to each of the alternative forms of holding reserves, and in a wide sense anything that can be exchanged for money is an alternative to holding reserves in the form of cash balances. For practical purposes, these alternatives can be grouped into three main classes: fixed-return assets (bonds); variable-return assets (equities and titles to producers' goods); and non-perishable consumers' goods. The cost of holding cash balances with respect to any of these alternatives is the difference between the money return on a cash balance and the money return on an alternative that is equivalent in value to the cash balance. The money return on a cash balance may be zero, as it typically is for hand-to-hand currency; negative, as it is for demand deposits when there are service charges; or positive, as it is for deposits on which interest is paid. The money return on bonds includes interest and on equities includes dividends, as well as any gains or losses due to a change in the money value of the assets. Variations in the cost of holding cash balances when the alternative is to hold consumers' goods can be determined solely by the change in the real value of a given nominal cash balance – the rate of depreciation in the real value of money. The variation in the real value of goods because of their physical depreciation is fairly constant and can be ignored.

The only cost of holding cash balances that seems to fluctuate widely enough to account for the drastic changes in real cash balances during hyperinflation is the rate of depreciation in the value of money or, equivalently, the rate of change in prices. This observation suggests the hypothesis that changes in real cash balances in hyperinflation result from variations in the expected rate of change in prices.

To be valid, this hypothesis requires that the effects of the other variables discussed above be negligible during hyperinflation. For the most part statistical tests uphold the hypothesis that variations in the expected rate of change in prices account for changes in desired real cash balances. For the periods in which the data do not conform to the hypothesis, what evidence there is suggests that taking account of changes in real income would not remedy the limitations of the hypothesis. Another explanation of why the hypothesis fails to hold for these periods is offered instead as a plausible possibility.

In order to test the hypothesis statistically, the two variables, desired real cash balances and the expected rate of change in prices, must be related to observable phenomena. The assumption made about the former is that desired real cash balances are equal to actual real cash balances at all times. This means that any discrepancy that may exist between the two is erased almost immediately by movements in the price level.[2] The assumption

2. This assumption can be formulated as follows: Let M^d/P and M/P represent desired and actual real cash balances. Then write

$$\frac{d}{dt} \log \frac{M}{P} = \pi \left(\log \frac{M^d}{P} - \log \frac{M}{P} \right), \qquad 1$$

where π is a positive constant. This says that, when desired and actual real cash balances differ, the percentage change in the latter is proportional to the logarithm of their ratio. Prices rise and diminish the actual balances when the latter exceed desired balances. Prices fall and increase the actual balances when the latter fall short of desired balances. If we write the equation as

$$\log \frac{M^d}{P} = \log \frac{M}{P} + \frac{1}{\pi} \frac{d}{dt} \log \frac{M}{P}$$

127

made about the expected rate of change in prices is that it depends on the actual rate of change [in such a way that the expected rate of change in prices is revised per period of time in proportion to the difference between the actual rate of change in prices and the rate of change that was expected].

With the above two assumptions, the hypothesis asserts that time series for the price level and the quantity of money are related by some equation that determines real cash balances. An equation of the following form is able to account for most of the changes in real cash balances in seven hyperinflations:

$$\log_e \frac{M}{P} = -\alpha E - \gamma. \qquad 2$$

Equation 2 shows the demand for real cash balances for different levels of the expected rate of change in prices. M is an end-of-month index of the quantity of money in circulation, and P is an end-of-month index of the price level. α (which is necessarily positive) and γ are constants. E represents the expected rate of change in prices and is assumed to be a function of the actual rate of change, denoted by C. C stands for $(d \log P)/dt$ and is approximated by the difference between the logarithms of successive values of the index of prices. This difference represents the rate of change in prices per month, compounded continuously, if the logarithms have the base e.[3]

E, being the expected level of C, has the same units of measurement as C, namely, a pure number divided by the number of months. M/P is an index and therefore a pure number. Consequently, the unit of α is 'months'.

An implication of the above relation is that variations in the expected rate of change in prices have the same effect on real cash balances in percentage terms regardless of the absolute

---

the assumption in the text is equivalent to asserting that π is so large that

$$\frac{1}{\pi}\frac{d}{dt}\log \frac{M}{P}$$

is always almost zero.

3. If we view the change in prices from P_{i-t} to P_i in t months as a continuous rate of change at a rate of C per month, $P_i = P_{i-t}e^{Ct}$. When t is one month, $P_i = P_{i-1}e^C$; hence $C = \log_e P_{i-1}$.

amount of the balances. This follows from the fact that equation 2 is a linear relation between the expected rate of change in prices and the logarithm of real cash balances. This implication seems proper for an equation that is supposed to provide an accurate approximation to the true demand function.

If we write equation 2 in the equivalent form,

$$\frac{M}{P} = e^{-\alpha E - \gamma}, \qquad\qquad 3$$

the elasticity of demand for real cash balances with respect to the expected change in prices, implied by the above relation, is

$$\left(\frac{d}{dt}\frac{M}{P}\right)\frac{E}{M/P} = -\alpha E, \qquad\qquad 4$$

where αE is a pure number. The elasticity is proportional to the expected rate of change in prices. It is positive when E is negative, and negative when E is positive. The elasticity is zero when E is zero.

[. . .]

Summary of Findings: The Theory of Hyperinflation

This study set out to explain the monetary characteristics of hyperinflation as displayed by seven such episodes following the two World Wars. These characteristics are summarized by the pattern of time series for money and prices: 1. the ratio of the quantity of money to the price level – real cash balances – tended to fall during hyperinflation as a whole but fluctuated drastically from month to month and 2. the rates at which money and prices rose tended to increase and in the final months preceding currency reform reached tremendous heights. This second pattern supplies the identifying characteristic of hyperinflation, but the explanation of the first holds the key to an explanation of the second and logically comes first in order of presentation.

1. *Elucidation in real cash balances*

The evidence [. . .] verifies the hypothesis that these fluctuations result from changes in the variables that determine the demand for real cash balances. With a change in demand, individuals cannot alter the nominal amount of money in circulation, but they can alter the real value of their collective cash balances by spending or hoarding money, and so bid prices up or down, respectively. Only one of the variables that determine this demand has an amplitude of fluctuation during hyperinflation as large as that of the balances and could possibly account for large changes in the demand. That variable is the cost of holding money, which during hyperinflation is for all practical purposes the rate of depreciation in the real value of money or, equivalently, the rate of rise in prices.

To relate the rate of price rise to the demand for the balances, it is necessary to allow for lags. There are two lags that could delay the effect of a change in this rate on the demand. First, there will be a lag between the expected and the actual rate of price rise; it may take some time after a change in the actual rate before individuals expect the new rate to continue long enough to make adjustments in their balances worthwhile. Second, there will be a lag between the desired and the actual level of the balances; it may take some time after individuals decide to change the actual level before they achieve the desired level. The method used to take account of these lags relates actual real cash balances to an average of past rates of price change, weighted by an exponential curve, so that price changes more recent in time are given greater importance. The weights never fall to zero, but past price changes sufficiently distant in time receive too small a weight to have any influence on the weighted average. The steepness of the weighting pattern indicates the length of period over which most of the weight is distributed. This method of allowing for the two lags does not distinguish between them. However, the period of time required for adjusting the balances to desired levels seems negligible compared with the past period of time normally reviewed in forming expectations. For this reason I have assumed that the actual level of real cash balances always equals desired levels and that the weighted average of past rates of price change measures only the 'expected rate of price change'. But there is no direct evidence on the relative importance of the two lags, and the name given to the weighted average may be lacking somewhat in descriptive accuracy.

The specific form of the hypothesis, restated to allow for lags, asserts that variations in the expected rate of price change account for variations in real cash balances during hyperinflation, where the expected rate is an exponentially weighted average of past rates. The hypothesis was tested by fitting a least-squares regression to time series for the balances and the expected rate. The regression fits the data for most months of the seven hyperinflations with a high degree of accuracy, and thus the statistical results strongly support the hypothesis.

The regression functions derived from these fits provide good approximations to the demand function for the balances and so reveal certain characteristics of this demand during hyperinflation. The elasticity of demand with respect to the expected rate of price change increases in absolute value as this expected rate rises. This contradicts the often stated view that the degree to which individuals can reduce their holdings of a depreciating currency has a limit. The demand elasticity indicates that they reduce their holdings by an increasing proportion of each successive rise in the expected rate. Indeed, the reason why issuing money on a grand scale does not almost immediately lead to extreme flight from the currency is not due to inelasticity in the demand for it but to individuals' lingering confidence in its future value. Their confidence maintains the lag in expectations, whereby the expected rates of price change do not at first keep pace with the rapidly rising actual rates. However, the weighting pattern for the lag appears to become much steeper in the later months, indicating that the lag in the expected behind the actual rates tends to shorten in response to continual inflation.

Thus the large changes in the balances during hyperinflation correspond to large changes in the rate of price change with some delay, not simultaneously. The demand function that expresses this correspondence can be interpreted to represent a dynamic process in which the course of prices through time is determined by the current quantity of money and an exponentially weighted average of past rates of change in this quantity. The process implies that past and current changes in the quantity of money cause the hyperinflation of prices. This link between changes in prices and money is only broken when the absolute value of the slope of the demand function is especially high or the lag in expectations is especially short. In that event price increases become self-generating. What this means is that the rise in prices immediately produces a proportionately greater decline in real cash balances. Then the effect of percentage changes in prices and the balances on each other does not diminish, as a stable moving equilibrium of prices requires, but grows. Such a process sends up the *percentage* change in prices at no less than an exponential rate, even if the quantity of money remains constant. Apparently the demand slope and the lag never reached the critical level in the seven hyperinflations, for none had self-generating price increases. Instead of running away on their own, price increases remained closely linked to past and current changes in the quantity of money and could have been stopped at any time, as they finally were, by tapering off the issue of new money.

2. *The tremendous increase in money and prices*

If in fact price increases were not self-generating, what accounted for their tremendous size? The above explanation of their behavior in terms of large increases in the quantity of money only raises the further question, 'Why did this quantity increase so much?' Clearly, issuing money on a large scale serves as a major source of funds for government expenditures. The inflation resulting from new issues places a tax on cash balances by depreciating the value of money. The revenue in real terms raised by this tax is the product of the rate of rise in prices (the tax rate) and real cash balances (the tax base). By setting the rate of increase in the quantity of money, the note-issuing authorities indirectly determine the rate of tax through the process implied by the demand function. The simplicity of administering this tax undoubtedly explains why governments resorted to continual issues of money in the difficult periods after the two World Wars. An explanation of why those issues became so large, however, is found in the response of the tax base to the tax rate.

If the tax rate remains constant, the tax base and, therefore, the revenue ultimately become constant. Among all constant rates, there is one that yields a maximum ultimate revenue. With a tax rate that increases rapidly enough, however, the revenue forever exceeds this maximum amount for a constant rate because of delays in adjusting the tax base produced by the lag in expectations. In the beginning and closing months of the seven hyperinflations, the authorities successfully pursued a policy of inflating at increasing tax rates to take advantage of this lag and collected more revenue thereby than they could have obtained with any constant rate. This policy led to actual rates far above the constant rate that would have maximized ultimate revenue and produced the tremendous increases in money and prices characteristic of hyperinflation.

In the middle months the rate of increase in the money supply tapered off, for what reason it is not entirely clear, and the revenue temporarily decreased. As a result, the revenue collected with the actual tax rates was not greater on the average than the amount that could have been obtained with a constant rate. The resumption of increasing rates in the closing months restored the revenue to amounts at least as large as those in the beginning months. In order to compensate for the low level to which the tax base fell after many months of hyperinflation, the tax rates rose to astronomical heights. This explosion of the rates in the final months completely disrupted the economy and forced the Government to substitute a traditional tax program for a policy of printing money.

In section I it was suggested that the seven hyperinflations represent the same economic process because of the similarity in the ratios of the average change in prices to the average change in the quantity of money (row 9 in Table 1). The model of hyperinflation described above depicts the nature of this process. But these ratios of averages cover up an extraordinary dissimilarity. Rows 13 and 15 also present ratios involving prices and the quantity of money but not averages, and they differ widely. The model shows that these differences originate, not in the differing responses of the public to a depreciating currency, but in the varying rates at which money was issued. The average share of national income that these new issues procured for the different governments was 3 to about 15 per cent, except in Russia, which had the unusually low percentage of 0·5. The differences in these percentages are not large when compared with the very much larger differences between the hyperinflations in the rates at which money rose. To some extent the governments may have collected less revenue than was planned. But, in so far as the actual collections met budgetary plans, the rates required to procure the intended amount in any month roughly equal the actual rates. The differences between the hyperinflations in the required rates that can be derived from the model thus account to a great extent for the corresponding differences in the actual rates at which money rose.

The model used has definite limitations: it only applies accurately to large price increases, and it fails to describe the closing months in four of the hyperinflations. In the closing months real cash balances sometimes rose when the model indicates they should have fallen. This limitation likely results from expectations that current price increases would not last very long. Such expectations are not related in any direct or obvious way to past changes in prices. To take account of this limitation of the model does not seem to require revisions that would contradict the premise of this study that domestic monetary factors alone explain hyperinflations.

Many prevailing theories of economic disturbances emphasize external monetary factors like the foreign-exchange rate, as well as real factors like the level of employment and real income, the structure of trade unionism, the rate and extent of capital formation, and so on. These factors are prominent primarily in discussions of depression. Yet they also enter into discussions of inflation. The theory of the cost–price spiral, which borrows its concepts and framework from theories of income and employment common in discussions of depression, has been applied to inflation with the suggestion, sometimes explicit, that it applies to hyperinflation as well. Closely related and often identical to the theory of the cost–price spiral is the explanation of hyperinflation in terms of the depreciation of the foreign-exchange rate.[4]

4. References to discussions of the cost–price spiral are too extensive to give even a partial list here. The most explicit application of this theory to hyperinflation that I have found is by Mrs Joan Robinson in 'Review of Bresciani–Turroni's *The Economics of Inflation*', *Economic Journal*, vol. 48, (September 1938), pp. 507–13.

To my knowledge no one has argued that depreciation of the foreign-exchange rate alone is sufficient to explain hyperinflations, but it is often considered to be a causal factor. The attempts to find statistical confirmation of this view are inadequate and unconvincing. Probably the best attempt is that by James Harvey Rogers (see his *The Process of Inflation in France*, Columbia University Press, 1929, chap. 7), on which Frank Graham based his interpretation of the German episode (see his *Exchange, Prices, and Production in Hyper-inflation: Germany, 1920–23*, Princeton University Press, 1930, esp. p. 172).

These theories postulate that a rise in prices results from increases in wages or prices of imported goods and precedes increases in the quantity of money. This study points to the opposite sequence and indicates that an extreme rise in prices depends almost entirely on changes in the quantity of money. By implication, the rise in wages and the depreciation of the foreign-exchange rate in hyperinflations are effects of the rise in prices. Extreme changes in a short period of time in exchange rates will primarily reflect variations in the real value of the currency. It is quite true that the public might well expect depreciation of the currency to show up more accurately in depreciation of exchange rates than in any set of readily available commodity prices and so follow these rates in adjusting their balances. Circumstances are easy to imagine in which *for a short time* the exchanges might depreciate faster than prices rise and so appear to move in advance of prices. But this result would not mean that the rise in prices had become the effect rather than the cause of exchange depreciation. Real cash balances would be related to this depreciation only so long as it remained a good indicator of price changes.

The model suggests in addition that the spiral theory places emphasis on the wrong factors. *Hyper*inflation at least can be explained almost entirely in terms of the demand for money. This explanation places crucial importance on the supply of money. While the monetary authorities might capitulate to pressures for sustaining wage increases, as the spiral theory presumes, they will typically attend to many other considerations. The most important of these in hyperinflation is the revenue raised by issuing money, which was analysed above. More precise analysis than this of the determinants of the money supply goes beyond a mechanistic account of the inflationary process and involves the motives of governments, with whom the authority to open and close the spigot of note issues ultimately lies.

8 M. Friedman

Monetary Theory and Policy

M. Friedman, 'Statement on monetary theory and policy', in *Employment, Growth and Price Levels* (Hearings before the Joint Economic Committee, 86th Congress, 1st session, May 25–8, 1959), pp. 605–12, U.S. Government Printing Office.

Unless we can achieve both a reasonably stable economy in the short run and a reasonably stable price level in the long run, our free enterprise economy is unlikely to be permitted to survive. And without a predominantly free enterprise economy, we shall neither preserve political freedom nor attain healthy economic growth, which in a free society means the possibility for individuals to use their resources effectively to promote their own aspirations.

The past three decades have seen first a sweeping revolution against previously accepted economic thought about the role of monetary factors in economic change and then a counter-revolution that is still incomplete but promises to be no less sweeping. As with any successful counter-revolution, the result has not been simply to restore the *status quo ante*. In the process, views initially held rather uncritically have been re-examined and improved, and some elements of the revolutionary interlude absorbed.

Before the great depression of the early 1930s, accepted economic doctrine attached great importance to the stock of money as a determinant of the level of money income and of the price level. This view rested on experience covering centuries in time and spanning the globe in space. On numerous occasions, substantial increases in the stock of money relative to output had been associated with substantial increases in prices, and substantial decreases in the stock of money relative to output with substantial decreases in prices. And there were no known cases in which substantial changes in either money or prices had occurred without a similar change in the other magnitude.

The theoretical relation suggested by this experience was generally termed 'the quantity theory of money'. Like most established orthodoxies, it became unduly rigid in form and structure and thereby gave rise to expectations that were bound to be disappointed. In particular, in the 1920s, it was a major element in the widespread belief that the Federal Reserve System could and, what is even more extreme, would succeed in producing for an indefinitely prolonged period a high degree of economic stability, itself a major ingredient in the belief in a new era.

The great depression spawned a revolution in views. Though on a retrospective examination the depression is a tragic testimonial to the potency of monetary factors – the stock of money fell by a third from 1929 to 1933 – the failure of the monetary authorities to stem the depression was taken as evidence that they could not have done so. And in any event, the obvious disorders in the economy and the urgent need for a remedy made the world in general and the economic profession in particular receptive to new ideas.

John Maynard Keynes was the chief architect of the subsequent intellectual revolution. He shifted emphasis from the relation between the stock of money and the flow of income which was at the heart of the quantity theory to the relation between different flows, in particular between the flow of capital expenditures and the flow of income. He regarded changes in the stock of money as of minor importance in times of unemployment, and as exercising a significant influence only in times of full employment. His disciples, as disciples will, went much farther than the master. The view became widespread that 'money does not matter', that the stock of money was a purely passive concomitant of economic change and played no independent part except as it might affect interest rates, and that hence the only role for monetary policy was the minor one of keeping interest rates low so as to avoid interfering with the investment regarded as needed to offset the secular stagnation that was confidently expected to be the major problem for the future.

Two forces combined to produce a counter revolution in ideas. One was strictly academic. Scholarly criticism and analysis of Keynes' ideas demonstrated a logical fallacy in one of his central propositions; namely, the proposition that, for a given stock of money, there might, even in principle, exist no price and wage level consistent with full employment; or, to put the proposition differently, that even in the economist's never-never land of the long run, and even if all prices and wages were perfectly flexible, a free market system might have no inherent tendency to full employment.

It has turned out on analysis that Keynes' proposition involved an error of omission. He neglected to take account of the effect of different levels of prices on the real value attached by the community to its wealth relative to its income, and of the effect of changes in this ratio, in its turn, on consumption expenditures. When this effect is taken into account, there is always in principle a price and wage level consistent with full employment, though of course frictions or other disturbances may prevent the economy from attaining such a position at any point in time. Unemployment, that is, cannot be attributed to an inherent 'flaw in the price system'; it requires explanation in terms of such other forces as rigidities in adjustments, external disturbances, and the like.

The second, and more obvious, though perhaps not more important, factor that produced a counter-revolution was the brute force of events. Many countries in the postwar period, including the United States, pursued cheap-money policies, partly under the influence of the ideas derived from Keynes that I have so briefly sketched. Every such country experienced either open inflation or a network of partly effective, partly ineffective, controls designed to suppress the inflationary pressure. In every case, the stock of money rose as a result of the cheap-money policies and so did prices, either openly or in whatever disguise was most effective in circumventing the controls. No country succeeded in stemming inflation without adopting measures that made it possible to restrain the growth in the stock of money. And every country that did hold down the growth in the stock of money succeeded in checking the price rise.

Western Germany's 'economic miracle' after the monetary reform of 1948 was the most dramatic episode, but the experiences of Italy, of Great Britain, and of the United States differed only in detail. And French experience, prior to the monetary reforms at the turn of this year, is equally striking testimony by its contrast in both policy and outcome.

These developments in the world of scholarship and of affairs have produced a rebirth of interest in monetary changes. It is by now clear, and widely accepted, that money does matter and matters very much. There has been an increasing amount of research by economists during recent years on just how monetary forces operate, on what the relation is between monetary changes and other economic changes, and on the structure and operation of our financial system. I venture to predict that this trend will continue.

The modern version of the quantity theory that has been developed as a result of this work is more sophisticated and subtle than the earlier version. Like that earlier version, however, it attaches great importance to the quantity of money as a determinant of prices and like it, also, it is consistent with centuries of experience.

An examination of the role of money must distinguish sharply between the arithmetic and the economics of the relation between money and other magnitudes.

As a matter of arithmetic, we can always express national income in two different ways:
First, as the product of the amount of money and its velocity of circulation.
Second, as the product of an index of the quantity of goods and services produced and an index of the average price of these goods and services.

The two products are always equal, which gives the famous quantity equation: $MV = Py$, in its income form, where M is the stock of money at any time; V, the income velocity of circulation of money; P, the price level, and y, the rate of flow of real income.

As it stands, this equation is simply a definition of velocity; for any values of the price level, real income, and the stock of money, all of which can be observed directly, we can compute the value of V that will make it true. It says nothing about the factors that might produce a change in the stock of money or about the effect of such a change. Conceivably, such a change might be absorbed entirely in V, without affecting prices or output at all – this is the result implicit in the views of the extreme and rigid disciples of Keynes. Or the change in M, the stock of money, might be entirely absorbed by prices, without affecting velocity or output at all – this is the result predicted by the extreme and rigid quantity theorists. Or the change in money might be partly offset by a change in velocity, and the remainder reflected partly in prices, partly in output – this is the result experienced in the United States in the longer period movements of the past century. Or the change in money might be reinforced by a change in velocity in the same direction, the combined effect being reflected in both prices and output, but in widely varying proportions, depending on circumstances – this is the result experienced in the United States during the shorter period movements, the so-called business cycles, of the past centuries. And still other combinations are possible.

The economic issue concerns the circumstances under which one or another of these outcomes is likely to occur and the process whereby it does occur. This in turn depends on the factors that determine the quantity of money, the problem of the supply of money; the factors that determine the amount of money people want to hold, the demand for money; and the factors that determine the process whereby the amount of money people want to hold is adapted to the amount available, the adjustment between demand and supply.

Under present conditions in the United States, the Federal Reserve System essentially determines the total quantity of money; that is to say, the number of dollars of currency and deposits available for the public to hold. Within very wide limits, it can make this total anything it wants it to be. Of course, it cannot do so instantaneously or to the precise dollar, and it frequently expresses its proximate objectives in terms of other magnitudes, letting the quantity of money be whatever is consistent with these other objectives. But there is no doubt that, if it wanted to, it has both the formal power and the actual technical capacity to control the total stock of money with a timelag measured in weeks and to a degree of precision measured in tenths of 1 per cent.

Broadly speaking, therefore, the public cannot by itself affect the total number of dollars available to be held. For any one individual separately, it both appears to be true and is true that he can control the amount of cash that he holds. He can increase his cash balances by selling some assets for cash or spending less than he receives from other sources. He can reduce his cash balances by spending on assets or for other purposes more than he receives. For all individuals combined, however, the appearance that they can control their cash balances is an optical illusion. One individual can reduce or increase his cash balance only because another individual or several others are induced to increase or reduce theirs; that is, to do the opposite of what he does. If individuals as a whole were to try to reduce the number of dollars they held, they could not all do so, they would simply be playing a game of musical chairs. In trying to do so, however, they would raise the flow of expenditures and of money income since each would be trying to spend more than he receives; in the process adding to someone else's receipts, and, reciprocally, finding his own higher than anticipated because of the attempt by still others to spend more than they receive. In the process, prices would tend to rise, which would reduce the real value of cash balances; that is, the quantity of goods and services that the cash balances will buy.

While individuals are thus frustrated in their attempt to reduce the number of dollars they hold, they succeed in achieving an equivalent change in their position, for the rise in money income and in prices reduces the ratio of these balances to their income and also the real value of these balances. The process will continue until this ratio and this real value are in accord with their desires.

Conversely, if individuals were to try to increase the number of dollars they held, they could not do so if the Federal Reserve System did not increase the number available to be held. But in their attempt to do so, individuals would try to spend less than they received, which would lower the flow of spending and reduce the level of money income and of prices. This would raise the ratio of cash balances to income and the real value of cash balances.

This essential difference between the situation as it appears to the individual, who can determine his own cash balances but must take prices and money income as beyond his control, and the situation as it is to all individuals together, whose total cash balances are outside their control but who can determine prices and money income, is perhaps the most important proposition in monetary theory and certainly the source of greatest confusion to the layman.

It follows from this analysis that if the nominal stock of money changes, but the public at large wants to hold the same real stock of money, the monetary change will be reflected fully and proportionately in prices after adjustment has been made to the change. In the interim, the effect on prices might be less or more and real income might also be affected. However, systematic discrepancies over any period between movements in prices and in the stock of money must reflect changes in the real stock of money that the public at large wishes to hold.

The main factors affecting the real stock of money the public wishes to hold are:

1. The level of income.
2. The cost of holding money.

The level of real income affects desired real cash balances in two ways:

In the first place, a change in real income affects the total volume of transactions to be effected; that is, the amount of work, as it were, for money to do. This effect would lead to a change in the desired real stock of money in roughly the same proportion as in output.

In the second place, if there is a change not only in total real income but also in *per capita* income, it means that people are at a higher or a lower level of living. With such a change in the level of living, they may want to increase their stock of money more or less than proportionately, just as an increase in level of living means a less than proportionate increase in expenditures on bread but a more than proportionate increase in the stock of durable consumer goods. It turns out empirically that in this respect money is like durable consumer goods rather than like bread, so that an increase in real level of living is on the average associated with a more than proportionate increase in the real stock of money.

A very recent and rather novel finding is that the income to which cash balances are adjusted is the longer term level of income that can be expected, rather than the income currently being received. This finding goes far to explain much that has hitherto been puzzling in the cyclical behavior of the stock of money relative to income.

The cost of holding cash balances depends mainly on two factors: the rate of interest that can be earned on alternative assets, and the expected rate of change of prices.

If a government bond, for example, yields 4 per cent, it costs an individual $4 a year to hold $100 in cash instead of in the form of a bond. If prices are rising at the rate of 4 per cent per year, for example, it will take $104 in cash to buy at the end of the year as much as $100 at the beginning, so that it costs an individual $4 a year to hold $100 in cash instead of in goods initially worth $100. In consequence, the higher are interest rates and the higher is the expected rate of change in prices, the greater is the incentive for individuals to economize on cash balances, and conversely.

Empirical evidence suggests that interest rates have a systematic effect in the expected direction but that the effect is not large in magnitude. The experienced rate of change in prices has no discernible effect in ordinary times, when prices are not expected to change by much. On the other hand, the rate of change in prices has a clearly discernible and major effect when price change is rapid and long continued, as during extreme inflations and deflations.

In recent years, both interest rates and the expected rate of change in prices have been working in the same direction in the United States. Expectations of inflation have become more and more widespread and, partly for that reason, interest rates have risen. These changes doubtless help to explain the recent tendency for the ratio of the stock of money to income to decline despite a rise in real income *per capita*.

Of course, even after allowance is made for changes in real income *per capita* and in the cost of holding money, the ratio of cash balances to income is not perfectly steady. But the remaining fluctuations are minor, certainly far smaller than those that occur in the stock of money itself.

In concluding this statement, I should like to emphasize two points that seem to me of central importance in fashioning a wise national monetary policy.

The first is the closeness, regularity, and predictability of the relation among the stock of money, the level of price, and the level of output over any considerable period of years.

The second is our present inability to predict at all accurately this same relation over very short periods, from month to month, quarter to quarter, even year to year.

The first proposition means that in order to attain a reasonably stable price level over the long pull, we must adopt measures that will lead to a growth in the stock of money at a fairly steady rate roughly equal to or slightly higher than the average rate of growth of output.

The second proposition means that in the present state of our knowledge we cannot hope to use monetary policy as a precision instrument to offset other short-run forces making for instability. The attempt to do so is likely merely to introduce additional instability into the economy, to make the economy less rather than more stable.

It should be emphasized that this conclusion about short-run changes is valid not only for monetary policy but also for fiscal or other policies. All these policies operate with a long lag and with a lag that varies widely from time to time. We know too little about either these lags or about what the economic situation will be months or years hence when the chickens we release come home to roost, to be able to be effective in offsetting the myriad of factors making for minor fluctuations in economic activity. This is one of those cases in which the best can be the enemy of the good.

As I examine the past record of stability in the United States, I am impressed by the number of occasions on which major fluctuations have been a consequence of changing and at times erratic governmental policies with respect to money. This record offers much support for the view that, if the monetary framework were stable, our private enterprise economy is sufficiently adaptable to the other changes that occur to yield a high degree of economic stability in the short run as well as the long run.

For this reason, the urgent need, I believe – and here I am venturing farthest from any academic ivory tower – is to keep monetary changes from being a destabilizing force, as they have been through much of our history. In my view, this can best be done by assigning the monetary authorities the task of keeping the stock of money growing at a regular and steady rate, month in and month out. This would at one and the same time provide a stable monetary background for short-run adjustments and assure long-run stability in the purchasing power of the dollar.

The elimination of monetary uncertainty would promote healthy economic growth by providing a stabler environment for both individual planning and social action. But it would be no panacea. The springs of economic progress are to be found elsewhere: in the qualities of the people, their inventiveness, thrift, and responsibility, in public policies that give a free field for private initiative and promote competition and free trade at home and abroad. Mistakes in monetary policy can render these forces impotent. A stable monetary environment can give them an opportunity to be effective; it cannot create them.

Part Three Demand and Cost Inflation

The issue of whether inflation is caused by the upward push of costs or the upward pull of demand began to be debated immediately after the war. According to the demand-pull theory, prices rise in response to an excess of aggregate demand over existing supply. Cost push, on the other hand, assumes that inflation is caused by factors of production trying to increase their share of the total product by raising their prices. One variant of cost push advanced by Schultz (Reading 12) to analyse the creeping inflation of the 1950s assigns sectoral shifts in demand the primary role – inflation resulting from the downward inflexibility of prices in the sector losing demand. Others generalized this by arguing that regardless of the initial pull or push, inflation continues because both management and labour are able to mark up prices and wages to protect their shares of total product.

The importance of the debate between demand pull and cost push stems largely from the difference between the policy recommendations which the two views on the causes of inflation imply. The former leads to a recommendation of monetary restraint and fiscal orthodoxy involving a higher level of unemployment (e.g. Paish's proposal, Reading 13). Cost push, on the other hand, leads to such recommendations as administrative restraint on price increases and incomes policies: measures aimed at halting inflation without sacrificing employment.

Some economists have argued that the issue between cost and demand inflation is largely spurious. The former, it is said, could never generate a sustained inflation unless the Government is prepared to create the additional money required to permit the cost push, without further unemployment. However, postwar experience in both the U.K. and the U.S. shows that the velocity of circulation is sufficiently flexible to permit rising prices without a major increase in the money supply. Another issue, discussed by Machlup and Streeten (Readings 9 and 10), is the effect of increased productivity on prices and employment. If, as Streeten believes, productivity increases in an industry are accompanied by an equivalent rise in factor payments, with no reduction in prices, then gains in productivity have the pessimistic result of increasing rather than reducing inflationary pressures.

9 F. Machlup

Cost Push and Demand Pull

F. Machlup, 'Another view of cost-push and demand-pull inflation', *Review of Economics and Statistics*, vol. 42 (1960), pp. 125–39.

It is with some hesitation that I join the discussion and thus contribute to the galloping inflation of the literature on the creeping inflation of prices. My excuse is probably the same as that of most of my fellow writers: dissatisfied with much of what others have written, I have, perhaps presumptuously, decided that my way of thinking would be more successful. Hence, I am presenting another view of cost-push and demand-pull inflation.

The Current Debate

Before I set forth the controversial issue and the most widely held views, I shall indulge in a few preliminaries by referring briefly to the old squabble about what should be meant by inflation.

Inflation of what?

Some people regard 'inflation' as a *cause* (explanation) of a general rise in prices (and of some other things too), while others use the word as a *synonym* (equivalent) for a general rise in prices. In times when governments undertake to control prices by prohibitions with threats of sanctions against unauthorized price raising, many writers realize how awkward it is to use the term inflation to signify price increase, because then they want to discuss the 'latent' or 'repressed' inflation – one that does not show up in a general price index, or does not show up adequately. Also when one talks about inflation and deflation as apparent opposites, a definition in terms of general prices is quite inconvenient, inasmuch as the problem of deflation is so serious largely because it shows up in falling volumes of production and employment instead of falling prices.

One solution would be to use the word inflation always with a modifying word that tells exactly what is blown up: currency, credit, spending, demand, wages, prices, etc. This would be a great help; indeed some controversial problems would disappear, because the disputants would find out that they were talking about different things, and other problems would be greatly clarified. The most lively issue of our times, whether 'our' inflation in the last four years has been due to a demand pull or to a cost push, would lose some of its muddiness if the analysts had to qualify all their pronouncements with regard to the inflation of credit, spending, demand, wholesale prices, consumer prices, and so forth.

A search of the learned literature would yield scores of definitions of inflation, differing from one another in essentials or in nuances. A search of the popular literature, however, reveals no realization of the differences in the meanings experts give to the term. The differences apparently have been reserved for the treatises and the quarterlies; the daily papers and the weeklies were not to be encumbered with 'technicalities'. Now that inflation has become such a widely debated topic, with many scholars participating in the debates, the popular meaning of inflation, denoting an increase in the consumer price index, has been increasingly adopted by the professional economists. Although this is probably bad for analysis, we may have to accept it. But at the risk of appearing pedantic I shall continue to speak of various kinds of inflation and to specify which I happen to be speaking about.

The controversial issue

Opinion is divided on whether consumer prices in recent years have increased chiefly because industry has invested too much and government has spent too much (relative to the nation's thrift) or because big business has raised material prices and/or big labor has raised wage rates too high (relative to the nation's increase in productivity). The issue is partly who is to be 'blamed' for the past rise in consumer prices, and partly what policies should be pursued to avoid a continued increase.

If demand-pull inflation is the correct diagnosis, the Treasury is to be blamed for spending too much and taxing too little, and the Federal Reserve Banks are to be blamed for keeping interest rates too low and for creating or tolerating too large a volume of free reserves, which enable member banks to extend too much credit.

If cost-push inflation is the correct diagnosis, trade unions are to be blamed for demanding excessive wage increases, and industry is to be blamed for granting them, big business may be blamed for raising 'administered prices' of materials and other producers' goods to yield ever-increasing profit rates, and government may be assigned the task of persuading or forcing labor unions and industry to abstain from attempts to raise their incomes, or at least to be more moderate.

Not everybody draws the appropriate conclusions from the theory which he espouses. And not everybody is willing to adopt policies to correct the undesirable situation. (Nor does everybody find the situation sufficiently undesirable to get seriously worried.) The ambivalent position of many partisans of labor unions is noteworthy. They reject the wage-push diagnosis because, understandably, they do not wish to take the blame for the inflation. But they also reject the demand-pull diagnosis, because this diagnosis would militate against the use of fiscal and monetary policies to bolster employment. They want effective demand to be increased at a rate fast enough to permit full employment at rapidly increasing wage rates; but they do not want to attribute increasing prices either to the increase in demand or to the increase in wage rates. The only way out of this logical squeeze is to blame the consumer-price increase on prices 'administered' by big business; but in order to support this hypothesis one would have to prove that the profit margins and profit rates of the industries in question have been rising year after year – which they have not. But we shall see later that matters are not quite so simple and cannot be analysed exclusively in these terms.

Our first task is to deal with the contention that the distinction between cost-push and demand-pull inflation is unworkable, irrelevant or even meaningless.

'Cost push no cause of inflation'

There is a group of outstanding economists contending that there cannot be such a thing as a cost-push inflation because, without an increase in purchasing power and demand, cost increases would lead to unemployment and depression, not to inflation.

On their own terms, these economists are correct. The rules of inductive logic say that if A and B together cause M; and if A without B cannot cause M, whereas B without A can cause M; then B, and not A, should be called the cause of M. Make A the wage-raising power of the unions and the price-raising power of the corporations; make B the credit-creating and money-creating power of the monetary system; make M the successive price increases. It should be quite clear that without the creation of new purchasing power a continuing price increase would be impossible. Hold the amount of money and bank credit constant (relative to real national product) and all that the most powerful unions and corporations can do is to price themselves out of the market.

Having admitted all this to the economists who reject the possibility of cost-push inflation we can shift the weight of the argument to the question whether, given the power of the monetary system to create money and credit, the power would be exercised to the same extent if strong trade unions and strong corporations desisted from raising wages and prices as it actually is exercised when wages and prices are being pushed up. There would probably be quick agreement that, given our present system, the exercise of the wage-raising power of strong unions and the price-raising power of strong corporations induces, or adds impetus to, the exercise of the ability of the banking system to create purchasing power.

The point then is that an increase in effective demand is a necessary condition for a continuing increase in general prices, but that a cost push under present conditions will regularly lead to an expansion of credit and to that increase in effective demand which will permit the increase in consumer prices.

There remains, however, an important question of fact. Assume it is decided not to exercise the power to create money and credit – more than is needed to maintain a constant ratio to real national product – even at the risk of severe unemployment that might result if wages and prices increased; would we then have to expect that the strong unions and corporations would continue to make use of their wage-raising and price-raising powers? Some economists are convinced that unions and business firms would adopt much more moderate policies if they had to fear that any lack of moderation would lead to unemployment and stagnation. This does not mean that a considerable level of unemployment would be required to impress industry and unions with the desirability of moderation. Industrial firms would know that, under an unyielding monetary policy, they could not hope to pass increases in labor cost on to consumers and they would therefore refuse to yield to union pressure. Unions, in turn, would not strike for higher wages if they were sure that industry could not afford to give in. Hence, no cost push and no extra unemployment.

Acceptance of this view by any number of economists would not yet make it a practicable policy. It could not work unless the monetary authorities embraced it without reservation, since any indication of a lack of faith and determination on the part of the authorities would remove the premise: unions could hope that industries would hope that an eventual relaxation of the monetary brake would 'bail them out' and by means of an expansion of demand avert the business losses and the unemployment that would threaten to arise in consequence of wage and price increases.

'Demand pull no cause of inflation'

Having shown that there is a sense in which the contention is correct that 'cost push is no cause of inflation, it takes a demand pull to produce it', we shall now attempt to show that the opposite contention may likewise be correct. There are indeed assumptions for which it would be appropriate to say that 'demand pull is no cause of inflation, it takes a cost push to produce it'. What are these assumptions and how do they differ from those of the traditional model?

In the traditional model, prices rise or fall under the impact of anonymous market forces. They rise when at their existing level the quantity of goods demanded exceeds the quantity supplied. Not that producers, noticing the increased demand, would decide that they could do better if they 'charged' more; rather the mechanism of a 'perfect market' would automatically lift prices to the level where the consumers would not want to purchase any more than was supplied. Sellers, in this model, don't ask higher prices, they just get them. The same thing happens in the model of the perfect labor market. When the demand for labor increases, workers don't ask for higher wages, they just get them as a result of competition.

In a large part of our present economy, prices and wages do not 'rise' as if lifted by the invisible hand, but are 'raised' by formal and explicit managerial decisions. Assume now that prices and wage rates are administered everywhere in the economy in such a way that changes in demand are not taken into account; instead, they are set in accordance with some 'rules of thumb'. Prices and wages may then be so high (relative to demand) that inventories accumulate, production is cut, and labor is unemployed; or they may be so low (relative to demand) that inventories are depleted, production is raised, customers must patiently wait for delivery or their orders are rejected, and there are plenty of vacancies, but no workers to fill them. If the rules of thumb are universally observed by producers, distributors, and labor unions and take full account of increased cost of production and increased cost of living, but disregard all changes in demand, then there can be no demand pull upon prices. In such circumstances an increase in effective demand leads to unfilled orders and unfilled vacancies, but not to higher prices.[1]

One may object, of course, that such a model cannot possibly apply to all markets; that there exist numerous competitive markets in which no producer has enough power to 'set' or 'charge' a price; that in many markets in which prices are administered the would-be buyers, in periods of increased demand, offer higher prices in order to be served and sellers are glad to accept them even though they exceed their list prices; and that this regularly happens when the demand for labor is brisk, so that wages paid can be higher than the rates agreed in collective bargaining. Thus, demand pull is likely to work despite the existence of administered prices and wages.

Although the objection may be sustained on practical grounds, this does not destroy the value of the model. If there are, in actual

1. '. . . if all prices were administered on the basis of markup over direct cost – then excess demand might exist in all markets, yet without effect on the price level.' Gardner Ackley (1959), p. 421.

fact, *many* industries where backlogs of orders accumulate while prices fail to rise and where job vacancies grow in number while wages fail to rise, then the model has some relevance, and it is legitimate to speculate about the functioning of an economic system in which *all* prices and wages are administered on the basis of cost calculations and held at the set levels even in the face of excess demand. It is not easy to decide whether on balance the institutions in our economy are such that a model featuring 'market-clearing prices' or a model featuring 'cost-plus prices' fits better the purposes of speculating about the over-all performance of the entire economy.

In any case, the contention must be granted that there may be conditions under which 'effective demand' is not effective and won't pull up prices, and when it takes a cost push to produce price inflation. But this position disregards an important distinction, namely whether the cost push is 'equilibrating' in the sense that it 'absorbs' a previously existing excess demand or whether it is 'disequilibrating' in the sense that it creates an excess supply (of labor and productive capacity) that will have to be prevented or removed by an increase in effective demand. Thus we are back at the crucial issue; a 'monistic' interpretation cannot do justice to it.

Statistical tests

It is possible to grant the usefulness of the distinction between cost push and demand pull in building theoretical models for speculative reasoning, and yet to deny its usefulness in identifying the causes of general price increases in concrete situations. It may be that the concepts are not operational, that statistical tests are either unavailable or unreliable.

Some have proposed to answer the question whether wage push or demand pull had 'initiated' the upward movement of prices, by looking to see which has *increased first*, prices or wages. But 'first' since what time? If prices and wages have risen in turn, in successive steps the choice of a base period is quite arbitrary and a conclusion assigning the leading or initiating role to one factor or the other would be equally arbitrary. (This is especially so if our statistical information is limited to annual data.)

Not much better is the idea of looking to see which of the two, money-wage rates or consumer prices, has *increased more*. The arbitrary choice of the base period for this comparison is again a serious difficulty. But even more important is the fact that the annual rise in productivity (output per labor hour) normally secures increases in real wages over the year. Hence it is to be expected that wage rates increase relative to consumer prices regardless of whether there is inflation, and regardless of whether prices are pulled up by demand or pushed up by wages.

Even some highly seasoned economists have fallen victim to another logical snare: that any increase in money-wage rates that *exceeded the increase in labor productivity* was a sure sign of a wage push. Yet, even if there were not labor union in the country and no worker ever asked for higher wages, a demand-pull inflation would eventually pull up the wage level; and if the demand pull were such that prices and wages rose by any percentage above two or three a year – and it may well be five or ten or twenty per cent – money-wage rates would be up by more than the rate of increase in productivity. This, then, would have been the result of demand pull only, without any wage push at all. Hence the proposed statistical test is completely inconclusive.

A test which is based on a fundamentally correct chain of reasoning would compare profit rates with wage rates, and diagnose demand pull when *profit rates increase faster than wage rates*. A slight variant of this test uses the relative shares of profits and wages in national income. The theory behind these tests is simply this: when an expansion of effective demand – without a wage push – pulls up product prices, an increase in profits and profit rates would result until wage rates are pulled up by the derived demand for labor. On this theory, an increase in consumer prices associated with increased profit rates, but with wage rates lagging, would reliably indicate the existence of a demand-pull inflation. The operational difficulties with a test based on this theory are the same as those connected with other statistical tests: the arbitrary selection of the time periods. The theory, moreover, applies to an economy in which most prices are the result of anonymous market forces, not of administrative decisions. If most prices were administered and the price setters decided to raise their 'profit targets' (perhaps at the same time that trade unions were out to engineer a wage boost, but a little faster or by a bigger jump) we could find – given the present monetary regime guided by the high-level-employment goal – that prices and profits rates increase ahead of wage rates even though the movement was not started by an autonomous expansion of demand. Hence, the lead of profit rates is not a reliable indication of demand pull; it may occur also in conjunction with a cost push in which price setters take a leading part.

Widely accepted as reliable symptoms of demand-pull inflation are over-employment and over-time payments. The statistical operations proposed to establish these symptoms are, for over-employment, to see whether *job vacancies exceed job applications* and, for over-time pay, to see whether *average hourly earnings have increased faster than wage rates*. Some critics rightly point out that the presence of these symptoms does not rule out that some cost push has contributed to the inflation of prices. Indeed it would have been possible that a cost push actually initiated the process and that the compensatory monetary injection, expanding demand to avoid the threatening unemployment, turned out to be heavier than necessary. Thus while these tests can verify the existence of an inflation of demand, they cannot prove that it was excess demand that precipitated the inflation of consumer prices.

Proposed Concepts and Distinctions

The diversity of expert opinion and the absence of any good statistical tests to support a diagnosis may in part be due to the lack of precise definitions. It is clear that an inflation of effective demand is a necessary condition not only for a demand-pull inflation of consumer prices but also for a cost-push inflation. Without an expansion of demand the cost boost would result in less production and less employment, not in a continuing rise of the level of consumer prices. Should one then speak of a demand-pull inflation only when the expansion in demand is clearly the initiating factor and any administrative cost increases are clearly induced? Or should one also speak of a demand-pull inflation if administrative wage and material-price increases start and lead the procession of events, but are then joined and over-taken by induced or compensatory expansions of demand?

Autonomous, induced and supportive demand inflation

It is useful to distinguish autonomous from induced and supportive expansions of demand. *Autonomous* would be expansions which are not linked to previous or to expected cost increases; hence, disbursements which would also occur if no cost increases had been experienced or anticipated. *Induced* expansions of demand are direct consequences of a cost increase, in that those who receive the increased cost-prices or those who pay them will make larger disbursements than they would have made otherwise. For example, the industrial firms yielding to union pressure for a wage increase may borrow from banks (or dig into cash reserves) in order to pay the higher wage bill; or the recipients of higher wages may increase instalment purchases and induce an expansion of consumer credit. *Supportive* (compensatory) expansions of demand would be those which are engineered by monetary or fiscal policy designed to reduce the unemployment arising, or threatening to arise, from cost increases. For example, the monetary authorities may reduce reserve requirements or create reserves in order to allow banks to extend loans, or the fiscal authorities may increase government expenditures in an attempt to expand effective demand and employment.

Without wishing to restrict the freedom of choice of those who formulate definitions, I submit that the choice should be appropriate to the purposes for which the concept is used. If the concept of a demand-induced inflation, or demand-pull inflation, is to serve for diagnostic and prognostic purposes in the development of economic policies, it would seem preferable to confine it to autonomous expansions of demand. This would not obstruct but rather aid the analysis of instances in which cost-induced expansions or supportive expansions of demand should turn out to be excessive in the sense that they create more employment opportunities than are destroyed by the cost increases, and hence give rise to some of the symptoms of a demand-induced inflation.

Aggressive, defensive and responsive cost inflation

Similar obscurities due to a lack of essential distinctions surround the concept of the cost-induced inflation. Perhaps so much is clear that the term refers to increases in consumer prices that are the (direct or indirect) result of cost increases – labor cost, material cost, or any other cost. But it is not clear whether these cost increases have to be *autonomous* in the sense that they would not have come about in the absence of any monopoly power (price-making power), merely as a result of competitive demand. For it is quite possible that formal administrative decisions are behind cost increases which, however, do not go beyond what would have occurred without such decisions. For example, a trade union may achieve a 'victory' in its negotiations with an employer group bringing home the same raise in pay which the individual employers would have offered (without collective bargaining) in trying to get or keep the labor force they want. Let us decide to call these cost increases *responsive* (or competitive) to distinguish them from those that could *not* be obtained in a purely competitive market.

It would be misleading to denote all non-responsive (non-competitive) price or wage increases as 'autonomous', since they may well be 'induced' by some changes in the economic situation. And the adjectives 'autonomous' and 'induced' are usually used as opposites. A wage-rate increase, for example, is not responsive unless it is in response to an excess demand (short supply) in the particular labor market; but an increase which is not 'demand-induced' (and which therefore presupposes some 'autonomy' with respect to competitive market forces) may yet be induced by (a) an increase in the employer's profits, (b) an increase in wage rates obtained by other labor groups, or (c) an increase in the cost of living. I propose to call (a) a 'profit-induced' wage increase, (b) an 'imitative' (or 'spill-over') wage increase, and (c) a 'defensive' wage increase. Any one of these increases may act as either an 'impulse' or a 'propagation' factor in the inflationary process.

Profit-induced and imitative increases as well as spontaneous increases may be called *aggressive* because they are designed to achieve a new advance in the real wage rates. A *defensive* increase merely restores real earnings which the group in question has long been enjoying; an aggressive increase raises real earnings above that level. The specification of a time interval is necessary in the definition so that one avoids calling 'defensive' what really is a battle to defend the ground just gained in an aggressive action. For example, an aggressive wage-rate increase of ten per cent is likely to be partially eroded within less than a year through the resulting cost-push inflation (aided by induced and supportive expansions of demand). If the same trade unions then demand 'cost-of-living raises' to restore their real wages, it would be somewhat ironic to call these new wage adjustments 'defensive'. But there will always be a wide range in which cost increases may as legitimately be considered defensive as aggressive, especially since trade unions take turns in their actions, each defending the real earnings of its own members that have suffered in consequence of the aggressive actions of other unions, and at the same time attempting to obtain a net improvement.

Administrative price increases by industries producing materials and other producers' goods which enter as significant cost items into the prices of many other products can likewise be characterized as responsive (competitive), defensive, or aggressive. Purely responsive increases cannot occur in an industry with much unused productive capacity; only when plants are working at capacity and orders are piling up can administrative price increases be merely responsive; in such circumstances it is economically irrelevant that these prices are administered. Defensive increases leave real profit rates substantially unchanged; these increases take account of increased production cost and no more. Needless to say, the rates of return must be calculated on the basis of the reproduction cost of the required capacity; that is to say, the book values of the fixed capital may be too low if reproduction cost of buildings and equipment is higher than at the time of their acquisition, or too high if assets are included which are not required for current production. Thus, price increases designed to defend, in periods of falling production, a profit rate that is calculated on the basis of the value of assets inclusive of unused capacity are really aggressive; and price increases designed to raise the money rate of return on capital just enough to take care of increased replacement costs are really defensive.

Should all kinds of wage increase and price increase be included in the concept of a cost-push inflation whenever they are collectively negotiated, unilaterally announced, or otherwise the result of administrative action? I submit that increases which are merely responsive (competitive) do not belong there at all.

Defensive increases do of course play an important role in the process of price inflation and the economist will surely not leave them out of his analysis. But in an explanation of an inflationary process going on year in, year out the aggressive increases have a more substantive role to play than defensive increases; and when it comes to assign 'blame' for an inflation of consumer prices, the aggressive cost boosts will obviously be the more eligible candidates.

The basic model sequences

With the help of the proposed concepts the two basic model sequences of consumer-price inflation can be easily described.

(A) *Demand-pull inflation:*	Autonomous expansions of demand (government spending, business spending, consumer spending) are followed by responsive (competitive) price and wage increases.
(B) *Cost-push inflation:*	Aggressive increases of wage rates and/or material prices are followed by induced and/or supportive (compensatory) demand expansions.

Cost-push models are relatively simple as long as they contain only a single impulse – either wage or price increases – with all sequential changes in the nature of adjustments.

(B-1) *'Pure' wage-push inflation:*	Aggressive increases of wage rates are followed by induced and/or supportive demand expansions, and by responsive increases of material prices and other wage rates.
(B-2) *'Pure' price-push inflation:*	Aggressive increases of material prices are followed by induced and/or supportive demand expansions, and by responsive increases of other materials prices and wage rates.

Models become more complicated as more discretionary actions are included in the sequence of events, especially imitative

161

and defensive increases of cost elements, or even aggressive increases, requiring further adjustments. For example, an autonomous demand expansion may be followed by administered wage and price increases more drastic than merely competitive increases would be; thus, the increases would be partly responsive and partly aggressive, requiring further demand expansions, induced or supportive, if unemployment is to be avoided. Or, aggressive wage and price increases may be followed by excessive demand expansions, perhaps because a nervous government rushes in with overdoses of supportive injections of buying power; some of the effective demand thus created would then be in the nature of an autonomous expansion, resulting in further (responsive) upward adjustments of costs.

Attempted Application

Even the most complicated model sequence will probably still be much simpler than the actual course of events as reflected in the data at our disposal. Since reality is so messy that no neat and simple model will fit at all closely, whereas various complex models will fit approximately, it is not surprising that even impartial analysts arrive at divergent interpretations of the so-called facts.

The postwar inflation

In the narrow scope of this article no attempt can be made to sift the data, to assess the comparative applicability of the various models, and to award first prize to the best-fitting model. But I shall not dodge this question and shall indicate briefly what impressions I have derived from the data presented by governmental and private researchers.

I believe that for an explanation of the consumer-price inflation from 1945 to 1948, and from 1950 to 1952, the basic model of the demand-pull inflation does as well as, or better than, any of the other models, simple or complicated. On the other hand, for the period 1955–9 several cost-push models appear to do better, and I am prepared to regard the consumer-price increases of these four years as a result of a cost-push inflation.

The choice among the various cost-push models is a hard one, especially in view of the controversy about the behavior of administered material prices. The periodic increases in steel prices have sometimes been regarded as the most strategic impulse factor in the inflationary process. A special theory of 'profit-target pricing' assuming 'periodic raising of the target' has been devised in support of this diagnosis and an array of empirical material has been added in its support.

Wage or profit push?

Neither this theory nor the statistical data seem to me to make the model of the 'material-price-push inflation' a plausible explanation of the period in question. While many of the administered price increases may have hampered the performance of our economy and accelerated the inflationary process, I doubt that all or most of them have been 'aggressive' in the sense defined. The reported data on profit rates and profit margins do not, in my judgement, indicate that the price increases were aggressive. Of course, few, if any, of the increases since 1955 have been in the nature of responsive adjustments to excess demand – but probably most of them were defensive in nature, taking account of cost increases without raising real profit rates. I cannot verify this impression of mine to everybody's satisfaction, and perhaps not even to my own. But my impression is strengthened by the deduced consequences of certain assumptions which I consider plausible, concerning the policies and objectives of business managers.

There is, in my opinion, nothing invidious in contending that there are essential differences between most wage increases obtained by strong labor unions and most increases of material prices announced by strong corporations. Nor is it meant to be critical of union policies or uncritical of business policies if many wage increases are held to be aggressive, and many administered price increases defensive. The point is that the situation of most businesses is such that a series of aggressive price increases would be either injurious to them in the long run or downright impossible. A series of aggressive wage increases, on the other hand, may be both possible and beneficial to the labor groups concerned.

To hold that most administered price increases have been defensive rather than aggressive, does not mean (a) that the prices in question were not too high – they probably were, (b) that the increases did not speed up the inflationary process – they certainly did, or (c) that they were 'justified' – which they were not if a competitive market model is used as the standard. But if the question is only whether these price increases were the 'impulse factors', the 'initiating forces' of the price inflation, then I believe the answer is negative.

Wage Increases and Productivity

I do not expect serious exception to the proposition that most of the wage increases obtained by strong trade unions in the last four years, whether spontaneous or profit-induced or imitative, have been aggressive in the sense defined. (This is in contrast to most wage increases between 1945 and 1952, which were responsive.) We must now inquire whether aggressive wage increases are inflationary if they do not exceed the relative rate at which productivity increases.

Aggressive wage increases to capture average productivity gains

According to accepted doctrine, the consumer price level can be held approximately stable, and full employment maintained, if the average increase in money-wage rates does not exceed the average increase in productivity in the economy as a whole. Some of the necessary qualifications to this proposition are not relevant to the issues under discussion. For interested readers they are presented in a footnote.[2] One qualification, however, that

2. There is first the qualification for the sacrifice of fixed-income recipients. The existence of contractual payments in fixed amounts makes it possible for wage rates to increase a little more than productivity. Assume, for the sake of a simple arithmetical illustration, that of a national product of $1,000 a share of $700 is distributed in the form of wages, $100 in the form of profits, and $200 in the form of fixed interest, rent, and pension payments. If now net national product rises by $20 (or 2 per cent) and the recipients of fixed money incomes get no share in the increased product (because prices are held stable), 20 per cent of the increased product, i.e. $4, becomes available as a possible bonus for labor in addition to their

may matter here to some extent concerns the additional profits needed as returns on the additional investments required for the increase in national product. It is sometimes possible for total product per worker to increase thanks to a progress of technology, organization, or skills, without any increase in capital investment. More often, however, it takes some additional investment to achieve an increase in productivity. If such investments were not allowed to earn a return, progress might be stopped short; but if they are to earn a return, total profits must increase lest the rates of return on capital are cut, which could lead to reduced investment and employment. Hence, as a rule, wage increases must not absorb the entire increase in output. And if the additional investment were so large that capital per worker has increased at a percentage rate greater than that of output per

---

70 per cent share or $14. Total wage payments can thus increase by $18 or 2·57 per cent.

A second qualification relates to possible improvements in the terms of trade. Assume that the price of imports (relative to the price of exports) falls by 2 per cent and that imports had amounted to 10 per cent of the net national product, or $100. If the entire gain of $2 is seized as another bonus for labor, wages can rise by $20 or 2·86 per cent.

A third qualification concerns the possible effects of increased tax revenues. Assume that the effective tax rate on profits (distributed plus undistributed) is 50 per cent while the marginal tax rate on wages is 20 per cent. The additional profits are (10 per cent of $20 =) $2 and the taxes on this are $1. The taxes on additional wages are (20 per cent of $20=) $4. If the Government kept expenditures constant despite increased revenues, another bonus of $5 could be distributed in the form of wages, bringing the total addition to $25 before taxes, or more than the entire increase in net national product. (We neglect now the tax on the third bonus.) Wages before taxes could with all three bonuses be increased by 3·57 per cent, compared with a 2 per cent increase in national income.

The second and third bonuses, however, cannot be counted upon; the second bonus may just as likely be negative since the terms of trade may deteriorate rather than improve. Even the first bonus is likely to disappear in an economy with perpetual inflation, because contractual incomes might gradually be made subject to automatic cost-of-living adjustments. All three qualifications are probably less important than the one presented in the text and this one works in the opposite direction.

This exposition has been freely adapted from Lutz (1958), pp. 9–10. The adaptations were necessary because I believe Lutz's argument to be partly erroneous.

worker, wage rates cannot even increase by as much as output per worker and still allow price stability with full employment.[3]

The following formulation will steer clear of such technicalities and express the essential points. Apart from a few modifying influences, such as a squeezing of quasi-rents in stagnant industries, a whittling down of the real claims of recipients of contractual incomes, or a lucky improvement in the terms of foreign trade, real wages per worker cannot increase faster than product per worker. If *money*-wage rates are raised faster than productivity, and the monetary authorities supply the money needed to pay the increased wages without unemployment, prices will rise enough to keep *real*-wage rates from rising faster than productivity. To say that the price inflation has the 'function' of keeping the increase in real wages down to the rate at which productivity increases may help some to understand the mechanism. But it is not really an appropriate expression, for nothing has to 'function' to 'prevent from occurring' what cannot occur anyway. Either prices rise (with the help of supportive expansion of demand) to cut the real wage rates to the level made possible by the productivity increase, or unemployment occurs (if demand expansion is prevented or restrained) and cuts total real wages even lower.

If money wages were not increased at all and all increments to the net national product that are due to technological progress were distributed to consumers in the form of lower prices, *all* income recipients – wage earners, owners of businesses, and fixed-income recipients – would share in the increased product. If money wages all over the economy are increased approximately by the rate at which average productivity has increased, prices on the average will neither fall nor rise and hence the fixed-income recipients (bondholders, landlords, pensioners, perhaps also civil servants, teachers, etc.) will be cut out of their share in the increment. Thus, aggressive money wage increases which, on the average, equal the average increase in productivity in the

3. If wage rates were to increase as much as output per worker while prices were kept from rising, total output would not be large enough to allow any return to be earned by the new capital; employers, then, might not want to maintain the level of investment and employment. See Lutz, (1958), p. 4.

economy will improve the relative income share of labor at the expense of the receivers of contractual income.

Aggressive wage increases to capture individual productivity gains

The 'rule' that price stability and full employment can be maintained if all money wage rates are increased by the same percentage by which average productivity has increased in the economy as a whole is frequently misunderstood and mistakenly applied to advocate increases in money-wage rates in individual firms or industries by the same percentage by which productivity has increased in these firms or industries. In other words, the rule is perverted to the proposal that the benefits of advancing productivity should accrue to the workers in the industries in which the advances take place. It is twisted into a proposition justifying

union demands in those industries, which, because of improved technology and consequent cost reductions can afford to pay higher wages without charging higher prices for their products. This proposition is thoroughly unsound. It misses completely the economic function of prices and wages; its realization would sabotage the economic allocation of resources without serving any purpose that could be justified from any ethical or political point of view (Machlup, 1952, p. 403).

A sensible allocation of resources requires that the same factors of production are offered at the same prices to all industries. It causes misallocations if industries in which technology has improved are forced to pay higher wages for the same type of labor that gets lower pay in industries where technology has not changed. Wage rates should be temporarily higher in fields into which labor is to be attracted, not in fields where labor is released by labor-saving techniques. It is economic nonsense to advocate that wage rates should be forced up precisely where labor becomes relatively abundant.

One might accept an economically unsound arrangement if it were ethically much superior. But no one could claim that the proposition in question satisfied any ethical norm. If five industries, let us call them A, B, C, D, and E, employ the same type of labor; if any of them, say Industry A, develops a new production process and is now able to make the same product as before with half the amount of labor; then this

167

Industry A could afford to raise its wage rates without raising its selling prices. Should now workers in Industry A get a wage increase of 100 per cent while their fellow workers in Industries B, C, D, and E get nothing? Should the coincidence that the technological advance took place in A give the workers there the windfall of the entire benefit, raising them above the rest of the people? I can see no ethical argument that could be made in favor of such a scheme.

But as a matter of practical fact, apart from economics and ethics, the scheme could never be consistently applied, because the workers in other industries would not stand for it, . . . similar wage increases would have to be given in all . . . firms and industries regardless of their ability to pay, regardless of whether their selling prices would remain stable or go up slightly or a great deal. It simply would not be fair if a favored group were to be the sole beneficiary of progress while the rest of the population would have to sit back and wait for better luck. (Machlup, 1952, pp. 404–405.)

No fair-minded person would ask them to sit back and wait; every labor union with any power at all would press the claims of its members, and where no unions existed workers would eventually appeal to their employers and to the public to end the injustice. Yet, any 'equalizing' wage increases would be clearly of the cost-push type and would, if unemployment is prevented, lead to consumer price increases which take away from the originally privileged worker groups some of the real gains they were first awarded (with the approval of short-sighted commentators and politicians).

This spill-over of money-wage increases and the cost-push inflation which it produces (with the help of a supportive demand inflation) serve to redistribute some of the productivity gains first captured by the workers in the industries where the gains occurred. This redistribution by means of consumer-price inflation cuts back the real wages of the first-successful labor groups, whose unions will then complain about the erosion of their incomes and will call for seemingly defensive wage increases to regain the ground lost through inflation (though they rarely lose all of their gain in real income and often keep a large part of it).

In short, a policy that condones wage increases in industries which, because of increased productivity, can afford to pay increased wages without charging increased prices, is actually a policy that accepts a rising cost–price spiral without end.

Price Reductions Essential for Stability

A wage increase obtained by a particular labor group may initiate an inflationary process, but the speed of this process will depend largely on the incidence of defensive price increases and of imitative and defensive wage increases. If nothing but responsive (competitive) price and wage increases were to occur, the rate of inflation initiated by an isolated wage boost would be very small, perhaps negligible. It is, nevertheless, interesting to examine models of price inflation that include neither defensive nor imitative increases.

Inflation without spill-over wage push

In the inflationary process described in the last section, the industries that were forced to pay the increased wages (out of the economies provided by improved techniques) were assumed for the sake of the argument not to increase their selling prices. The price inflation was chiefly the work of a spill-over of the wage increases into fields where productivity had increased less or not at all. But even in the absence of any spill-over, even if no worker in the country were to receive a raise that did not come from economies in production, some degree of consumer-price inflation would be inevitable in an economy in which (a) wage rates are never reduced in any sector, even in the face of unemployment, (b) wage rates are increased to capture productivity gains entirely in the industries where they accrue, and (c) full employment is secured, if necessary, through expansion of effective demand. Now when workers are released in the industries where productivity increases, but production, with unchanged prices and unchanged demand, is not increased, it will take an inflation of demand to create employment for the workers set free by the advance of technology. In other words, the 'technological unemployment' will have to be cured by an expansion of demand, which in turn will cause a rise in consumer prices.

Does not this argument overlook the increase in demand on the part of workers who receive wage increases? It does not. Since the wage increases were gained just to offset the cost reduction made possible by the increase in output per worker, the workers who stay employed receive their raise out of funds no longer paid out as wages to the workers who lost their jobs. A little arithmetic may clarify this point. If 90 workers can now produce the output previously produced by 100, and are now paid the total wage that was previously paid to 100, the total purchasing power in the hands of the workers stays the same. The 10 workers who were released get nothing, and what was saved on them is being paid to the 'more productive' 90. The firm, paying the same wage bill (though to fewer workers), finds its costs neither increased nor reduced and keeps its selling prices unchanged. Since at these prices demand is the same as before, the firm has no use for the 10 workers; nor has anybody else if wages rates are nowhere reduced. If the authorities want them re-employed, a demand inflation has to be engineered. True, the 10 workers will produce something once they are employed, but only after increased prices have created incentives for employers to use more labor; or they will have to be employed (and paid for with new money) in the production of public services not sold in the market.

The assumptions built into the model underlying this chain of reasoning have excluded growth (of labor force and capital stock) and excess capacity. If there were adequate excess capacity in each and every line of production, the demand created (in order to re-employ the labor released by the more productive industries) could be satisfied without price increases anywhere. But no inflation model can reasonably include the assumption of ubiquitous excess capacity; limited facilities (bottlenecks) are implied in any explanation of inflation. Thus, no exception should be taken to the assumption that the new wages paid to the re-employed workers will not all be spent for their own products, but largely for other things, and that prices will be bid up in the process.

The exclusion of a growing labor force and a growing capital stock have served merely to simplify the reasoning. When inputs and outputs are increasing, a certain increase in the money supply and in aggregate spending will be required to manage the increase in output and trade at given prices. An expansion of money demand to effect a re-absorption of technological unemployment would be over and above the money demand required to take care of the growth in labor force and capital stock. To combine the analyses of such growth and of technological unemployment would be an unnecessary complication; the other growth factors can be disregarded without vitiating the conclusions derived in an isolated treatment of 'technological unemployment'.

The price inflation to be expected from a demand inflation engineered to absorb 'technological unemployment' will of course be quite moderate in this case, where all the spill-over wage increases are ruled out. Here is a type of inflation that cannot be characterized as a cost-push inflation, and not as a demand-pull inflation either, if that term is reserved for autonomous expansions of demand. To be sure, aggressive wage increases are involved in the process, but these increases, merely offsetting the growth of productivity, will push up only the cost per labor hour, not the cost per unit of output, and thus no price increases can be said to result from cost increases.

Inflation without any wage increases

One may easily jump to the conclusion that technological unemployment, and the need to resort to demand inflation as its only cure, is entirely due to the aggressive wage increases giving to the workers in the technically advancing industries the entire benefit of the productivity gain. This conclusion would be wrong. The consequences will be the same if in the absence of any wage increase the firms in question find their profits increased but for some reason fail to let consumers benefit in the form of lower selling prices.

Does this argument rely on lower marginal propensities to spend, or on insufficient investment opportunities, or on excessive liquidity preferences? It does not. Even if it is assumed that corporations spend all of their retained profits and stockholders spend all their dividends – just as the workers would have spent their wages – the workers released in the industries where technology has advanced will not be re-employed without the help of demand inflation unless prices to consumers are lowered. The case is almost the same as that in which the workers captured the productivity gain, except that now the corporations and their owners pocket the entire benefit.

Why 'almost' the same, why not exactly the same? Because there is the possibility that an increase in retained earnings, as an increase in capital supply, raises the marginal productivity of labor and thus the demand for labor at given wage rates. But it would be absurd to expect that this would suffice to re-employ all the released labor. Assume that the entire amount saved on the wage bill is spent on new machinery; this new demand for machinery (and indirectly for the labor that goes into its manufacture) merely takes the place of the former workers' demand for consumer goods (and indirectly for the labor that went into their production). Thus the spending of the retained profits – earned by reducing the wage bill – constitutes no increased demand for labor. Only the resulting increase in productive facilities may eventually help the demand for labor to the extent of a small fraction of the technological unemployment created by the (labor-saving) increase in productivity. Hence the conclusion is the same as it was in the case of wage increase: only if consumers get a chance through lower prices to buy more product with their given money incomes will the released workers get a chance to find jobs in the absence of demand inflation.[4]

But why should firms refuse to lower their prices when production costs fall? The well-known theoretical models of a monopolist responding to a lowering of his cost curve show with no reasonable exceptions that he would reduce his selling price and increase his output. If firms can be observed acting otherwise, what is wrong with the model or what is wrong with the firms? One possible hypothesis would be that the firms of the real world had been in 'disequilibrium', charging less than profit-maximizing monopoly prices and waiting for a good occasion to adjust their position. If now their costs are reduced, inaction, failure to reduce their prices, may be an easy way to adjust. Another hypothesis would be that the firms of the real world are in positions of not firmly coordinated oligopoly, where the safest rule is always 'not to rock the boat', that is, never to reduce prices lest a rival mistake it for an outbreak of price competition. A third hypo-

4. This does not mean that the entire increase in productivity must be passed on to consumers in the form of reduced prices. Technological unemployment will neither be perpetuated nor require a price-inflating demand expansion for its cure if wage rates are raised by the national average increase in productivity. This will still permit price reductions in the industries where productivity has increased. The money the consumers save in buying these products at reduced prices will be spent on other goods and will drive up some other prices, without however raising consumer prices on the average.

thesis would be that the 'administered' prices in modern business cannot be explained by any models based on intelligent considerations, but are set by some fixed rules of thumb, and that one of these rules is never to reduce a price. There are perhaps still other hypotheses to explain the fact of 'downward inflexibility' of prices – if indeed it is a fact. But no matter which hypothesis is accepted, the conclusion remains valid that if prices are not reduced when productivity has increased, technological unemployment arises and cannot be absorbed except through demand inflation and consequent consumer-price inflation.

Stabilization of individual prices necessitates inflation

The argument of the preceding pages was designed to demonstrate that the failure to reduce prices in industries where productivity has increased will result in an inflationary increase of general prices, which

(a) will be most rapid if the productivity gains are captured by the workers of these industries by way of wage rate increases – because of the practically inevitable spill-over of the wage increases to other worker groups; but

(b) will also occur, though much more slowly, in the absence of such spill-over, because it will take a demand expansion to re-employ the workers released when the wage bill of the progressive industries is distributed over fewer workers; and

(c) will not be avoided even in the absence of any wage increases, because a demand expansion will be required to re-employ the workers released when the entire part of the wage bill that is saved through the technological advance is transformed into profits without giving consumers a chance to buy more product.

An economist willing to rely on the most abstract and general principles of economic theory can derive this 'inevitability' of inflation from a simple set of theorems. He can deduce from the equilibrium conditions in a system of general equilibrium that general prices must rise if individual prices are maintained in industries where productivity increases. For a fall of production cost in one industry will call forth a reduction of the price of its product relative to the prices of all other products; this adjustment of relative prices will, in a money economy, proceed either through a fall in the money price of the product that now requires less labor per unit than before or through an increase in all other money prices (or through a combination of both); hence, stabilization of the money price of the more economically produced product implies that equilibrium will be restored through a general increase in money prices.

I do not propose to use this technical way of reasoning to convince trade union leaders, business executives, or members of Congress. But the previous argument was, I trust, understandable before I added the sophisticated demonstration of its conclusion.

The O'Mahoney plan to check inflation

It should now be clear that the only way to prevent inflation of consumer prices, and prevent unemployment too, is to make prices more flexible in the downward direction and, in particular, to encourage price reductions in industries where productivity has increased. Senator O'Mahoney's plan, partly incorporated in Senate Bill 215 of April 1959, and receiving serious consideration by several members of Congress, would achieve exactly the opposite. According to the preamble of the Bill, its author believes that 'inflation will be checked if the pricing policies of these [dominant] corporations are publicly reviewed before increased prices may be made effective'. On this theory the Bill provides for public hearings and investigations of large corporations whenever they want to raise prices. But the harder it is made for firms to raise prices the more surely will they avoid ever reducing their prices.

If a nation is committed to a full-employment policy, that is, to a policy of using demand inflation to create employment, it can avoid inflation only by avoiding anything that may create unemployment. Since economic growth proceeds chiefly through technological progress, and technological unemployment can only be avoided through price reductions, the prime requirement of a non-inflationary full-employment policy is to prevent the workers, owners, and managers of the progressing industries from capturing all the productivity gains accruing in these industries in the form of increased money wages and increased profits, respectively, and to encourage the dispersion of most of these gains to consumers in the form of reduced prices.

The O'Mahoney policy in effect encourages the trade unions in the industries in question to get out and capture the entire productivity gains for their workers. It does so implicitly because, if the firms are prevented from raising prices after the aggressive wage increases have absorbed 'only' the new economies, the labor unions will no longer be blamed by the public for causing or precipitating higher prices. The 'visible link' between these wage increases and price inflation is removed, and the union leaders will have even less compunction in pressing for these supposedly non-inflationary wage increases. The firms, losing all or most of the productivity gains to their workers, will hardly be eager to reduce prices. But even if they should, by means of tough bargaining, succeed in keeping a good deal of the gains, they will surely not dream of sharing any part of them with the consumers, because they would consider it foolish to reduce prices that cannot be raised again except after expensive, cumbersome, and perhaps embarrassing public inquisitions.

The O'Mahoney plan to check inflation would actually tend to make inflation perennial and perpetual. The only thing that can be said for the proposed policy is that it might in the short run, perhaps for a couple of years, slow down the progress of the price inflation. But even this is doubtful since, apart from encouraging trade unions to fight for the productivity gains accruing in their industries, it does nothing to check the spill-over wage increases, which in genuine cost-push fashion engender many chains of defensive, 'approvable' price increases and necessitate continual resort to supportive demand inflation.

Conclusion

It was not the purpose of this article to lead up to a critique of a proposed policy; this was a mere by-product. The intention was to examine the conceptual framework employed in recent discussions and, in view of its inadequacies, to propose some improved theoretical tools that may serve better in the analysis of the inflationary process of our time.

Analysis requires the following distinctions: an administered cost increase may be 'equilibrating' in the sense that it merely 'absorbs' a previously existing excess demand, or it may be 'disequilibrating' in the sense that it creates an excess supply that may be prevented or removed only by an expansion of demand. To facilitate the analysis, three kinds of demand expansion are distinguished: *autonomous*, *induced* and *supportive*. Likewise three kinds of cost increase are distinguished: *responsive*, *defensive* and *aggressive*. Any one of these cost increases may be 'administered'; but the responsive ones would also occur in a fully competitive market. Neither defensive nor aggressive increases are in response to excess demand, and both therefore presuppose monopolistic power; defensive increases, however, attempt merely to restore previous real earnings of the group concerned, while aggressive increases raise real earnings above previous levels.

With the aid of these new concepts one can construct models of the inflationary process of various degrees of complexity. It may be possible to develop empirical tests for the choice of the model that fits best the recorded data of particular periods. The author believes that the price inflations of the periods 1945–8 and 1950–52 were of the demand-pull type, but that for 1955–9 a cost-push model would fit better. He tentatively suggests that wage push was more effective than profit push.

Finally the relation of inflation to increases in productivity was examined. The popular idea of a 'non-inflationary' distribution of productivity gains by way of wage increases to the workers employed in the industries in which technology has advanced was found to be untenable. Imitative wage increases would lead to a brisk inflation. But some degree of inflation would occur even without such 'spill-over' wage increases, because the distribution of the productivity gains to the workers or owners in the progressing industries would result in technological unemployment, and remedial full-employment measures would inflate the price level. The only way of avoiding inflation is through price reductions in industries where productivity has improved.

References

ACKLEY, G. (1959), 'Administered prices and the inflationary process', *American Economic Review*, Papers and Proceedings, vol. 49, no. 2, pp. 419–30.

LUTZ, F. A. (1958), 'Cost- and demand-induced inflation', *Banca Nazionala del Lavoro*, no. 44 (March 1958), pp. 217–228.

MACHLUP, F. (1952), *The Political Economy of Monopoly*, Johns Hopkins.

10 P. Streeten

Productivity Inflation

P. Streeten, 'Wages, prices and productivity', *Kyklos*, vol. 15 (1962), pp. 723–31.

Labour and Inflation

The tremendous improvement of the position of Labour in the Welfare State has been accompanied, paradoxically, by increasingly severe criticism of the trade unions. While human relations in industry have come under Royal patronage, the activities of the unions have been condemned as traitorous. At least one outspoken writer went so far as to suggest that they should be abolished, since they no longer fulfil any useful function (Wiles, 1956). They have been accused of sabotaging technical progress and of debauching the currency.

More specifically, it has been argued that

(a) the present *method* of collective bargaining,
(b) the *structure* of trade union organization, and
(c) the *objectives* of bargaining

are ill-adapted to keep wage increases within the bounds permitted by rises in productivity, and that they therefore cause, or contribute to, inflation. The above factors have also been said to lead to unfairness, rigidity, and lack of mobility, and to be therefore detrimental both to social peace and economic progress.

These arguments have been used to support the case for the introduction of some form of centrally planned and centrally imposed 'wage policy'. At present a wage policy would be strongly opposed by the Trades Union Congress (T.U.C.) and its constituent unions, and there seems to be little support for the idea among business men or the public at large. However, the question of whether such a policy is in principle desirable is an important one.

The main reason for advocating a wage policy has been stated in a White Paper (1956):[1]

'We all want full employment, and we all want stable prices. But we have not yet succeeded in combining the two.'

Immediately after the Second World War there was a sharp rise in prices in the United Kingdom; and since the middle of 1947 the cost-of-living index has nearly doubled. Many people believe that such a rate of increase in prices is harmful. Since the behaviour of prices depends to a large extent on what happens to wage rates and salary rates, any reasonable degree of price stability depends on moderating the increase in these rates. The advocates of a wage policy claim that this aim cannot be reconciled both with full employment and with free collective bargaining. They argue that price stability can be made compatible with free collective bargaining only if there is unemployment; it can be made compatible with full employment only if there is a wage policy.

There are several reasons for believing this to be true. First, the effect of full employment is to strengthen trade union bargaining power very considerably, and to make employers less reluctant to concede wage increases. Second, the effect of unregulated collective bargaining, in a period when prices are rising, is to make the determination of wages a competitive process. A further source of competition is the uneven incidence of the 'wage drift'. Local negotiations bring far greater benefits to the engineer than to the railwayman, who tries to catch up by a further increase. Each union's success improves its situation in relation to other workers, and at the same time causes the cost of living to rise. In both these ways it reacts upon other unions causing them in turn to formulate claims in order to restore 'differentials' and to offset or anticipate increases in the cost of living. Their claims, when granted, will themselves have a similar result; and it is difficult for employers not to meet the claims at least in part. If they fail to do so, they run the risk either of losing labour which they cannot afford to spare, or of a strike. Alternatively, even if they stand firm, the unions can take them to arbitration, where their decision may be over-ruled. Each group of employers has to try to keep in step, just as each union does.

1. It should be added that this White Paper does not advocate the adoption of a wage policy in the sense in which the phrase is used here.

It is often said that the ability to pass on wage increases in the form of higher prices presupposes excess demand and inflationary monetary policies. Otherwise employers would fear reductions in sales and would resist more vigorously wage claims. This view has been formulated at various levels of sophistication. Professor John Kenneth Galbraith (1957) discovered 'unliquidated monopoly gains'. Others, too, have pointed to the structure of competition, to administered prices, to conflicts between short and long-run objectives, etc., and a previous attempt to analyse the situation by Mr Balogh and myself has followed similar lines (Balogh and Streeten, 1957).

But the assumptions in these arguments are not necessary to explain the facts. The situation is analogous to that analysed recently in connexion with expanding investment in underdeveloped countries by the theory of balanced growth. An investment which would be unprofitable if carried out by one firm only, may be profitable if attempted simultaneously by a large group of firms, because demand for each other's products is thus created. Whether this theory is true or not of investment in underdeveloped countries, it applies to the granting of wage claims in a fully employed advanced economy. What could not be done by one employer if he acted in isolation, can be done by a large group. It is not necessary to assume excess demand in the initial situation. Since wages are normally negotiated on an industrywide basis, each employer knows that his rivals will have to pay higher wages too when his own wages go up. He may even suspect that the general round of wage increases will generate sufficient demand to absorb an undiminished supply at higher prices. But whether he suspects this or not, he need not fear that he will reduce his sales by raising his prices. Nor need limitations of finance present a crucial obstacle since there are many methods of short-circuiting at little cost those institutional devices that restrict credit. The existing or even a reduced stock of money can be used to do more and more work, both by circulating more rapidly and by being assisted by substitutes. The view that there must be some upper limit to increases in the velocity of circulation of money and to the introduction of substitutes is a mere article of faith.

We thus see that the competition which results from unregulated negotiations, together with the bargaining situation which full employment creates, gives rise to the danger that price stability may be difficult if not impossible to achieve.

Productivity Inflation

Economists disagree on the question whether the price inflation of the nineteen-fifties has been predominantly the result of excess demand or of trade union pressure. According to the demand-pull school, the rise in money wages, and particularly in earnings, reflects excessive demand in the markets for final products. According to the cost-push school, wages have risen even at times when aggregate demand was no more than adequate or was even deficient. It is ironical that in this country those whose sympathy has been with the employers, have tended to blame the employers' 'demand pull', whereas those normally aligned with Labour have held the unions' cost push responsible for the declining value of money. Indeed, the demand-pull school have often gone as far as to say that prices would have risen faster in a fully competitive labour market, and that our system of collective bargaining, with its delays, has slowed down the rise in basic wage rates, while the cost-push school have stressed that monopolistically administered prices have been lower than they would have been in a competitive product market.

Most writers would, of course, be ready to admit not only that our post-war inflation has contained elements of both demand pull and cost push, but also that the interaction of the two constitutes the characteristic impetus of the inflationary 'spiral'. But even so, the dichotomy oversimplifies the complex forces that have led to persistent price rises since the war, and neglects one important factor which cannot easily be fitted into either theory.

Let us begin by considering a typical sequence of events. Bill Brewer and his mates, who are engineering workers, get a wage increase because their *productivity* has increased. This may be the result of higher earnings of workers in piece rates or of some other form of sharing the higher profits earned. Stewer, who lives next door to Brewer but who works on the railways and whose productivity has not risen, belongs to a union which claims an increase on the ground of *fair shares*. Why should Brewer, who does much the same job with better machines, in easier conditions, get so much more than Stewer? Stewer gets his rise and the cost of living rises, for wages have moved ahead of productivity. Then Bill Brewer, Jan Stewer, Peter Gurney, Peter Davy . . . old Uncle Tom Cobley and all put in claims on the ground of a rise in the *cost of living*. Sometimes the circle is shorter, and is described as 'leap-frogging'. The dispute over the claims of the provincial and London bus drivers cannot be solved as long as the former want greater equality and the latter special rewards. Sometimes the process is started by particular employers offering various bonus payments in order to attract or keep labour (one aspect of 'wage drift'). In the ensuing scramble living costs rise and everybody rushes in with claims to maintain real incomes. But among the diverse possibilities, it is frequently an *increase in productivity* in some process, some type of production, or some industry that sets off the chain reaction.

However much the demand-pull school disagree with the cost-push school, they seem to agree on one point: that rises in productivity are anti-inflationary. The demand-pull school would argue that a rise in productivity accompanied by a rise in production will generate an additional £x worth of supply and, of course, an extra £x of incomes and therefore potential demand. But a large fraction of the extra incomes will be taxed away and saved by companies and individuals, so that only a fraction of x will be added to demand. The total disequilibrium between demand and supply will thus be reduced. The cost-push school would argue that the increase in productivity makes it possible to pay the asked-for higher money wage rates, without having to raise prices, since labour costs per unit of output have fallen. But both arguments neglect the important fact that it is the dynamic sectors (in particular the engineering industry) where productivity rises rapidly, which lead to automatic wage increases where piece rates are paid and which set off wage demands. The tendency of earnings to rise is not independent of productivity rises, as both schools assume. It is, on the contrary, an increasing function of productivity increases.

Moreover, it is not even true that the interaction of claims on grounds of productivity, fair shares, and cost-of-living (described above) must be postulated in order to get inflation. Even a system that accepted only the principle that wages should rise in those industries in which productivity has risen would not be able to maintain price stability (Hicks, 1956). Let the engineers again be the group whose productivity has risen and whose earnings have moved up proportionately.[2] Prices of engineering products can then be kept stable. But the engineering workers do not spend their whole incomes on engineering products. Some part of their incomes will be spent on, say, railway travel where productivity has not risen. The engineering industry will now no longer be able to sell all its products at the prices it was charging, and the railways will be faced with a shortage of labour. If now railway wages and railway fares rise, both problems will be solved. Workers will be attracted from engineering to railways and total demand will rise to absorb more engineering products. This adjustment will be assisted by engineering workers buying less railway travel as a result of the rise in fares. But in the process the general price level must rise. The 'productivity principle' will not have resulted in stable prices. If we adhere to the principle that wages must rise only with productivity (in particular industries), wages in the static sector cannot rise. There will be both an excess demand for the product of the static sector and a shortage of labour. And there will be a surplus of labour in the dynamic sector and deficient demand for its product. This difficulty could be overcome only if a transfer of labour from the dynamic to the static industry could be brought about without raising wages in the latter. Otherwise the static industry will be unable to recruit enough labour to satisfy demand and the dynamic industry will be unable to sell all its output, unless it reduces prices and profit margins. But there must be a limit to the lowering of profit margins and beyond that limit prices can fall only if money wages rise less than productivity

It thus appears that the linkage of wages to productivity in each industry is not normally sufficient to stop inflation or unemployment. Either prices must be reduced in the dynamic sector or wages raised in the static sector. An increase in productivity in a

2. It is assumed that the rise in productivity is not simply induced by higher demand and larger output, so that overheads are spread over a larger volume of production. The rise in productivity is assumed to be autonomous, and to precede demand increases.

particular industry or process must, in the interest of maintaining stable prices, be allowed to show itself in lower prices. It follows that, beyond a certain point, labour costs, as well as prices, must be reduced in the dynamic sector, which means that wages there cannot rise in the same proportion as productivity.

Yet, a rise in productivity in a particular sector provides the conditions in which a harmony of interests in raising wages prevails between employers and employees. Without the presence of either excess demand or excessive union pressure, higher wages can be claimed and will tend to be granted. It is true that the ability to pay higher wage rates may be contingent upon getting rid of redundant labour, but reluctance to declare workers redundant, fears of future labour shortage, or hopes of a sufficient eventual increase in sales may prevent the sacking, without weakening the inclination to grant wage increases. It is therefore often to this kind of situation – an autonomous rise in productivity – that we have to look for the impetus to inflation, which is, of course, reinforced if claims on grounds of fair shares and rises in cost of living are added by other workers in the same industry or in other industries.

It is true that the 'productivity principle' violates the principle of 'supply and demand'. An increase in the productivity of labour in an industry is not always accompanied by a more than proportional increase in production and sales, and in the argument above we have assumed that it is not, because workers do not spend their whole income on their own product. Only if planned production and sales rose more than productivity would the demand for labour in the industry under consideration rise; only then are wage increases warranted on the 'supply and demand' principle. An equiproportional increase in planned production leaves the demand for labour unaffected, while a less than proportional increase reduces the demand for labour. But institutional forces such as piece rates and psychological forces such as reluctance to sack will tend to raise earnings even when total labour requirements fall.

Precisely the situation in which the temptation to raise wages is strongest may also be that in which the economic justification to do so is weakest. The economic argument against raising wages with sectional productivity is reinforced by the human or moral argument that an increase in productivity in a particular process may be in no way attributable to the efforts of the workers concerned, and may indeed make their work easier and more pleasant. In such a case to grant an increase in wage rates would be unfair, as well as inflationary.

If the argument is accepted, it follows that the common distinction between demand-pull and cost-push inflation can be misleading. In searching for the sources of inflation, we find no opposition between pulling employers and pushing workers.

Wages Linked to Global Productivity Rises

Once the difficulties of linking wage increases to sectional productivity rises are recognized, it is only a short step to advocating that global productivity rises, averaged over the economy as a whole, should be reflected in global money wage increases, which would be distributed among different groups of workers according to other principles than that of productivity. One of these other principles would have to be the maintenance of equilibrium in the sectional labour markets, so that the high-productivity sectors may have to raise wages by less than productivity.

As a matter of economic logic, the proposal to link global productivity increases, as calculated by some council of economists and statisticians, to global wage increases (leaving relative wages to be determined by other principles) makes better sense than the proposal for sectional links. The case against it is that the benefits of higher productivity would be more widely dispersed if they were reflected in lower prices, with money wages constant (or rising by less than productivity), rather than in higher money wages. On the other hand, there are some difficulties in letting the price level fall with rising productivity.

1. It would increase the real burden of debt.
2. It would imply reducing piece-rates and this may cause friction.
3. Prices are often sticky; to make them fall, full employment may have to be abandoned.
4. Keeping the average level of wages constant makes it more

difficult to adjust differentials, for some wages would have to be cut; if wages are allowed to rise with productivity, these relative adjustments are easier.

5. One of the most important traditional functions of the trade union movement would be eliminated if increases in real wages were received in the form of price reductions.

Whatever the theoretical case for and against such policies may be, it is clear that both stable and, *a fortiori*, falling prices would require a national wage policy. Only general agreement on a national wage structure combined with the determination not to allow aggregate wage increases to exceed aggregate productivity increases can secure price stability. In other words, there must be a national policy with respect to both *relative* wages and the course of the *absolute* wage level.

The argument of this article is not that such policies are practical possibilities, but that, if they are not, stability of prices, too, is not a practical possibility, even if a sufficiently rapid growth of productivity could be achieved, and that productivity increases, far from being necessarily brakes on inflation, may actually accelerate it.

References

BALOGH, T., and STREETEN, P. (1957), 'A reconsideration of monetary policy', *Bulletin of the Oxford University Institute of Statistics*, vol. 19, no. 4, pp. 331–9.

GALBRAITH, J. K. (1957), 'Market structure and stabilization policy', *The Review of Economics and Statistics*, vol. 39, pp. 124–33.

HICKS, J. R. (1956), 'The instability of wages', *Three Banks Review*, vol. 31, pp. 3–19.

WHITE PAPER (1956), *The Economic Implications of Full Employment*, Cmnd 9725, H.M.S.O.

WILES, P. (1956), 'Are trade unions necessary?', *Encounter*, vol. 7, no. 3, pp. 5–11.

11 E. H. Phelps Brown

Wage Drift

E. H. Phelps Brown, 'Wage drift', *Economica*, vol. 29 (1962), pp. 339–56.

1. When attention began to be directed to the progressive rise in
unit labour cost under full employment, through pay rising more
than productivity, only part of the rise in pay was found to be
brought about by awards and collective agreements: a substantial
remainder was seen to be arranged less formally, not at the bargaining headquarters but at the place of work. This remainder,
since it came about continuously and was under no central control, became known as wage drift. It has been conspicuous in the
democracies with predominantly industry-wide settlements – in
Scandinavia, the Netherlands, the United Kingdom, and
Australia. For these countries at least it was something new. In
the 1930s it had been 'a nuisance to the planning authorities in
the suppressed-inflation, full employment economies of Germany
and the U.S.S.R.' (Hansen and Rehn, 1956); but elsewhere,
though very likely the locally effective rate often did diverge from
the centrally negotiated, the divergence seems not to have been so
great as ever to pose a problem of policy. Under full employment,
however, there certainly has been such a problem. In the countries
we have named, any policy designed to stop the rise in unit labour
costs would evidently have informal as well as scheduled rises in
rates of pay to cope with. More than this, some observers have
argued that so long as rates tend to get raised informally,
restraint of the scheduled rises will do little to reduce the ultimate
rise: if awards and negotiations move rates up more slowly, drift
will only go on more rapidly. The grounds for this apprehension
lie in the very fact of drift. If rates do in fact continue to be raised
locally, it is said, even after central negotiations have already
raised them, it can be only that they are being pulled up by
demand: but in that case the awards and negotiations are only

mediating part of a rise whose full extent is demand-determined, and so long as demand remains unchecked this rise will come about in one way if not another. As against this it has been held that scheduled rises and drift are not alternative ways of arriving at a fixed sum, but additive components of a sum whose size depends on how much each component brings to it. On this view, drift proceeds from whatever level negotiations set from time to time, at a rate that is largely independent of that level: and in this case smaller scheduled rises will mean smaller ultimate rises despite continuing drift. The object of this paper is to survey some of the studies that have been made of the extent and origins of drift, and to consider the implications for policy.

The Nature of Drift and the Possibility of Measuring It

2. The essence of drift is that the effective rate of pay per unit of labour input is raised by arrangements that lie outside the control of the recognized procedures for scheduling rates. These procedures issue in awards, statutory orders or – most often – negotiated agreements, that lay down time-rates or piece-rates, or changes in them, throughout a field of employment. But during a period in which unchanged scheduled rates continue to apply, the rates actually being paid for a given labour input prove to rise. This rise may come about in various ways. The employer may simply agree with an individual workman or a group a higher rate than that scheduled; or where the scheduled rate is sacrosanct he may still raise the effective rate by contriving overtime, loosening standards of grading and payment by results, and providing various kinds of bonus and benefit. Advances for particular men or tasks may be claimed and conceded at the place of work. An important instance of this is the negotiation of piece-rates; but payment by results will in any case generally yield higher pay per unit labour input as time goes on, solely through gradual improvements in materials, equipment and organization which enable the job to be done more easily than when it was first timed. In these ways the scheduled course of rates of pay is superseded by variations made locally, and they clearly lie within drift. Another source of divergence between earnings and rates lies on the borderline – the rise of earnings that follows upon

increased effort by the worker through overtime or payment by results. The overtime here must be not contrived but indispensable for the achieved output, and the higher earnings under payment by results must be attained without loosening of standards or improvement of the arrangements for the work. Rises of earnings that come about in these ways hardly 'lie outside the control of the recognized procedures for scheduling rates' but are attained in accordance with scheduled provisions; they depend upon an increased effort by the worker; and they may be reversed by changes in activity. Especially when a large part of the rise of earnings over rates is due to an increase in overtime on recovery from recession does the distinction seem significant between those rises in earnings that are and those that are not directly a function of labour input. Yet the rises that are a function of labour input are knit up with drift proper, and assimilated to it, because they inspire comparisons and spread out, and because in practice they are not always reversible.

3. To measure drift we need to compare the actual movement of earnings with the rise that would have come about, at the actual level of activity, from the scheduled provisions alone. But this rise is hard to estimate. The contribution of changed levels of activity through overtime and payment by results is not easy to assess. To quantify the intended effect of scheduled changes is often harder still. In Norway and Sweden these changes generally take the form of percentage rises in the actual earnings prevailing at the time of the settlement, so that the intended effect on earnings is largely apparent from the outset; but even so it was found advisable in Sweden to ascertain the outcome more exactly by direct inquiry (Hansen and Rehn, 1956, p. 101; Rehn, 1959, p. 3). But very commonly elsewhere, all that we have is an index of scheduled rates, and the changes that are announced in rates indicate only imperfectly the intended and consequential effects upon earnings. They may indicate too little: a rise in overtime, for instance, consequent upon a negotiated reduction in the standard week, will have been foreseen by the parties, and envisaged as providing effectively a higher hourly rate of pay than figured in the agreement. But the changes in scheduled rates may also be greater than the intended rise in earnings. For the effect of a new scheduled rate depends on whether it will raise all present effec-

tive rates however high, or only so many as otherwise would lie below it. In the latter event, the new rate is said to 'consolidate' part or all of the unscheduled rise. To the extent that consolidation occurs, the gap that drift opens up between rates and earnings gets closed again from time to time, and over a span of years drift may appear negligible. But besides these difficulties in assessing the effect of scheduled changes, there are difficulties in tracing the actual movement of earnings in the form we need. An index of earnings will usually trace the average earnings of the workers in a certain field of employment, taking them as they come from time to time in their changing deployment between different grades and occupations, and the average will rise as more workers come to be employed in the higher-paid jobs. If they have got there because they have acquired the existing qualifications for those jobs, there is no element of drift, but drift does occur when employers contrive to pay more by upgrading workers who would not have made the grade before; and we have no means of separating the two sorts of upgrading. For all these reasons the available records of scheduled changes and actual earnings generally afford us only a rough measure of drift, and one that we must supersede by more detailed inquiry before we can arrive at an understanding of each case. But for a first and broad international survey rough measures must suffice.

4. Such a survey is provided by the figures below. Column 1 gives the rise in the effective rates of pay, that is, in actual earnings per hour (or, in Australia, per week), as an average annually compounded rate. Column 2 gives the proportion of the total rise in earnings over the whole span that appears unaccounted for by scheduled changes.

	1	2
NORWAY, first quarter 1950 – first quarter 1961, men in industry, land transport, and construction (Norsk Arbeidsgiverforening, 1961)	6·9%	0·54
SWEDEN, November 1949–November 1960, all wage-earners in mining and manufacturing (O.E.E.C., 1961, p. 400)	8·1%	0·36
DENMARK, 1948–58, all wage-earners in L.O.–D.A.F. sector (O.E.E.C., 1961, p. 301)	5·5%	0·23
AUSTRALIA, 1945–46 to 1958–59, all wage-earners (Hancock, 1960, Table II)	9·3%	0·23

	1	2
UNITED KINGDOM, 1948–57, all wage-earners in manufacturing, public utilities and public administration (Dicks-Mireaux, 1958, Table I)	7·1%	0·21
WEST GERMANY, February 1953–February 1960, male wage-earners in manufactures, mining and building (O.E.E.C., 1961, p. 332)	6·4%	0·17
NETHERLANDS, 1945–61, all wage-earners (Central Planbureau, 1962, Tabel 3·8)	6·9%	0·16

To these we can add a finding based not so much on inquiries as on their absence – that in the United States drift has been exceptional. There is, it is true, no general index of wage rates to compare with the monthly earnings series, but expert opinion has no doubt that these series mainly reflect changes in negotiated rates. We shall note later (paragraph 16) one instance of drift; but in industry generally so much excess of earnings over rates as has appeared seems to have been due only to increases in output and hours during expansions (Hildebrand, 1959). Conceivably, effective rates might move ahead of scheduled when the schedule is a plant contract no less than when it is an industry-wide agreement; but in the United States they seem not to have done so generally (Maher, 1961).

Are any Factors Bearing on Drift Suggested by Comparisons of Drift in Different Sectors of the Economy?

5. A first comparison is between the men and women in the labour force. We have the following estimates of the part of the rise in earnings not accounted for by scheduled rises:

	Men	Women
SWEDEN, manufacturing industries 1945–55 (S.A.F.–L.O., 1957, p. 24)	0·37	0·26
DENMARK, 1948–58 (O.E.E.C., 1961, p. 301)		
On piece-rates in Copenhagen, unskilled	0·31	
On piece-rates in Copenhagen, all		0·28
On piece-rates in provinces, unskilled	0·25	
On piece-rates in provinces, all		0·16
On time-rates in Copenhagen, unskilled	0·20	
On time-rates in Copenhagen, all		0·12
On time-rates in provinces, unskilled	0·05	
On time-rates in provinces, all		0·09

	Men	Women
UNITED KINGDOM, engineering, January 1948– June 1959 (Lerner and Marquand, 1962)		
Men, fitters, on piece-rates	0·39	
Men, fitters, on time-rates	0·47	
Men, labourers, on piece-rates	0·40	
Men, labourers, on time-rates	0·35	
Women, on piece-rates		0·26
Women, on time-rates		0·14

Lerner and Marquand (1962, pp. 37–8), pointed out that women get less overtime and fewer long-service and merit increments than men: in so far as increases in these elements have been sources of drift, women have been less able to participate. Lerner and Marquand also suggested that shop stewards, feeling 'that women do not really need to earn as much as men', do not press as hard for women's rises as for men's; and the women are less able than men to defend or improve their rates, especially piece-rates, under the requirement of the grievance procedure in engineering, that in the first instance 'they must stand up to a foreman alone, without the aid of their shop steward or workmates'. Turner (1960, p. 108), held that women are unlikely to have benefited much from 'the upgrading of workers consequent on techno-logical progress', 'since they are generally confined to relatively unskilled jobs, and their employment on shifts is restricted.' It will be seen that these suggestions rest upon the way institutions work – if they provide an explanation of drift being less for women, we must infer that the amount of this drift is not deter-mined by forces such as the pull of demand for labour which if blocked on one path by, say, a particular method of wage pay-ment, is likely to break through on another.

6. The figures just examined may depend on differences not of sex only but of skill. Thus the Danish figures of which some were quoted above show not only generally higher drift for men than women, but among the men themselves higher drift for the skilled than the unskilled. The explanation given is that the scheduled rises, as a matter of policy at the centre, lifted unskilled rates towards the skilled, and greater drift for the skilled was the means of restoring the differential customary in the workshop. But elsewhere that process of restoring the wage structure might

191

call for greater drift for the unskilled. 'The current extent of overtime working,' said Turner (1956, p. 113), 'varies widely – at least, among men, whose average hours in particular industries currently exceed their standard weeks by anything from nil to thirteen. The variation seems more closely (and, of course, inversely) connected with the wage-levels of particular trades than with their activity. Overtime has clearly become a systematic method of raising lower male wage-rates.' Again, skilled labour may show more drift only because it happens to be scarcer than unskilled in the local market at the time – as generally it seems to have been in Sweden (S.A.F.–L.O., 1957, c. 7) and West Scotland (Behrend, 1960, p. 123).

7. The difference between skilled and unskilled is in its turn entangled with that between piece-rates and time-rates. The high rates of drift in Scandinavia have been connected with the high proportion of workers paid by results. In Denmark 40 per cent of the wage-earners in manufacturing and construction were on piece-rates in 1959, and a further 29 per cent were on 'minimum wage systems' in which merit rates are left to be agreed between the employer and worker individually (O.E.E.C., 1961, pp. 291–2, 298). Fifty-nine per cent of all hours of both men and women in Norwegian industry in 1961 were paid by piece-rates or other systems of payment by results (Norsk Arbeidsgiverforening, 1961). In Sweden more than 60 per cent of the wage-earners in manufacturing and construction are on piece-rates, and most of the remainder are on the 'minimum wage system' (O.E.E.C., 1961, p. 396). These proportions compare with the 42 per cent of all wage-earners in British manufacturing paid by results in 1961, or 33 per cent when we include construction, the public utilities, and public administration (*Ministry of Labour Gazette*, September 1961); and with the 27 per cent of production and related workers in United States manufacturing in May 1958 (Lewis, 1960). But within any one country, have the industries in which the proportion is high experienced more drift? In Sweden this has been markedly so, though the correlation is far from complete (Hansen and Rehn, 1956, p. 131). In Britain, one study has found that in 1948–55 the correlation was if anything negative (Dicks-Mireaux, 1958), but another calls attention to drift over 1948–59 having been well below average in five industries, in four

of which the proportion of workers paid by results was conspicuously low (Dicks-Mireaux, forthcoming). In any case, a lack of correlation does not prove that the industries with high proportions did not take the lead and set the pace: it may only mean that the others were not slow to follow. In Denmark, for instance, 'it is quite possible that a general tendency for the earnings of workers with flexible methods of wage payment to drift upwards between bargains was offset by smaller negotiated increases resulting from the implementation of the central agreements' (O.E.E.C., 1961, p. 298). The tendency for earnings under payment by results to drift upwards has been traced to three sources. First, improvements in equipment and processes generally loosen rates as time goes on. When a marked change is made the job may be re-studied, but the new rate is still likely to be rather easier than the old, for this exposes it less to the charge of disguised rate-cutting, and helps gain acceptance for any displacement of labour. There are many improvements, moreover, that are not individually big enough to warrant re-studying the job, or are made in the organization of the process rather than in the job itself, but whose effect on the rate of output obtainable in the job accumulates as time goes on. Second, the facts that rates are generally set at the place of work, and that in some firms many new rates are being set week by week, gives an immediate opening to local pressures towards higher earnings that is lacking in time-rates.[1] With this goes the third source, that employers are more ready to raise piece-rates than time-rates – thereby they can meet pressure at particular points without, initially at least, having to apply the rise widely; the adjustments appear more reversible than rises in time-rates if the climate should change; and there may be less evident transgression of the line drawn by the employers' association. Firms wishing to raise earnings as a matter of policy may adopt or extend methods of payment by results as the most flexible means (Behrend, 1960, p. 129). But the British and German building industries are cited as showing that

1. A. Nove comments: 'This was and is certainly a factor in Russia, and it gets mixed up with productivity statistics because of the tendency to give the highest possible relative value to any new product, or even to choose that variant among possible alternatives which will add most to gross output as conventionally measured.'

employers competing for labour will find ways of raising earnings even where payment by results is exceptional.

8. Any one industry is a mixed bag of the factors we have been considering, but comparing the extent of drift industry by industry may bring to light the influence of some factor not considered yet – for instance, has drift been greater in the more prosperous and expansive industries? On the whole it has been in Denmark, but the engineering and chemical industries are striking exceptions (O.E.E.C., 1961, p. 299). In Sweden the industries that have reported less unfilled demand for labour have generally shown less drift, but there has been no similar association between drift and the rise of productivity (O.E.E.C., 1961, pp. 401, 404). What is most apparent in West Germany is the similarity of the drift in different industries. That holds, too, of a number of industrial orders in the United Kingdom, though not of the five already mentioned. An association with the demand for labour was found by Marquand (1960): instances of outstanding drift 'were associated with a particularly high level of advertised unfilled vacancies'. No more than in Sweden does any correlation appear between drift and the rise of productivity industry by industry (Dicks-Mireaux, 1958). In sum, the differences between industries in the extent of drift show some association with their prosperity, as that has shown itself in their demand for labour, but the differences are by no means so marked or general as to suggest that the particular state of demand has been of itself a predominant factor. The comparison of industries, moreover, brings us back to institutional factors: we have already noticed the possible effect of the extent of payment by results, and Marquand (1960) found that British industrial orders with a propensity to higher drift were those 'with small plants, with many piecemeal local negotiations after a central wage bargain has been struck and with low relative earnings.'

Are any Factors Bearing on Drift Suggested by Comparison of Drift in Different Periods?

9. So far we have been looking for possible associations between the extent of drift and contemporary situations and circumstances, but we must also ask whether any factors have been

found to be associated with the variations of drift in the course of time. It is necessary first to clear up one misunderstanding. This arises from reckoning drift as a percentage rise in earnings, or as the difference between the percentage rises of indexes of earnings and of scheduled rates. It is natural to do this when index numbers are readier to hand than absolute figures, but it has its pitfalls. For to the extent that drift has been going on in an industry already, its earnings will be above its scheduled rates, and a scheduled rise that adds the same absolute amount to both rates and earnings will raise earnings by the smaller percentage, so that drift as measured by the difference between the two percentages can appear as negative, even though the effective rate has continued to move ahead of the scheduled. Consider a case where in each of two years drift raises the average weekly earnings in an industry by 4s., and the scheduled rate goes up by 6s. in the first year but by 21s. in the second.

		Year	
	0	1	2
1. Scheduled weekly rate	300s.	306s.	327s.
2. Element of cumulated drift	100s.	104s.	108s.
3. Weekly earnings (1 + 2)	400s.	410s.	435s.
4. Index of scheduled weekly rate (1)	100	102·0	109·0
5. Index of weekly earnings (3)	100	102·5	108·75
6. Drift takes as (5 − 4)		+0·5	−0·25

This property of the arithmetic may account for much of the inverse relation between scheduled rises and drift that has been found in a number of studies of time-series – when the scheduled rises have been bigger, drift has appeared to be smaller.

10. In this survey no series of the year to year changes in the absolute excess of earnings over scheduled rates has come to light with such a compensatory movement. Of Denmark it is reported that 'wage-drift has not been systematically higher or lower in the years in which there were no negotiated increases than in the years when new agreements were signed' (O.E.E.C., 1961, p. 298). Hansen and Rehn (1956, p. 102) found some support in Swedish figures 'for the conclusion that wage-adjustments through organisational negotiations seem neither to reduce the rate of wage-drift during the period immediately following the negotia-

tions nor to hasten it by stimulating local activity; or, rather these two tendencies – which undoubtedly do exist – seem to cancel out.' In the United Kingdom Dicks-Mireaux (forthcoming) has found no tendency for the size of the rise in scheduled rates to vary in response to that of the current and immediately preceding rise in earnings.

11. Some studies of time-series have looked for a possible association between the variations in drift and the rate of rise of productivity. Hansen and Rehn (1956) and Rehn (1959) found none such in Sweden. In the United Kingdom the figures given by Turner (1960, Table V) show an association between the change in output per operative hour and the rise in the 'actual wage' per hour, over spans of twelve months, that is markedly negative – the biggest rise in the 'actual wage' came about when output per operative hour actually fell. But Marquand (1960, pp. 92, 97–8) found that among the sixteen industrial orders considered 'in a considerable number of instances, the increases in productivity from year to year, even with the extreme assumption that all the wage-drift was concentrated in the pieceworkers' wage payments, were sufficient to account for the wage-drift.' In British engineering, Lerner and Marquand (1962, pp. 39–45) found 'nothing to suggest that changes in productivity have a direct quantitative effect upon wage-drift for any category of male workers', but such an effect did appear among women, especially those paid by results.

12. A number of studies of time-series have found a marked association between the variations in drift and in the demand for labour as that is evidenced by vacancies or unemployed or both. For Sweden, Rehn (1959) found a high correlation, nearly $+0.8$, between wage drift by industry and labour shortage as that was reported annually by employers, the deviations from this relation 'being explained by the influence of the elastic or rigid wage systems in the different industries'; but it is understood that since 1957 the correlation is no longer evident. For Denmark in 1949–60, Hoffmeyer (1961) found a correlation of -0.35 between drift and unemployment. In West Germany a significant negative correlation has been found (O.E.E.C., 1961, p. 356) between drift and seasonally adjusted unemployment lagged nine or twelve months. 'Perhaps more than in most countries, wage drift in the

Netherlands has been concentrated in the periods of excess demand for labour' (O.E.E.C., 1961, pp. 369–70). For the United Kingdom, Marquand (1960, p. 98) found that many elements of drift remaining after taking overtime and productivity into account 'were associated with a particularly high level of advertised unfilled vacancies'. Lerner and Marquand (1962, p. 60) found a marked negative association between drift (inclusive of overtime) and the rise in the number of unemployed, over spans of twelve months, for men but not for women. There is thus evidence that the state of demand for labour has often exerted a strong influence on drift; but it has not done so invariably, and attention has been drawn especially to Denmark, as showing that drift can continue in the presence of high rates of unemployment. It is true that over 1953–7, through which the prevailing national rate of unemployment was over 6 per cent, drift made up a third of the rise in wages for all workers and more than 40 per cent of that for the skilled (Dahl, 1959). But the incidence of unemployment was uneven: the prevailing rate, nearly 10 per cent among the unskilled, was only 3·3 per cent in engineering. Jobs for the skilled were increasing in number relatively to those for the unskilled. It may be going too far to ascribe the drift of skilled wages to the pull of demand, but certainly it occurred in a setting of much less unemployment than the national average suggests. On the other hand, we must note that among the unskilled, where unemployment was generally high, drift, though smaller, was still substantial.

13. Even where significant associations have been found between the variations of drift from year to year and those of labour shortage or productivity, part of the drift has remained unaccounted for. This part persists through the ups and downs of the economy: it has gone on even when the forces that foster drift have been weakest. In seeking to account for it, we may note that the setting too has had its persistent element – the state of managerial expectations associated with the commitment of governments to full employment, practical experience of sales rising year by year despite higher prices, and the sight of costs and prices rising abroad. In this state of expectation, the prospective dangers of raising a particular rate of pay are diminished, the prospective costs of any loss of output are enhanced.

Factors Bearing on Drift Suggested by Inquiries Conducted in the Firm

14. Some investigators have also reported the replies that trade unionists and managers have given to questions about the causes of drift in their experience at the place of work. In Sweden, the trade unionists laid most stress on increased effort by the workers, but also attached significance to local labour shortage, and the extension of payment by results. These factors were likewise significant in the experience of the managers, who also ascribed importance to the normal course of improvements in organization and methods, and to 'internal considerations', that is, to the restoration of the wage structure; but they gave by far the greatest weight to labour shortage (Rehn, 1959). In Denmark it was found that 'arguments for wage increases at the factory level were mainly productivity increases and wage increases in other companies or for similar kinds of work. It is suggested that as human relations in the work place are of mounting importance the majority of companies feel it necessary to grant such increases which means that increases take place, even though there may be unemployed persons' (Hoffmeyer, 1960, p. 292). A Norwegian inquiry (Aarvig, 1961) has brought out the distinction between primary and secondary drift. Primary drift was found to come about mostly through labour shortage and payment by results. Secondary drift occurred to rectify a wage structure that had been distorted by primary. Typically, within the firm, the earnings of workers paid by results went up while those of workers on time-rates, including some whose relative pay is customarily high, did not, and then the sense of what was fair, and the need to avoid trouble, alike prompted a lieu bonus or other rise in effective rates for the timeworkers. But drift was also imparted from one firm to another: to meet their workpeople's sense of what was fair, and to maintain their labour supply in the long run, firms compared their own levels of earnings with those of other firms in the same industry or district, and took care not to get left behind. Both sorts of drift took place within the knowledge and control of management. Perhaps the long-run rising trend of earnings under payment by results that arises from general improvements, such as do not justify the revision of rates

for particular jobs, was automatic; but otherwise, drift occurred with the connivance or on the initiative of management. Firms whose business had been unprofitable had been more rigorous in revising the rates of jobs for which methods had been improved. In Britain, Lerner and Marquand (1962, p. 53) found 'that workshop bargaining over piece-rates tends to act as a catalyst in the engineering wage-drift. It appears that skilled male payment-by-result workers are in the strongest position in the workshop; the increases which they receive set in motion factory wage claims for other workers. But it cannot be emphasised too strongly that the increases which they receive are in no way directly related to increases in productivity; the occasions when the bulk of the increases are awarded are occasions when there are discontinuities of production, but these discontinuities need not be associated with increases in productivity and the size of the increases awarded does not seem to be in any way related to a previous, contemporaneous, or anticipated increase in production. Skilled timeworkers' earnings rise as pieceworkers' earnings rise, partly through successful negotiations over lieu increments and partly through overtime work. The same pattern applies, in a modified form, to unskilled male workers, and in a more modified form still to women, whose bargaining position is considerably weaker than that of men.'

15. Studies of detailed instances bear out the importance of secondary drift. Lerner and Marquand (1962, pp. 26–7 and 51), for instance, in their study of British engineering, found that 'the greatest part of the wage-drift ... for male timeworkers in the 45 firms examined arose out of workshop bargaining between shop stewards and management', and the great majority of the agreements reached in the preceding ten years had been intended to re-establish the wage structure – to keep up with pieceworkers, or other timeworkers who had already received a 'lieu increment', and to raise factory rates or earnings to the modal level of the district, or to the average level reported for the industry. The same authors call attention to the quarterly district meetings of shop stewards of the Amalgamated Engineering Union to exchange information about wages, and to the co-ordinating committees formed by shop stewards in large concerns with plants in different regions: 'the knowledge of the increases won in high-

wage plants acts as an inducement to stewards employed in low-wage plants to try to catch up.' Turner (1956, p. 111) recorded that the reduction of the differential for skill that the scheduled rises tended to bring about in British shipbuilding 'has been somewhat offset by the general extension of piecework to craftsmen'. This kind of interplay between scheduled rises and drift has occurred on the national scale in Denmark: the 'solidaristic' policy of the trade unions has shaped central agreements so as to raise unskilled rates relatively to skilled, but the Danish wage-structure in terms of actual earnings has changed extremely little, because the skilled workers have obtained much more drift (O.E.E.C., 1961, pp. 300–303). The interplay may run the other way, from drift to the scheduled rise; in Sweden, for instance, a function 'of the central agreements has increasingly been to iron out distortions in the wage structure arising from drift' (O.E.E.C., 1961, p. 412). If the interplay runs both ways it can perpetuate a spiral. Lydall (1958, p. 295) has described such a case. A rise in productivity in Sector A 'causes piecework earnings in Sector A to rise, followed by the "lieu" rates of timeworkers in piecework firms in Sector A, followed again by the special "bribery" rates in other (non-piecework) firms in Sector A. Now earnings in Sector A as a whole have gone ahead of earnings in Sector B. But earnings in Sector B can only be increased in an orderly way by increasing wage rates in Sector B's industries. So the wage rates of the busmen, the railwaymen, the shop workers, the agricultural workers and the civil servants are gradually pushed up. But this in turn causes further repercussions in Sector A itself. The workers in engineering, etc., argue that their increased earnings are the result of greater productivity. They know that profits in their industry are booming. The newspapers tell them that various groups and workers in Sector B are getting increases in their agreed *rates*. So they also demand that their rates shall go up; and a new round of repercussions may begin.'

Some Common Features Apparent in the Evidence

16. In the findings we have surveyed, the sources and incidence of drift have, in one way, been perplexingly various. No one factor has exercised a constant influence, no one type of labour or

industry has experienced more drift in all times and places. What has seemed predominant in one setting has been negligible in another. But in another way this very variety indicates the underlying and pervasive presence of common influences, of permissive if not active factors that will account both for the generality of drift within certain bounds of time and space and for its comparative absence beyond them. The contrast between the years before and since the Second World War suggests that one of these factors is the state of managerial expectations prevailing internationally in the post-war years (paragraph 13 above): most drift could not have occurred if managers had reckoned a rise in unit labour costs more harmful than a loss of output. The contrast during the post-war years between the countries studied here and the United States suggests that another necessary condition for drift has been the need and the opportunity to alter particular rates at the place of work when only the broad lines of the wage structure are prescribed by centralized collective bargaining. Some allowance is due for the lower level of employment in the United States, and we do not know how American practice would have held out against European pressures; but the American setting in 1947–61 was still such as to permit an average annual rise in unit labour costs of more than $2\frac{1}{2}$ per cent.[2] One reason why next to none of this took the form of drift is likely to lie in differences of institutions rather than of pressures, and more particularly in the characteristic American institution of the plant contract, by which the wage structure of the plant is fixed in realistic detail until a stated date for renegotiation. It is significant that in one instance of pay being scheduled at the national level in the United States there has been a great deal of drift. For about a million Federal classified employees, a fifth of them professional and the rest mostly in clerical and administrative work, basic rates of pay are determined by Congress. Between 1939 and 1961 the average rate, after taking account of changes in the numbers at different points within each grade, rose by about 125 per cent, but the average of all salaries rose by 189 per cent. Some of the

2. *Annual Report* of the Council of Economic Advisers (Washington, D.C., January 1962), Table 20, p. 175: private non-agricultural industries, all employees, percentage change per year, 1947–61, average hourly compensation 5·1, output per man-hour 2·5.

divergence arose from changes in the occupational composition, but the rest is ascribed to upgrading, 'a liberalisation of classification reflecting a tightening of the labor market' (B.L.S., 1962). No such drift has appeared in the other major branches of Federal employment – the Postal Field Service, in which the bulk of the employees are in a single grade; and the manual workers, whose rates are adjusted locally by 'fair comparison'.[3] In Denmark, some industries explicitly treat their negotiated rates as minima only, and in the engineering agreement a 'promise clause provides that increases shall be given when conditions permit: in such industries drift has been greater than in those whose negotiated rates are intended to be effective (Hoffmeyer, 1960, p. 134). Primary drift in particular seems generally to have been greater where management has exerted less control over the wage structure within the firm, whether because it has not maintained uniform standards in payment by results, or because it has bought its way out of immediate threats or shortages without regard to the consequent disturbance of relativities.

17. Another common feature that may be traced in the detail we have been examining is the distinction between primary and secondary drift. Primary drift has had three main sources: a rise in the hourly earnings of pieceworkers in the course of the general improvement of organization and methods; action initiated by employers to attract and retain scarce labour; and the pressing of claims by particular workers or groups at points where management is likely to prefer a limited rise in labour costs to a loss of output. The three sources are more distinct in principle than practice: a shop steward's claim for a rise for a particular group of workers may be met by a loosening of standards when rates are revised, and management may be the more ready to meet the claim because other employers are competing for this type of labour. But in the first source alone is drift connected with higher productivity; in the second the essential is an excess demand for labour; in the third there may be no excess demand, but in the prevailing state of expectations managers are willing to buy off an immediate threat to production. What is common to all three sources, marks them off as primary and gives them a special significance for policy, is that the rises they bring initiate a

3. Communication from Dr H. M. Douty.

disturbance of customary relativities. It is to restore these relationships that secondary drift arises: whether the wage-earner enters
his claim first or management is beforehand, the motive force is
the sense of injustice that a change in customary parities or margins inspires, or the conviction that what one firm can afford
another can, and the object of the rise is to re-establish a wage-
structure that meets both labour's sense of equity and management's need to attract and retain labour, mark status and provide
incentives. The comparisons that actuate secondary drift may be
between different groups within one firm, between firms within
the same industry or region, or between industries; and the
instigation may be either primary drift or a scheduled rise –
which itself may have been instigated by primary drift (Corina,
forthcoming).

18. These findings enable us to attempt an answer to the question whether drift is additive or alternative. Can the rise of
scheduled rates be slowed down without drift being made greater?
Can drift be reduced without generating more pressure to raise
scheduled rates? We have seen that some observers have answered
no to both questions, on the ground that the very fact of drift
supervening upon scheduled rises shows that the effective rate of
pay is being pulled up by demand, and the demand price will be
arrived at in one way if not another. Again, it has been argued
that there is at any time a certain total rise that labour means to
get in one way or another, and if drift is smaller there will be more
push for scheduled rises, and conversely. We can agree that,
whether the force raising pay is a pull or a push, the size of a
further rise will in some cases tend to vary inversely with that of
the rise just effected. However much an employer is concerned
with how his rates compare with others', he may also be concerned with how much they have risen recently, and the greater
that rise, the less ready will he be to go on for the time being. A
wage-earner may be less moved to press for a rise when he has
just had one, even though it failed to restore a customary
relativity; or he may have in mind the exact sum needed for such
a restoration, and the more one mode of rise contributes to it, the
less is left for another to make up. In all such cases, in which the
size of the total rise to be obtained at any time has some definite-
ness, different modes of rise are alternative. But these are not the

only cases that recent years reveal. Since higher costs have so often proved in practice to be coverable by higher prices, employers competing for labour may count on the relation continuing to hold, so that their bidding does not bring pay nearer and nearer to a limit, but itself advances their notion of where the limit lies: the greater the excess of demand, the more likely is this to be the current state of expectations. A disturbance of relativities, again, may provoke in the wage-earner a resentment that a rise which leaves the disparity unchanged will not assuage. In such cases as these the size of the total rise is not felt to be potentially limited at one time, or is not the object in view, and here different modes of raising pay are not alternative but additive: employers competing for labour, for example, will not feel a scheduled rise that affects them all alike as reducing the competitive pressure on them, nor will mounting drift stiffen their resistance to scheduled rises. So long as we look at particular points within the ongoing process of recent years, both kinds of case appear plentifully. But if we suppose a widespread change, it is the second that seems likely to predominate. Whatever has been happening to particular rates, the general level of pay has not been being pulled or impelled towards a given limit. The evidence does not show that the subsequent drift has been generally greater when the scheduled rise was smaller, or conversely (paragraph 10); and if the prevailing amount of scheduled rises varies at all with that of the antecedent drift, it does so directly and not inversely, for less drift will have brought less of the disturbances of relativity that are a major instigation to claim scheduled rises (paragraph 15). It seems unlikely that an incomes policy would be nullified by higher drift, or that general action to check drift would only build up pressure to raise scheduled rates.

The Possibility of Action to Check Drift

19. What form can this action take? Drift is diffused, spontaneous, pervasive; it goes on in many forms and countless workplaces; it is unamenable to central control. Some might say that attempting to check it is not only futile but unnecessary. The object of any such attempt, they would point out, is not to stop money incomes rising at all, or stop them rising in any particular

way, but only to ensure that the total rise is not too great: if only the scheduled rises at the national level can be sufficiently moderated, then drift could simply be allowed to go on, at such rates as have prevailed in recent years, without money incomes going up too fast. It is a sufficient objection to this that any policy towards the scheduled rises at the national level itself needs the support of action to reduce drift, because drift generates claims to restore the relativities it disturbs. But this action must be initiated by management. The present survey of how drift has come about indicates that it has occurred sometimes on the initiative and generally without the active resistance of management, and that where management has had the means and the will to work out and maintain a wage structure drift has been smaller. Drift will be checked only as managers accept responsibility for their domestic wage structures, and move away from extemporization and its chain reactions towards, for instance, the negotiation and consistent application of works agreements. Those who have done this will generally say they have gained by it, but in the cost-plus climate of the post-war years those who only bought their way out of difficulties from day to day ran little risk themselves, and forced the hand of the rest. The climate, however, can change; the market environment has its phases. There are signs that the association between a high level of activity and a soft market environment that prevailed for twelve years or so after the war was only contingent, and that high levels of activity can be maintained when managers no longer count on being able to cover higher costs by higher prices without loss of business. Drift seems to depend not on the level of activity so much as on the consensus of managers' expectations about how much risk they take if they let their own costs rise.

Summary

20. (a) Wage drift has been mainly a problem of the economies with centralized wage-fixing procedures under full employment (1). It consists in a rise in the effective rate of pay per unit of labour input that is brought about by arrangements outside the control of the recognized procedures for scheduling wage-rates (2). To measure drift we need to compare the actual movement of

earnings with the rise that would have come about, at the actual level of activity, from the scheduled provisions alone; but this is hard to do (3). A broad international comparison shows the prevalence of drift and suggests substantial differences in its extent in different countries (4).

(b) For light on what determines that extent we must turn to comparisons in more detail. The reasons given for women's drift being smaller than men's imply the importance of the particular methods of wage payment customarily followed (5). There are instances of drift being greater for skilled than unskilled and also the opposite, and in both cases the function of drift has been to restore the wage structure (6). For several reasons methods of payment by results foster drift (7). Differences between industries in the extent of drift show some association with their prosperity, but this association is not strong enough to imply that the demand for labour has been a predominant factor, and the differences also call our attention again to institutional factors (8).

(c) We also look for factors associated with the variations of drift over time. At the outset we must avoid a pitfall in the reckoning of drift that may account for some of the inverse correlation that has been found between scheduled rises and drift (9); direct inquiries into the impact of scheduled rises on drift have found none (10). An association between variations in drift and in productivity has appeared in some cases but not in others (11). Variations in the state of demand for labour have often been found to exert a marked influence on drift, but in Denmark there has been drift for unskilled workers in the presence of substantial unemployment (12). After variations of drift have been accounted for a persistent element has remained: it may be associated with the prevailing state of expectations about the possibility of passing on rises in cost (13).

(d) Inquiries among those with direct knowledge of how drift comes about at the place of work have found emphasis laid especially on labour shortages, and rises of earnings under payment by results; they have also brought out the distinction between primary drift which raises particular earnings ahead of others, and secondary drift which then restores customary relativities (14). Many studies bear out the importance of secondary drift, and the possibility of its perpetuating a spiral (15).

(e) Amid all the variety of the evidence certain common features appear. Drift is seen to depend on the consensus of managers' expectations about the risk brought by a rise in costs; and on the lack of close application of the scheduled rates to local circumstances (16). The interplay of primary and secondary drift is also a common feature (17). A general reduction of either scheduled rises or drift seems unlikely to be offset by an increase of the other (18).

(f) Drift can be checked only as managers exert themselves to establish and maintain a sound domestic wage structure (19).

References

AARVIG, L. (1961), 'Inquiry on wage drift 1958/59'. (Mimeographed: Oslo; Norsk Arbeidsgiverforening.)

BEHREND, H. (1960), 'Some aspects of company wage policy', *Journal of Industrial Economics*, vol. 8, no. 2, pp. 122–32.

B.L.S. (1962), 'Salary trends, Federal classified employees, July 1960–July 1961', Supplement to B.L.S. Report 200 (1961), Bureau of Labor Statistics, Washington.

CENTRAL PLANBUREAU (1962), *Centräal Economisch Plan*, 's-Gravenhage.

CORINA, J. (1965), *Trade Unions and Wage Restraint*, Blackwell.

DAHL, A. H. (1959), 'Lonstrukturen i Dansk Industri siden 1946', *National-φkonomisk Tidskrift*, 3–4, 1959.

DICKS-MIREAUX, L. A. (1958), 'Wage-earnings and wage-rates, 1954–57', *London and Cambridge Economic Bulletin*, vol. 27, no. 3, pp. 10–11.

DICKS-MIREAUX, L. A. (1959), 'The relationships between wage earning and wage rates', *London and Cambridge Economic Bulletin*, vol. 28, no. 2, pp. 9–11.

DICKS-MIREAUX, L. A., and DOW, J. C. R. (1959), 'The determinants of wage inflation: United Kingdom, 1946–56', *Journal of the Royal Statistical Society* (A), vol. 122, part 2, pp. 145–84.

DOW, J. C. R., and DICKS-MIREAUX, L. A. (1958), 'The excess demand for labour: A study of conditions in Great Britain', *Oxford Economic Papers*, vol. 10, pp. 1–33.

EARL LEWIS, L. (1960), 'Extent of incentive pay in manufacturing', *Monthly Labor Review*, vol. 83, no. 5, pp. 460–64.

HANCOCK, K. (1960), 'Wages policy and price stability in Australia, 1953–60', *Economic Journal*, vol. 70, no. 279, pp. 543–60.

HANSEN, B., and REHN, G. (1956), 'On wage-drift: A problem of money-wage dynamics', in *Economic Essays in Honour of Erik Lindahl*, Ekonomisk Tidskrift.

HILDEBRAND, G. H. (1959), evidence 29 September 1959, before Joint

Economic Committee, Congress of the United States, 86th Congress, First Session, Part 8.

HOFFMEYER, E. (1960), *Stabile Priser og Fuld Beskaeftigelse*, c.8, Copenhagen.

HOFFMEYER, E. (1961), 'Lønteori og empiriske sammenhaenge', *National-økonomisk Tidskrift*, 1–2, 1961.

LERNER, S. W., and MARQUAND, J. (1962), 'Workshop bargaining, wage drift and productivity in the British engineering industry', *Manchester School*, vol. 30, pp. 15–60.

LYDALL, H. F. (1958), 'Inflation and the earnings gap', *Bulletin of the Oxford Institute of Statistics*, vol. 20, no. 3, pp. 285–304. [Reprinted in B. J. McCormick and E. Owen (eds.), *The Labour Market*, Penguin Books, 1968.]

MAHER, J. E. (1961), 'An index of wage rates for selected industries 1946–1957', *Review of Economics and Statistics*, vol. 43, no. 3, pp. 277–83.

MARQUAND, J. (1960), 'Earnings drift in the United Kingdom 1948–57', *Oxford Economic Papers*, vol. 12, pp. 77–104.

NORSK ARBEIDSGIVERFORENING (1961), 'Lønnstatistikk for Arbeidere', 1 Kvartal (1961).

NOVE, A. (1958), 'The State and the wage-earner', *Soviet Survey*, vol. 26, no. 3, pp. 28–34.

O.E.E.C. (1961), *The Problem of Rising Prices*, by W. Fellner, M. Gilbert, B. Hansen, R. Kahn, F. Lutz and P. de Wolff. (Paris; O.E.E.C., C(61) 12.)

PENRICE, G. (1952), 'Earnings and wage-rates since 1938', *London and Cambridge Economic Bulletin*, vol. 1, no. 4, pp. 4–6.

PENRICE, G. (1955), 'Earnings and wage-rates, 1948–55', *London and Cambridge Economic Bulletin*, vol. 16, p. 11.

TURNER, H. A. (1956), 'Wages: Industry rates, workplace rates and the "Wage Drift"', *Manchester School*, vol. 24, no. 2, pp. 95–123.

TURNER, H. A. (1960), 'Wages, productivity and the level of employment: more on the "Wage Drift"', *Manchester School*, vol. 28, no. 1, pp. 84–123.

12 C. L. Schultz

Sectoral Shifts and Inflation

Extract from C. L. Schultz, 'Recent inflation in the United States', in *Employment, Growth and Price Levels*, (Hearings before the Joint Economic Committee, 86th Congress, 1st session, May 25–8, 1959), pp. 4–10, U.S. Government Printing Office.

The Current Controversy: Demand Pull Versus Cost Push

The purpose of this study is to examine the nature of the gradual inflation to which the American economy has been subject in recent years. There is relatively little controversy over the basic features of a wartime or reconversion inflation; rising prices are attributed to an increase in the effective demand for goods and services over and above the capacity of the economy to furnish them. There is wide disagreement, however, about the nature of and remedies for the more gradual rise in prices which has occurred during the postwar period. Most of the discussion has centered on the merits of the 'cost-push' versus the 'demand-pull' theories of inflation. Proponents of the cost-push thesis attribute the major blame for the price increases, particularly those of the 1955–7 period, to autonomous upward movements in either wage rates or administered prices or both. The demand-pull theorists on the other hand, assert that price increases currently, as always, are reflection of aggregate excess demand for goods and services, including the services of the factors of production.

We have been and shall be using the concept of excess demand throughout this study in a dynamic sense. In an economy characterized by steadily improving technology and substantial net investment, the supply of goods and services forthcoming at full employment is continually growing. Hence an absolutely stable demand could only be consistent with full employment if prices declined. Excess aggregate demand, in a dynamic context, only exists, therefore, when monetary demands for goods and services are rising *faster* than the constant dollar value of supplies of goods and services at full employment. The degree of excess demand will, of course, be influenced by the composition of the aggregate: an increased output in some industries can more easily be supplied than in others. Moreover, we can have a situation in which output is below its potential even though the labor force is fully employed. If, for example, there is large-scale hiring of salaried employees, those employees may be retained even when output does not rise as expected – we have under-employment. But these refinements aside, the essential point to remember is that the term 'excess aggregate demand' is used throughout in the context of a growing full employment supply.

In analysing the process by which price increases are generated there are two major sets of factors to be considered:

1. The impact of rising prices and wages on aggregate demand for goods and services.

2. The impact of changes in the demand for goods and for factors of production on prices and wage rates. Put more simply, how does the growth of excess capacity and unemployment affect prices and wages?

Prices and wages have a dual nature when considered in the aggregate: they are costs to buyers and incomes to sellers. Thus an increase in the general level of prices does not automatically mean a reduction in the quantity of goods and services demanded as it normally would in the case of a single commodity. The increased cost of purchasing any article or any factor of production is matched by the higher incomes received by the seller. So long as the increase in prices is accompanied by an equal increase in money expenditures, *real* purchases of goods and services will not be affected and employment will not be reduced. There are, however, indirect influences on the level of real demand exerted by a rising price level. If the tax system is progressive, the higher money incomes lead to a higher proportion of income taken in taxes. With a constant money supply, higher prices normally lead to a tighter money market, which in turn has some depressing influence on investment demand. If these and other indirect effects are important, their depressing influence on demand must continually be offset by demand increases from other sources, if the rising price level is not to result in rapidly growing unemployment. If, on the other hand, these indirect effects are relatively unimportant, then a rising price level will not bring about excess capacity and unemployment, or at least will do so only very slowly.

If prices and wages are *sensitive* to changes in demand, then no inflation can continue unless aggregate excess demand is constantly being renewed. The appearance of unemployment and excess capacity would quickly halt any price rise. Consequently the strength of the indirect influences discussed above determines how large an inflation will result from a given initial excess demand. There can be no inflation without the excess demand, however. Hence monetary and fiscal policy, appropriately handled, can achieve full employment and price stability; all that needs to be done is to prevent the excess demand, without which wages and prices would cease to rise. If, on the other hand wages and prices are relatively *insensitive* to changes in demand, then the indirect influences of the price level on aggregate demand will determine not how large the price rise will be but how much unemployment it will generate. For if prices and wages do not respond to growing excess capacity and unemployment, then the limitation of aggregate demand will not halt the inflation – it will only lead to unemployment.

The responsiveness of prices and wages to changes in demand is thus the central issue. Let us call prices and wages which are sensitive to changes in demand 'flexible' and those which do not respond to demand, 'cost-determined'. The latter category includes both those cases in which prices and wages adjust solely to changes in costs[1] and those in which there occur autonomous increases in prices and wages. We can distinguish four types of situations, depending on the nature of price and wage behavior and the impact of rising prices and wages on demand.

I. Rising prices and wages tend to reduce demand and employment:

1. Prices and wages *flexible*.
2. Prices and wages *cost-determined*.

1. Changes in consumer prices are equivalent to changes in costs for the purpose of wage determination.

II. Rising prices and wages do not tend to reduce demand and employment:

1. Prices and wages *flexible*.
2. Prices and wages *cost-determined*.

So long as prices and wages are cost-determined, then a cost-push inflation is possible, regardless of whether case I or case II holds. If the indirect effects of a cost-push inflation are relatively weak, so that real aggregate demand is not reduced (case II), then the inflation is self-validating – a cost-push inflation will not, of itself, lead to unemployment. If the indirect effects of rising prices and wages on aggregate demand are significant (case I), then unemployment and excess capacity will result. But since prices and wages are not flexible, the inflation will continue. In this situation, the maintenance of full employment requires a positive Government monetary and fiscal policy to provide the validating demand. In either situation the failure of aggregate demand to keep pace with a growing full employment output would not eliminate the inflation, so long as price and wage decision making does not respond to demand conditions.

If, on the other hand, prices and wages vary in response to changes in demand as well as costs, then the failure of demand to match full employment supply will quickly bring an inflation to a halt. The effect of rising prices and wages on aggregate demand determines how much of an inflation will result from a given initial excess demand. If a general price and wage rise leads to a large reduction in demand, then the economic system has a built-in self-correction factor. The Government need only exercise self-restraint; so long as excessive deficits and money supply increases are avoided, inflation is not a serious problem. If, on the other hand, the self-corrective influence of a rising price level is weak, then positive government counterinflationary policy may be a recurrent necessity. In either event, the flexibility of prices and wages implies that full employment can be maintained without price inflation. If prices and wages start to rise, a restriction of aggregate demand will lead to a cessation of price and wage gains rather than a growth in unemployment.

The controversy between the demand-pull and cost-push theorists is in reality, therefore, a debate about the consistency of full employment and price stability. 'Given an appropriate monetary-fiscal policy, the answer to the question whether we can continue to enjoy a large, growing, and reasonably stable volume of production and employment . . . lies in the relations of prices, costs, and profits' (Mason, 1959, p. 189). Do labor unions and monopolistic firms largely disregard the state of the market in setting prices and wages? Are prices marked up as costs rise with little regard for demand conditions? Does a rise in the cost of living lead to an equivalent wage increase even in periods of unemployment? Few would take an extreme position on these questions. There is rather a spectrum of opinion. Toward the one end of the spectrum are those who feel that prices and wages do respond rather quickly to changes in demand. The possibility that strongly organized groups can push up their cost prices in the absence of *ex ante* excess aggregate demand is not 'an empirically important possibility' (Friedman, 1951, p. 244), according to these demand-pull theorists. Further, according to this theoretical approach, the existence of inflation implies that the excess demand must be an *aggregate* excess. If prices and wages are responsive to demand conditions, excess demands in particular areas of the economy, balanced by deficient demands in other sectors, will merely lead to a realinement of relative prices. Only if demands in the aggregate are too high will the general level of prices rise.

Toward the other end of the spectrum are those who feel that prices and wages are, within a substantial range, set independently of demand conditions. No one would deny that there is some level of unemployment and excess capacity which would halt a price–wage spiral. But the cost-push theorists feel that the degree of unemployment and excess capacity required to break through the cost-determined nature of wages and prices is quite large. The power of big business and big labor to determine prices and wages is so great, that under conditions of relatively full employment, even without excess demand, a secular rise in the price level is unavoidable.

The validity of either approach in this controversy cannot be discovered from the historical relationship of a few large aggregates. The fact that in recent years wages have risen faster than productivity, for example, is often cited as evidence that we have been experiencing a cost-push inflation. But this relationship tells us absolutely nothing about the nature of inflation. In the purest sort of demand-pull inflation, wages would also rise more rapidly than productivity. By the same sort of 'reasoning' we could cite the fact that money expenditures rose more rapidly than output as a proof of demand-pull inflation. An equally strong condemnation applies to demonstrations which point to the rise in the money supply or its velocity as proof of the demand-pull nature of inflation.

Even the timing of wage and price increases cannot be offered, by itself, as evidence of the nature of the inflationary process. Suppose, for example, that prices are marked up mainly in response to rising wages. Then an excess demand inflation will first lead to a rise in wage rates through its impact on the labor market, and only thereafter in a price rise. The historical data would indicate that the increase in wages preceded the rise in prices, yet the inflation would be one which was initiated by excess demands.

A cost-push inflation need not arise solely from an *autonomous* upward push of administered wages or prices. If prices are set by applying a constant margin to costs, and if wages are determined by movements in the level of consumer prices, then an initial general price rise, stemming from any source, can perpetuate itself, as wages and prices successively adjust upward to each other. The greater the insensitivity of the price and wage 'markups' over cost to unemployment or excess capacity, the greater the inflationary possibilities. The shorter the lag between the mutual adjustment of prices to wages and wages to prices, the faster the inflation will proceed.

The response of prices and wages to changes in demand cannot, in reality, be forced into the simple categories of 'flexible' and 'cost-determined'. The most important fact about their behavior, for the purpose of analysing creeping inflation, is its asymmetry. Prices and wages tend to be more flexible upward in response to increases in demand than they are in a downward direction in response to decreases in demand. As a consequence, the composition of demand as well as its aggregate magnitude, takes on a central role in the generation of inflation. The further development of this point is one of the major features of the present study.

C. L. Schultz

The Nature of the Recent Inflation

An examination of recent economic history suggests that creeping inflation is not a phenomenon which can be dealt with in aggregate terms. In particular the price increases from 1955 to 1957 stemmed, in the main, neither from autonomous upward 'pushes' of administered prices or wages nor from the existence of an aggregate excess demand. Neither of these explanations can satisfactorily account for a number of apparent paradoxes during this period: The dissipation of a relatively modest 5 per cent per annum rise in money expenditures in a $3\frac{1}{2}$ per cent price rise and only $1\frac{1}{2}$ per cent output gain; the apparent correlation of price increases with demand increases industry by industry, but with an upward bias, so that the overall level of prices rose while the overall level of demand was not excessive; the fact that prices rose more rapidly than unit wage costs, while at the same time net profit margins were shrinking; and finally the high level of investment activity followed by disappointing gains in productivity and consequent increases in unit costs.

The theoretical and empirical analysis of the economic processes which lead to creeping inflation is not easily summarized. It is not a relatively simple matter which can be condensed into a short formula, like the popular 'too much money chasing too few goods'. Nor is it a 'devil' theory in which abound the villains of most cost-push theories – the union boss and the greedy monopolist. We shall attempt to sketch the characteristics of economic behavior which lead to creeping inflation and indicate briefly the application of the analysis to the 1955–7 period.

The importance of the composition of demands

Prices and wages in the modern American economy are generally flexible upward in response to excess demand, but they tend to be rigid downward. There is, as we noted earlier, an asymmetry in their behavior. Even if demands in the aggregate are not excessive, a situation of excess demand in some sectors of the economy balanced by deficient demand in other sectors will still lead to a rise in the general level of prices. The rise in prices in markets characterized by excess demand will not be balanced by falling prices in other markets.

Excess demand in particular industries transmits its impact to the rest of the economy through its influence on the prices of materials and the wages of labor. Crude materials prices are normally quite sensitive to changes in demand, and are unlikely to rise significantly unless demands for them in the aggregate are excessive. Prices of intermediate materials supplies and components, on the other hand, are more likely to be rigid downward, but flexible upward in response to an increase in demand or costs. Prices of those materials chiefly consumed by industries with excess demand rise, since excess demand for the final goods usually implies excess demand for specialized materials. Materials used mainly in industries with deficient demand will not fall in price, unless the demand deficiency is quite large. Thus excess demand in particular sectors of the economy will result in a general rise in the prices of intermediate materials, supplies, and components; industries which are not experiencing excess demands will find themselves confronted with rising materials costs.

Wages will also be bid up in excess demand industries. Wages in other industries will tend to follow. Even though demand for labor is not excessive, firms cannot allow the wage differential between themselves and other firms to get too large; this is not because they fear the wholesale desertion of their work force, but because they do not wish to experience the inefficiencies and lowered productivity which result from dissatisfaction over widening differentials. Rising wage rates, originating in the excess demand sectors, thus spread throughout the economy. Because productivity gains in the short run are greatest where demand and output are increasing, firms in those sectors where demand is rising slower than capacity will often be faced with even larger increases in unit wage costs than firms in the areas of excess demand. In some cases the size of wage increases will be determined by long-term contracts concluded in earlier periods. Except as such increases are modified by changes in the cost of living (through escalator clauses) they will have little relationship to the current state of the market.

The spread of wage increases from excess demand sectors to other parts of the economy accentuates the rise in the price of semifabricated materials and components. Thus the influence of rising costs and the resistance of prices to declining demands will be larger at the later stages of the production process, other things being equal. The opportunities for rigidities to build up and for rising costs, particularly labor costs, to affect prices are multiplied as products approach the finished state.

Producers of finished goods will be confronted with a general rise in the level of costs, even when the demand for their products and their own demands for materials and labor are not excessive. The more cost determined are the pricing policies of the industries involved, the greater will be the price rise. In competitive sectors of the economy the rising costs will be at least partly absorbed. But in very many industries they will be more fully passed on in higher prices. Markups will of course be shaded when excess capacity begins to rise. As inflationary pressures spread out from excess demand sectors, their force will be somewhat damped in the absence of excess aggregate demand. Similarly the tendency of wages to follow the pattern set in the rapidly expanding industries will be modified as unemployment rises. But so long as markups and wages are more sensitive in an upward than in a downward direction, a rise in the general level of prices can be initiated by excess demand in particular industries.

This kind of inflationary process cannot be neatly labeled. It arises initially out of excess demand in particular industries. But it results in a general price rise only because of the downward rigidities and cost-oriented nature of prices and wages. It is not characterized by an autonomous upward push of costs nor by an *aggregate* excess demand. Indeed its basic nature is that it cannot be understood in terms of aggregates alone. Such inflation is the necessary result of sharp changes in the composition of demand, given the structure of prices and wages in our economy.

The downward rigidities and cost-oriented nature of prices and wages act like a ratchet on the price level. Most maladjustments of prices relative to each other and of prices relative to wages tend to be corrected by upward movements in the out-of-line prices or wages rather than by a mutual adjustment to a common center. The short-run inflationary mechanism which we have been describing thus imparts a long-run secular bias to the price level. A floor is placed under each higher level, from which later increases take off. During earlier periods in our history, the recurrence of substantial and lengthy depressions broke through these rigidities and forced large declines in the levels of prices and wages. The widespread bankruptcies and reorganizations of depression periods also led to massive writedowns in the value of fixed assets. This removed an additional feature of the ratchet mechanism. Moreover, a much larger proportion of total value produced originated in the demand-sensitive raw materials industries – particularly agriculture. Even if rigidities in the industrial sector were as great then as now, they played a smaller role in the overall economy.

References

FRIEDMAN, M. (1951), 'Some comments on the significance of labour unions for economic policy', in D. M. Wright (ed.), *The Impact of the Unions*, Kelley and Millman, pp. 204–34.

MASON, E. (1959), *Essays in Honor of John H. Williams*, Harvard University Press.

13 F. W. Paish

Unemployment and Price Stability

F. W. Paish, 'The limits of incomes policies', in F. W. Paish and J. Hennessy, *Policy for Incomes* (4th edn), Hobart Paper 29, Institute of Economic Affairs, 1968, pp. 13–49.

I. Introduction

Many differences of opinion on matters of economic policy are caused by disagreements about the relative importance of ultimate ends. Thus, those for whom greater equality of incomes is more important than a maximum rate of growth of national product will naturally disagree with those who would give first priority to growth. And those who believe that extreme full employment is desirable, not only for its own sake, but also because they think that rapid growth is possible only with some degree of inflation, will differ from those who believe that inflation is not only grossly unjust in its effects, but also leads to the inefficient use of resources and to the survival of inefficient managements, and thus in the long run tends to slow down growth.

The difference of opinion analysed in this *Hobart Paper* is, however, not of this sort. In this discussion both sides agree in giving first priority to the prevention of inflation, that is to say, to preventing rises in money incomes from outstripping the sustainable growth of output. We can therefore say that both sides agree on the necessity of an incomes policy: where they disagree is about the way in which it can be carried out. One side believes that its common objective can best be achieved by inducing trade unions and employers' organizations to agree to limit rises in wages and profits to rates which are compatible with the growth of output and with long-term price stability. The other holds the view that such an agreement, even if achieved, would be ineffective so long as there was an excess demand for labour and unnecessary if there were not. It believes that the only way to

219

prevent wages and other incomes from rising too fast is to prevent the emergence of an excess demand for goods and services, including an excess demand for labour. This requirement implies a level of unemployment as high as would be consistent with the absence of inflation with a fully competitive labour market. In this paper the attempt is made to examine the assumptions which lie behind the two views and to see how far they can be reconciled.

II. Inflation

Causes of inflation

One, though not the only, cause of the disagreement is a conflict of opinion about the ways in which an inflation can start. Both sides agree that an inflation *can* be generated by an excessive rise in the demand for goods and services, whether by public authorities or by the private sector. This is the so-called 'demand inflation'. Where they disagree is on whether inflation can also be initiated by an excessive rise in wage rates forced on reluctant employers by the use of monopoly power by the trade unions – the so-called 'cost inflation'.

The way in which cost inflation is supposed to operate seems simple. Employers are forced by trade union pressure to grant increases in wage rates in excess of the rise in output per head. To maintain profit margins, employers are forced to increase prices. Their higher wages enable consumers to buy as much as before, in spite of the higher prices, while the increase in prices induces further demands by the unions – and so *ad infinitum*. If this view is accepted it follows that, if trade unions can be persuaded not to press claims for excessive wage increases, a cost inflation can be prevented from starting, and can be arrested even after it has begun.

This apparently simple description of a cost inflation, however, conceals some implicit assumptions which are by no means obviously true. If an inflation is to be *initiated* by rising costs, it must start from a condition where there is no excess demand – that is to say, a condition in which output is rising by no more than its sustainable rate of growth and incomes are rising no faster than output. In such conditions, no employer, under pressure to grant an increase in wages larger than the expected increase in output per head, can expect in advance to be able to pass on his higher costs in the form of higher prices without losing sales. He will therefore do his best to resist the demand, even at the risk of a strike, and if he is forced to accept it will consider that some marginal activity, either existing or projected, has been made unprofitable. He will therefore reduce his output and his demand for labour, or more probably, in a growing economy with a rising working population, will not increase them as much as he would otherwise have done. He will also tend to restrict his plans for new investment below what they would otherwise have been, thus causing demand for investment goods to be less than expected and intensifying the effects on the profits of investment goods industries of their own wage increases. The higher wages, even if general, are thus achieved only at the cost of lower business profits and rising unemployment. Only if employers confidently expect that they will be able to pass on their higher costs in higher prices without losing sales will they maintain their output and demand for labour at the levels at which they would have stood but for the excessive increases in wages. Excessive wage demands will therefore be granted without rising unemployment only if inflation is already expected. 'Cost inflation' thus becomes the way in which inflations are perpetuated rather than initiated.

Inflation and the money supply

Even when an inflation is already in progress, a further assumption is necessary to enable a cost inflation to continue indefinitely. Each rise in money incomes will require the holding of more money to finance consumption, while each rise in prices of physical assets, and of titles to their ownership, will require additional money to be held for financing investment. If the total quantity of money is not rising, or rising only as fast as real output, money will have to be withdrawn from idle balances in order to increase the average velocity of circulation, and this will be accompanied by a rise in interest rates.[1] As the excessively rapid rise of incomes proceeds, the velocity of circulation must

1. For a discussion of the relationship between changes in national money income, the quantity of money and the rate of interest, see Paish (1962), chapter 1, p. 3.

continue to increase, and rates of interest will continue to rise until they reach a level which checks the rise in investment and reduces the demand for labour. It is true that if the economy starts from a condition of high liquidity and low interest rates, such as existed in 1946, the process may continue for a long time before it is checked; but to make any inflation truly self-perpetuating requires a suitably expansionary monetary policy.

The checking of an inflation through a shortage of money, often slow, can of course be swiftly speeded up by government fiscal policy. If part of the money flow can be diverted, so that it ceases to create increased incomes on its next circuit, the rise in incomes can be directly prevented from perpetuating itself. Such a policy is effective even though it is implemented by a rise in indirect taxes, of which the impact effect is to raise prices further. Unlike higher prices received by producers, the proceeds of which are paid out in increased wages or dividends or used to finance increased investment, a rise in prices due to higher indirect taxes is not self-perpetuating, *provided that the Government does not use the proceeds to increase its own income-creating expenditure*. The effects of a larger budget surplus will be particularly marked if the increase is used to repay short-term government debt to the banks, thus also reducing the quantity of money and accelerating the rise in interest rates.

Trade unions as monopolists of labour

The case for a policy of attempting to induce the unions to refrain from pressing for wage increases in excess of the rise in output per head does not, however, depend only on a belief in the existence of cost inflation. Even if we believe that, in the absence of demand inflation, the unions cannot enforce excessive increases in wages without causing a rise in unemployment, there is still a strong case for trying to persuade them to limit wage increases to amounts which can be paid without either raising unemployment or raising prices. It pays any monopolist to raise his prices even at the cost of some reduction in the volume of his sales, and if the unions are in fact effective monopolists of the supply of labour, the same will be true of them. When only a *minority* of occupations is effectively unionized, their unions can raise wages above the level at which they would stand in a fully competitive labour market at the cost of some reduction in the number employed in those occupations. They can do this without raising the general level of unemployment provided that those who are prevented from working in the unionized occupations are able to obtain employment in non-unionized occupations, thus driving wages there down below what they would have been in a fully competitive system. If, however, *all* occupations are strongly unionized, the general level of real wages can be kept above its competitive level only by forcing some potential workers out of employment altogether. It is possible, with suitable assumptions, to construct hypothetical cases where the combination of strong and ruthless unions with a government determined to prevent inflation at any cost will result in an unemployment level of 5 per cent, or even 10 per cent (Finch, unpublished). On such assumptions those still employed would obtain so much larger a share of the national product, at the cost partly of those rendered unemployed and partly of profits, that the rise in the size of their share would more than offset the fall in the size of the product, so that, at least in the short run, they would be better off. Whether they would be better off also in the long run depends on what assumptions we make about the effects on the rate of growth of output.

It is probable, of course, that long before unemployment had reached the levels which, on these assumptions, would be needed to reconcile the unions' policies with the absence of inflation, the Government would find the rise politically intolerable. If they could not induce the unions to change their policies, the Government would be forced to seek a cure for the unemployment by increasing expenditure or reducing taxes, thus expanding demand and profits, and at the same time raising prices and depriving union members already in employment of part of the rise in real wages which their rise in money wages would otherwise have brought to them. This would no doubt bring increased union pressure for wage increases and new measures to expand demand, and so on. In this sense it is perhaps possible to speak of a self-perpetuating 'cost-push' inflation.

III. Appropriate and Inappropriate 'Incomes Policies'

Control of wages

If it could be shown that in fact there existed conditions in which the trade unions were able and willing, even in the absence of demand inflation, to force wage rates up well above the level which would have existed in a competitive labour market, there would be every argument for the Government to try to escape from the choice between inflation and a high level of unemployment by attempting to induce the unions to abandon this use of their monopoly power. If the arguments in favour of a 'wages policy' were based on the need to escape from such a dilemma, the discussion would turn merely on whether the unions, in that particular economy at that particular time, were in fact able and willing to hold the rest of the community up to ransom in this way. Once the facts were ascertained, there could be no further argument about the desirability of a 'wages policy', though there could, of course, be differences of opinion about methods of implementation. These would no doubt depend largely on how much the activities of the trade unions were thought to be adding to the cost, in terms of unemployment, of preventing inflation. If it could be shown that this cost was anything like the theoretically possible 5 per cent or more, public opinion would probably support a revision of trade union law; while if the additional unemployment were shown to be relatively small, the support for a revision of the law would be correspondingly less, and the methods used to implement a wages policy would probably continue to be limited to attempts at persuasion.

It would, however, seem that some advocates of a 'wages policy' go further than this and wish, not only to prevent the level of unemployment (consistent with the absence of inflation) from being forced above what it would have been in a competitive labour market but also to hold the levels of wages and unemployment down below their competitive equilibrium levels. The desirability of such a policy is doubtful, its practicability more than doubtful. If it could be implemented, its effects would be identical with those of an employers' monopoly designed to keep wage rates down below their competitive level, and therefore the exact opposite of the effects of a trade union monopoly designed to keep wages above their competitive level. Those already employed would lose part of the wage increases they would otherwise have received, there would be less unemployment, and profits would increase.

On the credit side of such a policy can be set a fall in unemployment which, if the policy could be really effectively enforced, might be to an extremely low level. In addition, a fringe of workers, who would otherwise not have taken paid employment at all, may be recruited, often on a part-time basis, to help to meet the excess demand for labour. Thus output, at least in the short run, would be higher than it would have been with a competitive labour market. At the same time there would be rises in retained profits, very possibly in tax yields and in the Government's budget surplus, and possibly also in personal saving, if the increase in the savings of those receiving higher dividends more than offset the fall in the savings of those receiving lower wages and salaries. Thus it is likely that total saving would rise, and with it total investment, so that there might be a tendency not only for current output to be higher but also for it to grow faster.

On the debit side can be set the lower real incomes and standards of living of the great bulk of the population and also, perhaps, some loss of dynamism in the economy. In conditions in which wage rates are held artificially low and profits artificially high, it is easy for even inefficient managements to stay in business. The pressure for greater efficiency would thus be relaxed, and it is possible that, in spite of the higher rates of saving and investment, in the long run the rate of growth might be slower than in an economy where efficiency was enforced by competition.

Of more practical importance than the desirability of such a policy is its feasibility. The difficulties of its inauguration are largely political, while those of its subsequent maintenance are mainly economic. The most obvious difficulty is to persuade the unions to agree to collaborate in keeping wages below the levels at which they would have stood in a competitive labour market. The only argument likely to have any effect in persuading them to accept such a policy is that this is the only way in which unemployment can be kept at an extremely low level without inflation. From the unions' point of view, the chief argument against it is that it would not only keep down wages but also increase profits; and there is a danger that, in trying to meet this objection, the Government might offer measures, especially in the form of profit and price controls, which would reduce the advantages and increase the disadvantages of the policy itself.

Control of prices or profits

There is no need to consider in detail any proposal for the direct limitation of profits. To try to peg profit margins would mean that every firm would be working on a cost-plus basis and would lose all incentive to keep down costs. To attempt to fix all prices at levels which, given the agreed rates of wages, would give normal profits to the reasonably efficient firm would, perhaps, be slightly less impracticable; but if the attempt were successful it would frustrate the whole purpose of the operation. Unemployment can be kept abnormally low only by keeping the demand for labour abnormally high; and the demand for labour can be kept abnormally high only by keeping the employment of labour abnormally profitable. If profits are held down to the same level as would obtain with a competitive labour market, the demand for labour will be correspondingly restrained and unemployment will not fall.

It is more probable that the unions would be offered an agreement whereby, though profits would be allowed to rise, the extra profits would be removed by increased taxation. Such a policy, while technically enforcible, would greatly add to the debit side of a wages policy. A high rate of profits tax has no effect on the inefficient firm which is only just managing to stay in business, while it increases the difficulty of efficient firms in obtaining the finance they need for expansion, both from internal sources and, very probably, in the market. It also reduces the incentive to keep down costs, especially in the form of expenditures such as advertising, which may still be yielding some residual benefit to the firm after the tax, it may be hoped, is reduced or removed. No system could be better designed to slow down growth than one which keeps the inefficient alive, prevents the efficient from expanding, and reduces for everyone the incentive to keep down costs.

Alternatively, the Government might offer, as an inducement to the unions, higher taxation, not of all profits but of distributed profits only. Such a measure, while avoiding some of the disadvantages of heavy taxation of all profits, introduces some new ones of its own. A system of heavier taxes on distributed than on retained profits causes few problems for the well-established but slowly-growing company, which is able to finance its capital requirements entirely out of its own resources, but makes it more expensive, and probably more difficult, for a fast-growing company, which needs more capital than it can save, to raise new capital in the market. It also tends to induce companies which are growing little if at all to retain profits for which they have no real use. It thus tends to cause capital to be used for less productive rather than more productive purposes. It also keeps the aggregate market value of a company's securities below the value of its net assets and so provides an ideal situation for the take-over bidder; indeed, it is only by take-over bids that assets can be put to their optimum use and that shareholders can realize anything approaching the full value of their investments.

Difficulties of enforcement

Even if the political difficulties of obtaining the agreement of the trade unions could be overcome, it is unlikely that a wages policy would be successful for long in holding wages and unemployment below their competitive equilibrium levels. As time went on, the administration of the policy would encounter increasing difficulties. These would arise basically because an attempt was being made to hold wages below the level which would equate the demand for labour with the supply. Although such a policy might be effective for a limited period of emergency, an attempt to maintain it permanently would face the employers, the trade unions, and probably also the Government with difficulties so great that they would lead ultimately to its breakdown.

With the demand for labour in excess of the supply at the price, many employers will find themselves with plant and equipment they cannot man, and profitable orders they cannot fulfil, for lack of labour. In these conditions it is extremely difficult, even by penal legislation, to prevent employers from attempting to attract the labour they need by methods which raise their labour costs.

227

Even if standard wage rates can be effectively controlled, the other methods of offering higher remuneration, in cash or kind, are innumerable: guaranteed overtime; upgrading; piece rates; merit payments; bonus or incentive schemes; profit sharing; pension schemes and other fringe benefits; even improved canteen and other amenities. All these methods (however desirable some of them may be in themselves) add to labour costs, and to the real, even if not the money incomes, of employees; and all are means of bidding up the price of labour, the excess of which over standard wage rates is likely to become increasingly apparent the longer the wages policy is maintained.[2]

The only effective way yet found to stop such a 'wage drift' is to have a firm agreement between employers for allocating scarce labour, so that they may no longer bid for labour in the market but must draw it from a central pool, sharing the labour shortages on some agreed basis. A scheme of this sort has been successfully operated for many years by the South African mining industry, with the object and result of keeping African wages below the level at which they would have stood if the mines had competed freely with each other for African labour. But it is difficult to believe that a scheme of this sort could be successfully established in this country.

Just as the employers' associations would find it increasingly difficult to ensure that their members kept the spirit, if not the letter, of the agreement, so the trade unions would find it increasingly difficult to prevent their members from taking unofficial action to secure wage increases greater than provided for. As time went on, the unions would find their branches and members increasingly out of sympathy with headquarters; unofficial strikes and other means of bringing pressure on employers would become increasingly common; breakaway unions would be formed with increasing frequency; and finally, unless the agreement had already broken down as the result of breaches by employers, the unions would be faced with the choice of abandoning the agreement or losing all control over their members.

The Government's difficulties, apart from those caused by unofficial strikes and by the threat of inflation as the agreement

2. For example, see the divergent movements of earnings and wage rates in 1949–50 (Figure 3b and Table 4, pp. 245 and 246).

gradually collapsed, would arise largely from the need they would feel to set a good example to employers in the private sector, by keeping the agreement strictly in negotiations with their own employees and by trying to insist that local authorities and the managements of nationalized industries did the same. Consequently, as the agreement broke down in the private sector, employees' earnings in the public sector would tend to fall increasingly behind. The result would be not only unofficial strikes and other labour troubles, frequently in occupations where they would cause the maximum of inconvenience to the public, but also an increasing inability to recruit and retain labour for the public service in the numbers and of the quality required. This would be the more disastrous in that most of the really essential public services are now under the control of public authorities.

IV. The Extent of Unemployment

Even if we accept that, while there is every justification for trying to dissuade trade unions from using their monopoly power to force wage increases larger than would have been consistent with the absence of inflation in a competitive labour market, an attempt to keep wage increases below the equilibrium competitive level is of doubtful desirability and unlikely to succeed for long, we still need the answers to two further questions before we can formulate a practical policy:

first, what, in the existing situation, is the minimum level of unemployment consistent with the absence of inflation?
second, what would that level be with a competitive labour market?

If the existing minimum level were found to be substantially higher than the competitive level, it would imply that the unions were exercising considerable monopoly power, and that there would be a strong case for a wages policy; if, on the other hand, the difference were found to be small, the case for a wages policy would be correspondingly less strong. In no case, however, would an attempt be justified to keep wage increases and unemployment below the levels which would have existed in a noninflationary competitive market.

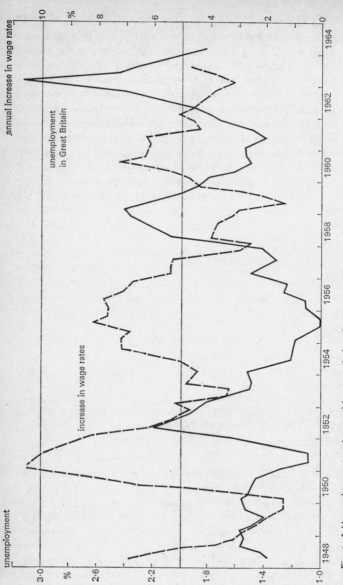

Figute 1 Unemployment and annual increase in hourly wage rates

How much unemployment to prevent inflation?

On the first of these two questions we have a good deal of evidence. It is clear that both before and since the war the rates of increase in wages have varied widely with changes in the level of unemployment. In Figure 1 and Table 1 changes in the rates of increase of wage rates are compared with changes in the average level of unemployment in Great Britain. Since in certain years, and especially since 1959, increases in wage rates have taken the form of reductions in the number of hours worked for a given weekly wage as well as of increases in weekly wage rates, the chart and table show the increases in hourly, rather than weekly, rates. Unemployment percentages are seasonally adjusted quarterly averages, while changes in wage rates are measured over periods of twelve months, starting six months before the dates of the unemployment figures and ending six months after them.

It will be seen that rates of increase of wage rates generally rise as unemployment falls and fall as unemployment rises. Thus a rise in the unemployment percentage from 1·08 in the second quarter of 1951 to 2·24 in the second quarter of 1952 is accompanied by a fall in the annual rate of wage-rate increase from 10·6 per cent to 6·6 per cent, and is followed by a further fall to 3·2 per cent in the third quarter of 1953. In the next cycle the changes are even more marked. Between the third quarter of 1955 and the first quarter of 1959 unemployment rose from 1·00 per cent to 2·43 per cent; during the same period the rate of rise of wage rates fell from 8·2 per cent to 3·1 per cent, with a further fall to 1·3 per cent in the second quarter of 1959. In the latest cycle the slowing down of the rise of wage rates, though less than in 1955–9, was again very marked. Between the third quarter of 1960 and the second quarter of 1963 (when it may still have been affected by the after-effects of the severe winter) unemployment rose from 1·53 per cent to 2·47 per cent; the rate of rise of wage rates fell from 7·4 per cent to 3·6 per cent.

The inverse relationship shown in Figure 1 and Table 1 between the percentage of unemployment and the rate of rise of wage rates is confirmed by the much more refined statistical investigations carried out by Messrs L. A. Dicks-Mireaux and J. C. R. Dow (1959), and by Professor A. W. Phillips (1958, see

Table 1

Unemployment and Annual Increases in Hourly Wage Rates in Great Britain, from 1948 to 1964

Year and quarter	Unemployment[1] %	Increase in wage rates[2] %	Year and quarter	Unemployment[1] %	Increase in wage rates[2] %
1948 1	1·37	6·9	1956 1	1·11	7·6
2	1·44	5·7	2	1·11	7·7
3	1·58	3·9	3	1·27	7·0
4	1·56	3·1	4	1·24	6·8
1949 1	1·58	2·8	1957 1	1·53	5·3
2	1·49	2·3	2	1·43	5·3
3	1·39	1·9	3	1·30	5·2
4	1·55	1·4	4	1·40	2·9
1950 1	1·58	1·3	1958 1	1·71	2·4
2	1·52	3·1	2	2·05	4·0
3	1·50	7·0	3	2·23	3·9
4	1·46	8·2	4	2·39	3·7
1951 1	1·30	9·4	1959 1	2·43	3·1
2	1·08	10·6	2	2·21	1·3
3	1·08	10·0	3	2·03	2·2
4	1·36	9·0	4	1·92	4·3
1952 1	1·72	8·1	1960 1	1·79	4·8
2	2·24	6·6	2	1·60	5·6
3	2·09	5·4	3	1·53	7·4
4	1·91	4·7	4	1·57	6·2
1953 1	1·82	5·2	1961 1	1·57	6·1
2	1·65	3·3	2	1·39	6·3
3	1·50	3·2	3	1·46	4·2
4	1·51	4·9	4	1·71	4·5
1954 1	1·55	4·4	1962 1	1·80	5·1
2	1·35	4·9	2	1·90	4·5
3	1·20	5·9	3	2·17	4·2
4	1·20	7·2	4	2·37	3·9
1955 1	1·18	7·2	1963 1	3·18	3·0
2	1·10	6·8	2	2·47	3·6
3	1·00	8·2	3	2·34	4·5
4	1·01	7·7	4	2·07	(4·3)
			1964 1	1·81	
			2	(1·60)	

1. Seasonally adjusted.
2. Measured from six months before to six months after the date shown.

Reading 15). Dicks-Mireaux and Dow conclude that 'a change of 1 per cent in excess demand (or, roughly, of unemployment) is associated with an increase or decrease in the percentage rate of wage-rate change of 3·5 per cent' (op. cit., p. 166). Professor Phillips's curve (op. cit., p. 297, Reading 15, p. 277), which is constructed on the basis of earlier data but which also fits almost exactly the post-war data up to the date on which he wrote, indicates that a rise in unemployment from 1 to 2 per cent will be accompanied by a fall in the rate of wage-rate increase from 9 to 3 per cent a year; a rise in unemployment from $1\frac{1}{2}$ to $2\frac{1}{2}$ per cent by a fall from $4\frac{1}{2}$ per cent a year to just under 2 per cent; and a rise in unemployment from 2 to 3 per cent by a fall from 3 to just over 1 per cent. While, therefore, he estimates that only a moderate amount of unemployment is needed to keep the annual rate of rise in wage rates down to 3 per cent, a much larger amount is needed to keep the rise down to 1 per cent. While the rate of rise in average output per man-hour is now probably more than 3 per cent a year, the gradual fall in the number of hours worked per week and the tendency towards longer holidays mean that annual output per head is probably rising at rather less than 3 per cent a year. A rise in weekly wage rates of 3 per cent, representing a rise in hourly wage rates of at least $3\frac{1}{2}$ per cent, is therefore probably rather more than can be absorbed indefinitely without a rise in the price level. On the basis of Professor Phillips's estimates, the level of unemployment which is compatible with a rate of wage increase no higher than the rise in output per head is thus probably rather more than 2 per cent, but almost certainly less than $2\frac{1}{2}$ per cent. If we put it at $2\frac{1}{4}$ per cent, or a little less, we shall probably not be very far out.

How much unemployment in a competitive labour market?
The next question we have to attempt to answer is by how much, if at all, this figure of $2\frac{1}{4}$ per cent of unemployment is in excess of the level which would be consistent with the absence of inflation in a competitive labour market. The general impression given by the way the atmosphere in the labour market changes as soon as unemployment falls appreciably below 2 per cent suggests that, although the competitive equilibrium rate is probably below $2\frac{1}{4}$ per cent, it is not much, if at all, below 2 per cent. It is, however,

not easy to get statistical confirmation of this impression. One possible line of approach to the problem presents itself. If in practice the trade unions are able, by the exercise of monopoly power, to keep wage rates above the level at which they would have stood in a competitive labour market, at the cost of a higher level of unemployment, we should expect to find, at the level of unemployment which is now just consistent with the absence of inflation, a supply of labour in excess of the demand at the ruling level of wage rates. We have a measure of the available supply of labour in the number of unemployed registered at the employment exchanges; we likewise have a measure of the demand for labour in the number of vacancies registered. If the figures of unemployment and vacancies could be taken at their face value, all we should have to do would be to find the level of unemployment at which the numbers of unemployed and of vacancies were equal.

Unfortunately, we cannot take the figures at their face value. The total of unemployed includes a substantial number who, for one reason or another, are not in fact available for employment. There are always a certain number who, though registered as unemployed, are not capable of doing a full day's, or, often, any work. Even in the worst years of the war, with the services of every man and woman urgently needed and with conscription and direction of labour in force, the unemployment percentage never fell below about 0·7 per cent. With the present level of civil employment, 0·7 per cent is equivalent to about 160,000, who must be regarded as not available for work, often through no fault of their own, even in conditions of the acutest excess demand for labour.

Secondly, a large proportion of those who are available for work is concentrated in the North of England, Scotland, Wales, and Northern Ireland, and is not available in the places where it is needed. There have been twelve quarters since the end of 1947 in which unemployment in Great Britain has reached or exceeded 2 per cent. In these quarters the average number of unemployed has been 487,000, and the average unemployment level 2·2 per cent (of 22·05 million). In the same periods, unemployment in the Midlands and South of England averaged 227,000, or just over 1·5 per cent (of 14·67 million), while in the North of England, Scotland, and Wales it averaged 259,000, or 3·5 per cent (of

7·38 million). Even if we allow for the effects of migration from the high to the low unemployment areas, which between 1959 and 1962 averaged 36,000 a year, it is clear that a good deal of the unemployment in the high unemployment areas cannot in present conditions be regarded as available for filling vacancies in the low unemployment areas. We must probably regard something like 30 per cent of the unemployed in high unemployment areas, or say 75,000, as not having been available for filling the vacancies which actually existed. If we add these to the 0·7 per cent assumed to be incapable of normal employment, we arrive at a total of rather over 1·0 per cent to be deducted from the total percentage unemployed before comparing it with the vacancies available.

The most recent period in which unemployment stood at $2\frac{1}{4}$ per cent was in May and June, 1963, when the number of unemployed averaged 517,000 out of a civilian labour force of 22·9 million. In the same period the average number of vacancies was 205,000.[3] If from the total unemployment figure of 517,000 we deduct the 230,000 estimated not to be available, we are left with 287,000 to fill vacancies of 205,000. This gives a surplus of available unemployed over vacancies of 82,000, or 0·35 per cent of the civilian labour force. Even this figure may be rather too high, since some vacancies, including those in many white-collar occupations, the police and the armed forces, are not registered with the employment exchanges. Allowing for these vacancies, we may perhaps put the excess of the number of available unemployed over the number of vacancies at about 60,000, or 0·25 per cent of the civilian labour force. Since this excess is measured at a time when unemployment stood at the estimated actual equilibrium rate of $2\frac{1}{4}$ per cent, we can put the competitive equilibrium rate at about 2 per cent. This, therefore, is the estimated level at which a 'wages policy', if it could be made politically acceptable, would cease to be self-frustrating.

If we put the amount of unemployment consistent with the absence of inflation (given the present rate of growth of produc-

3. This is very close to the average figure of 213,000 vacancies during the five periods since the war in which unemployment has stood at approximately $2\frac{1}{4}$ per cent: the second quarter of 1952; September–October 1958; April–May 1959; October–November 1962; and May–June 1963.

tive potential and the present regional distribution of unemployment) at 2 per cent[4] with a competitive labour market and at $2\frac{1}{4}$ per cent in the conditions actually ruling, it follows that we estimate the additional unemployment due to the monopoly power of the trade unions at not much more than 50,000. This figure is admittedly highly tentative; but even if we double it to 100,000 (almost certainly too high), it is doubtful if it would make the harmful effects of trade union monopoly power so obvious that public opinion would support a drastic revision of trade union law. If this view is correct, it seems likely that 'wages policies', even when applied in appropriate conditions, will continue to be implemented by the not very effective means of exhortation and persuasion.

We may summarize the conclusions to be drawn from the foregoing discussion as follows:

1. With the present rate of growth of productive potential and the present distribution of unemployment between regions, and excessive rate of wage increase with unemployment below 2 per cent must be restrained by restricting demand.

2. With unemployment between 2 per cent and $2\frac{1}{4}$ per cent restriction of demand can be usefully supplemented (though probably not replaced) by a 'wages policy'.

3. With unemployment above $2\frac{1}{4}$ per cent, a 'wages policy' becomes unnecessary, though harmless, and demand can safely

4. The estimate of 2 per cent for the level of unemployment needed to prevent inflation with a competitive labour market depends on the assumption that both the rate of growth of productive potential (which is equal to the long-term rate of growth of output) and the regional distribution of unemployment remain as at present. If, with the present distribution of unemployment, the rate of growth of productive potential could be increased substantially above the present rate (probably nearly $3\frac{1}{2}$ per cent a year), money incomes could rise faster than at present without inflation, and the level of unemployment needed to prevent inflation would consequently fall.

Again, if, with the present rate of growth of productive potential, the level of unemployment in the high unemployment areas could be reduced to equality with the average for the whole of Great Britain, the level of unemployment needed to prevent inflation in a competitive labour market would be reduced from 2 per cent to perhaps 1·7 per cent. This would mean that, instead of 1·5 per cent in the Midlands and South and 3 per cent in the North and Wales, it would become 1·7 per cent throughout.

be expanded. (If it were found that wages were still rising too fast with unemployment above $2\frac{1}{4}$ per cent, restriction of demand, whether or not supplemented by a 'wages policy', would have to be continued to a higher level.)

V. Implementing an 'Incomes Policy'

The questions of principle concerned in the concept of an 'incomes policy' have so far been discussed in the customary terms of unemployment and wage rates. When, however, we come to the implementation of policy, we find that both these bases of measurement have considerable disadvantages as guides to action. This is because unemployment rates and increases in wage rates, though showing a high degree of inverse correlation, have little direct causal relationship, but are both the consequences, after variable but often considerable time-lags, of changes in the demand for labour, themselves generated by changes in the demand for final products. If therefore action is postponed until the effects of these changes appear in unemployment and wage rates, it will often be taken much later than if it had been based on earlier indications of changes in the underlying state of demand. We can frequently find such earlier indications if we look to changes in weekly *earnings*, not wage *rates*; and if we look, not to unemployment, but to the whole of the margin, to which unemployment contributes only a part, between output and what the Treasury, in its *Economic Report 1963*, calls the 'productive potential' of the country, that is to say, what output *would have been* if there had been no limits to demand.

Time-lag: earnings and wage rates

The time-lag between changes in earnings and in wage rates arises from three causes. In the first place, when the demand for labour first increases faster than the supply, longer hours are worked and weekly earnings therefore rise faster than weekly wage rates; secondly, since a larger proportion of the total hours worked is at overtime rates, average hourly earnings rise faster than average hourly wage rates; and thirdly, when employers are, or fear to be, short of labour, they find one means or another of making extra payments in order to attract or retain workers. The gap between wage rates and earnings is the so-called 'wage drift'. When the demand for labour begins to decline, the movements are reversed; employers no longer find it necessary to offer anything, or so much, in the way of extra payment, and both total hours and

Table 2

Wage Rates and Earnings, Great Britain, from October 1958 to 1963

| | 1 | 2 | Percentage change on a year earlier | | |
| | | | 3 | 4 | 5 |
	Average weekly wage earnings	Average hourly wage earnings	Average hourly wage earnings excluding the effect of overtime	Average hourly wage rates	'wage drift' = col. 3 minus col. 4
October 1958	+2·3	+3·1	+3·1	+3·7	−0·6
October 1959	+5·1	+3·5	+2·7	+1·3	+1·4
October 1960	+6·6	+8·1	+7·6	+5·5	+2·1
October 1961	+5·4	+7·0	+6·9	+6·4	+0·5
October 1962	+3·2	+4·1	+4·4	+4·1	+0·3
October 1963	+5·3	+4·2	+3·6	+2·3	+1·3

Source: H.M. Treasury, *Economic Report 1963*, H.M.S.O., March 1964, p. 15.

Notes: The Table covers all full-time workers in the industries in the Ministry of Labour's earnings inquiry, i.e. all manufacturing industries *plus* mining and quarrying (excluding coal), construction, gas, electricity and water, public administration, and certain services.

The figures in column 3 are calculated by assuming that the amount of overtime in October of each year is equal to the difference between the average of actual hours worked and the average of normal working hours, multiplying this figure by $1\frac{1}{2}$ (the assumed rate of overtime pay) and adding the resultant figure to the average of normal working hours to produce a 'standard hours equivalent' of actual hours worked. Average weekly earnings divided by the standard hours equivalent gives a reasonably satisfactory estimate of average hourly earnings exclusive of overtime. From this series of figures the percentage changes in column 3 are calculated.

hours worked at overtime rates decrease. Meanwhile, the slow course of wage-rate negotiations may cause the rate of rise in wage rates to continue to increase for some time after the rate of rise in earnings has begun to fall, and to continue to fall for some time after the rate of rise in earnings has begun to accelerate again.

In its *Economic Report 1963* the Treasury published the table of changes in wage rates and earnings reproduced as Table 2.

It will be seen that, whereas the rate of rise in hourly wage rates reached its peak in 1961 and its lowest points in 1959 and 1963, the rise in weekly earnings reached its peak in 1960, with lowest points in 1958 and 1962. The estimates for wage drift reach their highest and lowest points in the same years as weekly earnings. Since changes in weekly earnings reflect the level of demand and affect money incomes more directly than do changes in wage rates, and since these changes appear a year earlier than changes in the rate of rise of wage rates, it is clear that here we have an index which is both more prompt and more relevant than wage rates. Hitherto, its usefulness has been limited by the fact that earnings figures have been available for only two months in each year, April and October, and only after several months' delay. Since January 1963, however, the Ministry of Labour has published, with much less delay, a monthly index of earnings. Now that this has been running long enough to begin to make possible comparison over 12 months, and especially when it begins to be possible to make seasonal corrections, the earnings index is certain to prove an invaluable source of information for purposes of incomes policy.

Time-lag: demand and unemployment

The time-lag between changes in the demand for final products and changes in the level of unemployment is due to the time it takes employers to make adjustments to the size of their labour force as the result of changes in their volume of sales. When demand first begins to decline, employers are reluctant to release labour until they are sure that the check to demand is likely to persist for a considerable time, especially if there are appreciable costs, psychological and other, both in enforcing redundancies and in re-employing labour. This reluctance to discharge labour will be particularly marked where employers have had recent experience of labour shortages. And secondly, quite apart from this reluctance to discharge labour, it will often take a considerable time to reorganize the work so that the reduced output can be produced by fewer workers. Meanwhile, the fall in output is reflected in a fall per head in the output of those remaining in employment.

With some industries still expanding and taking on labour while others continue to retain potentially redundant employees, total unemployment may continue to fall for some time after the rise in output has been checked. This is very likely to happen in present-day Britain, since output of heavy capital goods, produced largely in the heavy unemployment areas of the North and Wales, normally continues to rise for many months after the rise in output of consumption goods, produced largely in the low unemployment areas of the Midlands and South, has been checked; for employers in the low unemployment areas, with their recent experience of acute labour shortage, are particularly likely to retain employees until they are convinced that the check is likely to be prolonged.

In the upward phase of the cycle, the lag between rising output and falling unemployment is less regular and usually smaller than that between falling output and rising unemployment. Where it occurs, its cause is presumably that the size of the labour force has never been fully adjusted to the previous check to demand, so that employers are still holding redundant labour. They are particularly likely to do this in industries where the long-term trend of demand is sharply upwards and where they have had previous experience of labour shortages.

Estimating 'productive potential'

To obtain, as an improved substitute for the unemployment ratio, an estimate of the unused margin of 'productive potential' we need three sets of data:

1. Frequent and up-to-date estimates of total output (which is usually interpreted as meaning gross domestic product).

2. Reasonably reliable estimates of the rate (or rates) of growth of productive potential.

3. At least one date on which the proportion of productive potential actually in use can be identified.

For the first requirement, quarterly estimates of gross domestic product, derived from estimates of final expenditure on goods and services at market prices and adjusted for imports, taxes, subsidies, and price changes, are officially published with a time-lag of up to six months. More satisfactory, because less subject to random fluctuations, is an index of gross domestic product based on direct estimates of output. This index is officially published only for calendar years; but quarterly estimates on the same basis are prepared by the Department of Applied Economics, Cambridge.[5] This index is consistent with the Index of Industrial Production, which constitutes the most variable part of it; and indeed a close approximation to it can be calculated as soon as the Index of Industrial Production is available, by giving half the weight to the Index of Industrial Production and half to an index of non-industrial production assumed to rise at 3 per cent a year.

The index of productive potential is obtained by calculating rates of growth of output between pairs of years with similar levels of unemployment at similar stages of different trade cycles.[6] The rates of growth used here are 2·5 per cent a year up to 1953, 2·9 per cent a year from 1953 to 1956, 3·1 per cent a year from 1956 to 1959, and 3·5 per cent a year from 1960 onwards. From 1959 to 1960 there is a discontinuous check, the result of contra-cyclical reduction in the number of hours actually worked per week, apparently due to the sharp reductions in the length of the standard working week agreed to in the wage negotiations of 1959–60.

Finally, the relationship between this index and that of gross domestic product is established by assuming that in the last quarter of 1955, when unemployment in Great Britain was down to 1 per cent, the whole of the productive potential was being used. The resultant quarterly indexes of productive potential and gross domestic product are set out in Figure 2 and Table 3

5. Published in the *National Institute Economic Review* and in the *London and Cambridge Bulletin* (quarterly supplement to the *Times Review of Industry and Technology*).

6. For particulars of the method of constructing this index, under a slightly different name, see Paish (1962), pp. 318–22.

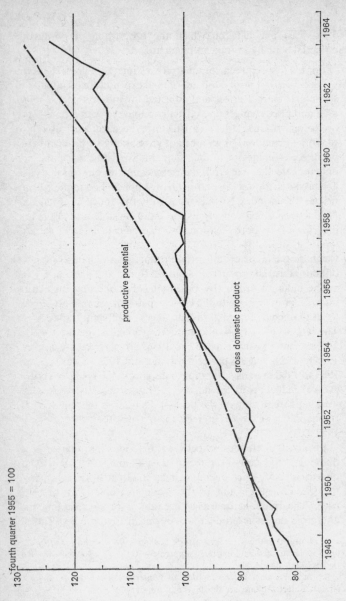

fourth quarter 1955 = 100

productive potential

gross domestic product

Figure 2 Indexes of gross domestic product and productive potential

Table 3

Gross Domestic Product[1] and Estimated Productive Potential,[1] Great Britain, from 1948 to 1964

(Percentages of fourth quarter of 1955)

Year and quarter	Gross domestic product	Estimated productive potential	G.D.P. as percentage of productive potential	Year and quarter	Gross domestic product	Estimated productive potential	G.D.P. as percentage of productive potential
1948 1	79·3	82·3	96·3	1956 1	99·3	100·7	98·6
2	80·2	82·8	96·8	2	99·4	101·4	98·0
3	80·7	83·3	96·9	3	99·3	102·1	97·2
4	81·3	83·8	97·0	4	99·5	102·9	96·8
1949 1	82·7	84·3	98·0	1957 1	100·8	103·6	97·4
2	83·7	84·8	98·5	2	101·3	104·4	97·1
3	84·0	85·3	98·3	3	101·7	105·1	96·6
4	83·7	85·8	97·3	4	100·8	105·9	95·2
1950 1	85·8	86·4	99·3	1958 1	100·9	106·7	94·5
2	86·6	86·9	99·2	2	100·5	107·5	93·5
3	87·2	87·4	99·7	3	100·7	108·3	93·0
4	87·8	87·9	99·9	4	101·9	109·1	93·4
1951 1	88·1	88·5	99·6	1959 1	102·5	109·9	93·2
2	89·0	89·0	100·0	2	104·8	110·8	94·5
3	89·0	89·6	99·3	3	106·1	111·7	95·0
4	88·2	90·1	97·8	4	108·6	112·6	96·4
1952 1	88·0	90·7	97·0	1960 1	110·4	113·0	97·6
2	87·1	91·2	95·3	2	111·1	113·4	97·9
3	88·0	91·8	95·8	3	111·4	114·3	97·5
4	88·0	92·3	95·4	4	111·6	115·3	96·8
1953 1	89·4	92·9	96·1	1961 1	112·6	116·3	96·7
2	90·7	93·4	97·0	2	113·3	117·3	96·5
3	91·7	94·0	97·4	3	113·2	118·3	95·6
4	93·1	94·5	98·4	4	113·0	119·3	94·7
1954 1	93·5	95·1	98·2	1962 1	113·3	120·3	94·2
2	94·6	95·7	98·7	2	114·7	121·4	94·5
3	95·7	96·4	99·2	3	115·5	122·4	94·4
4	96·8	97·0	99·6	4	114·9	123·5	93·1
1955 1	97·0	97·7	99·3	1963 1	113·3	124·5	90·9
2	98·0	98·4	99·4	2	117·3	125·6	93·3
3	98·8	99·2	99·4	3	119·2	126·6	94·0
4	100·0	100·0	100·0	4	121·4	127·7	94·9
				1964 1	(123·0)	128·8	(95·5)

1. Seasonally adjusted.

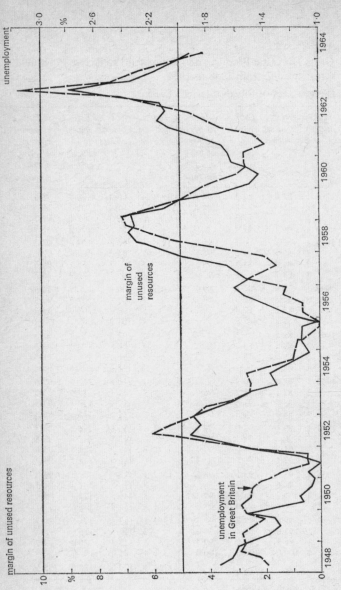

Figure 3a Margin of unused resources and unemployment

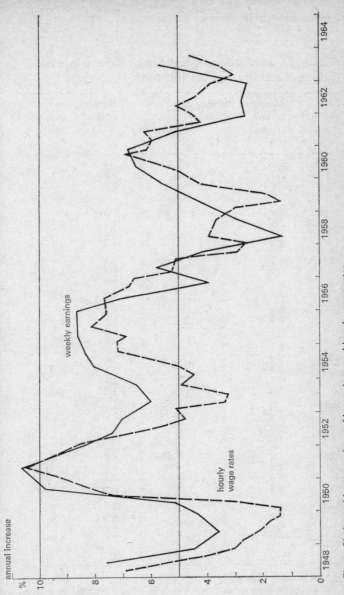

Figure 3b Annual increases in weekly earnings and hourly wage rates

Table 4

Margin of Unused Resources and Annual Increase in Weekly
Earnings, Great Britain, from 1948 to 1964

Year and quarter	Margin of unused resources[1] %	Increase in earnings[2] %	Year and quarter	Margin of unused resources[1] %	Increase in earnings[2] %
1948 1	3·7		1956 1	1·4	
2	3·2	7·7	2	2·0	7·1
3	3·1		3	2·8	
4	3·0	4·5	4	3·2	3·8
1949 1	2·0		1957 1	2·6	
2	1·5	3·6	2	2·9	5·9
3	1·7		3	3·4	
4	2·7	4·3	4	4·8	4·1
1950 1	0·7		1958 1	5·5	
2	0·8	5·3	2	6·5	1·2
3	0·3		3	7·0	
4	0·1	9·8	4	6·6	3·0
1951 1	0·4		1959 1	6·8	
2	0·0	10·7	2	5·5	4·3
3	0·7		3	5·0	
4	2·2	8·5	4	3·6	5·7
1952 1	3·0		1960 1	2·4	
2	4·7	7·5	2	2·1	6·6
3	4·2		3	2·5	
4	4·6	7·0	4	3·2	6·8
1953 1	3·9		1961 1	3·3	
2	3·0	6·0	2	3·5	5·0
3	2·6		3	4·4	
4	1·6	6·4	4	5·3	2·7
1954 1	1·8		1962 1	5·8	
2	1·3	8·1	2	5·5	2·8
3	0·8		3	5·6	
4	0·4	8·5	4	6·9	2·5
1955 1	0·7		1963 1	9·1	
2	0·6	8·7	2	6·7	5·8
3	0·6		3	6·0	
4	0·0	8·7	4	5·1	6·9
			1964 1	(4·5)	

1. Seasonally adjusted.
2. Measured from six months before to six months after the date shown.

(pp. 242–3). If we now express the index of gross domestic product as a percentage of the index of productive potential, we obtain an estimate of the percentage by which actual output falls below potential output. This gives us an estimate of the unused margin of productive resources in the economy.

In Table 4 (p. 246) we compare fluctuations in this margin of productive resources with fluctuations in the annual rate of increase of weekly earnings. In Figure 3(a) and (b) we plot these series, adding, for comparison, the series for unemployment and for the rate of increase of hourly wage rates shown in Table 1. For unemployment we use a scale five times as large as that used for the margin of unused resources.

From Figure 3 a number of conclusions can be drawn. The first is that fluctuations in the margin of unused resources and in the rate of increase of weekly earnings usually lead fluctuations in unemployment and in the rate of increase of hourly wage rates, sometimes by as much as a year, and never lag behind them. Their use, instead of unemployment and wage-rate data, would therefore often enable appropriate action to be taken many months earlier. It may well have been this lag which induced undue delay in re-expanding demand early in 1958 and in checking it early in 1960.

A second conclusion is that the magnitude of the fluctuations in the general margin of unused resources is almost exactly five times that of fluctuations in the percentage of unemployment. If we equate 1 per cent of unemployment with a zero general margin of resources, we can regard a 5 per cent general margin as the equivalent of 2 per cent unemployment, and a 6 per cent general margin as the equivalent of just under 2¼ per cent unemployment.

Thirdly, we find that, in the last two cycles, the lower turning points in the rate of increase of weekly earnings occur at very much the same level as those in the rate of increase of hourly wage rates. We can therefore treat a 3 per cent rate of rise in earnings as the equivalent, for purposes of policy, of a 3 per cent rise in wage rates.

The policy proposals made on page 236 can now be restated as follows:

1. With the present rate of growth of productive potential and the present distribution of unemployment between regions, an exces-

sive rate of earnings increase, with the margin of unused resources below 5 per cent, must be restrained by restricting demand.

2. With the margin of unused resources between 5 per cent and 6 per cent, restriction of demand can be usefully supplemented (though probably not replaced) by a 'wages policy'.

3. With the margin of unused resources above 6 per cent, a 'wages policy' becomes unnecessary, though harmless, and demand can safely be expanded. (If it were found that earnings were still rising too fast with the margin of unused resources above 6 per cent, restriction of demand, whether or not supplemented by a 'wages policy', would have to be continued to a higher level.)

VI. Incomes Policy and the Balance of Payments

Throughout this paper incomes policy has been discussed in relation only to the pressure of internal demand and the rate of rise in money incomes, without mention of foreign trade or the balance of payments. This treatment is justified by the fact that, in recent years, the United Kingdom's balance-of-payments difficulties have been merely one of the symptoms of an excess of internal demand and an over-rapid rise of money incomes.

This condition is of course not true of all countries at all times. It is possible for a country's balance of payments to worsen sharply even in the absence of any tendency towards internal inflation. Such a development could, for instance, result from an economic depression in the rest of the world; from an excessive depreciation of foreign currencies or (as in the United Kingdom in 1925–31) from an overappreciation of the home currency; or, especially in countries exporting mainly primary products, from a fall in export prices and a consequent worsening of the terms of trade. But in the United Kingdom there has been no year since the devaluation of 1949 in which the balance of payments on current account has worsened which has not also been a year in which money incomes were rising much faster than productive potential, the margin of unused resources was well below 6 per cent, and unemployment was well below $2\frac{1}{4}$ per cent. It is no accident that the years in which the largest adverse balances of payments were recorded – 1951, 1955, 1960, and (probably)

1964 – were also years of rapidly rising money incomes and low unemployment. It is therefore justifiable to treat balance-of-payments difficulties not as an independent problem but merely as part of the same problem as an over-rapid rise of internal money incomes.

There is, indeed, a case for thinking that the introduction of balance-of-payments considerations simplifies the problem of dealing with an over-rapid rise in incomes within any one country (though not, of course, in all countries simultaneously). In a country with a completely open economy and negligible transport costs it would be impossible for incomes to rise much faster (in relation to output) than in the rest of the world; for the larger part of any increase in expenditure would be absorbed in the purchase of additional imports (and possibly in the diversion of exports to home consumption) and relatively little would be left for raising domestic incomes. It would then almost certainly require a less drastic restriction of demand to convert the adverse balance of payments back into a favourable one than to bring down again a level of wage rates, costs, and prices which had once been allowed to go too high. In a partially open economy, the effects of excess demand are shown partly in a worsening balance of payments and partly in an excessive rise of incomes, costs, and prices; but the more they are shown in the balance of payments and the less in incomes, costs, and prices, the more reversible are they likely to be.

Another reason for welcoming the diversion of part of the effects of excess demand away from the internal economy on to the balance of payments is that public opinion and governments seem to react more quickly to balance-of-payments deficits than to excessively rapid increases in money incomes. There is therefore a better chance of an incipient inflation being checked in its early stages if its effects are seen partly in the balance of payments than if they were entirely restricted to the internal economy.

Postscript

Developments since 1964

Nothing that has occurred in the four years which have elapsed since this paper first went to press in the summer of 1964 has given any reason to reconsider either its argument or its conclusions.

In the last quarter of 1964 the Labour Government inherited an economy in which the margin of unused resources had already fallen to a dangerously low level. For nearly two years it struggled desperately to prevent money incomes from rising faster than the long-term trend of output while at the same time maintaining conditions of extreme full employment. The attempt inevitably failed. Throughout this period weekly earnings rose at an average rate of over 7 per cent a year, while, partly as the result of a reduction in the number of hours worked a week, the rise in output slowed down to not much more than 2 per cent a year and retail prices rose by nearly 5 per cent a year. Meanwhile, in spite of various *ad hoc* measures to improve it, the balance of international payments remained persistently adverse, and the country was able to meet its foreign obligations only by heavy borrowing from the International Monetary Fund and the realization of part of the Government's holdings of dollar securities.

In July 1966, the Government, under the pressure of a violent sterling crisis, abandoned its attempt to maintain extreme full employment and introduced a highly disinflationary collection of measures. These broke the boom. Output fell in the second half of 1966, the margin of unused productive potential is estimated to have risen from 1·4 per cent in the first quarter of 1966 to 5 per cent in the first quarter of 1967 and the (seasonally corrected) number of unemployed in Great Britain from under 300,000 to over 500,000.

At the same time, the Government took power to enforce a compulsory six months' standstill on wages, salaries, prices, and dividends, followed by a further six months of severe restraint. At the time, there seemed grounds for hope that these measures, when used in conjunction with a severe disinflation, would have the effect of keeping rises in incomes below what they would have been with the disinflationary measures by themselves. For a time it looked as if these hopes might be fulfilled, for during the second half of 1966 the rises in wage rates and earnings were completely checked and in the first half of 1967 they were small. Unfortunately, the increases prevented in 1966–7 proved to have been merely deferred. The relaxation of the controls in July 1967 was followed by a rapid rise of both wage rates and earnings, and by early in 1968 all the ground gained had been lost. Although later in 1968 the rate of rise seems to have fallen again, for the whole period from the second quarter of 1966 to the second quarter of 1968 the rises in both wage rates and earnings have been rather higher than during the corresponding periods of previous cycles. The acceleration of the rise in wages and earnings in the second half of 1967 may have contributed to the general loss of confidence in sterling which culminated in the devaluation of November 1967.

Table 5

Increases in Wage Rates and Earnings, 1957–68

Year and quarter	Average margin of unused productive potential (%)	Average unemployment in Great Britain (%)	Increases in	
			hourly wage rates (%)	weekly earnings (%)
1957–II to 1958–II	4·7	1·6	3·1	4·6
1958–II to 1959–II	6·0	2·3	3·4	4·0
1957–II to 1959–II	5·3	2·0	6·6	8·7
1961–II to 1962–II	4·0	1·7	4·5	3·9
1962–II to 1963–II	5·6	2·5	4·0	2·8
1961–II to 1963–II	4·8	2·1	8·7	6·8
1966–II to 1967–II	4·3	2·0	2·8	1·7
1967–II to 1968–II	5·0	2·4	7·5	8·1
1966–II to 1968–II	4·6	2·2	10·4	9·9

Revision of statistics

While no amendments are needed to the main arguments of this paper, information published since it was written makes it possible to improve the statistical material used to quantify the argument. On page 234 an attempt was made to estimate the number of those who, while included in the unemployment statistics, were not really available for employment. This number was very tentatively put at 160,000, or 0·7 per cent of the employed population. The results of a survey conducted in 1964, published in the *Ministry of Labour Gazette* of April 1966, put the number of those who would have difficulty in obtaining work whatever the state of the labour market at about 180,000, or 0·8 per cent. So close a confirmation of so tentative an estimate is surprising.

A number of minor improvements to Table 3 (page 243) are made possible by the Central Statistical Office's publication of quarterly index numbers of total output, which from 1955 onwards can now replace the unofficial quarterly estimates, based on the official annual indexes, which were used in the original paper. These revised figures are used in Table 6 below.

A more important change is necessitated by the article by Godley and Shepherd (1964). Their estimates, based on a much more refined statistical technique than I had been able to use, showed that my estimates of the rate of growth of productive potential were too high (partly because I had failed to make sufficient allowance for the fall in the length of the standard working week in 1959–61), so that by 1963 my cumulative over-estimate of the level of productive potential was as much as 2 per cent. The economy is therefore now estimated to have been much more fully employed in 1961–4 than is shown in Table 3 of the original paper, so that the margin of unused potential is estimated to have fallen to the critical 5 per cent level in the second quarter of 1963 instead of in the last quarter of that year. These revised estimates of potential, and my extrapolation for 1964–8, are shown in Table 6, together with recent (seasonally adjusted) increases in weekly earnings and hourly wage rates.

The outlook

In view of the continuing need for large balance-of-payments surpluses to repay the heavy short-term foreign debts incurred as the result of the deficits of 1964–8, it is unlikely that any British Government for several years to come will be able to take the risk of allowing the re-appearance of internal excess demand. If so, it seems likely that, for the first time since the war, a margin of 5 per cent or more of unused productive potential will be maintained for long enough to test its continuing effect on the rate of rise of incomes. Even this test will not necessarily be con-

Table 6 (Revised)[1]

Output, Productive Potential, Unemployment, Earnings, and Wage Rates, 1962–8

Year and quarter	Gross domestic product (4th quarter of 1955 = 100)	Productive potential	G.D.P as a percentage of productive potential	Margin of unused resources	Unemployment	Annual increases (a) in weekly earnings	Annual increases (a) in hourly wage rates
			%	%	%	%	%
1962							
1	113·3	118·7	95·4	4·6	1·8		5·0
2	114·5	119·7	95·6	4·4	1·9	2·4	4·5
3	115·6	120·7	95·8	4·2	2·2		4·3
4	114·8	121·7	94·3	5·7	2·4	2·8	4·3
1963							
1	113·6(b)	122·7	92·6(b)	7·4(b)	3·2(b)		3·1
2	117·7	123·8	95·0	5·0	2·5	5·1	3·4
3	120·3	124·7	96·5	3·5	2·3	7·9	4·6
4	122·1	125·6	97·2	2·8	2·1	7·1	4·5
1964							
1	123·8	126·5	97·9	2·1	1·8	7·6	5·6
2	125·4	127·4	98·5	1·5	1·6	6·3	5·5
3	126·0	128·2	98·2	1·8	1·6	7·8	5·3
4	127·1	129·0	98·4	1·6	1·5	7·1	5·8
1965							
1	128·9	129·9	99·2	0·8	1·4	6·3	7·0
2	128·0	130·8	97·8	2·2	1·3	7·6	7·3
3	128·9	131·6	97·9	2·1	1·5	7·2	8·1
4	130·1	132·4	98·2	1·8	1·4	7·8	7·6
1966							
1	131·3	133·2	98·6	1·4	1·3	6·7	6·2
2	130·8	134·0	97·5	2·5	1·2	4·5	4·9
3	131·4	135·1	97·2	2·8	1·4	2·4	3·2
4	130·4	136·2	95·7	4·3	2·2	1·7	2·8
1967							
1	130·7	137·3	95·1	4·9	2·2	3·7	4·4
2	132·0	138·4	95·3	4·7	2·3	5·9	5·8
3	132·4	139·6	94·8	5·2	2·5	8·1	7·8
4	134·4	140·8	95·4	4·6	2·4	8·1	7·5
1968							
1	135·7	142·1	95·4	4·6	2·4		
2	136·3	143·4	95·0	5·0	2·4		

1. See Table 3, p. 243.

(a) Measured from six months before to six months after the date shown.

(b) Figures affected by exceptional weather.

Columns 1 to 5 seasonally adjusted.

clusive. The continuation of a policy of limiting, possibly by compulsion, the rates of increase of wages, salaries, prices, and dividends would make it difficult to attribute with certainty the credit for such moderation of the rise in incomes as may occur. On the other hand, if the rate of rise in incomes returned to the level customary during past periods of excess demand, both methods of restraint would be discredited.

One development which will facilitate the maintenance of an adequate margin of unused productive potential is the marked acceleration which appears to have occurred in the growth of potential itself. Between the second quarter of 1963 and the second quarter of 1968, which are closely comparable both in their margins of unused potential and in their levels of unemployment, total output of goods and services per man-hour worked rose by 18 per cent, or at an average rate of 3·4 per cent a year, compared with average rates of increase of 2·8 per cent between 1959 and 1963 and of 2·0 per cent between 1952 and 1959. It is therefore reasonable to hope that during the coming years output per man-hour will rise at an annual rate of $3\frac{1}{2}$ per cent a year or more, especially since one effect of the reduced pressure of demand will be to compel employers to give more attention to keeping down costs, including labour costs. This improvement would enable output to rise faster than in the past without reducing the margin of unused potential, and so permit a faster rise of incomes to be maintained without a rise of labour costs and prices than at any time since the war – or, probably, in British history.

References

DICKS-MIREAUX, L. A., and DOW, J. C. R. (1959), 'The determinants of wage inflation in the United Kingdom, 1946–56', *Journal of the Royal Statistical Society*, series A, vol. 122, part 2, pp. 145–84. Republished as *National Institute of Economic and Social Research Reprint Series*, no. 23.

FINCH, C. D. (unpublished), 'Some problems of wages policy', London Ph.D. thesis.

GODLEY, W. A. H., and SHEPHERD, J. R. (1964), 'Long-term growth and short-term policy', *Economic Review*, August.

PAISH, F. W. (1962), *Studies in an Inflationary Economy*, Macmillan.

PHILLIPS, A. W. (1958), 'The relation between unemployment and the rate of change of money wage rates in the United Kingdom, 1861–1957', *Economica*, vol. 25, pp. 283–99. [Reading 15.]

14 W. G. Bowen

The Dilemma Model Re-examined

Abridged from W. G. Bowen, *The Wage–Price Issue: A Theoretical Analysis*, chapter 21, Princeton University Press, 1960.

The dilemma model suffers from two closely related weaknesses. First, each of the individual assertions that comprise the model leaves something to be desired. These assertions all appear to be half-truths, which at best are somewhat misleading and at worst provide a highly dangerous basis for public policy decisions. Second, the way in which these assertions interact is unduly neglected in the basic dilemma model.

Both the rationale behind this rather sweeping indictment and the more positive picture of the dilemma process that emerges from the discussion can best be described with the aid of Figure 1, which appears below. The function of this figure is to provide an over-all view of the way in which the various parts of the model interact, and where within the dilemma framework other factors and considerations exert their influence.

The solid heavy lines that appear in the center of the figure identify the main events that make up the basic dilemma model described in chapter 3. [Chapter 3 is not included here.] The solid heavy arrows illustrate the sequence of events usually emphasized in this model: wage determination is followed by an increase in unit labor costs and unit total costs; these higher costs are then mediated through the price determination process and transmuted into upward pressure on the price level; and, the monetary-fiscal authorities then decide whether this trend of events is to culminate in inflation or unemployment. The dotted heavy lines show the aggregate money income and spending links, which are given less attention in the basic dilemma model. The remaining lines and arrows indicate both the points in the dilemma process at which various factors exogenous to the basic model exert their impact and the ways in which various endogenous factors interact. The specific links or lines of impact are discussed below. The arabic numbers that appear on the arrows serve only to facilitate the exposition, and have no substantive significance.

It is convenient to organize the following conclusions concerning the over-all dilemma model around the same three assertions that have provided the framework for the body of this study. And, it is again useful to begin with the wage determination assertion.

The Wage Determination Assertion

The first and most basic conclusion about this aspect of the dilemma model that emerges is that the empirical sort of wage determination assertion frequently encountered – to wit, that so long as unemployment does not rise above some 'critical' level wages will in fact increase more rapidly than productivity in general can advance – is both unsatisfactory and unnecessary. It is unsatisfactory for two reasons: first, the magnitude of wage adjustments is dependent on many facets of the economic environment and is not nearly such an independent variable as implied in the empirical type of assertion; and, second, an understanding of the determinants of wage adjustments is absolutely imperative if wise public policies are to be formulated and costly mistakes avoided.

The empirical type assertion is also unnecessary because, while admittedly complex, the wage determination process is not totally undecipherable. It is possible to single out six factors that seem especially crucial for determining the general magnitude of wage adjustments. The arrows illustrating the impact of these wage-determining factors are grouped at the extreme left of Figure 1, and bear numbers 1 through 6.

It would, of course, be extremely naïve to think (and unfair to suggest) that existent writings on the subject of the wage–price issue have failed to consider the significance of these factors. The single wage-determining factor that has probably received the most attention is the level of unemployment (the arrow connecting the level of unemployment with wage determination is labelled 1 in Figure 1). Particularly noteworthy is the large number of quests for the 'critical' volume of unemployment at which wage pressures will cease to exceed the rate of productivity

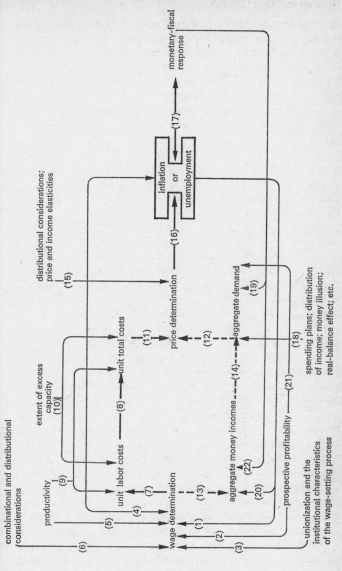

combinational and distributional considerations

distributional considerations; price and income elasticities

monetary-fiscal response

inflation or unemployment

(17)

(16)

(15) price determination

extent of excess capacity (10)

unit total costs

(11)

(12)

aggregate demand

(19)

productivity

(9)

unit labor costs

(8)

(14) aggregate money incomes

(18)

spending plans; distribution of income; money illusion; real-balance effect; etc.

(7)

(22)

(4)

(13)

(20)

(5)

wage determination

(1)

prospective profitability

(21)

(2)

(6)

(3)

unionization and the institutional characteristics of the wage-setting process

Figure 1 The dilemma model re-examined

improvement. Without intending to disparage the efforts of these searchers, it is necessary to point out that the value of such a parameter (assuming, for the moment, that it in fact exists) must not be overestimated. What would really be useful is a nice, well-defined, *continuous* function relating levels of unemployment to movements of aggregate wages.

Unfortunately, however, there are a number of theoretical reasons for doubting the existence of such a convenient function: (a) The existence of other important wage-determining factors makes it very unlikely that a precise relationship between wage adjustments and any single wage-determining factor can be found. (b) The volume of unemployment is *not* always a good index of labor market pressures, since it tells us nothing about the number of unfilled jobs that exist concurrently with people seeking job openings. Unemployment data are particularly unsatisfactory as an index of the total situation in the labor market when the number of unemployed is low, since in such periods striking shifts in the demand for labor can take place with little or no variation in the unemployment figures. (c) Even when unemployment data do serve as accurate indices of shifts in the demand for and supply of labor, there may not be a close correlation between such shifts and changes in either the wages paid by particular firms or the general wage level. This is because: (i) within particular firms, there are a number of sound reasons for thinking that certain changes in labor market pressures will often have little or no direct effect on wages; and (ii) within the economy as a whole, there is the additional complication introduced by the fact that the distribution of a given volume of unemployment among various sectors and industries may be extremely important.

This is not, of course, to deny that high levels of employment are conducive to substantial wage increases, and that 'enough' unemployment will moderate the magnitude of wage adjustments. However, it should be pointed out that this may be more a consequence of the *associated effects* of the employment situation than of the alteration in labor market pressures *per se*.

More precisely, the apparent importance of the employment situation may stem to a large extent from the fact that the volume of unemployment serves as a very rough index of movements in a second wage-determining factor – namely, the *prospective profitability* of firms (labelled 2 in Figure 1). One of the main wage-determination hypotheses developed in the course of this study is that prospective profitability coupled with the opportunity cost of the proposed wage adjustment serves as an important determinant of (a) the reaction of firms possessing unilateral wage-setting power to the wage pressures they encounter, and (b) both the magnitude of the proposed wage adjustment and the resistance of the firm to the wage demand in cases where collective bargaining is the mode of wage determination. It must be emphasized that prospective profitability is most certainly not an exogenous variable, but is dependent on such factors as the level of aggregate demand – and, for this reason, arrow 21 links aggregate demand and prospective profitability together.

A composite wage-determining factor that has received at least as much attention as the amount of unemployment is the institutional characteristics of the wage-setting process (arrow 3). In particular, the question of the impact of the union has been the subject of heated debate. Without pretending to have resolved the complex methodological problems that beset anyone brave enough to attempt to unravel the independent significance of this institution, it can be suggested that the visible and dramatic nature of union activities has resulted in some exaggeration of the importance of this whole question. It must be remembered that the trade union is but one of the parties to a collective bargaining agreement – trade union wage policy most emphatically cannot be identified with wage determination – and that, to some extent at least, the union mediates economic pressures which would have taken their toll in its absence. This is not to deny that unions probably exert some upward pressure on wages, but rather to warn against an uncritical exaggeration of union impact. The ability of the union to increase the cost to the employer of not agreeing to a hypothetical wage increase would certainly suggest, on *a priori* grounds, that in most circumstances unions encourage upward wage adjustments. However, the empirical magnitude of this impact must be classed as an unsolved problem.

This preoccupation with the impact of the union *per se* has diverted attention from certain other institutional characteristics of the wage- and price-setting process that may serve to impart added upward thrust to the over-all wage level. These characteristics include: (a) the strength of non-price competition in product markets, the accompanying incentive to maintain production at almost any cost, and the concomitant reduction in employer resistance to union wage demands; (b) the growth of longer-term contracts which, coupled with the importance of inter-union and inter-firm wage comparisons, may serve to lessen the tendency for wage adjustments to be moderated by mild recessions; and (c) the existence of an apparent tendency for workers to expect a significant wage increase each year as the 'normal' thing – annual wage increments have come close to achieving an 'habitual' status.

By following arrow 4 back to its origin, another wage-determining factor which has received considerable attention is identified – namely, inflation itself, or movements of the cost-of-living index. There is little doubt but that this wage-determining factor magnifies upward price adjustments which have received their impetus elsewhere, and that workers will make every effort to see that their wages at least keep pace with the cost of living so that real wages are maintained. However, it must also be remembered that wage changes attributable to increases in the price level constitute a 'play back' effect and cannot instigate an upward movement of wages and prices. At the same time, it is equally important to recall that *ex post* statistics showing that wages and prices have increased at the same rate prove absolutely nothing concerning the direction of impact. Such equivalent increases are perfectly compatible with either a wage→price model or with a price→ wage model, and in no way demonstrate that the wage-setting institutions have merely reacted passively to price changes originating elsewhere rather than instigating the upward movements of wages and prices themselves.

The fifth wage-determining factor portrayed in Figure 1 is productivity itself. One of the key questions raised – but left unanswered – in the basic dilemma model is whether wage adjustments and changes in productivity are independent or functionally related. The only general answer which can be given to this question is that wages and productivity are both partly inter-related and partly independent. Remembering that productivity is defined as the ratio of output to labour input, it is first necessary to recognize that there are a number of ways in which an increase in productivity can come about, and that not all of these sources of productivity gains have the same implications for wage determination.

It is also necessary to recognize that, except in cases where workers are paid on a piece-rate basis, there is no visible link between productivity changes and wage adjustments. Productivity actually exerts its impact indirectly, by influencing other wage-determining factors. It is generally thought that the main link through which productivity changes are transmitted is the demand for labor – however, closer examination has suggested that it is rather difficult to predict the impact of a change in output per man-hour on the firm's demand for labor; and, as already pointed out above, whatever change in the demand for labor does occur will often have a minimal effect on wages. Instead, it appears that the more important link between productivity improvements and wage adjustments is the profit position – or, more precisely, the prospective profitability – of the firm.

In short, while an increase in productivity is likely to lessen the upward pressure on the price level to some extent, this cost-reducing impact will be moderated by the tendency of productivity gains to call forth still larger wage adjustments.

This brings us to arrow 6, which identifies the final wage-determining factor depicted in Figure 1 – namely, 'combinational and distributional considerations'. The inclusion of this somewhat nebulous-sounding category is intended to emphasize that the magnitude of wage adjustments cannot be adequately understood by considering each of the other wage-determining factors individually. The important points to be noted here are: (a) within the individual firm, the *combinations* in which these factors appear are vitally important for determining the magnitude of the resultant wage adjustment; and (b) throughout the economy as a whole, the *distribution* of various factors – such as unemployment and profitability – among sectors, areas, and industries cannot be neglected.

While it is impractical to summarize the detailed characteristics of the schema developed to take account of these inter-relations, it is still possible to emphasize the central point of this analysis –

to wit, the real source of significantly large wage increases is the existence of certain 'potent' or 'deadly' groupings of wage-determining factors. To illustrate, large productivity increases by themselves may not be overly significant, but when they are combined with an aggressive union, a high capital-to-labor ratio, and little price competition in the product market, but sufficient non-price competition to encourage the maintenance of production at almost any cost, sizeable wage increases are likely to result.

The Cost and Price Determination Assertions

At this point, it is appropriate to note that, as Figure 1 indicates, any change in the general level of money wages affects both costs and aggregate money incomes; consequently, the decision to continue along the main route laid out by the basic dilemma model and consider wages-as-cost prior to wages-as-income constitutes a somewhat arbitrary – albeit convenient – procedure.

Proceeding along the upper branch of Figure 1, the links initially encountered are those which join wage determination to unit labor costs (arrow 7) and unit labor costs to unit total costs (arrow 8). The first thing to note about the wages→unit-labor-cost link is that the behavior of productivity is, as the dilemma model explicitly recognizes, an important determinant of the extent to which upward wage adjustments are translated into higher unit labor costs. And, apart from certain detailed problems involved in computing a useful labor cost index (such as the proper treatment of salaried personnel and fringe benefits), there is little else to be said about this link.

The link between unit labor costs and unit total costs is, however, much more complex, and there are several significant points to be made here. The basic point is simply that the connexion between unit labor costs and unit total costs cannot normally be expected to be as 'tight' or rigid as has often been implied in discussions of the dilemma model. This is primarily because considerations associated with changes in productivity may bring about changes in non-labor costs. And, it is in recognition of this possibility that link 9 in Figure 1 joins productivity to unit total costs as well as to unit labor costs.

More specifically, a given change in unit labor costs will necessarily result in an equal absolute increase in unit total costs only if (a) the proportions in which labor and non-labor variable factors are combined do not vary as relative factor prices and technology change; (b) the prices of non-labor factors do not change; and (c) there is no change in capital costs per unit of output as a consequence of technological innovations. In addition, it should be observed that so long as unit labor costs and unit total costs are thought of as arithmetic ratios, their actual magnitudes will also vary with changes in the rate of output – unless, of course, the cost schedules turn out to be perfectly horizontal. Hence, arrow 10 indicates that the extent of excess capacity must also be recognized as a factor influencing both per-unit cost figures.

While it is certainly worthwhile knowing that the unit-labor-cost→unit-total-cost link is likely to be somewhat elastic, there is a still more interesting and useful conclusion to be noted here: in most cases it is reasonable to expect changes in unit labor costs to be *smaller* than the associated changes in unit variable costs and unit total costs. This is because the pressure of rising labor costs would normally encourage firms to substitute other factors for labor, and this increased demand may well bring about an increase in the per-unit price paid for these other factors as well as an increase in the number of units employed.

Turning now to the impact of unit costs on prices (arrow 11), we immediately run head-on into the price-determination assertion of the dilemma model – namely, that changes in the general price level are geared mainly (if not exclusively) to changes in unit costs. Here the central issue is the validity of the cost-plus pricing doctrine.

Since in our economy changes in the general price level are the result of a myriad of individual price decisions, it is necessary, in the first instance, to look at this question from the vantage point of the individual firm and to evaluate the famous cost-plus pricing controversy. The main conclusion that we can draw from this controversy is that available evidence does not justify dethroning traditional price theory and replacing it with a rigid cost-plus formulation. And, the most important corollary to this finding is that demand considerations still play some role in the price-setting process. Hence, it is necessary to picture demand (arrow 12) – along with costs – as a determinant of the magnitude of price adjustments.

However, restoration of demand to its accustomed position in the price-determination process fortunately does not exhaust the conclusions of this study germane to the price-determination assertion. The depressing aspect of the entire cost-plus controversy is that so much time has been invested in attacking and defending various people's conceptions of 'traditional theory' rather than in fusing the insights of traditional theory and the cost-plus investigations into a more useful model of price behavior. Such a fusion has been attempted in this study, and, while it would be impractical and unwise to condense the resulting formulation still further in order to summarize it here, certain conclusions stemming from this analysis can be listed. [These issues are discussed at length in other chapters of Bowen's book.]

The first conclusion is that changes in costs are in general more likely to inspire a price adjustment than are shifts in demand, and that rising costs are especially likely to lead to a price increase of approximately the same dollar amount per unit and possibly the same percentage magnitude. The rationale for this conclusion includes the following points: (a) the 'usual' shape of cost and demand functions suggests that a firm seeking only to maximize short-run profits will receive clearer and sharper instructions from an increase in costs than from a shift in demand; (b) the existence of uncertainty encourages price increases based on rising costs because of the strong desire to maintain profit margins and because cost increases are relatively knowable, predictable, and permanent; (c) cost increases are often fairly uniform among industries and competitors, and price increases based on rising costs are not terribly likely to upset relationships among firms or to start a price war; and (d) price increases based on higher costs are fairly acceptable on 'ethical' grounds and are easier to 'justify' before Congress and the public than price adjustments geared to 'what the market will bear'.

A second conclusion is that decreasing costs are not nearly so likely to bring about price reductions as rising costs are to precipitate price increases. And, there are some grounds for suspecting that it is downward shifts in demand rather than in costs which are the key element in inspiring price reductions. This may be because decreases in demand are 'unfavorable' events; consequently, once a certain action threshold is passed, the firm may succumb to the pressure to 'do something', and price cuts may thus result.

A third, closely related point, is that the existence of a 'turn-over lag' coupled with the desire of firms for security imparts a certain upward bias to price decisions even apart from long-run tendencies for costs to rise and governments to prevent serious deficiences of demand from lasting for an extended period of time.

It is important to remember that these comments pertain to price setting within the individual firm. In order to arrive at a picture of the behavior of the general price level – which, after all, is the main concern of the dilemma model – several additional observations are required.[1] For one thing, it is necessary to recognize the existence of more than a single mode of price determination. Agricultural prices, for example, are very important in the Consumer Price Index and yet are determined quite differently from the prices of such durable goods as automobiles. And, a general weakness of the price determination aspects of the dilemma model is that price behaviour in the 'competitive' sectors of the economy is unduly neglected.

The main implication resulting from the addition of explicit recognition of the sectored nature of the economy to the preceding analysis of microeconomic price determination is that neither the strict cost-plus pricing doctrine of the dilemma model nor the aggregative excess demand (inflationary gap) model provides a satisfactory framework within which to study changes in the general price level. The difficulty with both these hypotheses is that they are able to deal only with special cases and cannot serve as useful general descriptions of macroeconomic price behavior. The cost-plus model not only suffers from certain

1. At this juncture it should be noted that at the macroeconomic level the interdependence of costs and demand can no longer be completely ignored. That is, the existence of arrows 13 and 14 must now be recognized, even though a discussion of the determination of aggregate demand and aggregate money income is postponed until later. For the present, only the proximate determinants of price level changes are being considered.

difficulties when applied to the 'administered price' sector of the economy, but is totally inapplicable to other sectors such as agriculture and the service trades. The excess demand model, on the other hand, is useful only in dealing with the competitive sector of the economy.

Thus, it is necessary to turn to a less aggregative approach which recognizes the sectored nature of the economy and which supplements an understanding of microeconomic price behavior with an appreciation of the importance of the composition or distribution of changes in aggregate demand and aggregate cost indices (these distributional considerations are represented by arrow 15 in Figure 1).

The importance of distributional considerations is illustrated by the fact that the impact of a given increase in an aggregate index of unit costs[2] will depend on: (a) the distribution of cost increases among modes of price determination – the immediate price reaction will be strongest if rising costs are concentrated in sectors where cost-plus pricing is prevalent and weakest if most of the cost increases occur in the competitive sector; (b) the distribution of cost increases *vis-à-vis* the demand situation in various sectors and industries – an adverse situation in the product market may force firms that 'usually' set prices on a cost-plus basis to depart from this policy; and (c) the uniformity of the cost increase among sectors – the tendency of prices to respond more quickly to cost increases than cost reductions suggests that a given increase in aggregate costs comprised of a great number of moderate price increases may lead to less pressure on prices than a combination of cost reductions and larger cost increases.

Distributional considerations are at least equally important in determining the impact of shifts in demand. It seems reasonable to suppose that a given decrease in aggregate demand will exert more downward pressure on prices in general the more heavily it is concentrated in the 'competitive' sectors of the economy. Conversely, the general price index will increase more rapidly in

2. It is necessary at this point to append a comment concerning the need for a clear definition of any aggregate cost index used in making cost-price comparisons. Unless the cost index is constructed in the same manner as the price index, very misleading results may be obtained.

response to an increase in the demand for such items as farm products than in response to an increase in orders for structural steel. At the root of shifts in the distribution of demand are, of course, price and income elasticities of demand as well as shifts in the distribution of income and secular changes in tastes. The preceding analysis suggests that these rather unexciting and frequently neglected considerations may be important determinants of price level movements.

The Monetary Policy Assertion

The links in Figure 1 that still remain to be considered are all related to the third and last assertion contained in the dilemma model – namely, the monetary policy assertion, which states that the awesome responsibility for deciding whether the wage and price behavior of individual economic units is to culminate in inflation or unemployment rests with the monetary authorities (or, more precisely, with the monetary-fiscal authorities). The arrows numbered 16 and 17 indicate the relationships usually envisioned in discussions of the dilemma model. Arrow 17 points in both directions in order to show that the initial pressures on prices and the level of employment influence the monetary-fiscal authorities, who in turn help determine whether inflation or unemployment finally results from the dilemma process.

The fundamental objection to the conception of the role of the monetary authorities embodied in the dilemma model is that it is seriously incomplete – there is no explanation of the mechanism whereby monetary policy affects wage, price, and employment decisions. It is to remedy this deficiency that links 18–22 have been added to Figure 1, and an examination of the characteristics of these links included in the following discussion of the monetary policy assertion.

However, before looking at specific links, it is necessary to have a clear understanding of the general role played by the monetary authorities. In this connexion, the first point to be noted is that the dilemma model is entirely correct in emphasizing the importance of the monetary environment as a determinant of price level movements. It is clearly improper to ignore monetary considerations by arguing (as some have done) that what is cost to one man is income to another, and so a cost-induced price increase is self-financing and self-sustaining in that money incomes are automatically raised in tune with rising prices. The difficulty with this rigid linking of wages to aggregate money income to aggregate demand (links 13 and 14) is that the monetary authorities *may* inhibit such self-financing by keeping the supply of money under tight control and letting the increasing demand for transactions balances bid up interest rates (or reduce the 'availability' of credit) sufficiently to dampen some spending plans.

However, this point must be counterbalanced immediately with a second observation. It is equally improper to move from this laudatory recognition of the significance of the monetary environment to the position that price-level movements can best be understood by concentrating attention solely on the money supply and the behavior of the monetary authorities. The difficulty with this purely monetary approach is that it leaves unanswered too many fundamental questions such as: (a) What is the probability that changes in velocity will offset changes in the stock of money? (b) What factors influence the size of the money supply, and to what extent is the quantity of money dependent on wage and price behavior, rather than the other way around? and (c) What is the mechanism whereby changes in the money supply exert their impact, and what are the social and economic costs involved in controlling the level of prices and employment in this manner? In order to answer these questions it is necessary to examine the interactions of monetary policy and wage–price behavior – concentration on either to the exclusion of the other precludes the possibility of finding satisfactory answers.

Furthermore, it is necessary to note the existence of still a third set of factors (in addition to wage–price behavior and monetary-fiscal policy) which affect the outcome of the dilemma process – namely, the group of factors which affect private decisions to spend out of a given level of aggregate income and which are linked to aggregate demand by arrow 18 in Figure 1. An unfortunate consequence of the dilemma model's concentration on the production side of the economic process is the tendency to forget that aggregate income and aggregate spending are *not* rigidly bound together, and that a cost–price spiral can be either interrupted or hastened by a change in private spending plans due to: (a) exogenous factors such as the world political situation or the climate; (b) the possible existence of a money illusion; (c) the so-called 'real-balance effect'; (d) redistribution of aggregate income; (e) temporary disparities between the composition of plans to spend and plans to produce; and (f) price expectations. An important implication of the existence of such factors is that it is by no means obvious that an 'elastic' or 'easy' money policy is sufficient to insure the uninterrupted progression of a series of cost–price increases.[3]

Having bounded the significance of monetary policy somewhat, it is now possible to concentrate on the two basic questions here: (a) What actions are the monetary-fiscal authorities likely to take in the face of upward pressures on the general price level? and (b) What will be the impact of these actions?

The first of these questions falls at least as much in the province of the political scientist as it does in the province of the economist; however, at the risk of transgressing, it seems reasonable to suppose that the monetary authorities will not support an on-going inflation indefinitely, but instead will make an effort to preserve price-level stability. The weapons used in this anti-inflation campaign may range all the way from a simple refusal to supply additional reserves to the banking system (such a 'do nothing' policy will eventually put pressure on the banking system because of the need for increasing transactions balances that accompany rounds of cost and price increases) to more overt actions such as raising the discount rate, selling governments in the open market, and raising reserve requirements.

The next question is *where* within the dilemma model this response of the monetary authorities exerts its impact. In very general terms, this question is answered by arrow 19 – the initial and direct impact of a restrictive monetary policy will be on aggregate demand. A restrictive monetary policy will exert a direct impact on the wage and price determination processes

3. At this point it should be noted that, in addition to the above factors, the existence of both a progressive federal income tax and a foreign component in aggregate demand may also serve to slow up an on-going inflation.

proper *only* if the 'anticipatory' or 'announcement effects' impinge significantly on individual wage and price decisions – and earlier discussions have suggested that it would be unwise to pin much hope on this possibility. Hence, there are no arrows that lead directly from monetary-fiscal policy to wage and price determination; as will be seen below, these processes feel the impact of a restrictive monetary policy only in a more circuitous manner.

This brings us to the important and exceedingly complex issue of *how* monetary policy affects aggregate demand. For our present purposes, it is sufficient to note three of the main conclusions that stem from this analysis.

First, it is extremely important not to exaggerate the speed and the ease with which the central bank can control aggregate spending. The monetary authorities have to rely on control of bank reserves and the quantity of money to achieve their objectives – and, both the banking system and the private sector in general possess the incentive and the capacity to bring about increases in velocity that will offset (at least partially and temporarily) central bank control of the money supply. It may take considerable time and effort for the central bank to 'wear down' the liquidity of the private sector sufficiently to permit effective control of aggregate spending.

Second, the attempt to control aggregate spending by monetary policy is quite likely to necessitate a significant increase in interest rates, which will in turn hamper a restrictive monetary policy both by inducing additional increases in velocity and by lessening public and governmental support for a tight money policy.

Third, the initial impact of credit restraint will not be felt with equal severity by all sectors of the economy and all types of spending, but will be concentrated on private investment in general, and on such categories as residential construction, public utility expansion, and state and local government spending in particular.

So much for the link between a restrictive monetary policy and aggregate demand. The next question is how whatever diminution in aggregate spending does result from a restrictive monetary policy affects prices and employment. Our earlier analysis suggests that a restrictive monetary policy is much more likely to lead, in the first instance at least, to a reduction in output and employment within the sectors especially susceptible to monetary restraint rather than to much of a reduction in the upward pressure on the price level. Hence, we have now traversed the route by which the adoption of a restrictive monetary policy can precipitate unemployment; however, to see how such an anti-inflationary policy can actually halt inflation, a few additional steps are needed.

The initial reduction in employment will in turn lead to both a reduction in aggregate money incomes (arrow 20) and some tendency for the magnitude of wage adjustments to be reduced (arrow 1). The distribution of the initial volume of unemployment and the effect of the reduced aggregate demand on prospective profitability (arrow 21) will both be important determinants of the speed with which labor costs respond to the beckoning of the monetary authorities. The key question now is whether this combination of less upward pressure on costs and a further reduction in aggregate demand (due to the appearance of unemployment and possibly to continued pressure from the monetary authorities as well) will be sufficient to bring about price stability. If it is *not* sufficient, unemployment will continue to increase and will in turn induce another round of reductions in money incomes and demand as well as a bargaining climate less and less favorable to substantial wage increments.

If the monetary authorities are resolute in their determination to achieve price stability, this cycle will have to continue until either (a) the downward pressure on aggregate demand has been disseminated widely enough to bring price level stability even though the aggregate cost index may still be rising, or (b) the pressures exerted by unemployment, excess capacity, and lower prospective profitability have become strong enough to eliminate the upward pressure on prices attributable to rising costs. It must be emphasized that it is only by operating through these channels that a restrictive monetary policy can hope to halt the inflationary process.

However, it is far from certain that a restrictive monetary policy will in fact be carried this far. The monetary authorities (or the Federal Government in general) may become so concerned over the rising level of unemployment that they will seek to halt the above cycle by rescinding the anti-inflation policy – and it is this latter possibility that still remains to be considered.

The point here is simply that in our society the continuous attainment of high-level employment is at least as important a goal as price-level stability, and that when the two conflict, high-level employment may well receive preference. Arrow 22 illustrates the possibility that the monetary-fiscal authorities will react to the appearance of non-frictional unemployment by adopting tax and expenditure programs designed to bolster private incomes directly. And, while the oft-voiced fear that 'full' employment policies will operate to remove all barriers to inflation seems to have been considerably exaggerated (primarily because governments in fact have not been willing to adopt such unlimited commitments to a single goal), it is reasonable to expect that unemployment will be countered with at least a moderate anticyclical fiscal-monetary policy.

Anti-unemployment policies will, of course, increase inflationary pressures. For one thing, the direct impact of such policies on the level of employment and money incomes is bound to lessen downward pressures on costs and prices. Perhaps of greater long-run importance is the effect of anti-inflationary monetary and fiscal policies on the composition of private asset holdings and on the liquidity of the banking system and the public in general. That is, the by-product of attempts to fight unemployment may be a legacy of liquidity which, by paving the way for future increases in both the size and velocity of the money supply, will in turn accentuate the problems faced by the monetary authorities in combating subsequent periods of inflation.

In short, to predict the eventual outcome of the dilemma process it is necessary to know not only the initial monetary-fiscal policy adopted and the way in which the private sector reacts to this policy, but also to what lengths the monetary-fiscal authorities are prepared to carry their initial policy decision.

Our re-examination of the dilemma model is now complete. In the above all-too-sketchy synopsis an attempt has been made to point out some of the more significant weaknesses of this model – namely, an inadequate picture of the wage-determination process; neglect of the differences between labor costs and total costs; an overly rigid price-determination schema; undue neglect of the spending side of the inflationary process; and a failure to consider the *modus operandi* of monetary policy – and to indicate how some of the more important gaps may be filled. This analysis has, of necessity, been critical – perhaps overly critical – and at this juncture it is appropriate to redress the balance somewhat. For all its weaknesses, the dilemma model does serve a very worthwhile function in that it focuses our attention on an important macroeconomic problem and then encourages us to think about this problem from the vantage point of the ultimate decision-making units involved.

Part Four Econometrics

The analyses of inflation so far have largely been descriptive and qualitative with only occasional references to quantitative evidence. This part contains several papers which mark important developments in measuring and predicting price level changes. The 'Phillips curve' (Reading 15) has been the most widely applied technique on this front which predicts with remarkable accuracy changes in wage rates from data on the level and rate of change of unemployment. Phillips' original study led to further developments both in the United Kingdom and elsewhere which involved greater disaggregation and introduced additional variables. Lipsey, for example, concluded that the cost-of-living index as well as the level of unemployment helped significantly in explaining wage changes over the inter-war and post-war periods.

The two papers by Dicks-Mireaux (Reading 16) and by Klein and Ball (Reading 17) are simultaneous equation studies which are important in showing that the inflationary process is a result of the interaction of a number of economic relationships. The former is a two-equation model consisting of a wage-formation and a price-formation equation. The latter paper contains a four-equation model, which in turn is a subset of a more comprehensive econometric study of the United Kingdom. This estimates that the significant independent variables are the level of unemployment, the consumer price index and hours worked (as a proxy for changes in the demand for labour). Both papers attributed shifts in the wage equation to increased trade union militancy in the mid-1950s.

Eckstein and Wilson (Reading 18) also find that political factors play a role in determining wage changes in the U.S.

These enter the model implicitly through the important hypotheses of the key group and the wage round. Profits and the level of unemployment are significant on these hypotheses, primarily because they influence the wage negotiating position through reflecting economic conditions in the product and labour markets respectively.

15 A. W. Phillips

Unemployment and Wage Rates

A. W. Phillips 'The relationship between unemployment and the rate of change of money wage rates in the United Kingdom, 1861–1957', *Economica*, vol. 25 (1958), pp. 283–99.

I. Hypothesis

When the demand for a commodity or service is high relative to the supply of it we expect the price to rise, the rate of rise being greater the greater the excess demand. Conversely when the demand is low relative to the supply we expect the price to fall, the rate of fall being greater the greater the deficiency of demand. It seems plausible that this principle should operate as one of the factors determining the rate of change of money wage rates, which are the price of labour services. When the demand for labour is high and there are very few unemployed we should expect employers to bid wage rates up quite rapidly, each firm and each industry being continually tempted to offer a little above the prevailing rates to attract the most suitable labour from other firms and industries. On the other hand it appears that workers are reluctant to offer their services at less than the prevailing rates when the demand for labour is low and unemployment is high so that wage rates fall only very slowly. The relation between unemployment and the rate of change of wage rates is therefore likely to be highly non-linear.

It seems possible that a second factor influencing the rate of change of money wage rates might be the rate of change of the demand for labour, and so of unemployment. Thus in a year of rising business activity, with the demand for labour increasing and the percentage unemployment decreasing, employers will be bidding more vigorously for the services of labour than they would be in a year during which the average percentage unemployment was the same but the demand for labour was not increasing. Conversely in a year of falling business activity, with the demand for labour decreasing and the percentage unemployment increasing, employers will be less inclined to grant wage increases, and workers will be in a weaker position to press for them, than they would be in a year during which the average percentage unemployment was the same but the demand for labour was not decreasing.

A third factor which may affect the rate of change of money wage rates is the rate of change of retail prices, operating through cost-of-living adjustments in wage rates. It will be argued here, however, that cost-of-living adjustments will have little or no effect on the rate of change of money wage rates except at times when retail prices are forced up by a very rapid rise in import prices (or, on rare occasions in the United Kingdom, in the prices of home-produced agricultural products). For suppose that productivity is increasing steadily at the rate of, say, 2 per cent per annum and that aggregate demand is increasing similarly so that unemployment is remaining constant at, say, 2 per cent. Assume that with this level of unemployment and without any cost-of-living adjustments wage rates rise by, say, 3 per cent per annum as the result of employers' competitive bidding for labour and that import prices and the prices of other factor services are also rising by 3 per cent per annum. Then retail prices will be rising on average at the rate of about 1 per cent per annum (the rate of change of factor costs minus the rate of change of productivity). Under these conditions the introduction of cost of living adjustments in wage rates will have no effect, for employers will merely be giving under the name of cost-of-living adjustments part of the wage increases which they would in any case have given as a result of their competitive bidding for labour.

Assuming that the value of imports is one fifth of national income, it is only at times when the annual rate of change of import prices exceeds the rate at which wage rates would rise as a result of competitive bidding by employers by more than five times the rate of increase of productivity that cost-of-living adjustments become an operative factor in increasing the rate of change of money wage rates. Thus in the example given above a rate of increase of import prices of more than 13 per cent per annum would more than offset the effects of rising productivity so that retail prices would rise by more than 3 per cent per annum.

Cost-of-living adjustments would then lead to a greater increase in wage rates than would have occurred as a result of employers' demand for labour and this would cause a further increase in retail prices, the rapid rise in import prices thus initiating a wage–price spiral which would continue until the rate of increase of import prices dropped significantly below the critical value of about 13 per cent per annum.

The purpose of the present study is to see whether statistical evidence supports the hypothesis that the rate of change of money wage rates in the United Kingdom can be explained by the level of unemployment and the rate of change of unemployment, except in or immediately after those years in which there was a very rapid rise in import prices, and if so to form some quantitative estimate of the relation between unemployment and the rate of change of money wage rates. The periods 1861–1913, 1913–48, and 1948–57 will be considered separately.

II. 1861–1913

Schlote's index of the average price of imports (Schlote, 1952, Table 26) shows an increase of 12·5 per cent in import prices in 1862 as compared with the previous year, an increase of 7·6 per cent in 1900 and in 1910, and an increase of 7·0 per cent in 1872. In no other year between 1861 and 1913 was there an increase in import prices of as much as 5 per cent. If the hypothesis stated above is correct the rise in import prices in 1862 may just have been sufficient to start up a mild wage–price spiral, but in the remainder of the period changes in import prices will have had little or no effect on the rate of change of wage rates.

A scatter diagram of the rate of change of wage rates and the percentage unemployment for the years 1861–1913 is shown in Figure 1. During this time there were $6\frac{1}{2}$ fairly regular trade cycles with an average period of about eight years. Scatter diagrams for the years of each trade cycle are shown in Figures 2 to 9. Each dot in the diagrams represents a year, the average rate of change of money wage rates during the year being given by the scale on the vertical axis and the average unemployment during the year by the scale on the horizontal axis. The rate of change of money wage rates was calculated from the index of hourly wage rates

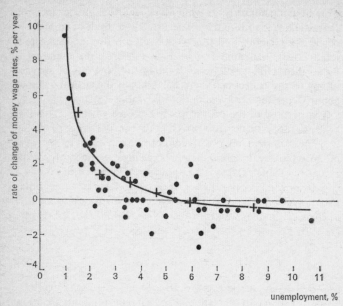

Figure 1 1861–1913

constructed by Phelps Brown and Sheila Hopkins (1950), by
expressing the first central difference of the index for each year as
a percentage of the index for the same year. Thus the rate of
change for 1861 is taken to be half the difference between the
index for 1862 and the index for 1860 expressed as a percentage of
the index for 1861, and similarly for other years.[1] The percentage
unemployment figures are those calculated by the Board of Trade
and the Ministry of Labour[2] from trade union returns. The cor-

1. The index is apparently intended to measure the average of wage rates
during each year. The first central difference is therefore the best simple
approximation to the average absolute rate of change of wage rates during
a year and the central difference expressed as a percentage of the index
number is an appropriate measure of the average percentage rate of change
of wage rates during the year.

2. *Memoranda upon British and Foreign Trade and Industrial Conditions*
(Second Series) (Cd. 2337), B.P.P. 1905, vol. 84; *21st Abstract of Labour
Statistics, 1919–1933* (Cd. 4625), B.P.P. 1933–34, vol. 26.

responding percentage employment figures are quoted in Beveridge (1960) Table 22.

It will be seen from Figures 2 to 9 that there is a clear tendency for the rate of change of money wage rates to be high when unemployment is low and to be low or negative when unemployment is high. There is also a clear tendency for the rate of change of money wage rates at any given level of unemployment to be above

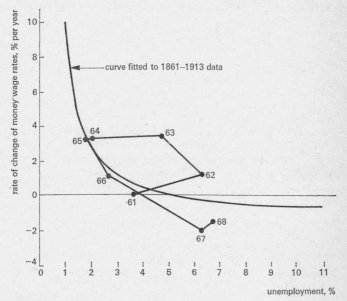

Figure 2 1861–8

the average for that level of unemployment when unemployment is decreasing during the upswing of a trade cycle and to be below the average for that level of unemployment when unemployment is increasing during the downswing of a trade cycle.

The crosses shown in Figure 1 give the average values of the rate of change of money wage rates and of the percentage unemployment in those years in which unemployment lay between 0 and 2, 2 and 3, 3 and 4, 4 and 5, 5 and 7, and 7 and 11 per cent respectively (the upper bound being included in each interval).

Since each interval includes years in which unemployment was increasing and years in which it was decreasing the effect of changing unemployment on the rate of change of wage rates tends to be cancelled out by this averaging, so that each cross gives an approximation to the rate of change of wages which would be associated with the indicated level of unemployment if unemployment were held constant at that level.

The curve shown in Figure 1 (and repeated for comparison in later diagrams) was fitted to the crosses. The form of equation chosen was

$$y + a = bx^c$$
or $$\log(y + a) = \log b + c \log x$$

where y is the rate of change of wage rates and x is the percentage unemployment. The constants b and c were estimated by least squares using the values of y and x corresponding to the crosses in the four intervals between 0 and 5 per cent unemployment, the constant a being chosen by trial and error to make the curve pass as close as possible to the remaining two crosses in the intervals between 5 and 11 per cent unemployment.[3] The equation of the fitted curve is

$$y + 0 \cdot 900 = 9 \cdot 638 x^{-1 \cdot 394}$$
or $$\log(y + 0 \cdot 900) = 0 \cdot 984 - 1 \cdot 394 \log x.$$

Considering the wage changes in individual years in relation to the fitted curve, the wage increase in 1862 (see Figure 2) is definitely larger than can be accounted for by the level of unemployment and the rate of change of unemployment, and the wage increase in 1863 is also larger than would be expected. It

3. At first sight it might appear preferable to carry out a multiple regression of y on the variables x and $\frac{dx}{dt}$. However, owing to the particular form of the relation between y and x in the present case it is not easy to find a suitable linear multiple regression equation. An equation of the form $y + a = bx^c + k\left(\frac{1}{x^m} \cdot \frac{dt}{dx}\right)$ would probably be suitable. If so the procedure which has been adopted for estimating the relation that would hold between y and x if $\frac{dx}{dt}$ were zero is satisfactory, since it can easily be shown that $\frac{1}{x^m} \cdot \frac{dx}{dt}$ is uncorrelated with x or with any power of x provided that x is, as in this case, a trend-free variable.

seems that the 12·5 per cent increase in import prices between 1861 and 1862 referred to above (and no doubt connected with the outbreak of the American Civil War) was in fact sufficient to have a real effect on wage rates by causing cost-of-living increases in wages which were greater than the increases which would have resulted from employers' demand for labour and that the consequent wage–price spiral continued into 1863. On the other hand

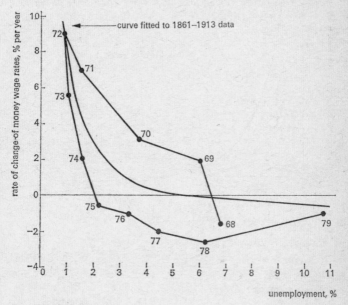

Figure 3 1868–79

the increases in import prices of 7·6 per cent between 1899 and 1900 and again between 1909 and 1910 and the increase of 7·0 per cent between 1871 and 1872 do not seem to have had any noticeable effect on wage rates. This is consistent with the hypothesis stated above about the effect of rising import prices on wage rates.

Figure 3 and Figures 5 to 9 show a very clear relation between the rate of change of wage rates and the level and rate of change of unemployment,[4] but the relation hardly appears at all in the cycle shown in Figure 4. The wage index of Phelps Brown and Sheila Hopkins (1950, pp. 264–5) from which the changes in wage rates were calculated was based on Wood's earlier index, which shows the same stability during these years. From 1880 we have also Bowley's index of wage rates (Bowley, 1937, table VII,

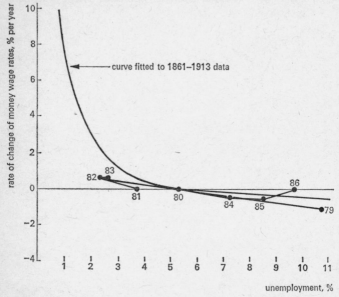

Figure 4 1879–86

p. 30). If the rate of change of money wage rates for 1881 to 1886 is calculated from Bowley's index by the same method as was used before, the results shown in Figure 5 are obtained, giving

4. Since the unemployment figures used are the averages of monthly percentages, the first central difference is again the best simple approximation to the average rate of change of unemployment during a year. It is obvious from an inspection of Figure 3 and Figures 5 to 9 that in each cycle there is a close relation between the deviations of the points from the fitted curve and the first central differences of the employment figures, though the magnitude of the relation does not seem to have remained constant over the whole period.

the typical relation between the rate of change of wage rates and the level and rate of change of unemployment. It seems possible that some peculiarity may have occurred in the construction of Wood's index for these years. Bowley's index for the remainder of the period up to 1913 gives results which are broadly similar to those shown in Figures 5 to 9, but the pattern is rather less

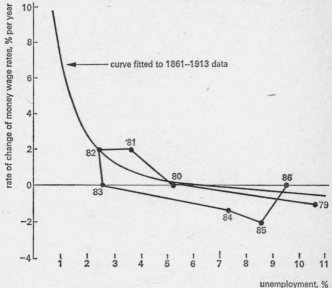

Figure 5 1879–86, using Bowley's wage index for the years 1881–6

regular than that obtained with the index of Phelps Brown and Sheila Hopkins.

From Figure 7 it can be seen that wage rates rose more slowly than usual in the upswing of business activity from 1893 to 1896 and then returned to their normal pattern of change; but with a temporary increase in unemployment during 1897. This suggests that there may have been exceptional resistance by employers to wage increases from 1894 to 1896, culminating in industrial strife in 1897. A glance at industrial history confirms this suspicion (see Roberts, 1958, chapter 4, especially pp. 158–62). During the

1890s there was a rapid growth of employers' federations and from 1895 to 1897 there was resistance by the employers' federations to trade union demands for the introduction of an eight-hour working day, which would have involved a rise in hourly wage rates. This resulted in a strike by the Amalgamated Society of Engineers, countered by the Employers' Federation with a lock-out which lasted until January 1898.

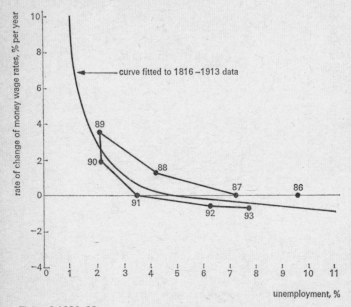

Figure 6 1886–93

From Figure 9 it can be seen that the relation between wage changes and unemployment was again disturbed in 1912. From the monthly figures of percentage unemployment in trade unions[5] we find that unemployment rose from 2·8 per cent in February 1912 to 11·3 per cent in March, falling back to 3·6 per cent in April and 2·7 per cent in May, as the result of a general stoppage of work in coal mining. If an adjustment is made to eliminate the

5. 21st *Abstract of Labour Statistics*, 1919–1933, loc. cit.

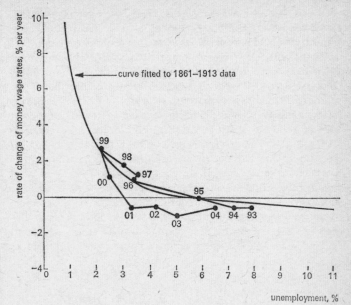

Figure 7 1896–1904

effect of the strike on unemployment the figure for the average percentage unemployment during 1912 would be reduced by about 0·8 per cent, restoring the typical pattern of the relation between the rate of change of wage rates and the level and rate of change of unemployment.

From a comparison of Figures 2 to 9 it appears that the width of loops obtained in each trade cycle has tended to narrow, suggesting a reduction in the dependence of the rate of change of wage rates on the rate of change of unemployment. There seem to be two possible explanations of this. First, in the coal and steel industries before the First World War sliding scale adjustments were common, by which wage rates were linked to the prices of the products.[6] Given the tendency of product prices to rise with an increase in business activity and fall with a decrease in business activity, these agreements may have strengthened the relation

6. I am indebted to Professor Phelps Brown for pointing this out to me.

between changes in wage rates and changes in unemployment in these industries. During the earlier years of the period these industries would have fairly large weights in the wage index, but with the greater coverage of the statistical material available in later years the weights of these industries in the index would be reduced. Second, it is possible that the decrease in the width of the loops resulted not so much from a reduction in the dependence of wage changes on changes in unemployment as from the introduction of a time lag in the response of wage changes to changes in the level of unemployment, caused by the extension of collective bargaining and particularly by the growth of arbitration and conciliation procedures. If such a time lag existed in the later years of the period the wage change in any year should be related, not to average unemployment during that year, but to the average unemployment lagged by, perhaps, several months. This would have the effect of moving each point in the diagrams horizontally part of the way towards the point of the preceding year and it

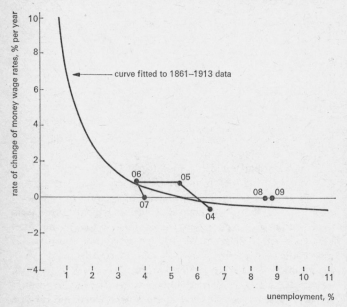

Figure 8 1904–9

can easily be seen that this would widen the loops in the diagrams. This fact makes it difficult to discriminate at all closely between the effect of time lags and the effect of dependence of wage changes on the rate of change of unemployment.

III. 1913–48

A scatter diagram of the rate of change of wage rates and percentage unemployment for the years 1913–48 is shown in Figure 10. From 1913 to 1920 the series used are a continuation of those used for the period 1861–1913. From 1921 to 1948 the Ministry of Labour's index of hourly wage rates at the end of December of each year (*Ministry of Labour Gazette*, April 1958, p. 133) has been used, the percentage change in the index each year being taken as a measure of the average rate of change of wage rates during that year. The Ministry of Labour's figures for the percentage unemployment in the United Kingdom have been used

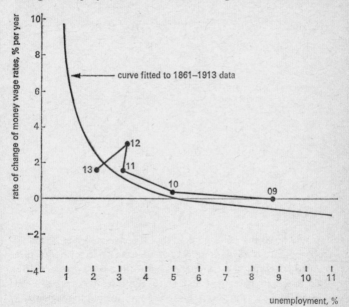

Figure 9 1909–13

for the years 1921–45 (*Ministry of Labour Gazette*, January 1940 and subsequent issues). For the years 1946–8 the unemployment figures were taken from the *Statistical Yearbooks* of the International Labour Organization.

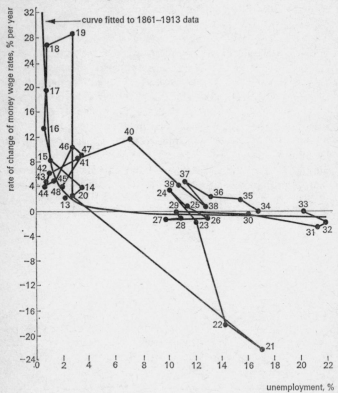

Figure 10 1913–48

It will be seen from Figure 10 that there was an increase in unemployment in 1914 (mainly due to a sharp rise in the three months following the commencement of the war). From 1915 to 1918 unemployment was low and wage rates rose rapidly. The cost of living was also rising rapidly and formal agreements for automatic cost-of-living adjustments in wage rates became widespread, but it is not clear whether the cost-of-living adjustments were a real factor in increasing wage rates or whether they merely replaced increases which would in any case have occurred as a result of the high demand for labour. Demobilization brought increased unemployment in 1919, but wage rates continued to rise rapidly until 1920, probably as a result of the rapidly rising import prices, which reached their peak in 1920, and consequent cost-of-living adjustments in wage rates. There was then a sharp increase in unemployment from 2·6 per cent in 1920 to 17·0 per cent in 1921, accompanied by a fall of 22·2 per cent in wage rates in 1921. Part of the fall can be explained by the extremely rapid increase in unemployment, but a fall of 12·8 per cent in the cost of living, largely a result of falling import prices, was no doubt also a major factor. In 1922 unemployment was 14·3 per cent and wage rates fell by 19·1 per cent. Although unemployment was high in this year it was decreasing, and the major part of the large fall in wage rates must be explained by the fall of 17·5 per cent in the cost-of-living index between 1921 and 1922. After this experience trade unions became less enthusiastic about agreements for automatic cost-of-living adjustments and the number of these agreements declined.

From 1923 to 1929 there were only small changes in import prices and in the cost of living. In 1923 and 1924 unemployment was high but decreasing. Wage rates fell slightly in 1923 and rose by 3·1 per cent in 1924. It seems likely that if business activity had continued to improve after 1924 the changes in wage rates would have shown the usual pattern of the recovery phase of earlier trade cycles. However, the decision to check demand in an attempt to force the price level down in order to restore the gold standard at the pre-war parity of sterling prevented the recovery of business activity and unemployment remained fairly steady between 9·7 and 12·5 per cent from 1925 to 1929. The average level of unemployment during these five years was 10·94 per cent and the average rate of change of wage rates was −0·60 per cent per year. The rate of change of wage rates calculated from the curve fitted to the 1861–1913 data for a level of unemployment of 10·94 per cent is −0·56 per cent per year, in close agreement with the average observed value. Thus the evidence does not support the view, which is sometimes expressed, that the policy of forcing the price level down failed because of increased resistance to downward movements of wage rates. The actual results obtained, given the levels of unemployment which were held, could have been predicted fairly accurately from a study of the pre-war data, if anyone had felt inclined to carry out the necessary analysis.

The relation between wage changes and unemployment during the 1929–37 trade cycle follows the usual pattern of the cycles in the 1861–1913 period except for the higher level of unemployment throughout the cycle. The increases in wage rates in 1935, 1936, and 1937 are perhaps rather larger than would be expected to result from the rate of change of employment alone and part of the increases must probably be attributed to cost-of-living adjustments. The cost-of-living index rose 3·1 per cent in 1935, 3·0 per cent in 1936 and 5·2 per cent in 1937, the major part of the increase in each of these years being due to the rise in the food component of the index. Only in 1937 can the rise in food prices be fully accounted for by rising import prices; in 1935 and 1936 it seems likely that the policies introduced to raise prices of home-produced agricultural produce played a significant part in increasing food prices and so the cost-of-living index and wage rates. The extremely uneven geographical distribution of unemployment may also have been a factor tending to increase the rapidity of wage changes during the upswing of business activity between 1934 and 1937.

Increases in import prices probably contributed to the wage increases in 1940 and 1941. The points in Figure 10 for the remaining war years show the effectiveness of the economic controls introduced. After an increase in unemployment in 1946 due to demobilization and in 1947 due to the coal crisis, we return in 1948 almost exactly to the fitted relation between unemployment and wage changes.

IV. 1948–57

A scatter diagram for the years 1948–57 is shown in Figure 11. The unemployment percentages shown are averages of the monthly unemployment percentages in Great Britain during the calendar years indicated, taken from the *Ministry of Labour Gazette*. The Ministry of Labour does not regularly publish figures of the percentage unemployment in the United Kingdom; but from data published in the *Statistical Yearbooks* of the International Labour Organization it appears that unemployment in the United Kingdom was fairly consistently about 0·1 per cent higher than that in Great Britain throughout this period. The wage index used was the index of weekly wage rates, published monthly in the *Ministry of Labour Gazette*, the percentage change during each calendar year being taken as a measure of the

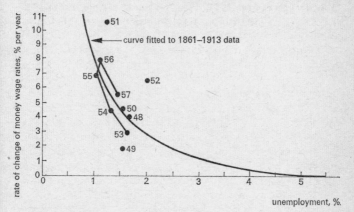

Figure 11 1948–57

average rate of change of money wage rates during the year. The Ministry does not regularly publish an index of hourly wage rates;[7] but an index of normal weekly hours published in the *Ministry of Labour Gazette* of September 1957 shows a reduction of 0·2 per cent in 1948 and in 1949 and an average annual reduction of approximately 0·04 per cent from 1950 to 1957. The percentage changes in hourly rates would therefore be greater than the percentage changes in weekly rates by these amounts.

It will be argued later that a rapid rise in import prices during 1947 led to a sharp increase in retail prices in 1948 which tended to stimulate wage increases during 1948, but that this tendency was offset by the policy of wage restraint introduced by Sir

7. An index of hourly wage rates covering the years considered in this section is, however, given in the *Ministry of Labour Gazette* of April 1958.

Stafford Cripps in the spring of 1948; that wage increases during 1949 were exceptionally low as a result of the policy of wage restraint; that a rapid rise in import prices during 1950 and 1951 led to a rapid rise in retail prices during 1951 and 1952 which caused cost-of-living increases in wage rates in excess of the increases that would have occurred as a result of the demand for labour, but that there were no special factors of wage restraint or rapidly rising import prices to affect the wage increases in 1950 or in the five years from 1953 to 1957. It can be seen from Figure 11 that the point for 1950 lies very close to the curve fitted to the

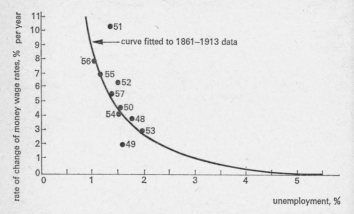

Figure 12 1948–57, with unemployment lagged 7 months

1861–1913 data and that the points for 1953 to 1957 lie on a narrow loop around this curve, the direction of the loop being the reverse of the direction of the loops shown in Figures 2 to 9. A loop in this direction could result from a time lag in the adjustment of wage rates. If the rate of change of wage rates during each calendar year is related to unemployment lagged seven months, i.e. to the average of the monthly percentages of unemployment from June of the preceding year to May of that year, the scatter diagram shown in Figure 12 is obtained. The loop has now disappeared and the points for the years 1950 and 1953 to 1957 lie closely along a smooth curve which coincides almost exactly with the curve fitted to the 1861–1913 data.

In Table 1 below the percentage changes in money wage rates during the years 1948–57 are shown in column 1. The figures in column 2 are the percentage changes in wage rates calculated from the curve fitted to the 1861–1913 data corresponding to the unemployment percentages shown in Figure 12, i.e. the average percentages of unemployment lagged seven months. On the hypothesis that has been used in this paper, these figures represent the percentages by which wage rates would be expected to rise, given the level of employment for each year, as a result of employers' competitive bidding for labour, i.e. they represent the 'demand-pull' element in wage adjustments.

Table 1

	1 Change in wage rates	2 Demand pull	3 Cost push	4 Change in import prices
1947	..	..	..	20·1
1948	3·9	3·5	7·1	10·6
1949	1·9	4·1	2·9	4·1
1950	4·6	4·4	3·0	26·5
1951	10·5	5·2	9·0	23·3
1952	6·4	4·5	9·3	−11·7
1953	3·0	3·0	3·0	−4·8
1954	4·4	4·5	1·9	5·0
1955	6·9	6·8	4·6	1·9
1956	7·9	8·0	4·9	3·8
1957	5·4	5·2	3·8	−7·3

The relevant figure on the cost side in wage negotiations is the percentage increase shown by the retail price index in the month in which the negotiations are proceeding over the index of the corresponding month of the previous year. The average of these monthly percentages for each calendar year is an appropriate measure of the 'cost-push' element in wage adjustments, and these averages[8] are given in column 3. The percentage change in

8. Calculated from the retail price index published in the *Monthly Digest of Statistics*. The figure for 1948 is the average of the last seven months of the year.

the index of import prices[9] during each year is given in column 4.

From Table 1 we see that in 1948 the cost-push element was considerably greater than the demand-pull element, as a result of the lagged effect on retail prices of the rapid rise in import prices during the previous year, and the change in wage rates was a little greater than could be accounted for by the demand-pull element. It would probably have been considerably greater but for the cooperation of the trade unions in Sir Stafford Cripps' policy of wage restraint. In 1949 the cost element was less than the demand element and the actual change in wage rates was also much less, no doubt as a result of the policy of wage restraint which is generally acknowledged to have been effective in 1949. In 1950 the cost element was lower than the demand element and the actual wage change was approximately equal to the demand element.

Import prices rose very rapidly during 1950 and 1951 as a result of the devaluation of sterling in September 1949 and the outbreak of the Korean War in 1950. In consequence the retail price index rose rapidly during 1951 and 1952 so that the cost element in wage negotiations considerably exceeded the demand element. The actual wage increase in each year also considerably exceeded the demand element so that these two years provide a clear case of cost inflation.

In 1953 the cost element was equal to the demand element and in the years 1954 to 1957 it was well below the demand element. In each of these years the actual wage increase was almost exactly equal to the demand element. Thus in these five years, and also in 1950, there seems to have been pure demand inflation.

V. Conclusions

The statistical evidence in sections II to IV above seems in general to support the hypothesis stated in section I, that the rate of change of money wage rates can be explained by the level of unemployment and the rate of change of unemployment, except in or immediately after those years in which there is a sufficiently rapid rise in import prices to offset the tendency for increasing productivity to reduce the cost of living.

9. *Board of Trade Journal.*

Ignoring years in which import prices rise rapidly enough to initiate a wage–price spiral, which seem to occur very rarely except as a result of war, and assuming an increase in productivity of 2 per cent per year, it seems from the relation fitted to the data that if aggregate demand were kept at a value which would maintain a stable level of product prices the associated level of unemployment would be a little under $2\frac{1}{2}$ per cent. If, as is sometimes recommended, demand were kept at a value which would maintain stable wage rates the associated level of unemployment would be about $5\frac{1}{2}$ per cent.

Because of the strong curvature of the fitted relation in the region of low percentage unemployment, there will be a lower average rate of increase of wage rates if unemployment is held constant at a given level than there will be if unemployment is allowed to fluctuate about that level.

These conclusions are of course tentative. There is need for much more detailed research into the relations between unemployment, wage rates, prices, and productivity.

References

BEVERIDGE, W. H. (1960), *Full Employment in a Free Society*, Allen and Unwin.

BOWLEY, A. L. (1937), *Wages and Income in the United Kingdom since 1860*, Cambridge University Press.

PHELPS BROWN, E. H., and HOPKINS, S. (1950), 'The course of wage rates in five countries, 1860–1939', *Oxford Economic Papers*, vol. 2, no. 2, pp. 226–96.

ROBERTS, B. C. (1958), *The Trades Union Congress*, 1868–1921, Allen and Unwin.

SCHLOTE, W. (1952), *British Overseas Trade from 1700 to the 1930s*, Blackwell.

16 L. A. Dicks-Mireaux

Inflation in Post-War Britain

L. A. Dicks-Mireaux, 'The interrelationship between cost and price changes, 1946–1959: a study of inflation in post-war Britain', *Oxford Economic Papers*, vol. 13 (1961), pp. 267–92.

1. Introduction

This study is concerned with changes in the general level both of wages and of prices during the period 1946–59. It is an attempt to explain, using regression techniques, the way in which they were influenced by the pressure of demand for labour and changes in import prices, and to describe the mutual reaction of prices on wages and of wages on prices.

Most previous empirical studies have been confined to explaining wage changes alone without taking full account of the mutual interaction of wages and prices.[1] It seems possible to get a little further than this by a simultaneous approach, and thereby test hypotheses relating to both the formation of wage changes and of price changes.

Regression techniques provide estimates only of the *short-term* influences on wages or on prices. These estimates need to be set in the context of the long-term development of wages and prices provided by the national income statistics. It then appears that the short-term statistical relationships may not give a complete picture of the cost–price mechanism, but need to be amplified on the grounds of somewhat more general reasoning.

The short-term equations describing wage and price changes imply that a 1 per cent change in the level of demand for labour – roughly equivalent to a similar change in the percentage level of unemployment – gives rise to an annual rate of change of about

1. Some of the recent studies concerned with data for the United Kingdom are: Dow (1956), Phillips (1958 and Reading 15), Dicks-Mireaux and Dow (1959), and Lipsey (1960).

3 per cent in wages. Similarly a change of 1 per cent in import prices appears to lead fairly quickly to a change of about ¼ per cent in final prices. The least certain results concern the estimates measuring the mutual influence of wages on prices and of prices on wages. Finally, the long-term model which is put forward to account for the inadequacies of the short-term results suggests that there may be further, delayed repercussions on wages and prices.

2. The Model and Method

The general hypotheses tested were:

(a) Changes in wages and salaries are determined partly by previous price changes, partly by changes in output per man, and partly by the pressure of demand for labour.

(b) Changes in prices are determined partly by past changes in labour costs, partly by past changes in import costs, and partly by changes in output per man.

Through the mutual reaction of wages on prices and of prices on wages there is some interdependence in the complete system defined by these two hypotheses. Figure 1 attempts to illustrate this causal set-up schematically.

It is probable that the effect of past changes in the determinant variables on the dependent variable, i.e. wage or price change, is distributed over several years (see p. 319). There may be an initial delay when little or no effect occurs, and then a series of past changes in the determinant variable each exerting some effect. The dependent variable will change in response to the combined influence of past changes in the determinant variables. The separate responses of the dependent variable to a unit change in the determinant variable, lagged at equidistant time intervals are often called the time-shape or time-form of the reaction.[2] In principle an estimate of the time-form of reaction is provided by the regression coefficients of each of the lagged values of the

2. See, for example, Koyck (1954), and A. W. Phillips (1956).

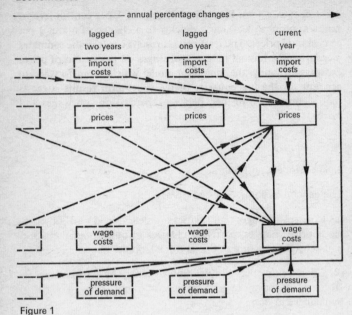

Figure 1

determinant variable.[3] But it would be difficult to allow for all the lagged determinant variables: the number of observed annual changes is far too small for such sophistication, since the analysis has been confined to fourteen post-war years. This being so, one of two solutions remains open. The first is to assume, *a priori*, the shape of the time-form and calculate a composite determinant variable based upon current and lagged observations of it. But since there are few clues about the shape of the time-form, a second solution was adopted. This consisted of estimating first the *short-term* relationships only, that is, changes from one year

3. This may be better seen if set out formally: if y is the dependent variable and x the determinant or independent variable the relationship described above may be written as:

$$y_t = a_0 x_t + a_1 x_{t-1} + a_2 x_{t-2} + \cdots + a_n x_{t-n}$$

or

$$y_t = \sum_{i=0}^{n} a_i x_{t-i}.$$

It follows that, in principle, the pattern described by the as, called the time-form of reaction, can be estimated by multiple regression methods.

to the next. In this way it seemed possible to isolate the major reaction, that is, the modal value of the time-form (Figure 1).

Consequently, only recent past changes in explanatory variables have been considered[4] (the parts drawn in bold lines in Figure 1). By the more general argument of section 5 the analysis is taken further to suggest a plausible general interpretation of the data for the post-war period.

These short-term relationships may be expressed formally as:

$$W_t = a + bP_{t-\theta} + cD_{t-\lambda} + fX_t + u_t \qquad 1$$

and

$$P_t = g + kW_{t-\mu} + mI_{t-\tau} + nX_t + v_t \qquad 2$$

where the following notation has been used:

W = average wages and salaries per person employed: annual percentage change between twelve-month averages.

P = final (factor-sale) prices: annual percentage change between twelve-month averages.

D = pressure of demand for labour:[5] annual percentage level.

I = import prices: annual percentage change between twelve-month averages.

X = output per man: annual percentage change between twelve-month averages.

u, v = error terms.

t = time subscript measured at yearly intervals.

$\theta, \lambda, \mu, \tau$ = initial delay periods measured in yearly units.

W and P are endogenous variables in the short-term wage–price mechanism described by the structural equations 1 and 2, and all other variables are considered here to be exogenous. A

4. The assumption is made here that the time-form is skew so that the modal value will correspond to the most recent past change in the explanatory variable.

5. See Dow and Dicks-Mireaux (1958); and the *National Institute Economic Review*, Appendix, table 3. Changes in the index of the pressure of demand are broadly similar to changes in the percentage level of unemployment. The average level of unemployment associated with the zero point of the index has been between 1·5 and 1·6 per cent during the period 1946–59. The index standing at zero does not necessarily imply that the over-all supply of, and demand for, labour are 'in balance'. But it does imply a level of unemployment which does not in itself exert a *short-term* pressure on wages.

full description of the series underlying these variables is given in Appendix A [not included in this Reading].

In the short-term relationships time-lags correspond to the interval between the modal reaction of the explanatory variable and the subsequent adjustment to it of the dependent variable. They are therefore referred to here as 'initial delay periods'. Thus the lagged response of a wage change, for example, to a price change implies that prices have little or no effect on wages for a period of some months. Experiment with different initial delay periods for both equations 1 and 2 showed that these periods were not considerable and were in all cases less than 1 year (see p. 312). The period θ between the wage change and the determinant price change in equation 1 appeared to be between 3 and 6 months, and the interval μ between a wage change and the dependent price change in equation 2 appeared to fall between 0 and 3 months.

These initial delays are important, for they determine the degree of interdependence of the short-term relationships. Price and wage changes have been measured annually, only because they are not generally available for shorter intervals. But since the interval θ between a given price change and the wage change it partly determines, plus the interval μ between this wage change and the price change it in turn causes, is less than one year, part of the initiating price change will be common to the final price change. In other words, neither the determinant price change and the determined price change, nor the determinant wage change and the determined wage change are independent.

This phenomenon of feedback means that neither equation 1 nor equation 2 may be properly estimated singly by the method of least squares, for in these circumstances the estimated regression coefficients of price change (in equation 1) and of wage change (in equation 2) would tend to be biased. An estimation procedure for overcoming this risk is provided by the 'two-stage least-squares method' developed by Theil.[6] Appendix B [not

6. A general description of the method of two-stage least squares is given in Theil (1958), pp. 334-61. The present analysis is a simple application of this method. The two-stage least-squares method is not, of course, the only procedure available for estimating interdependent systems for it is more usual to employ techniques based upon maximum likelihood methods. It is preferred here because of its computational simplicity.

included in this Reading] outlines the method in formal terms so that only a brief description is given here. The source of inter-dependence in the short-term wage–price mechanism stems from the endogenous variables, wage and price changes. But with some slight modifications the two structural equations 1 and 2 may be recast to give the *reduced form* equations in which each endogenous variable is expressed as a function of exogenous or predetermined variables only. Applying the method of least squares to each of these reduced form equations, calculated, as distinct from observed, values may be obtained of wage and price changes which will be devoid of any feedback element. This is the first stage. These calculated changes may now be substituted as explanatory variables into each of the structural equations 1 and 2. At this second stage the method of least squares may again be applied – this time to each structural equation – to obtain unbiased estimates of the structural coefficients.

The approach in this study has been to experiment with various forms of the structural equations estimated by what might be called the single-stage least-squares method, the risk of biased estimates being taken in order to isolate the preferable *form* of each equation. The two-stage least-squares method was then used to obtain unbiased estimates of the parameters.

3. The Short-Term Relationships: Statistical Results

The five equations, three estimated by the single-stage least-squares method, and two by the two-stage least-squares method, which accounted for most of the variation in wage and price changes during 1946 and 1959, are:[7]

(a) *Single-stage least squares*

$$W(t) = 4 \cdot 07 + 0 \cdot 41 P(t - \tfrac{1}{4}) + 2 \cdot 60 D(t - \tfrac{1}{4}) + u(t). \qquad 3$$
$$\quad\;\; (0 \cdot 37) \quad (0 \cdot 08) \qquad\quad (0 \cdot 49)$$

$$R^2 = 0 \cdot 91.$$

7. Following the usual practice an estimate of the standard error of each estimated coefficient is shown in parentheses beneath the estimate in question. However, in none of these equations can the standard errors be assumed to have been properly estimated so that conventional tests of significance cannot be applied. No test was made for autocorrelation in the residuals, mainly because of the relatively few observations available.

$$W(t) = 3 \cdot 72 + 0 \cdot 38 P(t) + 0 \cdot 14 P(t-1) + 2 \cdot 44 D(t-\tfrac{1}{4}) + u(t). \quad 4$$
$$(0 \cdot 51) \quad (0 \cdot 11) \quad\quad (0 \cdot 08) \quad\quad\quad (0 \cdot 66)$$

$$P(t) = 1 \cdot 95 + 0 \cdot 35 W(t) + 0 \cdot 20 I(t-\tfrac{1}{4}) - 0 \cdot 52 X(t) + v(t). \quad 5$$
$$(1 \cdot 03) \quad (0 \cdot 15) \quad\quad (0 \cdot 03) \quad\quad (0 \cdot 14)$$

$$R^2 = 0 \cdot 95.$$

(b) *Two-stage least squares*

$$W(t) = 3 \cdot 90 + 0 \cdot 30 P(t) + 0 \cdot 16 P(t-1) + 2 \cdot 78 D(t-\tfrac{1}{4}) + u(t). \quad 6$$
$$(0 \cdot 63) \quad (0 \cdot 13) \quad\quad (0 \cdot 10) \quad\quad\quad (0 \cdot 82)$$

$$P(t) = 2 \cdot 47 + 0 \cdot 27 W(t) + 0 \cdot 21 I(t-\tfrac{1}{4}) - 0 \cdot 54 X(t) + v(t). \quad 7$$
$$(1 \cdot 39) \quad (0 \cdot 04) \quad\quad (0 \cdot 04) \quad\quad (0 \cdot 16)$$

As the last two equations were simultaneously estimated a measure of the extent to which they jointly account for the variation in wage and price changes was calculated. Known as the coefficient of simultaneous correlation,[8] it is analogous to the ordinary multiple correlation coefficient and for the two estimated equations was equal to 0·99. For the purposes of the two-stage least-squares method the original short-term equations 1 and 2 had to be modified slightly. Hence equation 4 contains the current price change and the price change lagged one year as explanatory variables instead of the single price change lagged three months,[9] and equation 6 is the corresponding equation jointly estimated with the price relationship equation 7.

The reason for jointly estimating the short-term wage and price

8. Various measures have been suggested in, for example, Theil (1958), p. 347, and Hooper (1959). The particular measure adopted here is defined by:

$$(1 - S^2) = (1 - R_1^2)(1 - R_2^2)$$

where S is the coefficient of simultaneous correlation, and R_1 and R_2 are the multiple correlation coefficients of the two reduced forms. It is worth noting that S, as defined, will be close to unity even if the disturbances in the reduced form are large.

9. A non-integral time-lag of one quarter represents the annual percentage change between the average price level in a year lagged three months (October to September) and the average price level in the previous year lagged three months. For example, if $P_t(\mathrm{I})$ represents the price index for the first quarter in year (t), then:

$$P(t-\tfrac{1}{4}) = \left(\frac{P_t(\mathrm{II}) + P_t(\mathrm{III}) + P_t(\mathrm{IV}) + P_{t-1}(\mathrm{I})}{P_{t-1}(\mathrm{II}) + P_{t-1}(\mathrm{III}) + P_{t-1}(\mathrm{IV}) + P_{t-2}(\mathrm{I})} - 1 \right) \times 100.$$

Such lags were allowed for in a similar way with other variables.

relationships was to avoid biased estimates of the regression coefficients attached to the endogenous variables – wage and price changes – when they appeared as explanatory variables in the structural equations. But comparison of the coefficients of the current price change in equations 4 and 6 and of the coefficients of the current wage change in equations 5 and 7 do not suggest the presence of any marked bias. This validates the procedure, discussed below, of experimenting with ordinary least-squares methods on the single equations before combining the preferred forms for joint estimation. It seems probable that feedback is relatively unimportant in the aggregate wage–price mechanism described by the model, at least as far as these observations relating to the post-war period are concerned.[10]

The immediate implications of the short-term relationships may be summarized as follows:

(a) *The wage equation*

(i) The short-term effect of a change in prices is about one-third of the price change.

(ii) The level of demand plays an important role in the determination of wage changes. A 1 per cent point change in the level of demand is associated with a change of about $2\frac{3}{4}$ per cent in the annual percentage rate of wage change.

(iii) The constant term implies that wages will increase at a steady annual rate if prices do not change and if the index of demand is zero.

(b) *The price equation*

(i) A change in wages has an immediate short-term effect on the price change; this effect is about one-third of the wage change.

(ii) A change in import prices is also associated with a change in final prices, the effect, after a delay of three months, being about one-fifth of the import price change.

---

10. In an earlier paper by Dicks-Mireaux and Dow (1959) it was tentatively argued that over the earlier part of this period 1946–52 import changes were the main determinant of price changes, so that the feedback element through the mutual reaction of wages on prices would be small. The present results seem to support this belief.

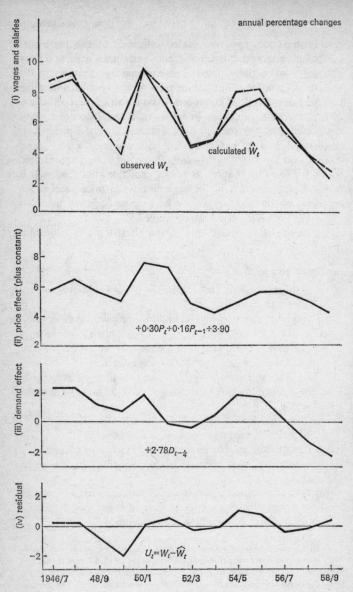

annual percentage changes

(i) wages and salaries

observed W_t

calculated $\hat{W}_t$

(ii) price effect (plus constant)

$+0.30P_t+0.16P_{t-1}+3.90$

(iii) demand effect

$+2.78D_{t-\frac{1}{4}}$

(iv) residual

$U_t=W_t-\hat{W}_t$

1946/7   48/9   50/1   52/3   54/5   56/7   58/9

Figure 2

(iii) Changes in output per man also influence changes in prices: about one-half the current change in output per man is reflected inversely in the current price change.

(iv) As with the wage equation, there is a constant term which implies that prices will rise at a steady annual rate if wages, import prices, and output per man do not change.

The jointly estimated equations 6 and 7 are shown in Figures 2 and 3, which compare the observed and calculated wage and price changes and give the contributions to these changes of the determinant variables. These are only the short-term relationships incorporating time-lags which represent the initial delay periods. The complete time-lags are considered later in section 5.

The reliability of these results is best judged from equations 6 and 7.[11] The standard errors of the price coefficients (in the wage equation 6) and of the wage coefficient (in the price equation 7) suggest that the estimates of both these coefficients are somewhat imprecise. This is not surprising. These endogenous variables are the source of interdependence in the system so that precise estimates of the internal links are unlikely. On the other hand, the relatively small standard errors of the coefficients of the remaining, exogenous, variables suggest that the external links are fairly well determined. In so far as the wage–price complex can be thought of as a single entity, the influence of these exogenous variables is perhaps the most important effect to estimate.

Variants of the short-term relationships

In the preliminary stages of working, different time-lags or initial delay periods were experimented with in both the wage and price relationships. Also the basic hypotheses were varied slightly and different variants were tested; and in particular the direct effect of changes in output per man on wages was examined.

11. It must, however, be emphasized that any attempt to assess the significance of the estimated regression coefficients can only be tentative at best. The deliberate exclusion of lagged explanatory variables from the short-term relationships gives strong grounds for suspecting auto-correlation in the residuals of the estimated equations (see in particular p. 109 of Phillips (1956), where this result is formally demonstrated). Consequently the estimated standard errors of the coefficients may contain considerable bias, although the coefficients themselves may be unbiased.

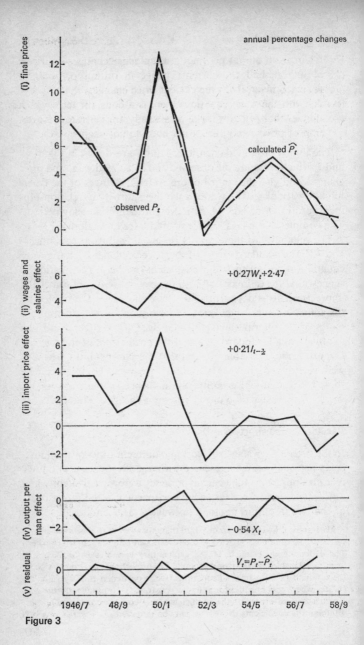

(i) final prices — annual percentage changes

calculated $\widehat{P_t}$

observed P_t

(ii) wages and salaries effect $\quad +0.27W_t + 2.47$

(iii) import price effect $\quad +0.21I_{t-\frac{1}{2}}$

(iv) output per man effect $\quad -0.54X_t$

(v) residual $\quad V_t = P_t - \widehat{P_t}$

1946/7   48/9   50/1   52/3   54/5   56/7   58/9

Figure 3

(a) *The wage equation*

Initial delay periods. The results obtained by allowing for different delay periods in the wage equation 3 are set out in Table 1. The effect of increasing the delay period is to reduce the coefficient b of price change and to increase considerably the demand coefficient c. The constant term a also becomes larger with longer delays. Since these equations have been estimated independently of the price relationship, the value of the multiple correlation coefficient R^2 is not strictly correct. None the less the estimated values permit the inference that there is an interval of between 0 and 6 months before the wage change responds either to a price change or to the pressure of demand.

Output per man. In the original hypothesis (equation 1) it was thought that changes in output per man would influence wage changes. In fact this variable was found to contribute very little to

Table 1

Effect of Different Initial Delay Periods: the Short-Term Equation for Wages and Salaries, 1946–59

Initial delay periods (months) for:		Estimated regression coefficients of:			
Price changes $P(t-\theta)$	Pressure of demand $D(t-\lambda)$	Price changes b	Pressure of demand c	Constant term a	Percentage of variation accounted for: $100R^2$
1. *Equation* 3					
(i) 3	3	0·41	2·60	4·07	91·2
2. *Variants*					
(i) 0	0	0·44	1·89	4·25	81·4
(ii) 3	6	0·37	2·59	4·19	87·0
(iii) 6	6	0·27	3·18	4·43	81·2
(iv) 9	6	0·17	3·63	4·72	75·5

Note: Standard errors have not been shown because of their dubious value. For equations other than the first, the standard errors were of the following order of magnitude:

	Coefficient	b	c	a
	Standard error	0·1	0·7	0·5

the estimated wage equation. Table 2 presents the results obtained including and excluding output per man as an explanatory variable.

Table 2

Effect of Productivity Changes: the Short-Term Equation for Wages and Salaries, 1946–59

$$W(t) = a + bP(t - \tfrac{1}{4}) + cD(t - \tfrac{1}{4}) + fX(t) + u(t).$$

| | *Estimated regression coefficients of:* | | | | |
Explanatory variables	*Output per man changes* f	*Price changes* b	*Pressure of demand* c	*Constant term* a	*Percentage of variation accounted for:* $100R^2$
1. $X = $ *Output (G.D.P.) per man*					
(i) $X(t)$	$-0{\cdot}25$	...	...	$7{\cdot}03$	$3{\cdot}3$
(ii) $P(t - \tfrac{1}{4})$	...	$0{\cdot}61$	...	$3{\cdot}89$	$66{\cdot}3$
(iii) $D(t - \tfrac{1}{4})$	...	...	$3{\cdot}78$	$5{\cdot}53$	$67{\cdot}3$
(iv) $X(t)$ and $P(t - \tfrac{1}{4})$	$0{\cdot}29$	$0{\cdot}68$	...	$2{\cdot}92$	$70{\cdot}1$
(v) $P(t - \tfrac{1}{4})$ and $D(t - \tfrac{1}{4})$	...	$0{\cdot}41$	$2{\cdot}60$	$4{\cdot}07$	$91{\cdot}2$
(vi) $X(t)$, $P(t - \tfrac{1}{4})$ and $D(t - \tfrac{1}{4})$	$-0{\cdot}03$	$0{\cdot}40$	$2{\cdot}66$	$4{\cdot}20$	$91{\cdot}3$
2. $X = $ *Industrial output per man*					
(i) $X(t)$	$-0{\cdot}13$	...	...	$6{\cdot}84$	$2{\cdot}9$
(ii) $X(t)$ and $P(t - \tfrac{1}{4})$	$0{\cdot}17$	$0{\cdot}68$	...	$3{\cdot}11$	$70{\cdot}2$
(iii) $X(t)$, $P(t - \tfrac{1}{4})$ and $D(t - \tfrac{1}{4})$	$0{\cdot}02$	$0{\cdot}43$	$2{\cdot}55$	$3{\cdot}97$	$91{\cdot}3$

Note: Although no standard errors are shown, it is worth noting that for changes in output per man the standard error was as large as the estimated coefficient when price change ($P(t - \tfrac{1}{4})$) and productivity change ($X(t)$) were the only explanatory variables, and much larger than the estimated coefficient in all other cases. For the coefficients of the other variables the standard errors were roughly the same as those shown in equation 3.

Two measures of output per man were used: gross domestic product per employee and industrial production per employee in industry. The results are very similar whichever measure is adopted. Only current changes in output per man were considered as an explanatory variable in Table 2.

Changes in output per man add very little to the explanation of wage changes (Table 2). The correlation between the two variables taken alone is negligible. Some slight contribution is found when changes in output per man are included jointly with price changes as explanatory variables. But if price changes and the pressure of demand are taken as explanatory variables the further inclusion of changes in output per man contributes practically nothing to the amount of variation in wage changes accounted for; and the coefficient of changes in output per man becomes negligible. No doubt this effect reflects some correlation between changes in output per man and the pressure of demand; but in fact – as might indeed be expected – this is not strong. On the basis of the results in Table 2 there seems to be little evidence that current changes in output per man directly determine *short-run* wage and salary changes.[12]

Additional explanatory variables. Further possible variants of the short-term wage equation were considered. The method, a somewhat crude one, consisted of correlating the residuals of equation 3 with various additional variables. The following results were obtained:

Additional variable	*Correlation coefficient*
Changes in:	
Overtime	−0·07
Consumer market prices (relative to final prices)	−0·13
Retail prices (relative to final prices)	0·08

The lack of correlation between the residuals of the wage equation and changes in overtime is somewhat surprising and must remain, in this analysis, unexplained. The remaining two additional variables were considered since it is likely that wages are most influenced by changes in consumer market prices[13] or by

12. Residuals of the estimated wage equation 3 were also correlated with changes in industrial output per man lagged 3 months, 6 months, 9 months, and one year. In none was any marked correlation detected. Also the same process was repeated for all the estimated wage equations shown in Table 1, and once again no marked correlation was observed. These tests are not completely conclusive, but in the absence of a more exhaustive analysis they provide strong evidence that changes in output per man do not play an important role in the direct short-run determination of wage and salary changes. (This conclusion is further strengthened by the preliminary results of an analysis of changes in wage drift during the post-war period which is being made at the National Institute.)

13. The average value of consumers' expenditure on goods and services at market prices.

changes in the official retail price index. However, the correlation coefficients obtained do not suggest that the substitution of final prices by either index of consumer prices would materially alter the explanation of wage changes.[14]

(b) *The price equation*

Initial delay periods. As a first step, changes in output per man were omitted from the short-term price equation, since it is not clear how changes in output per man influence price changes and whether their effect can be distinguished from the influence of demand. With this form of the equation, different initial delay periods were experimented with. The results, estimated independently of the wage equation, are given in Table 3.

Table 3

Effect of Different Initial Delay Periods: the Short-Term Equation for Changes in Final Prices, 1946–59

Initial delay periods (months) for:		Estimated regression coefficients of:			Percentage of variation accounted for:
Wage and salary changes $W(t - \mu)$	Import price changes $I(t - \tau)$	Wage and salary changes k	Import price changes m	Constant term g	$100R^2$
1. *Equation 5 (excluding output per man)*					
(i) 0	3	0·49	0·18	−0·02	88·0
2. *Variants*					
(i) 0	0	0·71	0·13	−1·20	84·2
(ii) 0	6	0·39	0·20	0·42	85·4
(iii) 0	9	0·83	0·09	−1·73	73·9
(iv) 3	6	0·09	0·25	2·13	82·8
(v) 3	9	0·44	0·14	0·42	59·9

Note: Standard errors are not shown because of their dubious value. In nearly all cases they were fairly low for the estimated coefficient of import price changes k, but for the estimated constant term they were as large or larger than the constant itself.

14. In each case deviations between changes in the consumer price series and changes in the final price series were correlated with the residuals of the wage equation 3.

These results are somewhat more erratic than those obtained for the short-term wage equation. In particular the estimated value of the coefficient of wage changes fluctuates quite considerably with different initial delay periods. Broadly the values of R^2 suggest delay periods of between 0 and 3 months for the wage change and between 0 and 6 months for the change in import prices. The estimated constant term also varies sharply with the delay period. In so far as it is negative it may provide a hint that changes in output per man should be taken into consideration. But before introducing such changes as an explanatory variable, it is necessary to test whether the level of demand and not the change in output per man contributes materially to the explanation of price changes. There is unfortunately no good indicator of the level of demand (in relation to supply) for goods and services; but a proxy measure is perhaps provided by the index of the pressure of demand for labour. As a first test, therefore, the residuals of the first price equation in Table 3 were correlated with (i) the current pressure of demand for labour, and (ii) the current change in output per man. The correlation coefficients obtained were:

Additional variable	*Correlation coefficient*
Pressure of demand for labour	−0·41
Change in output (G.D.P.) per man	−0·75

The pressure of demand for labour is not highly correlated with the residuals;[15] and in any case the negative sign is not what would be expected. On the other hand, the correlation coefficient with changes in output per man suggests that this variable exerts a strong and inverse influence on price changes.[16]

Output per man. When output per man was included as an explanatory variable in the short-term price equation, various initial delay periods were again experimented with. The results are shown in Table 4.

15. The conventional significance test, not strictly appropriate here, shows that the correlation coefficient is not significantly different from zero.

16. It is perhaps worth noting at this stage that changes in output per man bear little relationship to the pressure of demand which represents a *level* not a change. The coefficient of correlation between these two is as low as +0·22.

Table 4

Effect of Changes in Output per Man: the Short-Term
Equation for Changes in Final Prices, 1946–59

Initial delay periods (months) for changes in:			Estimated regression coefficients of:				
Wages and salaries $W(t-\mu)$	Import prices $I(t-\tau)$	Output (G.D.P.) per man $X(t)$	Wage and salary changes k	Import price changes m	Output per man changes n	Constant term g	Percentage of variation accounted for: $100R^2$
1. *Equation 5*							
(i) 0	3	0	0·35	0·20	−0·52	1·95	95·2
2. *Variants*							—
(i) 0	6	0	0·30	0·20	−0·43	2·04	90·5
(ii) 0	9	0	0·80	0·08	−0·34	−0·76	77·0
(iii) 3	9	3	0·30	0·20	−0·28	1·64	75·1
(iv) 3	12	3	0·98	0·03	−0·21	−1·99	60·2

Note: As in previous tables the standard errors of the estimated coefficients are not shown. For all variables, except changes in output per man, the standard errors of the estimated coefficients were similar to those indicated in the note to Table 3. For the coefficient of changes in output per man the standard errors ranged between 0·15 and 0·40, increasing as the initial delay periods increased.

The introduction of changes in output per man makes a definite contribution to the amount of variation in price changes accounted for. The extent of this contribution is shown in Table 5 (which compares the results of Tables 3 and 4).

Although it was not possible to experiment thoroughly with different initial delay periods in output per man changes, the first equation in which this variable is unlagged is perhaps to be preferred. The residuals of this equation were once again compared with the current values of the index of the pressure of demand for labour, but still no marked association was apparent.

(c) *The combined wage and price equations*

So far the testing of alternative hypotheses has not been strictly correct, because, by the approach adopted, each short-term equation was estimated singly without taking into account a counterpart price or wage equation. Two of the 'extra' variables seemed sufficiently important to be reconsidered at this stage. Thus (current) changes in output per man were correlated with the residuals of the *jointly estimated* wage equation 6; and the

Table 5

The Contribution of Changes in Output per Man to the Explanation of Changes in Final Prices, 1946–59

| Initial delay period (months) for changes in: | | | Percentage of variation accounted for: | |
Wages and salaries	Import prices	Output per man	Changes in output per man: Excluded	Included
0	3	0	88·0	95·2
0	6	0	85·4	90·5
0	9	0	73·9	77·0
3	9	3	59·9	75·1

Note: Quarterly series of output (G.D.P.) were not available for the full period 1946–59. In order to experiment with lagged productivity changes all other variables were taken with a lead on the annual changes in output per man, for example, $P(t + \frac{1}{4})$ with $X(t)$ gave productivity lagged 3 months. This means, however, that the comparison in the last line of this table is not strictly correct.

(current) pressure of demand for labour was correlated with the residuals of the *jointly estimated* price equation 7. The scatter diagrams are given in Figures 4 and 5. Figure 4 still shows the somewhat surprising lack of association between the wage equation residuals and changes in output per man (the correlation coefficient is −0·26). The influence of the level of demand,

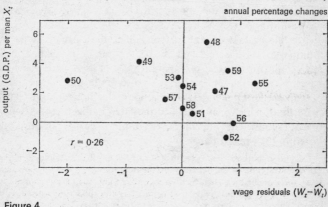

Figure 4

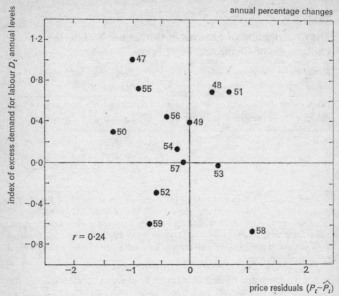

Figure 5

as approximated by the index used, on price changes also seems to be negligible in Figure 5 (the correlation coefficient is −0·24). The conclusion is that the estimated equations 6 and 7 seem the best description of the short-term changes in the wage–price mechanism.

The finding that only about one-half of the current change in output per man is reflected in the current price change may appear surprising. The explanation may be that entrepreneurs base prices not simply on the level of costs in the current year, but on the level expected over a somewhat longer term. This hypothesis, which may be called the 'standardized costs' hypothesis, is consistent with the present results; but it is not properly tested in the present paper.[17]

17. This hypothesis has been suggested privately by W. Godley of the Economic Section of the Treasury. In the long-term relationship suggested later (section 5 below), the lagged values of costs and output per man in the current and several past years are suggested as an explanatory variable for prices. This may be interpreted as a closer statistical proxy for expected costs.

Table 6

Estimated Coefficients in the Explanation of Wage-rate
Changes and of Wage and Salary Changes

Explanation of percentage changes in:	Sample period	Price coefficient	Demand coefficient	Constant term
Wage rates	1946–56	0·54	2·62	1·9
Wages and salaries[1]	1946–59	0·41	2·60	4·1
Wages and salaries[2]	1946–59	0·46	2·78	3·9

1. Single-equation least-squares estimates given in equation 3.
2. Two-stage least-squares estimates given in equation 6. The price coefficient shown here is the sum of the coefficients for current price changes and for price changes lagged one year.

4. Comparison with Previous Results

The present results for the short-term equations may be compared with two earlier sets of results.

Previous study of determinants of wage-rate changes

This attempt to consider jointly the determinants of changes in wages and in prices grew out of an earlier study, which dealt only with wage-rate changes in the post-war period.[18] Since the earlier model for wage-rate changes and the present model for average wage and salary changes are virtually of the same form, the estimated effects of similar explanatory variables are directly compared in Table 6.

The price and demand coefficients are remarkably similar and only the constant terms differ markedly. This is perhaps not sur-

18. Dicks-Mireaux and Dow (1959). In this paper quarterly changes in aggregate wage rates during the post-war period were shown to depend upon previous price changes, the level of excess demand for labour and some constant factor. Although the model adopted was non-linear, the range of percentage changes was such that it can be expressed fairly reasonably as a linear one comparable to the present analysis. Thus the estimated relationship accounting for quarterly wage-rate changes between 1946 and 1956 may be written approximately as:

$$W_t = 1\cdot9 + 0\cdot54P_{t-\frac{1}{2}} + 2\cdot62D_{t-\frac{1}{2}}$$

where

W = annual percentage change in the aggregate weekly wage-rate index,
P = annual percentage change in the retail price index,
D = annual level of the index of excess demand for labour.

prising. The difference between wage rates and average wages and salaries consists of two elements: first, the gap between wage earnings and wage rates, second, salaries. Apart from fluctuations in overtime earnings the first element is wage drift. Most studies of wage drift in the United Kingdom tend to show that the degree of correlation with price changes and the level of demand is slight.[19] But between 1946 and 1959 weekly wage earnings have increased at an annual rate of 6·5 per cent compared to 4·9 per cent for weekly wage rates.[20] Thus the difference of 1·6 per cent between these two rates of increase would help to explain most of the difference between the constant terms associated with the earlier explanation of wage-rate changes and the present one concerned with average wages and salaries. There is insufficient information to consider in any detail the effect of the inclusion of salaries in the equation; changes in the rate of increase of salaries are probably less than those in wages, so that the constant term would tend to increase. The present results therefore seem consistent with those of the previous wage-rate study.

Klein's study of wage and price changes

The only other attempt to consider wages and prices simultaneously for the United Kingdom is that by Klein and his colleagues.[21] Their analysis deals primarily with the *level* of prices

19. Preliminary results of an analysis of wage drift during the post-war period also tend to support this conclusion.

20. These percentages have been based on the Ministry of Labour's earnings inquiries for October 1946 and October 1959. They refer to 'principal industries', which account for some 60 per cent of operatives in the civilian labour force.

21. See Klein *et al.* (1961), pp. 114–26 and appendix III. The specific question of wage and price determination was also discussed in an earlier paper by Klein and Ball (1959). In both these works the model describing the wage–price complex consists of four equations:

(i) Changes in wage rates explained by price changes, the level of unemployment, and a political factor.

(ii) The difference between the level of wage earnings and the level of wage rates explained by the level of hours and of industrial output per man-hour.

(iii) The level of prices explained by the level of wage earnings, of import prices, and of indirect taxes.

(iv) The level of prices explained by the level of wage earnings, of import prices, and of indirect taxes.

and the *level* of wage earnings, so that comparison is not always straightforward. Nevertheless the conclusions drawn differ from the results presented here. Perhaps the two most distinctive features of Klein's analysis are (a) the price coefficient in the wage-rate equation, and (b) the role of productivity in the wage–price complex.

In Klein's model the estimated effect of price changes on wage changes is invariably greater than any of the estimates put forward here, and in the equation finally adopted is of the order of 0·8. This higher figure does not appear to be the result of more sophisticated estimation techniques. None the less the estimate is a fairly unstable one, considerably influenced by the time-lags attributed to the effect of demand, and once again illustrates the difficulty of obtaining precise estimates of the internal links in the wage–price complex (see also p. 312).

A puzzling feature of the wage–price system as estimated by Klein is the role attributed to productivity. While no such variable appears in the price equation, it is included as a determinant of the level of wage earnings.[22] Thus, it is implied that a rise in productivity leads to a *rise* in prices. It is true that when changes in wage earnings are considered, the productivity effect appears insignificant;[23] but since the price equation makes no specific provision for productivity, this still implies that the effect of productivity on the wage–price system is zero. The correlation between changes in output per man and changes in prices was so markedly negative in the present study (see p. 313) that Klein's results remain all the more puzzling. But Klein's model aims to account for quarterly changes in prices; and it is possible that such very short-term changes in productivity have little or no effect on price determination.

5. The Long-Term Implications of the Statistical Results

The two estimated wage and price equations 6 and 7 illustrated in Figures 2 and 3 describe the response of wages and prices only to

22. More precisely, the level of output per man-hour in the industrial production index industries is a determinant of the spread between the level of wage earnings and the level of wage rates, i.e. their difference.

23. See Klein *et al.* (1961), particularly Appendix III.

the fairly immediate changes in the determinant variables. It is only these immediate reactions that can be estimated, using multiple regression methods on the limited number of observations available. But they do not necessarily provide a complete picture of the wage–price mechanism; and something more can be learned by comparing the results with what is known about the behaviour of wages and prices over several decades.

An indication of the way wages and prices have developed in the long run is provided by:

(a) Official national income figures, available since 1938, and
(b) some previous studies based upon less reliable earlier estimates of national income and its components.[24]

These figures show that there has been no large cumulative shift in the share of wages and salaries in national income. Thus, *in the long run* the change in real wages/salaries has been equal to the change in productivity.

As estimated, the two short-term relationships are not inconsistent with stability of wage and profit shares. Nevertheless, the sizeable constants which appear in both equations, as estimated, are difficult to interpret. As they do not depend on the original hypotheses, some economic meaning has now to be found for them. They may, alternatively, be interpreted as:

(a) An institutional, bias-creating general pressure for wage increases: for example, some kind of wage push, or, for the price equation, a built-in tendency to raise prices, or as
(b) the average values of *delayed* responses to the explanatory variables, i.e. delayed effects of price changes on wages, or of cost changes on prices, which could not be included in the analysis of a short period such as 1946–59. (It could also be argued that the sustained high level of demand in the post-war period may account for these positive constants.)

On the first hypothesis, the constancy of shares in the national product would be an accident. The constancy of shares in the national income can more plausibly be taken as suggesting that

24. See, for example, Phelps Brown and Hart (1952). From this article the share of wages and salaries in home-produced national income can be derived for each year from 1870 to 1938.

in the long run changes in costs are fully passed on as price changes and that profit mark-ups are constant. This being so, the long-run coefficients of wage costs and import costs must sum to unity. As to their separate absolute values, an estimate can be inferred from the post-war detailed national income estimates.

For the period 1946–59 the average share of labour costs and import costs in total costs was, respectively, 74 and 26 per cent. This provides an estimate of each of the long-run cost coefficients: 0·74 for wage changes, −0·74 for changes in output per man, and 0·26 for changes in import prices.[25] On this hypothesis the difference between these coefficients and their short-term equivalents in the price equation 7 has then to be allocated over past changes in the explanatory variables. It seems probable that the short-term response is the greatest, so it was assumed that the response of past changes diminished the farther they were removed from the current period.[26] As to the time-span covered by these distributed responses, any assumption must be somewhat arbitrary. By way of illustration, a period of five years was taken and the long-term coefficients were distributed as follows:

| | | Changes in: | |
| | | | |
Explanatory variable:	Wages and salaries	Import prices	Output per man
Long-term coefficient	0·74	0·26	−0·74
Distributed as:			
Year (t)*	0·27	0·21	−0·54
Year $(t−1)$	0·20	0·020	−0·08
Year $(t−2)$	0·14	0·015	−0·06
Year $(t−3)$	0·09	0·010	−0·04
Year $(t−4)$	0·04	0·005	−0·02

* For year (t) the coefficients shown are the estimated short-term coefficients of equation (7).

25. If the coefficient of wage changes is less than unity the change in prices will be less than the change in wages, provided that there is no change in import prices. This would imply a shift in factor shares. But it would also imply a persistent shift in the terms of trade. In fact, though not impossible, this is not normal.

26. This particular skewed time-form of reaction is quite frequently assumed in the analysis of economic data. See, for example, Koyck (1954).

A price relationship completed in this way is necessarily somewhat arbitrary. None the less, it appears to provide a reasonable explanation of factor price changes during the period 1950–59, as shown in Table 7.

If prices go up as much as costs, this alone is enough to produce constant factor shares in the long run,[27] even without a similar assumption regarding the behaviour of wages. But similar assumptions could also be made about the wage equation. It could be assumed that in the long run there is full price compensation, so that every current wage change would be expected to be as large as some combination of previous price changes, all other things being equal. An experiment was made assuming the following responses:

Long-term coefficient of price change	1·00
Distributed over past price changes as follows:	
Year (t)	0·30*
Year ($t - 1$)	0·16*
Year ($t - 2$)	0·18
Year ($t - 3$)	0·18
Year ($t - 4$)	0·18

* As estimated in equation 6.

The results obtained from this form of equation are given in Table 8. In general the reproduction of actual percentage changes in average wages and salaries is not very successful – certainly not as successful as the earlier price relationship (Table 7). As might be expected, the long-term wage relationship still contains a constant term, equivalent to an annual percentage increase of 1·9 in average wages and salaries: this rate of increase is not far removed from the average increase in output per man (1·7 per cent) during the years 1950–59. The case for a long-term price coefficient of unity in the wage relationship, however, remains doubtful: the attempt, illustrated in Table 8, does not provide strong evidence for it.

These experimental calculations with the constant terms in both short-term equations suggest that there is no constant term in the price equation at least; instead current price changes appear

27. Provided there is no persistent shift in the terms of trade.

Table 7

Price Changes, 1950–59: a Long-Term Hypothesis
Annual Percentage Changes

Year	Long-term contribution to price change of:				Calculated price change	Actual price change
	Wage change	Import price change	Product-ivity change	Constant term*		
1951	5·7	7·3	−1·2	−0·6	11·2	12·4
1952	5·7	2·1	−0·1	−0·6	7·1	5·9
1953	4·8	−1·6	−1·9	−0·6	0·7	0·2
1954	4·4	−0·4	−1·7	−0·6	1·7	1·7
1955	5·1	0·7	−1·9	−0·6	3·3	3·2
1956	5·5	0·3	−0·5	−0·6	4·7	4·9
1957	5·0	0·7	−1·2	−0·6	3·9	3·8
1958	4·4	−1·6	−0·9	−0·6	1·3	2·5
1959	3·6	−0·5	−2·1	−0·6	0·4	0·3

* This constant has been calculated slightly artificially so that the differences between calculated and actual price changes should sum to zero over the period. It thus results from the fact that the hypothesis as stated is not exactly true: the share of import costs was slightly higher than assumed, and the share of profits fell slightly.

to be the result of a series of changes in costs extending over a fairly long period. In fact a number of prices are infrequently changed. These changes, when made, may relate to historical and not current cost changes. Since many goods take a long path to the final consumer, through several industrial processes, it would follow that changes in final prices were determined by some distribution of past changes in costs extending over several years. Moreover, the short-term changes in profit margins have been small, smaller possibly than would be generally accounted for by the price equation including a constant. The constant term in the wage equation is less easily explained by the inclusion of past changes in prices, so there remains some doubt as to the form the wage equation should take. This suggests two possible cost–price models; a first, in which neither equation contains a constant; and a second, in which the price equation does not contain a constant but the wage equation does.

The first kind of model implies in the long run full price

Table 8

Wages and Salary Changes, 1950–59: a Long-term Hypothesis
Annual Percentage Changes

| Year | Contribution to long-term wage and salary change of: | | | Calculated wage and salary change | Actual wage and salary change |
	Price change*	Level of demand	Constant term†		
1951	6·6	1·8	1·9	10·3	9·7
1952	5·7	−0·3	1·9	7·3	7·9
1953	4·2	−0·3	1·9	5·8	4·4
1954	4·3	0·5	1·9	6·7	4·9
1955	4·4	1·8	1·9	8·1	8·0
1956	3·2	1·7	1·9	6·8	8·3
1957	2·7	0·2	1·9	4·8	5·6
1958	3·0	−1·2	1·9	3·7	4·0
1959	2·6	−2·2	1·9	2·3	2·9

* The sum of present and past price changes multiplied by the coefficients, adding to unity, set out above.

† Obtained so that the sum of residuals, actual wage and salary change less calculated wage and salary change, should sum as near to zero as possible.

compensation in wage changes, the long-term coefficient of prices being unity, and full cost compensation in prices. But the combined system is an extraordinarily repetitive one, which, once set in motion by a wage or price change does not damp down very easily. This makes such a model somewhat difficult to believe, although the results given above do not mean it must be rejected. It is, therefore, not impossible that the second model may provide a more plausible description of post-war wage and price changes. In this model there is still a very close link between wage and price changes, but the whole system is subject to the influence of some inflationary element, represented by the presence of the constant term in the wage equation, causing an upward trend in wages and prices. Although the complete system is somewhat repetitive it will tend to damp down about this rising trend, since the price coefficient in the wage equation is not unity but smaller.

6. Conclusions

Some conclusions can be drawn less tentatively than others from the results obtained. The impact of the exogenous variables on the complete wage–price system can be assessed fairly well. The level of demand plays an important part, and the results suggest that the first effect of a one per cent change in the level of demand – roughly equivalent to a similar change in the percentage level of unemployment – gives rise to an annual rate of change of 3 per cent in average wages and salaries. Similarly, a change of one per cent in import prices appears to have a fairly quick initial effect on prices, raising them by $\frac{1}{4}$ per cent. The effect of demand has been estimated from a period during which there has generally been excess demand for labour. It is not at all certain that the same result would hold in a reverse situation of prolonged unemployment.

It is much more difficult to estimate the internal links and the lagged responses in the cost–price system. It seems fairly probable that some delayed responses exist, although it is difficult to verify their time-span. On this point it is quite possible that estimates of short-term reactions tell much less than the whole truth. It is quite possible that the generation of current changes in wages and prices is a longer than annual process, and it might indeed be very lengthy. This would mean that such changes reflect the effects not only of current economic measures, but also of measures taken earlier. The extent to which the effects of earlier measures will be inherited in the current situation finally rests on the internal links. The link between costs and prices, and that between prices and wages, could each, in the long-term, be very rigid. On the other hand, however, the likelihood of some 'semi-political' or non-economic factor operating in the cost–price system cannot be entirely discounted. A factor of this kind could be attributed to some institutional attitude exerting an upward pressure on costs, but this attitude may itself be determined by a long period of high demand, such as that obtaining in the post-war years.

This attempt to analyse wage changes and price changes simultaneously has made it possible to consider more closely the way in which they interact. Such an approach has illustrated the possible inadequacy of the short-term statistical relationships, which do not provide a complete picture of the cost–price mechanism. The internal links still need much further investigation, and it is possible that they could be improved upon by analysing a more complex cost–price system involving more than two equations. Also the rapidity and form of response of wages and prices to their determinants still requires more research. But these uncertainties do not detract from the assessment of the effect of the exogenous variables. Both the pressure of demand, and changes in import prices, are shown to have large immediate effects, even though their later repercussions still remain uncertain.

References

DICKS-MIREAUX, L. A., and DOW, J. C. R. (1959), 'The determinants of wage inflation in the United Kingdom, 1946–56', *Journal of the Royal Statistical Society*, series A, vol. 122, part 2, pp. 145–84.

DOW, J. C. R. (1956), 'Analysis of the generation of price inflation', *Oxford Economic Papers*, vol. 8, pp. 252–301.

DOW, J. C. R., and DICKS-MIREAUX, L. A. (1958), 'Excess demand for labour: A study of conditions in Great Britain, 1946–56', *Oxford Economic Papers*, vol. 10, pp. 1–33.

HOOPER, J. W. (1959), 'Simultaneous equations and canonical correlation theory', *Econometrica*, vol. 27, no. 2, pp. 245–56.

KLEIN, L. R., and BALL, R. J. (1959), 'Some econometrics of the determination of absolute prices and wages', *Economic Journal*, vol. 69, pp. 465–82.

KLEIN, L. R., BALL, R. J., HAZLEWOOD, A., and VANDOME, P. (1961), *An Econometric Model of the United Kingdom*, Blackwell.

KOYCK, L. M. (1954), *Distributed Lags and Investment Analysis*, North-Holland Publishing Co.

LIPSEY, R. G. (1960), 'The relation between unemployment and the rate of change of money wage rates in the United Kingdom, 1862–1957: A further analysis', *Economica*, vol. 27, pp. 1–31.

PHELPS BROWN, E. H., and HART, P. E. (1952), 'The share of wages in national income', *Economic Journal*, vol. 62, no. 246, p. 251–77.

PHILLIPS, A. W. (1956), 'Some notes on the estimation of time-forms of reactions in inter-dependent dynamic systems', *Economica* (N.S.), no. 90 (May), pp. 99–113.

PHILLIPS, A. W. (1958), 'The relation between unemployment and the rate of change of money wage rates in the United Kingdom, 1861–1957', *Economica*, vol. 25, pp. 283–99, [Reading 15].

THEIL, H. (1958), *Economic Forecasts and Policy*, North-Holland Publishing Co.

17 L. R. Klein and R. J. Ball

The Determinants of Absolute Prices and Wages

L. R. Klein and R. J. Ball, 'Some econometrics of the determination of absolute prices and wages', *Economic Journal*, vol. 69 (1959), pp. 465–82.

Introduction

Much of the discussion of the current problem of inflation in the Western Capitalist world is necessarily strongly coloured by awareness of the course of the leading statistical series on wages, prices, productivity, profits, and unemployment during the last decade, when the general inflationary situation has caused many series to move together. It is rather difficult, but of the utmost importance, to try to unravel the chains of relationship among the several variables in order to delineate *structural* relations that have a high degree of *autonomy*.

The annual figures on wage rates over the past ten years are correlated with those on productivity, but they are as highly correlated with employment, unemployment, or the price level. Many of the apparent correlations are derived relations obtained by combining more basic structural relations. Many such derived relations can be obtained from a given structure, and one must take great care in the conclusions drawn from empirical correlations. The problem is especially serious in this decade of annual observations when reversals of the broad trend give only delicate statistical movements that are not easily discerned with the use of blunt tools.

The present paper arises out of work being done by the authors on the construction of an econometric model of the United Kingdom economy as a whole.[1] This work involves the fitting

---

1. Our colleagues, A. Hazlewood and P. Vandome, of the Institute of Statistics, Oxford, have collaborated on the larger study, of which this paper is a part.

together of autonomous structural components, from which a partial sub-system of interest on the inter-relations between wages and prices emerges. The findings we have obtained on this part of the model seem to be relevant in assisting an understanding and interpretation of the post-war inflation. We are thus moved to put forward some of our results at this stage. The entire investigation is based on quarterly series covering a wide variety of economic activities in the United Kingdom. It is hoped that by refining the sample data to this unit of observation we have a more sensitive and adequate body of information for discriminating among alternative explanations of the phenomena at hand. We cannot claim, however, to have found *the single* explanation of the inflationary process. That is hardly ever possible in our subject, and statistical analysis alone on the very best samples of economic data have never been able to prove that a particular relationship or explanation dominates the field to the exclusion of all others. We do, however, feel that our results are reasonable and carefully backed up by *a priori* considerations of autonomous patterns of behaviour. We can also bring evidence to bear against *some* alternative hypotheses.

In the discussion of post-war inflation, a number of economists have taken strong sides on the question of whether we have *demand* or *cost* inflation. Unfortunately, the great lesson of Walras has been forgotten in this debate. We have tried to keep a picture of the inter-related network of equations in the economy as a whole in front of us constantly, in building each component of the United Kingdom model, and feel that this may be advantageous in the interpretation of wage and price movements. In our system, and by our method of approach, it is possible for both demand and cost elements to show their respective strengths.

Some observers would base their characterization of the type of inflation we have been having on the movements in such statistical series as the spread between wage rates and earnings, others on the share of profits in national income, others on the lead–lag relationship between price and wage indexes, and others on the relationship between productivity and earnings. We select no key series for our study of this problem but try to inter-relate several series as part of a comprehensive model.

L. R. Klein and R. J. Ball

A Model of the Wage–Price Mechanism

The central equation of the model dealing with the determination of wages is based on the purely conventional assumption that market prices move in order to wipe out excess demand or supply. Economic theory has given us no reason to say whether dynamic movements of *relative* or *absolute* prices are associated with market clearing. We assume that money wage rates move over time in response to excess supply or demand in the labour market. This latter concept is given a statistical representation in the figures for unemployment, but such measures as unfilled vacancies may also be used.[2]

Actual bargaining over wage rates takes place in terms of monetary units, but this is not to say that a 'money illusion' is involved. Both sides are only too aware of the 'real' nature of economic affairs. Movements in the cost of living are prominent facts at the bargaining table. Instead of saying that dynamic movements in real wage rates are functionally related to unemployment, we take the somewhat more general and more realistic view that the time rate of change in money wage rates is a function of the level of unemployment and the time rate of change of the price level. A further reason for expressing the relationship in this way is that a time lag may exist between price and wage movements. The nature, extent, and magnitude of this time lag is of key significance in the interpretation of inflation as being of either the demand or cost variety. With ten annual observations it is difficult to say anything very definite about the lag, but with quarterly data we may eventually hope to make a stronger inference, although not necessarily from the samples at hand.

Two other factors are frequently mentioned in connexion with wage bargaining – profits and productivity. To some extent price movements and the level of unemployment already indicate the profit position, but in one of our experimental computations we explicitly introduce a profit variable into the relationship.

Productivity, we believe, is more properly entered at a different stage of the process, but we do not rule out the possibility that it can be a variable in its own right in the bargaining equation and similarly include it in an experimental computation.

2. Vacancy statistics are used by Dow and Dicks-Mireaux (1958).

If workers try to keep pace with the cost of living and find their bargaining power sensitive to the state of excess supply or demand in the labour market, we would be inclined to call the resulting movement in wages an expression of demand inflation. They simply follow the ordinary laws of the market. If, however, workers are able to push wages ahead of price movements or the level dictated by the state of the labour market, we have evidence of cost inflation spurred by deliberate trade union action. It is often said that trade unions cooperated with the post-war Labour Government and moderated their demands in accordance with a tacit understanding about general economic policy. It is further claimed that the trade unions became more aggressive or militant in pressing their claims after 1952 under the Conservative Government. To the extent to which trade unions can turn off or turn on steam in forcing the outcome of wage bargains in pre-determined fashion we have cost inflation. In our equation we shall introduce a constructed statistical variable (sometimes called a 'dummy' variable) which assumes the value of zero before 1952 and unity thereafter, to take into account this dual character of the period under review. In this respect our model has some flexibility in describing events during the period 1948–57, but otherwise our system has the same structural coefficients at all times. We treat the whole group of quarterly periods since 1948 as homogeneous as far as the mechanism of inflation is concerned.

Another way of expressing the power of trade unions over and above their market-induced strength is to note that they force wage movements on an irreversible path upwards. Either a steady trend growth or some type of 'ratchet' variable could bring out this aspect of union strength on the side of cost-induced inflation. Our results do not have this irreversibility, and perhaps they are not typical of all business-cycle movements in this respect. In the framework of the post-war economy there are no adequate data for testing this hypothesis. The pre-war data are unsatisfactory because many basic series are not available for that period. The power of trade unions is believed to have changed greatly since the war, and the structure of the economy as a whole has similarly changed. For these reasons, we are not pursuing the aspect of irreversibility in the present model.

We formulate a wage-rate equation, in which changes in wage rates appear as a function of previous price changes, and of the level of excess demand for labour as indicated by our proxy measure, the level of unemployment.

The particular form that we have given to this equation originates from a suggestion made to us by L. A. Dicks-Mireaux, who has pointed out the implications of discontinuity in wage bargaining. Broadly speaking, workers in any particular sector of the economy bargain for changes in wage rates once a year. The extent of the change will depend on the current level of excess demand, but also on the change in the price level that has occurred since the workers in that particular sector last had an increase in wage rates, i.e. the price change in the previous twelve months, assuming that workers receive wage increases at roughly the same time in each year. This assumption is, of course, not strictly true, since in some years the roles of leader and follower in wage demands may have been altered. Nevertheless, it is close to the now familiar concept of the annual round of wage-rate increases. It follows from this argument that wage-rate increases in any one quarter for workers having a change in that quarter will depend on the level of excess demand, and the price change over the previous twelve months.

For workers not subject to change in wage rates during that quarter, their wage rates will be related to excess demand and prices of previous quarters, i.e. the time of their last negotiations. If we follow through this scheme of discrete adjustment we find that the *average* wage change for all workers of any quarter over the same quarter of the preceding year is a function of a weighted average of past levels of excess demand and past changes in the price level. The weights in the average will depend upon the number of workers coming up for negotiation in each quarter, but we assume an even distribution of numbers among the quarters.

The equation to be estimated takes the form,

$$(w_r)_t - (w_r)_{t-4} = \alpha_1 \left(\frac{U_t + U_{t-1} + U_{t-2} + U_{t-3}}{4} \right) +$$

$$\alpha_2 \left(\frac{p_t - p_{t-4} + p_{t-1} - p_{t-5} + p_{t-2} - p_{t-6} + p_{t-3} - p_{t-7}}{4} \right) +$$

$$\alpha_3 F_t + \alpha + \alpha_{s1} Q_{1t} + \alpha_{s2} Q_{2t} + \alpha_{s3} Q_{3t} + u_{1t} \quad 1$$

w_r = quarterly average of index of weekly wage rates;

U = index of unemployment;

p = quarterly average of index of consumers price level;

F = political factor, zero in quarters before 1952 and unity thereafter;

Q_i = seasonal factor, unity in the ith quarter and zero in any other quarter;

u_1 = disturbance.

It may be observed at once, from the form of (1), that the institutional character of wage bargaining has led to the formulation of an equation, in which there is, on the average, a six-month lag between wage and price changes. But this lag does not carry any implications about what most people have in mind on the existence of demand or cost inflation. Nevertheless, it does introduce a lag of rates behind prices.

The political factor F_t needs no explanation beyond that already given. For every equation of the entire United Kingdom model the data used are completely unadjusted for seasonal variation. In each equation, however, we include explicit seasonal variables. Inspection of graphs has led us to posit a linear additive seasonal component throughout. In this equation with four quarter changes and moving averages there is little, if any, scope for seasonal influence. Indeed, the empirical results indicate this below, but every equation was treated for seasonal variation on the same basis, and we include the Q_{it} variables here for the sake of uniformity.

Equation (1) is a key equation in the United Kingdom model because it displaces, in a sense, the money-balance equation for the absolute determination of prices and wages. It is difficult, again following the Walrasian idea, to say what determines what in a truly inter-related system, but the main function of equation (1) is to complete the system in respect of the determination of absolute wages or prices, while the cash-balance equation has the main function of completing the system in respect of the determination of the interest rate.[3] The state of the labour market displaces the state of the money market in determining the course of absolute prices or wages. 'It is hardly an exaggeration to say

3. These ideas are developed in connexion with similar American models in Klein (1954), and Klein and Goldberger (1955).

that instead of being on a Gold Standard we are now on a Labour Standard' (Hicks, 1955, p. 391).

To be as realistic as possible we have carefully formulated the bargaining equation of our model in terms of a wage-rate variable. Earnings, however, not rates, are the important cost variables to an entrepreneur. We therefore seek to establish a relation between the two concepts of wage payment. The spread between earnings and rates has, as noted above, become an important statistical indicator in the view of many people who are trying to diagnose the inflationary process. Our measure of wage rates used in this model is an index of weekly wages paid for a full-time standard work period. It is averaged to quarters for our purposes. The earnings variable is similarly an index of total wages paid for a week's work regardless whether that week's hours consist of short time, full time or overtime. It includes bonus or other premium payments as well. In some analyses an attempt is made to measure hourly earnings, in which case weekly earnings would have to be adjusted to a uniform number of hours worked, but we make no such adjustment.

If workers are paid, wholly or partially, on a piece basis, their earnings will rise with rising productivity; therefore the excess of the earnings index over the rate index is made to depend on the level of productivity. For those workers geared to a time rate of pay, their earnings will vary with hours worked. As they work more or fewer hours they will earn more or less per week. In addition, overtime work will provide a premium rate of pay. We make the spread between the two wage indexes a function of hours worked as well as of productivity. Hours worked are one of the most sensitive indicators of economic activity; therefore it is not necessary to introduce another variable into the relationship to indicate the level of demand pressure. The hours contribution to the earnings-rate spread seems to be a measure of demand pull, while the productivity contribution is perhaps more mixed in its cost and demand elements. Some writers, however, regard any positive movement in the spread as demand inflation. Our second equation takes the form

$$w_{et} - w_{rt} = \beta_1 h_t + \beta_2 \left(\frac{P}{hE_p}\right)_t +$$
$$\beta + \beta_{s1} Q_{1t} + \beta_{s2} Q_{2t} + \beta_{s3} Q_{3t} + u_{2t}. \quad 2$$

w_e = quarterly average of index of weekly earnings;

h = quarterly average of index of hours worked per week;

$\left(\dfrac{P}{hE_p}\right)$ = quarterly average of index of productivity (industrial production index divided by index of weekly man-hours in corresponding production industries).

In contrast with the previous equation, there is a significant seasonal factor in the excess of earnings over rates, and the seasonal variables introduced in this equation are more important than in the previous one.

Hours are introduced as an explanatory variable in equation (2); hence we include an equation in our sub-system to show how hours worked are related to some of the other variables included in the same sub-system. Short of a presentation of our entire model consisting of more than a score of equations, we cannot show how industrial production is related to other variables of the system. For the purposes of the present paper we leave the system open at the production end. It is a partial and not a complete analysis.

When output is high hours worked are high. Hours are fairly closely tied to the general business cycle. They are also related to the pressure on facilities. When activity is slack, short time is introduced, and when labour is very scarce overtime comes back into operation. Our third equation thus relates the hours index to indexes of industrial production and of unemployment.

$$h_t = \gamma_1 P_t + \gamma_2\left(\frac{U_t + U_{t-1} + U_{t-2} + U_{t-3}}{4}\right) +$$
$$\gamma + \gamma_{1s}Q_{1t} + \gamma_{2s}Q_{2t} + \gamma_{3s}Q_{3t} + u_{3t}. \quad 3$$

This equation shows that the hours variable in (2), accounting partially for the earnings-rate spread, is, in turn, related to the level of activity measured both by P_t and the average of unemployment.

The completion of our sub-system involves the construction of an equation giving a direct link between wages (earnings) and prices. It is, in effect, an equation of mark-up over prime costs. In the debates on the theory of the firm the adherents of full cost pricing as a pattern of behaviour would suggest an equation roughly similar to that which we propose below. An alternative approach, which we have not followed in this particular model, would be to construct equations proposed by the adherents of marginal analysis, i.e. marginal-cost or marginal-productivity equations. Such equations, transformed into equations of *labour's share* on the assumption of an exponential production function, have been estimated in the econometric models of the American economy (Klein and Goldberger, 1955). The equation of entrepreneurial behaviour introduced here is similar to that used in the model of the Dutch economy.[4] In our mark-up equation the index of price of final output is made a function of the earnings index, the import price index, and an index of indirect tax rates.

$$p_i = \delta_1(w_e)_t + \delta_2(p_i)_{t-2} + \delta_3 T_t + \delta + \\ \delta_{1s}Q_{1t} + \delta_{2s}Q_{2t} + \delta_{3s}Q_{3t} + u_{4t}. \quad 4$$

p_i = index of import prices;

T = index of ratio of indirect taxes less subsidies to consumer expenditures.

It is assumed that import prices affect final output prices with a time lag of two quarters, but a somewhat shorter lag, a somewhat larger lag, or even no lag at all would not have greatly altered our statistical results or the conclusions based on them.

It may be thought that the mark-up over costs varies cyclically, and we have looked into this possibility by adding a productivity variable to the equation in an experimental calculation. Increasing productivity enables producers to moderate mark-ups over costs and yet retain levels of profits. We should expect to find a negative coefficient of a linear productivity variable if one is added to an equation like (4). Other cost variables may be considered as well, but we have restricted the analysis to prime costs covering wages, imports, and taxes. To the extent to which fluctuations in import prices contribute to final price fluctuations we have a form of cost inflation (or deflation) but not one that is attributable in any sense to trade union power. In this equation and in our entire United Kingdom model import prices are treated as exogenous. While we attempt to close the system at many points in the trading accounts, we make no attempt to do so with respect to import prices.

4. See Central Planning Bureau (1956), pp. 70–73.

Statistical Estimates of the Model

The four equations outlined in the preceding section have all been estimated from quarterly data of the period since 1948. The method of estimation used is known, in technical terms, as limited information maximum likelihood, a variant of the well-known method of maximum likelihood. This method has the desirable property of taking into account the structure of an interdependent model when estimating any particular part of it. For this reason it avoids the problems of bias (large sample theory) prevalent in application of what might be called single-equation methods such as the familiar methods of multiple-correlation theory applied to any particular equation without reference to the fact that it is imbedded in a larger interrelated system. Our method also has desirable properties in forecasting for the economy as a whole and is being used to estimate the entire United Kingdom model. The present estimates are a by-product of this effort.[5]

The estimated set of four structural equations in our partial model with sampling errors noted in parentheses is

$$(w_r)_t - (w_r)_{t-4} = \underset{(0 \cdot 013)}{-0 \cdot 091} \left(\frac{U_t + U_{t-1} + U_{t-2} + U_{t-3}}{4} \right) +$$

$$+ \underset{(0 \cdot 092)}{0 \cdot 854} \left(\frac{p_t - p_{t-4} + p_{t-1} - p_{t-5} + p_{t-2} - p_{t-6} + p_{t-3} - p_{t-7}}{4} \right) +$$

$$+ \underset{(0 \cdot 40)}{2 \cdot 90 F_t} + \underset{(1 \cdot 41)}{10 \cdot 26} + \underset{(0 \cdot 57)}{0 \cdot 10 Q_{1t}} + \underset{(0 \cdot 57)}{0 \cdot 30 Q_{2t}} + \underset{(0 \cdot 57)}{0 \cdot 19 Q_{3t}}. \quad \text{(1e)}$$

$$(w_e)_t - (w_r)_t = \underset{(0 \cdot 54)}{2 \cdot 06 h_t} + \underset{(0 \cdot 150)}{0 \cdot 625} \left(\frac{P}{h E_p} \right)_t - \underset{(45 \cdot 80)}{272 \cdot 72} +$$

$$+ \underset{(0 \cdot 96)}{0 \cdot 001 Q_{1t}} + \underset{(0 \cdot 98)}{1 \cdot 58 Q_{2t}} + \underset{(1 \cdot 36)}{5 \cdot 54 Q_{3t}}. \quad \text{(2e)}$$

5. Substantive economic content and not econometric method occupies our main interest in this paper; therefore we shall not discuss the details of the estimation procedure. The method is explained and described in Klein (1953). An example of its application to similar problems is given in Klein and Goldberger (1955).

$$h_t = 0.089P_t + 0.0068\left(\frac{U_t + U_{t-1} + U_{t-2} + U_{t-3}}{4}\right) +$$
$$\quad (0.007) \quad (0.005)$$

$$+ 90.20 - 0.11Q_{1t} + 0.15Q_{2t} + 0.83Q_{3t}. \quad (3e)$$
$$\quad (1.13) \quad (0.20) \quad\quad (0.20) \quad\quad (0.22)$$

$$p_t = 0.421(w_e)_t + 0.216(p_i)_{t-2} + 0.013T_t + 35.65 +$$
$$\quad (0.013) \quad\quad (0.030) \quad\quad\quad (0.161) \quad\quad (13.03)$$

$$+ 0.94Q_{1t} + 2.06Q_{2t} + 1.18Q_{3t}. \quad (4e)$$
$$\quad (0.50) \quad\quad (0.50) \quad\quad (0.50)$$

All variables are measured as index numbers which average to 100 in the base period calendar year, 1948, except Q_{it} and F_t. These are constructed variables which take on the values of zero or unity in specified quarters.

The estimate of equation (1) gives a close correspondence between actual and computed four-quarter rates of change in wage rates. The degree of correlation, adjusted for degrees of freedom used up in estimation is 0.93 in our sample of 36 quarterly observations over the period 1948–56.[6] The residual variation appears to be slightly auto-correlated, thus indicating that we have not isolated all the non-random factors. We measure auto-correlation in residuals by the statistic $\frac{\delta^2}{s^2}$, known as the ratio of the mean square successive difference to the variance (Hart and von Newmann, 1942). For values above 1.4 in samples of our size we accept the hypothesis of non-auto-correlation at the 5 per cent level of significance. In the present case our value is estimated at 1.02. By another test using a statistic which is smaller than $\frac{\delta^2}{s^2}$ by the factor $\frac{N-1}{N}$ (N = sample size), we find an indecisive answer to the question whether or not there is significant auto-correlation (Durbin and Watson, 1951).

Our estimated equation suggests three positive conclusions:
1. Excess demand for labour as represented by a moving average

6. Although this is not an ordinary multiple-correlation estimate, we can compute an over-all correlation coefficient defined as $(1 - S_u^2/S_y^2)^{\frac{1}{2}}$, where S_u^2 is the estimated variance of disturbances (determined from the variance of residuals) and S_y^2 is the variance of the normalized variable in the equation (the variable with a unit coefficient).

of unemployment has been an important factor over the sample period. 2. Wage-rate adjustment to price changes has in effect roughly compensated for the effects of price increases between the times at which increases in wage rates have been obtained. 3. The behaviour of wage-rate changes before 1952 is markedly different from that after 1952. The latter point is illustrated by the magnitude and statistical significance of the coefficient of F_t in (1e). On the average, wage rates moved up over a four-quarter interval by 2·90 more index points after 1952 than before, *ceteris paribus*. This might be taken as evidence of the strength of cost inflation.

Since the change in wage rates is measured over a period of four quarters seasonal factors are effectively repressed. This is indicated by the small sizes and comparatively large sampling errors of the coefficients of the Q_{it} in (1e).

The main influence of demand inflation should be shown through the coefficient of $\left(\dfrac{U_t + U_{t-1} + U_{t-2} + U_{t-3}}{4} \right)$, the index of unemployment averaged over the past four quarters. As would be expected from *a priori* considerations, this coefficient is negative and has a relatively small sampling error. In earlier work we estimated (1e) in the form.

$$(w_r)_t - (w_r)_{t-4} = -0{\cdot}021 \left(\frac{U_t + U_{t-1} + U_{t-2} + U_{t-3}}{4} \right) +$$
$$(0{\cdot}017)$$
$$+ 0{\cdot}975(p_t - p_{t-4}) + 3{\cdot}88F_t +$$
$$(0{\cdot}115) \qquad\qquad (0{\cdot}48)$$
$$+ 2{\cdot}40 - 0{\cdot}31Q_{1t} - 0{\cdot}25Q_{2t} - 0{\cdot}030Q_{3t}. \quad (1e')$$
$$(2{\cdot}05) \quad (0{\cdot}67) \qquad (0{\cdot}67) \qquad (0{\cdot}67)$$

It will be noted that the principal difference between (1e′) and (1e) is the size and significance of the coefficient of the moving average of unemployment. There seems a pronounced tendency for this coefficient to increase in absolute size and significance as we increase the lag in the price change. The estimate of (1e′) was obtained using the method of limited information. We experimented, however, with an alternative form of (1e′) using $(p_{t-1} - p_{t-5})$ as our price variable, and making use of the method of least squares. As we have observed, least-squares estimates of an equation of the form (1e) or (1e′) will be biased estimates, but though they are biased, they probably give a good estimate of the change to be expected from introducing a new variable.[7] Using $(p_{t-1} - p_{t-5})$ as our price variable, the coefficient of

$$\left(\frac{U_t + U_{t-1} + U_{t-2} + U_{t-3}}{4}\right)$$

jumped to 0·06, and was significant as opposed to the estimate in (1e′), which is only just greater than its sampling error. Least-squares estimates of (1e′) gave us a coefficient of 0·039, which suggests that 0·06 represents an upward biased estimate; nevertheless, the added importance given to the influence of demand as a result of the introduction of a price lag appears to be firmly established.

This result indicates that the magnitude of the coefficient of the moving average of unemployment in (1e) is not unexpected, since we have, in effect, an average lag of price changes of six months. The actual size of the coefficient in (1e) indicates that if the average price change were zero, and $F_t = 1$ for all t, the index of the moving average of unemployment would have to be about 150 before the change in wage rates would become negative. The rise in the coefficient of $\left(\dfrac{U_{t-1} + U_{t-2} + U_{t-3} + U_{t-4}}{4}\right)$ in (1e) as compared to (1e′) has been partially offset by the increase in the constant term from 2·40 to 10·26, which represents the trend increase in wage rates.

This raises the question to what extent equation (1e′) can be considered reversible. It would undoubtedly be felt by some that even if the price level could be stabilized over the requisite period, a rise in the index of the moving average of unemployment to 150, representing an absolute level of unemployment of about 350,000, would not be sufficient to result in an actual decline in the wage-rate index. In the case of equation (1e′), unemployment would

7. It may be observed that the least-squares estimates of the coefficients in (1e) are hardly distinguishable from those obtained using a consistent method of estimation. The coefficient of the moving average of unemployment is 0·089 as against 0·091, and that of the distributed lag in prices, 0·812, as against 0·854, with the sampling errors being virtually unchanged.

have to be about 520,000 before this eventually would take place, with perfectly stable prices. Even in this case, many would doubt this conclusion.

We prefer to reserve judgement on this point. The ever-continuing upward movement in money wage rates is only an assertion by some economists, who can read basic trends from something like a decade or two of experience. We believe that logically equation (1e) is more satisfactory than equation (1e'), since it reflects more closely the institutional character of wage bargaining, although it increases the possibility of a fall in the wage-rate index when the price level is stable. On the basis of our sample we are unable to reach any positive conclusion on this matter. Other economists have emphasized that the relation between changes in wage rates and excess demand for labour is non-linear, so that a considerable rise in unemployment (say) may take place with the wage-rate index being unaffected.[8] We have seen no empirical evidence that justifies the fitting of a non-linear rather than a linear function to the sample data, though to some this procedure is highly plausible on *a priori* grounds.

In assessing the responsibility for inflation it is important to be able to specify the lags involved, if any. As already pointed out, the particular form of the wage-rate equation (1e) has a built-in lag of six months between wage-rate and price changes. However, our sample does not permit a statistical discrimination of any other lag.

We have already mentioned the possibility that either the level of profits, changes in productivity or both should be included as variables in our wage-rate equation. Utilizing the method of least squares, we have experimented with their introduction into equation (1e').

Productivity change over four quarters when introduced into (1e') leaves the estimates of the other coefficients nearly the same and itself carries a negative coefficient. As a result of this finding

8. In this connexion we may mention the work of Dicks-Mireaux and Dow (1959) and a recent paper by Phillips (1958). Phillips explains wage-rate changes in terms of unemployment alone, except in period of rapidly rising import prices. He estimates a non-linear (i.e. logarithmic) relation between wage-rate changes and unemployment.

we concluded that the inclusion of productivity change would not improve our basic model.

The influence of profits was assessed by a similar least-squares computation, using as a variable the average of our index of company profits over the last four quarters. The result was that a positive coefficient larger than its sampling error was obtained on the profit variable. The coefficients of the other variables were, however, reduced, and strong auto-correlation was introduced into the residuals. This seems to lend weight to the idea put forward above that the influence of profits is largely reflected already in the other variables. Accordingly, we have not included the profit variable in our unbiased computations. We have conducted these experiments in an equation of the form (1e′). We believe, however, that the results obtained may be extended to an equation of the form (1e), and have therefore not included either the change of productivity or our profits variable in our basic equation.

Equation (2e) above represents the spread between earnings and wage rates. As it stands, this is in terms of the levels. The degree of correlation is estimated at 0·93, which indicates a fairly close agreement between the actual and computed value of the spread. Unlike the previous equation, however, its residual variation is decidedly not free of serial correlation. For this equation the measure $\frac{\delta^2}{s^2}$ comes out as low as 0·73, which indicates a fairly high degree of auto-correlation in the residuals. The reason for this is not far to seek. Over the period covered by our sample, the spread has grown at a fairly steady trend rate. However, in explaining the spread we have used variables that are cyclical in character, the result being that we have introduced a cycle into the residuals which is inversely related to the cycle followed by the variables used.

In this case we have made an experimental calculation which removes the serial correlation of residuals, i.e. we have transformed all the variables to first differences.[9] With the first-difference transformations we have made a simple least-squares estimate of (2e) to compare with the same kind of estimate of the

9. These differences are from quarter to adjacent quarter and not over four quarter periods as in equation (1e).

equation expressed in its original form. The two least-squares estimates are,

$$(w_e - w_r)_t = \underset{(0·67)}{1·55h_t} + \underset{(0·118)}{0·538}\left(\frac{P}{hE_p}\right)_t - \underset{(56·95)}{211·38} - \underset{(0·93)}{0·414Q_{1t}} +$$

$$\underset{(0·94)}{1·10Q_{2t}} + \underset{(1·39)}{4·75Q_{3t}}. \quad (2e')$$

$$\Delta(w_e - w_r)_t = \underset{(0·365)}{1·737\Delta h_t} + \underset{(0·09)}{0·044\Delta}\left(\frac{P}{hE_p}\right)_t - \underset{(0·3275)}{0·00657\Delta Q_{1t}} +$$

$$\underset{(0·377)}{0·346\Delta Q_{2t}} + \underset{(0·87)}{0·205\Delta Q_{3t}}. \quad (2e'')$$

The estimated equation (2e') is roughly similar to that in (2e), and the degree of serial correlation in the residuals is equally high. On the other hand, (2e''), the estimate from transformed data, has no significant serial correlation in the residuals but gives a different figure for the relative importance of productivity in accounting for the spread. If anything, our estimates in (2e) are over-generous in attributing fluctuations in the spread to those in productivity.

Our results are not inconsistent with the hypothesis that the spread is largely influenced by the level of demand. As pointed out above, hours worked constitute a very sensitive indicator of the level of demand. In one sense hours worked contribute to the spread in a purely accounting manner, as do, other things being equal, increases in output per man-hour for piece-workers.[10] We are unable, however, to separate out the relative importance of these two influences. No doubt, overtime, bonus payment, premium rates, and changes in the length of the 'official' working week have all been important. On the demand side, it is often argued that a high level of demand has led to payments above the

10. Among other things equal here, would be the timing of particular jobs. The effects of higher productivity on the spread may be to some extent offset by re-timing and re-estimating after the introduction of new capital equipment. We are unable to make any reliable estimate of the importance of this factor in cancelling out productivity charges.

'official' rates to bid labour away from some firms into others. Our results are consistent with either hypothesis alone or a combination of both.

It is interesting to compare our results with those obtained by the Swedish economists Bent Hansen and Gösta Rehn (1956) in their study of the Swedish economy. They start from the assumption that wage rates are fixed institutionally, and that the influence of economic forces is reflected in the spread between earnings and wage rates, which they describe as the 'wage drift'. In our model we have not followed this assumption about rate fixing, putting forward instead the hypothesis that changes in wage rates are influenced by changes in the cost of living, by the demand for labour and by the political climate.

The procedure followed by Hansen and Rehn was to take a sample of annual data 1947–54, applied to eight main groupings within Swedish manufacturing industry. Briefly, their findings suggested that the main influence determining the 'wage drift' in Sweden over these years has been excess demand. They tested the further influence of 'excess profits', and the hypothesis that increases in productivity have contributed substantially to the drift in the manner outlined above. Neither was found to be significant.

The relations estimated were between the rate of change of the 'wage drift', the level of excess profit, the level of excess demand, and the rate of change of productivity. It may be pointed out that while in our model productivity makes a significant contribution to the spread between earnings and wage rates, when all variables are expressed as levels, productivity ceases to be a significant factor in our least-squares computation, in which rates of change were introduced. It would appear therefore that our findings are not inconsistent with those of Hansen and Rehn. However, it must be re-emphasized that we have included an index of hours worked in our computation, which is an indicator of the direct influence of demand in the spread, but which also reflects other influences, and we have used weekly and not hourly earnings. Hansen and Rehn, on the other hand, construct an index of excess demand for labour, in some cases by taking the difference between unfilled vacancies and numbers unemployed, in others, where the numbers unemployed in the industry could not be ascertained, by using vacancy statistics alone.[11] We have included an explicit labour-demand variable, in the form of an average of the last year's unemployment, in the wage-rate equation (1e). This reflects our belief that the demand for labour can affect the wage bargain as well as the 'wage drift'.

We include the equation for hours worked in the sub-system to illustrate one of the ways in which demand enters the inflationary process. Our estimates in (3e) produce a correlation coefficient of 0·93 and a serial correlation measure of 1·23. Again we find evidence of slight serial correlation in residual variation.

It appears that the most important factor explaining the level of hours worked is the level of production. The coefficient of production is small, but many times its sampling error. The small size of the coefficient is explained by the relative magnitudes of the range of the hours and production indices over the sample period. Hours worked are, on the whole, a fairly stable input into the productive process. Our estimates show that roughly a 10 per cent change in the industrial production index is required to produce a 1 per cent change in the hours index. The unemployment variable adds little to the computation. The coefficient is small, as one might have expected, but the sign differs from that anticipated, and the sampling error is sufficiently large to admit the hypothesis of either a positive or negative true value.

Thus it would be possible to substitute industrial production for hours worked in equation (2e), illustrating the relation of the spread between earnings and wage rates to the force of demand. Under the assumptions made in our model, this would, however, obscure the underlying chain of relationship.

Equation (4e) is the price or 'mark-up' equation. As pointed out above, the price index here used is that of the general price level of consumer goods. In the econometric model we also deter-

11. Hansen and Rehn attach significance to the use of vacancy statistics in addition to those on unemployment in order to measure excess demand during a period of sustained inflationary pressure. Following the suggestion of J. C. R. Dow, we have made experimental computations with a measure based on vacancy statistics (unemployment deflated by index of vacancies), and found the results on the basis of least-squares estimates not to be different in any essential way from those using ordinary unemployment figures. Compare Dow and Dicks-Mireaux (1958) for comparisons of vacancy and unemployment statistics.

mine the price of investment goods, as a function of earnings and imported non-ferrous metal prices. These two price indices can be weighted together to obtain an index of the general price level if so desired. The result established by the limited information estimate of (4e) is among one of the firmest in the model. The degree of correlation corrected for degrees of freedom is 0·996, which is very high. The measure of serial correlation $\frac{\delta^2}{s^2}$ is 1·16, which indicates a moderate amount of serial correlation in the residuals.

It will be observed that the coefficients of $(w_e)_t$ and $(p_i)_{t-2}$ are many times their sampling errors. The coefficient of our measure of the influence of indirect taxes, however, is small, and very much smaller than its sampling error. As stated, we have expressed total indirect taxes paid, less subsidies, as a proportion of consumers' expenditure. Variations in this ratio have, on the whole, been small compared to the substantial changes in the indexes of earnings and import prices, which are also included in the equation. Since the simple correlations between $(w_e)_t$ and p_i and between p_t and $(p_i)_{t-2}$ are so high, there is very little residual variation to be explained by the indirect tax variable. As changes in indirect tax rates are specifically directed, it might, perhaps, be argued that such changes tend to affect prices of, and expenditures on, particular goods, but will show little effect on the consumer price level as a whole, since the effects of the imposition of higher taxes on specific goods, may simply be to divert the expenditures elsewhere.

In the case of this equation there is remarkably close agreement between the results of the estimation by the method of limited information and by the method of least squares, which is largely a result of the high over-all level of correlation. Applying the least-squares procedure to the equation in the form presented above, we obtain the result

$$p_t = 0·418(w_e)_t + 0·217(p_i)_{t-2} + 0·023(T)_t + 34·83 +$$
$$(0·013) \qquad (0·030) \qquad (0·160) \qquad (12·92)$$
$$+ 0·94Q_{1t} + 2·06Q_{2t} + 1·18Q_{3t}.$$
$$(0·50) \qquad (0·50) \qquad (0·49)$$

In a prototype model, based on a decade of annual data, this equation was estimated using Theil's (1953) two-rounds method, in the form $p_t = \lambda + \lambda_1(w_e)_t + \lambda_2(p_i)_t$. Using annual data, the seasonal variables and the lag in import prices disappear. We then obtained $\lambda_1 = 0.48$ and $\lambda_2 = 0.34$, where the λ_i are estimates of the λ_i. There is thus a very close relation between these three results, all obtained using different methods of estimation, and in the latter case using annual rather than quarterly data.

We experimented, using least-squares estimates, with the introduction of productivity into the equation. In formulating the 'mark-up' in his statistical study, Dow (1956, p. 269) introduced productivity as an alleviating factor on the influence of a rise in earnings on prices. This follows the general custom of arguing that prices will be stabilized provided that earnings do not rise faster than productivity, or more generally that in times when productivity is rising fastest, prices will rise less fast than earnings. The least-squares estimate yielded a small coefficient of productivity with a positive sign contrary to expectations, and the sampling error was sufficiently large for the 'true' value to be assumed to be either positive or negative. We, therefore, concluded that our result afforded no evidence for the belief that the 'mark-up' varies in response to changes in productivity. Our results suggest that earnings have been roughly twice as important, at the margin, as import prices in determining the level of consumer prices over the period of our sample. It must not, however, be forgotten that in some sense we have established an average relationship, and this does not rule out the possibility that over certain periods within the sample, import prices may have contributed very much more than earnings to the rise in prices, as, for instance, at the time of the Korean War and shortly afterwards. How close we are to having established a basic structural relationship depends on the representative character of the sample, and as we have suggested elsewhere in this paper, there are reasons which give rise to doubt whether our sample is a representative one.

Conclusions

Our particular model of the inflationary process brings out points that have been raised by different authors and attempts to follow through some inter-related patterns of behaviour in the sphere of wage and price determination. This model contains elements of both cost and demand inflation. Our model is not unique, as judged by its agreement with observed data, and it contains flaws; nevertheless, it appears to be reasonable, and the difficulties that it encounters are inherent in the nature of our basic economic information. We are not able to discriminate between certain competing key hypotheses, but it does not appear that other methods of analysis will be able to do so either.

The weaknesses of our results, such as serial correlation of residuals and some relatively large sampling errors, may perhaps be erased in a model of the same general type that specifies different relations among the variables or uses some more complex methods of parameter estimation, but we know of no such findings. Our model is aggregative, as is most of the analysis of the inflation problem, but one disaggregative type of analysis has been mentioned by several writers, namely, that changes in productivity in certain leading and rapidly advancing industries have been influential in securing favourable wage bargains in those industries in the first instance and that such awards have later spread, on equity grounds, to other sectors of the economy where productivity has advanced less rapidly. Phenomena like these are not adequately handled by our aggregative model, but they are not necessarily contradictory with what we find.

The model we have presented does not have irreversibilities that often are ascribed to the behaviour of wage rates in modern society, but for the period under review a model with irreversibilities will probably not function much differently from ours. The test of the irreversibility hypothesis is yet to come, but we remain unconvinced of its correctness.

Our statistical analysis covers the post-war period as a whole. It gives a set of average relationships, which do not rule out dispersion. In the Korean period import prices were obviously of extraordinary significance. Some writers, such as Robbins, point to mainly demand inflation until the most recent months, when cost influences are considered to be dominant. Our only claim is that our model will tend to depict behaviour on the average.

We cannot say whether there is a lag of a quarter or more in the adjustment of wage rates to price changes (see equation 1e), but if there were definite evidence in favour of a lag we would lean more to the side of demand than to the side of cost inflation in the absence of substantial changes in import prices. The main element of demand inflation in this equation is through the effect of unemployment on wage rates. Our estimates of equation (1e) indicate the importance of the demand for labour, as represented by our variable on unemployment, on changes in wage rates.

Demand also enters the process through the strong influence of hours worked per week on the earnings-rate spread – the wage drift. Through the mark-up equation we have a measure of the influence of labour cost on price and import cost on price. These are both aspects of cost inflation, but the respective origins of cost must be kept firmly in mind when assessing the blame for inflation and formulating remedial policy action.

On the basis of our results we should be inclined to rule out the direct structural influence of productivity on wage-rate setting or on price mark-ups.[12] We similarly exclude profits from direct consideration in the rate equation. This is not to deny obvious chains of indirect influence of either variable throughout a larger and more complete inter-related system.

Our main point is that we should keep the inter-related structure of the economy more firmly in mind and not fall into the trap of ascribing our present difficulties with control of inflation to any single source in the economy.

As these pages are written, some countries in the Western World are experiencing a cyclical sag in output and accompanying growth in unemployment. Many people have been impressed by the fact that even during this cyclical phase, prices and wages have continued to rise, and they have taken this to be evidence that the prevailing structure should be described as cost, rather than demand, inflation.

Two points may be made in this connexion. In the first place with regard to changes in the general consumer price level, it has been pointed out by Clague (1958), that in the case of the United States, rising prices during the early stages have been a feature of

12. Subject to the above-cited influence of pace-setting industries.

previous recessions.[13] The American Consumer Price Index continued to rise for some time after the fall in production and employment and finally fell in the summer of 1958. The explanation of this is largely to be sought in the make-up of the index (which closely resembles the price index used in our computation). The food component carries a large weight, and the comparative volatility of food prices is well known. Although, as Clague shows, durable goods prices respond fairly quickly to changes in the level of production, food prices are closely related to seasonal factors, and to the prevailing weather conditions. A poor harvest prior to the onset of a recession may keep food prices rising, the over-all effect of which may offset falls in other prices to the extent that the total index rises rather than falls. The exceedingly great harvest of 1958 has been mainly responsible for the summer and autumn drop in American prices. In the longer run, it appears, food prices have adjusted themselves to the changed *general* economic conditions. Finally, a recession may get under way just before a normal seasonal pressure on food prices, so that the total index may still rise as output and employment fall. If the recession were sufficiently brief, it is possible that other prices may recover before the special factors keeping up the total index have worked themselves out, so that the impression is given that the recession has had no effect on prices. It follows that considerable care must be taken in interpreting movements in the consumer price level, when drawing conclusions about the character of current inflation. Wholesale prices, during the current American recession, did fall shortly after production turned down if food prices are excluded from the index.

Secondly, with regard to wage changes, it may be argued by those placing emphasis on demand that wage increases were much more difficult to obtain during the recession, and are much reduced in size. Bargaining power was distinctly impaired by unemployment. Both sides in the controversy have elements of truth in their arguments.

The dampening of demand had not fully checked inflation at the time of writing, and a simple theory leading to an equally

13. G. H. Moore (1958), in his work on statistical indicators of business cycles, confirms this laggard behaviour of consumer prices at the upper turning point.

simple policy proposal does not seem adequate to the situation. But neither would a 'deal' with the trade unions on a national wages policy, advocated by some extremists on the side of cost inflation, do the trick.[14] It is a very simple solution based on a very simple theory. Just as we argue here for more tolerance for alternative points of view on the matter of a theoretical description of behaviour, we feel that a broader approach to policy control based on both demand and cost aspects of the situation would lead to more fruitful results.

14. Roberts (1958) remarks that even if a sensible agreement is worked out on a national scale among government, employers, and trade unions, 'No trade unionist is able to stand silently by, as the Dutch have found out, when profits are rising rapidly.' We may prefer to cite another measure of activity besides *profits*, but the point of Roberts's observation remains well founded.

References

CENTRAL PLANNING BUREAU (1956), *Scope and Methods of the Central Planning Bureau*, The Hague.

CLAGUE, E. (1958), 'The consumer price index in the business cycle', *Monthly Labour Review*, vol. 81, pp. 616–20.

DICKS-MIREAUX, L. A., and DOW, J. C. R. (1959), 'The determinants of wage inflation: United Kingdom, 1946–56', *Journal of the Royal Statistical Society*, series A, vol. 122, part 2, pp. 145–84.

DOW, J. C. R. (1956), 'Analysis of the generation of price inflation', *Oxford Economic Papers*, vol. 8, pp. 252–301.

DOW, J. C. R., and DICKS-MIREAUX, L. A. (1958), 'The excess demand for labour: A study of conditions in Great Britain, 1946–56', *Oxford Economic Papers*, vol. 10, pp. 1–33.

DURBIN, J., and WATSON, G. S. (1951), 'Testing for serial correlation in least squares regression, 11', *Biometrika*, vol. 38, pp. 159–78.

HANSEN, B., and REHN, G. (1956), 'On wage drift, a problem of money wage dynamics', in *Economic Essays in Honour of Erik Lindahl*, pp. 87–139, Ekonomisk Tidskrift, Stockholm.

HART, B. I., and VON NEWMANN, J. (1942), 'Tabulation of the probabilities for the ratio of the mean square successive difference to the variance', *Annals of Mathematical Statistics*, vol. 13, pp. 207–14.

HICKS, J. R. (1955), 'Economic foundations of wage policy', *Economic Journal*, vol. 65, pp. 389–404.

KLEIN, L. R. (1953), *A Textbook of Econometrics*, Row Peterson & Co.

KLEIN, L. R. (1954), 'The empirical foundation of Keynesian economics', in K. Kurihara (ed.), *Post Keynesian Economics*, Ratger University Press.

KLEIN, L. R., and GOLDBERGER, A. S. (1955), '*An econometric model of the United States: 1929–1952*', North Holland Publishing Co.

MOORE, G. H. (1958), 'Measuring Recessions', *Journal of the American Statistical Association*, vol. 53, pp. 259–316.

PHILLIPS, A. W. (1958), 'The relation between unemployment and the rate of change of money wage rates in the United Kingdom, 1861–1957', *Economica*, vol. 25, pp. 283–99. [Reading 15.]

ROBERTS, B. C. (1958), 'Lessons of a national wages policy', *The Times Review of Industry*, May 1958, pp. 36–7.

THEIL, H. (1953), 'Estimation of parameters of econometric models', *Proceedings of the 28th Session of the International Statistical Institute*, Rome, vol. 34, no. 2, pp. 122–9.

18 O. Eckstein and T. A. Wilson

Money Wages in American Industry

Abridged from O. Eckstein and T. A. Wilson, 'The determination of money wages in American industry', *Quarterly Journal of Economics*, vol. 76 (1962), pp. 379–414.

This paper presents an empirical model to explain the behavior of wages in American manufacturing industry from 1948 to 1960. The wage theory advanced and empirically tested views inflation as a dynamic process different from the traditional pure demand-pull and cost-push theories. Our study focuses on money wages, not on real wages, since the present analysis is to be a building block in a general theory of money wages, costs, and prices in the American economy.

Issues in Wage Determination

Wage determination has been the subject of an immense amount of study and controversy in the last twenty years. Three issues have received particular attention:

1. *The effect of unionization.* Do unions make a difference in wage determination, or is the final result about the same as market forces would produce under perfect competition? It is generally agreed that some particular aspects of the structure of wages among occupations, regions, companies, and industries will be affected, and that the speed of adjustment of wages to disequilibria may be changed; but there is no agreement whether unionism affects the long-run level of average wages.[1]

2. *Economic versus political factors.* If unions are able to exercise some independent influence, does the typical union seek to maximize some economic variable like the income of its members;

1. See the useful survey articles on these issues by Kerr and Reynolds (1957). See particularly Friedman (1951).

or is it primarily a political organization in which the leadership strives to assure the survival and strength of the organization and to keep the rank and file content?[2]

3. *The significance of product versus factor market conditions.* If economic variables are important, is it the labor market or the product market which determines wages? According to classical supply-and-demand analysis, only conditions in the labor market (in part, reflecting the derived demand for labor) determine wages. Thus, if the product demand is high yet the labor market loose because of technological change or an expansion of the labor force, wages should not rise. On the other hand, the collective bargaining process provides new routes for the structure and the prosperity of the product market to exert an influence.[3]

No attempt is made here to construct a comprehensive theory of wages. Our efforts are limited to providing sufficient empirical hypotheses to account for the changes in industrial wages for the period of our analysis. Some limited conclusions will be drawn from our general findings about the above competing theories, though our major goal is not to enter the lists of past controversies, but rather to integrate wage determination into the general body of empirical macroeconomics, using simple, but realistic, microeconomic assumptions.

The analysis proceeds as follows: first, five hypotheses about economic and institutional aspects of wage determination are advanced. Second, the significance of the economic variables is tested by time series regressions which are so formulated as to incorporate the institutional hypotheses. Third, cross-section analyses are used to search for significant structural variables,

2. The classic references remain Dunlop (1950), and Ross (1948).

3. Dunlop (1950), chapters 5 and 6. Also see his Oxford Lecture, 'Wages Policy and General Economic Policy', in which profits and the cost of living are advanced as the chief determinants of key wage changes, May 1958 (unpublished). Reynolds (1951, p. 231) also stresses the product market, particularly prices of the product. While these issues have been discussed within the context of unionized industries, their importance extends to some unorganized industries as well. Factor immobility, ignorance of job opportunities, non-maximizing behavior by firms and workers, and other imperfections may lead to deviations from the classical mechanism, and consequently raise the question of the significance of variables other than the supplies of and demands for labor.

such as unionization and concentration, and to provide an additional test of the main theory. The basic data of the analysis are for two-digit industries in manufacturing, 1948–60, with some recourse to both finer and cruder levels of aggregation.

Hypothesis 1 (Institutional): Wage Rates are Set by a Bargaining Process

In much of modern industry, wage rates are determined by contracts reached through collective bargaining, a process which differs mechanically from the classical supply–demand adjustment processes. A theory of wages requires at least a primitive model of the bargaining process, and of the institutional, political, and economic forces which it reflects.

No new formal bargaining theory will be advanced here, nor will we apply any of the recent theories, such as those of Zeuthen, Nash, Harsanyi, Schelling or Pen,[4] except to draw on them for general concepts. We view the problem in terms of the utility functions of union leaders and corporate managements, particularly with respect to 1. wage settlements of different amounts, 2. the cost of a strike, and 3. the cost of losing a strike.

Hypothesis 2 (Economic): Both Product and Labor Market Factors Influence Wage Determination

With labor and product market factors influencing the costs of settlements and of strikes to the bargaining participants, variables pertaining to both markets must affect wage determination. Thus, a union's utility function with respect to the size of settlements will shift with economic conditions. Members expect large settlements in good times and make it impossible for union leaders to settle for less. The loss of jobs produced by the wage increases is likely to be greater when unemployment is high, since the degree of control over the labor supply by the union is likely to be weaker when employers find it easy to get non-union labor, or to shift the work to regions that are not organized;

4. In a general way, our model resembles that of Pen (1952). See also Pen (1958), in which he suggests that bargaining theory be used to isolate strategic variables for statistical analysis. Pen there favors unemployment and consumer prices, although he also mentions profits as a factor.

further, the disutility of any given employment effect is greater since the probability of the laid-off workers being absorbed elsewhere in the industry is smaller. Finally, non-wage benefits, particularly strengthened job security and improvements in the union's security as bargaining agent, are relatively more important under such conditions and unions will be willing to trade off wage gains for them.

Similarly, the disutility to management of large settlements varies with economic conditions. The share of any settlement which is paid out of profits rather than out of higher prices depends upon the elasticity of demand for the product. This elasticity depends upon the degree of tightness in the product market. When demand is high and the market is considered tight, firms have little concern that they will lose sales to their rivals; when demand is low and excess inventories hang over the market, prices cannot be easily raised and wage increases are more likely to come out of profits.

Where 'full cost' or 'target return' pricing is used, this relation is strengthened. In periods of high demand, price is likely to be below profit-maximizing levels and informal rationing may prevail. A wage rise will then be passed on with little or no loss of sales, and may even provide the opportunity for moving closer to a profit-maximizing price position. In periods of low demand, price is likely to be above the profit-maximizing level and a wage increase will cut into profits either by absorption or, if passed on, by loss of sales.

The disutility of sharing profits with employees through higher wages also varies with the level of profits. When profits are high and dividends and other financial requirements easily met, it costs management little to give away some of the profit; when profits are low, encroachment of wages on profits increases the risk of management's having to disappoint stockholders' dividend expectations and generally complicates management's financial problems. Thus, both the share of wage increases likely to come out of profits and the amount of discomfort that management experiences from any given loss of profits vary with economic conditions.

The cost of being tough in bargaining and running the risk of a strike also varies with economic factors, though the effects are mixed. In good times, when operating rates are high, the loss of profits during a strike is great; on the other hand, in many situations the hazard of losing customers to competitors is greater when the product market is not prosperous and competition is keener. On the union side, the loss of payrolls is greater in good times, but the employees may be better able to stand the loss. The hazard of losing the work to non-union employees is also greater in bad times.

The probability of a union winning a strike is unambiguously related to economic conditions in the two markets. The pressure on the companies to settle the strike is particularly great when supplies are short. Major customers exert increasing pressure as the strike interferes with their own operations and begins to affect their sales. The ability of the union to withstand a long strike depends among other things on its financial resources and the financial position of its membership, both of which are greater in good times than in bad.

Finally, economic conditions influence the cost of losing a strike to the two sides. In bad times when a union loses a strike, its position as a bargaining agent, which after all is its main function as an institution, is seriously threatened and it will try not to run this risk. In good times the companies are less likely to engage in long drawn-out struggles to win strikes since they have little hope of achieving any long-term gains in their relationships with their employees, but run the serious risks of large losses in profits and, perhaps more important, of ruining their everyday relations with the work force upon which they are dependent for efficient production.

The above does not exhaust the relations between economic conditions and collective bargaining, of course. It is merely meant to establish that there are relationships, both for product and factor market variables, and that, on the whole, good market conditions make for large settlements.

Hypothesis 3 (Economic): Two Variables, Profit and Unemployment Rates, are Sufficient to Explain Most of the Variation in the Rate of Increase of Wage Rates

The above discussion suggests that a statistical explanation of wage changes must include some labor and some product-market variables. One might wish to construct an elaborate system incorporating many variables, such as output and its rate of change, new and unfilled orders, profits and their recent history, and, on the labor market side, unemployment and its change, employment change, vacancy and turnover rates, and all of these variables both for local and national markets. However, there are far too few observations in the history since the rise of industrial trade unions for this approach; also, the variables inevitably are highly correlated with each other; nor is it sound methodology to use more than the necessary number of variables. Two variables have, therefore, been singled out, one for each market.

For the labor market, unemployment was chosen.[5] Besides the central role which unemployment plays in determining the division of bargaining power in wage negotiations, it also serves as an appropriate variable in those unorganized labor markets in which the classical supply–demand mechanism applies.[6] All industries contain some unorganized segments, and a statistical analysis must allow for them.

The profit rate was chosen as the strategic variable for the product market. First, it reflects the short-run conditions which affect bargaining power discussed above. Second, it reflects long-run structural characteristics of the product market, such as the degree of monopoly. Finally, although we do not attribute great significance to equity factors in wage determination, the desire of unions to maintain labor's share in industry income and, hence, to insist on large wage increases when profits are high is certainly a real factor.

Hypothesis 4 (Institutional): Wage Determination in a Group of Heavy Industries is Interdependent

Since 1948, wages in several industries, which might be characterized as heavy industries, moved almost identically. All of these

5. For evidence of the high correlation between unemployment and other labor market variables, see Knowles and Kalachek (1961).

6. Ideally, unemployment should be supplemented by measures of excess demand, such as job vacancy figures. See Dow and Dicks-Mireaux (1958), for an index using both unemployment and vacancy figures.

industries are high-wage industries, have strong industrial unions, typically consist of large corporations that possess considerable market power, and are geographically centred in the Midwestern industrial heartland of the continent. For our statistical analysis, the group was defined to include these two-digit industries: rubber, stone clay and glass, primary metals, fabricated metals, non-electrical machinery, electrical machinery, transportation equipment, and instruments. We call this group the 'key group'. This list does not define the group perfectly; in each of these two-digit industries some segments do not belong in the group, and conversely, some segments of two-digit industries not included should properly be put inside the group. However, the two-digit industry list is sufficiently accurate for the purpose of the statistical analysis.[7]

The industries in the group are interdependent in a number of ways. First, because of the considerable input–output connexions among them, they tend to prosper together. For example, when auto sales are high, rubber, plate glass, and metal fabricating sales are high. When there is much construction, steel and cement fare well. When there is a capital goods boom, machinery, steel, and metal fabricating are prosperous. Second, because of the geographical concentration and perhaps because of some general similarity in the kinds of mechanical skills required, the industries constitute at least a weakly linked labor market. Third, typically a wage pattern is known to exist in these industries. While no one industry is always the leader in establishing this pattern, autos and steel probably play more of a leadership role than the others. But whoever initiates the pattern, it has a very considerable influence on all subsequent settlements in the group. In some instances, the pattern setting and following are quite regular; for example, the cement and aluminium settlements follow the steel settlement, and rubber and plate glass tend to follow the auto settlement.[8]

The political relationships among unions are also close within

7. See Appendix I [not included in this reading] for a re-examination of the *a priori* list in the light of the statistical results.

8. In the latter case, the possibility of the auto companies going into the rubber or plate glass business makes the wage settlements in these supplier industries inevitable very similar to the auto settlement.

this group. Some unions are bargaining agents in several industries. Geographic proximity, including proximity of some large plants, makes the members of different unions aware of each others' settlements, and puts pressure on their leaders to achieve as good a settlement as the rest of the group.[9]

The industries outside the group do not exhibit as close patterns of interdependence, although there are considerable spillovers from the key group. On the whole, they are not so well organized, have lower wages, are dispersed more over the country including the lightly unionized South, and exhibit less interdependence both through input–output connexions and through the labor market. Our statistical hypotheses are also tested for these industries on an individual basis, and in some instances, simple hypotheses, including spillovers, do explain wage behavior. In some other cases, unique factors, such as technological changes, changes in the product mix, or large regional movements of the particular industry produce unusual industry wage patterns.[10]

9. Interdependence of this group has long been recognized by students of labor economics. A fuller account is given by Ross (1957). Ross finds that a group of 'hard-goods' industries, which corresponds rather closely to our key group, received virtually identical wage increases over the period 1939–52. Soffer (1959) has analysed some of the interactions within the group in detail.

Dunlop employs the concept of the 'wage contour'. He defines a contour as a set of bargaining units which are linked via product markets or labor markets, or which have a common labor market organization. Our key group, on these definitions, is a wage contour, and may perhaps be considered the central wage contour in manufacturing. Dunlop stresses the prevalence of these contours all through the economy. Our analysis is confined to manufacturing, which leaves out many of the important wage contours in the economy, and is limited to the two-digit level, at which many smaller contours, even in manufacturing, are not visible.

Ross (1948) speaks of 'orbits of coercive comparison'. The key group appears to be such an orbit, or perhaps should more properly be considered to be two or more linked orbits.

10. As this paper was completed, Maher (1961b) appeared. Maher, on the basis of a detailed analysis of contract terms, also finds the existence of the key group. He explores the interconnexions among the unions in the group and cites the same list of reasons as above. His independently derived list of industries is almost identical with our own, which is reassuring. Maher does not seek to explain the changes in the wage pattern of the group from movements of economic variables.

Hypothesis 5 (Institutional): Wages are Determined in Wage Rounds

The instrument of wage determination in organized industries is the contract that is negotiated between a union and its employers. Contracts have varied from one year to five years.[11] This institutional arrangement has significant implications. It means that the economic conditions prevailing and expected at the time of the negotiations play a particularly important role in wage determination, and this is true whatever theory of wages one chooses to embrace. A statistical investigation which ignores this crucial factor cannot hope to get very successful results.

Levinson (1959, 1960, 1962) has found that during the postwar period contracts were negotiated in a series of wage rounds. Chronologies of contract settlements show a clustering of settlements in time, and, in the case of the key industries, also in the characteristics of the settlements. These rounds have ranged from one to four years. Once the pattern for a round is set in

11. A contract specifies changes in wage rates, not in average hourly earnings, of course. However, recent studies have shown that there has not been much 'wage drift', i.e. changes in hourly straight-time earnings not imposed by contracts, in the United States. See Maher (1961), especially Charts 1 and 2. Maher finds considerable short-run deviations; they are partly caused by variations in overtime and seasonal factors.

We seek to explain a fixed weighted average of the changes in the wage rates paid for specific jobs. Not all wage drift need be eliminated in order to obtain such a wage variable. Wage drift resulting from a more favorable setting of piece rates at the local level is a true rate increase; similarly, wage drift arising from arbitrary upgrading of workers by firms attempting to attract and keep labor is effectively a rate increase.

The wage drift which should be eliminated results from changes in overtime, or changes in the occupational, industrial, geographical, or demographic composition of the sector's work force.

The variable used, straight-time average hourly earnings for two-digit industries, eliminates the effect of overtime and of changes in two-digit industry mix. Since the deviations between industry straight-time earnings and contracted rate increases have been small, the remaining kinds of wage drift must have been relatively unimportant.

Our analysis excludes fringe benefits. There are no data of sufficient detail to include them in our analysis. In the period we studied, they increased more rapidly than wages, but rose especially when wages rose by relatively large amounts. This pattern may be changing with the new emphasis on job security, and analysis in the future may not be able to leave them aside.

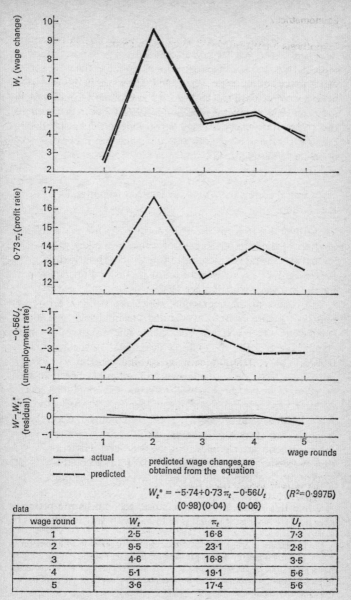

Figure 1 Wage determination in the key group

predicted wage changes are obtained from the equation

$$W_t^* = -5.74 + 0.73\pi_t - 0.56U_t \qquad (R^2 = 0.9975)$$
$$\quad\ \ (0.98)(0.04) \quad\ (0.06)$$

data

wage round	W_t	π_t	U_t
1	2·5	16·8	7·3
2	9·5	23·1	2·8
3	4·6	16·8	3·5
4	5·1	19·1	5·6
5	3·6	17·4	5·6

early key bargains, the movements of wages in the remaining months or years are largely determined until the next round is settled. Thus, to take the most extreme example, the wage settlements in the key industries up to 1958. The wages in this four-year period were determined largely by the economic conditions in 1955 and 1956, not by the recession of 1958. While in this instance the result was a particularly large long-term wage increase because of the timing accident, on some other occasion the opposite result might occur.[12]

The Central Result on Wages: Wage Determination in the Key Group

These hypotheses form the theoretical basis for the statistical analysis of the rate of increase of wages in the key group. The annual average rate of increase of straight-time hourly earnings in the key group was regressed against profits and unemployment for the five wage rounds since 1948.

The results of this regression, which are striking, are represented in Figure 1. Both profits and unemployment are highly significant; the regression coefficients are several times their standard errors, and the multiple determination coefficient R^2 is 0·9975. The correlation between the independent variables is fairly low, partly because after-tax profit rates have been affected by changes in tax rates as well as economic conditions, partly because neither profits nor unemployment are perfectly correlated with general prosperity. Thus, even though the correlation has only two degrees of freedom, the fit is so extraordinary that the coefficients are significant at the 0·99 level. Given the variation in the variables during the period, profits account for 57 per cent of the total explanation, unemployment for the other 43 per cent.

While this result is beyond chance, economists are properly skeptical of any result which is obtained with only two degrees of

12. The length of wage periods is the result of bargaining with sometimes one side, sometimes the other, pressing for a longer contract and willing to pay a price for it. A guessing game about coming economic conditions seems to be involved. We do not attempt to explain the length of the periods; we only identify them.

freedom.[13] Some supporting evidence, based on cross sections and on time series studies of individual industries, will be presented below. But we must stress that the fewness of observations represents historical reality. In the period under study, there were only five or six[14] actual episodes, i.e. five or six points which could be observed. Sample size could conceivably be increased by studying prewar data; however, since industrial unions did not achieve their present position until after World War 2, the same mechanism probably would not apply.

The result is consistent with the hypotheses. Both product and factor market variables are important; profit and unemployment appear to be the crucial variables in wage determination. The bargaining theory is not tested directly, that is, the variables could make their influence felt via some other route. However, the fact that an analysis of the key group by wage rounds gives more significant statistical results than time series analyses of annual data, or cross-section analyses of annual or cyclical period data, lends support to the institutional hypotheses which we have adopted.

Some Supporting Evidence: Time Series for Individual Industries Within the Key Group

If the hypothesis about the significance of the key group for industry wage determination is correct, time series analysis of wages in the individual industries should verify the group result. Using the same wage rounds as above, time series regressions were run for each of the industries, using both the profit and unemployment variables specific to the industry and the same variables for the group as a whole. Table 1 summarizes these regressions.

The statistical explanations of individual industry wage changes are better with group variables than with industry variables. More of the correlation coefficients are statistically significant (8 versus 4 significant coefficients at the 0·95 level, 4 versus none

13. See Appendix I [not included in this reading] for a detailed account of the statistical work.
14. A six-period regression was also fitted. Similar results were obtained. See Appendix I [not included in this reading].

Table 1
Regression Results for Industries in the Key Group*

Industry	Industry variables				Group Variables			
	Constant	Profits	Unemployment	R^2	Constant	Profits	Unemployment	R^2
Rubber	-0.70	0.37 (0.13)	-0.31 (0.26)	0.89	3.25	0.32† (0.06)	-0.90‡ (0.09)	0.99‡
Stone clay and glass	-84.47	2.12‡ (0.69)	9.57 (4.84)	0.94	-5.57	0.72‡ (0.07)	-0.57‡ (0.10)	0.99‡
Primary metals	4.09	-0.44† (0.12)	-1.57† (0.28)	0.98†	-5.94	0.81 (0.35)	-0.79 (0.52)	0.90
Iron and steel	-4.72	0.91† (0.27)	-1.57† (0.37)	0.96†	-11.76	1.18† (0.25)	-0.94 (0.36)	0.97†
Fabricated metals	4.89	0.26 (0.15)	-0.92 (0.46)	0.96†	-4.16	0.62‡ (0.05)	-0.46† (0.08)	0.995‡
Non-electrical machinery	-19.03	1.49 (0.87)	-0.13 (0.73)	0.62	-7.76	0.84† (0.19)	-0.51 (0.27)	0.96†
Electrical machinery	-13.68	0.94 (0.35)	0.16 (0.53)	0.87	-9.25	0.95‡ (0.20)	-0.73 (0.29)	0.97†
Transportation equipment	-5.54	-0.61† (0.10)	-0.51† (0.10)	0.97†	-5.56	0.66‡ (0.09)	-0.39 (0.14)	0.98†
Autos	6.98	0.20 (0.79)	-0.78 (1.25)	0.34	-11.85	1.02‡ (0.04)	-0.50‡ (0.06)	0.999‡
Instruments	-0.57	0.36 (0.25)	-0.03 (0.31)	0.62	-2.01	0.42 (0.24)	-0.05 (0.36)	0.72

* Throughout this study, the significance of R^2 was determined by the standard F ratio test. The significance of the regression coefficients was determined by one-tailed t tests.
† Indicates statistical significance at the 0·95 level.
‡ Indicates statistical significance at the 0·99 level.

at the 0·99 level), as are the regression coefficients (12 versus 8 and 6 versus 0). Group variables are clearly better in the case of rubber, stone clay and glass, fabricated metals, non-electrical machinery, and electrical machinery. In the case of instruments, neither explanation is satisfactory.

In the two biggest industries, primary metals and transportation equipment, separate regressions were obtained for steel and autos. For steel, group variables and industry variables do about equally well. For autos, the group variables explain wages very precisely, while industry variables provide no explanation at all. To some extent, the auto bargain reflects conditions in the group; however, errors in the unemployment estimates may have distorted the equation with industry variables.[15]

In summary, the analysis of individual industry time series supports the key group hypothesis. Profits and unemployment again prove to be significant variables. Group variables give a somewhat better explanation than industry variables, and the regression coefficients for the group variables are similar.[16]

The Significance of Other Variables

A. Productivity

Productivity does not appear to be an important independent variable in wage determination. Levinson found no correlation between interindustry differences in productivity gains and wage increases. The industries with the largest long-run productivity gains, chemicals, tobacco, lumber, and textiles, have not received particularly large wage increases. Although productivity is much discussed in connexion with wage demands, productivity statistics

15. The unknown errors in the synthetic unemployment series reduce the correlations for industry variables. Regressions using durables unemployment and industry profits – both reported figures – produced results intermediate between the results obtained by using all group and all industry variables. See Appendix II [not included in this reading].

16. Comparing the regression coefficients for the industries within the group, one can see that while they are similar, they are not identical. This is not surprising; we know that the wage changes were not completely identical; for example, iron and steel received a somewhat larger increase than electrical machinery (81 per cent versus 66 per cent over the total twelve years), the two extremes in the group.

are available for only a very few industries. And in these cases, the two parties do not agree on the figures.[17]

This is not to say that there are not some indirect connexions between productivity and wages. For example, the rapid growth of output in the early phases of upswings produces large productivity gains and large profits, which in turn affect wage demands. Also aggregate real wages are, of course, chiefly determined by aggregate productivity.

B. Consumer prices

Consumer prices have long been assumed to play an important part in wage determination. Certainly when inflation is rapid, the sense of inequity creates strong member support of union leaders' wage demands or pressure on the leaders to 'catch-up'. Under normal conditions, consumer prices should not be important; they bear no other relation to the bargaining power of either side, nor do they affect the companies' ability to pay.

To test for the significance of consumer prices during the period of our study, several statistical tests were run. (See Table 2.) The change in consumer prices and unemployment provides a statistically significant explanation of wage changes in the key group, though the correlation coefficient is somewhat below that of the profits–unemployment equation. If profits and prices are used as the explanatory variables, profits cease to be a significant variable because of their high collinearity with consumer price changes. At first blush it appears that consumer prices do play a large role.

More detailed examination revealed that this relation is largely based on the extreme observation of the wage round of 1950–51, when the entire price and wage structure of the economy, including material and food prices, got into rapid motion. Certainly the sharp rise of consumer prices contributed to the large wage demands that led to renegotiation of some contracts; escalator clauses were also important.

To analyse the importance of consumer prices under less extreme conditions, the same regressions were run omitting the extreme 1950–51 observation. Table 2 shows that the profit–

17. See Bowen (1960), chapter 5, for further reasons for reaching the same conclusion.

Table 2

Regressions Testing for Effect of Cost-of-Living*

Constant	Profits	Unemployment	Consumer prices	R^2
2·24	0·04 (0·30)		0·94† (0·28)	0·962‡
3·76		−0·14 (0·22)	0·89‡ (0·17)	0·966‡
−5·32	0·72‡ (0·05)	−0·61‡ (0·07)		0·994‡

Extreme Observation of July 1950–July 1951 Omitted

0·58	0·14 (0·45)		0·99† (0·36)	0·838
4·00		−0·17 (0·35)	0·82 (0·54)	0·848
−6·29	0·78† (0·16)	−0·62‡ (0·08)		0·975†

* These results are for the key group for six periods. The weakly defined period 3 was divided at the end of 1953. The regressions were also run on a five-period basis with similar results.

† Indicates statistical significance at the 0·95 level.

‡ Indicates statistical significance at the 0·99 level.

unemployment equation remains statistically significant; the price equations, however, cease to be so, suggesting that consumer prices are not an important influence on wages in conditions other than very rapid price change. In addition, the wage–price regression is biased by the simultaneous effect of wages on prices.

Escalator clauses are one of the possible routes for price effects. However, they can be a substitute for higher hourly wage rates or for fringe benefits and, thus, cannot be considered to be a completely independent factor. Because of the uncertainty of the future movements of the consumer price index during the life of a long-term contract, consumer prices can be an independent influence to the extent that their actual movements differ from what was expected by the bargainers. Thus, the wage increases of

Table 3

Regression Equations for Industries Outside the Key Group

Industry	A: Industry variables				B: Wage spillover and industry unemployment			
	Constant	Profits	Unemployment	R^2	Constant	Key wage	Unemployment	R^2
Food	-6·31	0·88 (0·89)	-0·32 (0·73)	0·19	2·04	0·78† (0·08)	-0·21 (0·14)	0·96†
Tobacco	12·18	-0·79 (0·31)	0·50 (0·18)	0·67	3·07	0·32 (0·19)	0·15 (0·14)	0·49
Textiles	0·05	0·69* (0·31)	-0·70 (0·54)	0·83*	1·83	0·90 (0·46)	-0·57 (0·65)	0·80*
Apparel	9·62	0·56 (0·44)	-1·43* (0·62)	0·60	-1·20	1·16† (0·20)	-0·25 (0·30)	0·94†
Lumber	-1·22	0·35† (0·08)	-0·08 (0·13)	0·88*	4·24	0·44† (0·10)	-0·34* (0·12)	0·87*
Furniture	-2·40	0·70† (0·17)	-0·65 (0·42)	0·89*	-2·52	1·53† (0·32)	-0·17 (0·43)	0·91†
Paper	-6·02	0·72 (0·82)	-0·25 (0·80)	0·57	2·28	0·73† (0·15)	-0·29 (0·20)	0·93†
Printing	8·29	-0·23 (0·53)	-0·12 (0·27)	0·05	4·98	-0·13 (0·41)	-0·15 (0·41)	0·03
Chemicals	-2·05	0·37 (0·38)	0·12 (0·31)	0·20	1·88	0·63* (0·19)	0·04 (0·17)	0·75
Petroleum	16·66	-0·40 (0·97)	-1·05 (2·56)	0·47	-0·58	1·21* (0·33)	-0·25 (0·33)	0·87*
Leather	24·31	-0·77 (0·46)	-0·23 (1·09)	0·54	-0·63	1·00† (0·21)	-0·18 (0·54)	0·88*

Table 3 – continued

Industry	C: Wage spillover and industry profits				D: Wage spillover, industry profits, unemployment				
	Constant	Key wage	Industry profits	R^2	Constant	Key wage change	Industry profits	Unemployment	R^2
Food	0·96	0·76† (0·10)	0·01 (0·23)	0·94†	−0·09	0·76† (0·09)	0·18 (0·21)	−0·27 (0·16)	0·97†
Tobacco	4·45	0·32 (0·22)	−0·04 (0·29)	0·37	9·80	0·21 (0·15)	−0·64 (0·30)	0·43 (0·17)	0·80
Textiles	−6·78	0·74† (0·22)	0·59* (0·18)	0·94†	−5·78	0·71 (0·31)	0·57* (0·22)	−0·10 (0·46)	0·94*
Apparel	−5·81	1·24† (0·13)	0·26 (0·13)	0·96†	−1·99	1·06† (0·09)	0·33* (0·08)	−0·43* (0·14)	0·99†
Lumber	−2·48	−0·07 (0·20)	0·42* (0·14)	0·87†	0·57	0·15 (0·48)	0·24 (0·39)	−0·16 (0·31)	0·88
Furniture	−6·47	1·06† (0·24)	0·36* (0·13)	0·97†	−4·66	0·93* (0·29)	0·37* (0·13)	−0·24 (0·26)	0·98†
Paper	−5·29	0·68† (0·10)	0·42† (0·14)	0·97†	−7·56	0·70† (0·11)	0·52 (0·26)	0·13 (0·26)	0·97†
Printing	5·61	0·02 (0·22)	−0·10 (0·43)	0·01	13·96	−0·31 (0·52)	−0·44 (0·67)	−0·45 (0·64)	0·15
Chemicals	2·99	0·67* (0·22)	−0·06 (0·25)	0·75	2·76	0·66* (0·26)	−0·05 (0·30)	−0·03 (0·20)	0·75
Petroleum	−13·44	1·41† (0·23)	0·56 (0·39)	0·90†	−12·64	1·39† (0·38)	0·54 (0·54)	−0·04 (0·39)	0·90
Leather	0·86	1·01† (0·17)	0·21 (0·18)	0·91†	8·13	0·86† (0·17)	−0·40 (0·19)	−0·81 (0·50)	0·95*

* Indicates statistical significance at the 0·95 level.
† Indicates statistical significance at the 0·99 level.

the wage round 1955–8 certainly were somewhat increased above the amounts bargained for by an unexpectedly large increase in consumer prices; a similar effect may have occurred in 1950–51 (Soffer, 1959b).

In summary, our limited evidence suggests that consumer prices do not play a major role in periods other than extreme price change, although they certainly have a minor influence through escalator clauses.

Wage Determination Outside the Key Group

The profit–unemployment explanation of wage changes was also attempted for the industries outside the key group. (See Table 3.) Since long-term contracts were less important in these industries a seven-period analysis was used, with periods 3 and 4 subdivided.

Regressions using only industry variables are significant at the 0·95 level for just three of the eleven industries. To obtain a successful explanation of wage changes in some of these industries, explicit allowance must be made for spillover from the key industries. A regression with key wages and industry unemployment provides statistically significant explanations for eight of the eleven industries, with four of the explanations significant at the 0·99 level, and similarly for industry profits. Key wages are statistically significant in eight cases; the industry variables are significant in only one and four cases respectively and take on the correct signs in all cases but one in the eight equations. These results are confirmed by a regression using all three independent variables.

Three industries remain without explanation at this stage: chemicals, tobacco, and printing. In chemicals, industrial chemicals belong inside the key group; the rest might yield to analysis at a more detailed level. Printing, a very highly organized industry on a craft union basis, provides a useful illustration that high correlations are not inevitable in the analysis of wages. It is not impossible to get correlations as low as 0·01!

Even in the industries where the regressions are significant, they do not account for all the wage changes by any means. In some of the industries, for example, increases in the minimum wage clearly led to jumps in the average wage in 1956.

Results of Cross-Section Analysis

In addition to the analyses of wage changes over time, the variation of wage changes among industries was studied. Because time series are influenced by cyclical developments and other short-run influences, and, more importantly, because the structure of labor and product markets has changed very little in the postwar period, one turns to cross sections with the hope of identifying the influence of structural factors such as unionization or concentration. Previous students of this problem have placed most of their emphasis on cross-section analysis.

In the event, however, these hopes are disappointed: cross-section analysis yields few positive results. Nor is this surprising in the light of the time-series findings. The presence of groupings and spillovers, even among industries with different structural characteristics, makes for a uniformity of wage changes which leaves very little variation among industries to be analysed. An analysis of the variance of wage changes shows that the interperiod variance was 5·44 while the interindustry variance was only 0·57. Whatever associations between wage changes and structural characteristics there may be, even when statistically identified, would be understated because the spillovers pull the wage structure toward uniformity. In addition, one should not expect to discover the time-series properties of the system – which are necessary for prediction and policy – from cross-section data alone (see Kuh, 1959).

On the other hand, cross sections also have the important advantages of more degrees of freedom and absence of serial correlation. Further, by being relatively free of short-run effects, cross sections may permit the estimation of long-run structural coefficients.

Two sets of cross sections were run. The first is a moving cross section, in which all the time-series data and cross-section data are pooled, and in which one set of dummy variables is introduced to measure the effects of time, and another set is used to measure the effects of structural characteristics associated with specific industries. Table 4 summarizes this analysis. It shows that the industry dummy variables are not significant and contribute so little to the correlation that the multiple correlation coefficient adjusted for loss of degrees of freedom is not increased by the introduction. The same result holds for unemployment, although in this instance the absence of the relationship may be due to errors in the industry estimates and also to the differences among industries in the amount of normal frictional and seasonal unemployment. Profits, on the other hand, are a significant variable

Table 4

Regression Analysis of Pooled Cross-Section – Two-Digit Industries, Five Wage Rounds

Constant	Profits	Unemployment	Time* dummies	Industry dummies	Corrected† R^2
−0·58	+0·46** (0·05)				0·50**
0·28	+0·43** (0·05)	−0·12 (0·09)			0·51**
1·41	+0·21** (0·05)	+0·002 (0·07)	−0·81 +3·88** +0·63 +0·74		0·74**
1·65	+0·22** (0·08)	+0·05 (0·09)	−0·84¶ +3·89** +0·72 +0·75	‡§	0·74**
−0·91	+0·58** (0·06)	−0·19¶ (0·10)		‖	0·56**

* Values for the periods 1–4; the dummy for period 5 is the constant.

† Corrected for degrees of freedom so that the successive R^2 can be compared.

‡ Eighteen industry dummies, one for each industry, were used. None was statistically significant.

§ Concentration and unionization dummies were also tested in place of the industry dummies. The coefficients (and their significance) for profits, unemployment, and the time dummies were little affected. Concentration dummies were not significant, but unionization was significant at the 0·95 level.

‖ When the industry dummies were introduced without the time dummies, one of the eighteen coefficients was significant at the 0·95 level, which one would expect by chance.

¶ Indicates statistical significance at the 0·95 level.

** Indicates statistical significance at the 0·99 level.

even when the time dummies bear the weight of most of the cyclical influences, and even though absolute rates of return are used as the variable without any normalizing adjustment to reflect interindustry differences, such as differences in risk premia or capital intensities. When concentration and unionization were used instead of the industry dummies, unionization was significant, concentration was not.

Cross-section analyses for each wage round were also run for several different equations. (See Table 5.) To characterize these results rather generally, statistically significant relationships were obtained for two to three of the five periods and very few regression coefficients were significant. However, many of the coefficients were substantially larger than their standard errors and some significance attaches to the results as a whole.

To test for the significance of concentration in the product market, a dummy variable was introduced into the regressions. This variable had the value of one if the concentration index [18] for the two-digit industry was over 50 per cent, and zero otherwise. [19] It is not statistically significant and has a negative sign in the first, second, and fifth periods. The coefficients for profits are more consistent, and are almost always larger than their standard error. While some of the differences in industry profits are due to differences in the degree of concentration, and thus concentration has an indirect influence on wages, our cross-section analysis yields no evidence that concentration has an independent impact on wages, other than through its effect on profits. Of course,

18. The concentration indices used were those computed and published by Levinson in his study paper. His two-digit concentration index measures the per cent of the shipments in the industry originating in component four-digit industries in which the top eight firms produced at least 50 per cent of the shipments.

19. This is a superior variable to the concentration index itself. The concentration indices follow a bimodal distribution and no real significance attaches to the variations within the two groups. For example, petroleum refining has a concentration index of 99 per cent and primary metals of 81 per cent, yet it is not clear that market power is greater in petroleum refining than in primary metals. As a test, however, regressions were also run using concentration indices. These yielded extremely small regression coefficients, which, with one exception, were only a small fraction of their standard error; in the fourth period the concentration ratio is significant at the 99 per cent level.

Table 5
Cross-Section Regressions, Separate Periods

Period	Constant	Profits	Union dummy	Concentration dummy	R^2	Corrected R^2
1	−0·07	0·28* (0·13)			0·20	0·11
2	6·48	0·14 (0·10)			0·10	−0·01
3	0·90	0·33† (0·09)			0·46†	0·40†
4	1·92	0·23† (0·07)			0·37†	0·30†
5	2·19	0·13* (0·07)			0·19	0·09
1	0·15	0·21 (0·20)	0·68 (1·38)		0·22	0·07
2	6·62	0·16 (0·11)	−0·73 (0·97)		0·13	−0·03
3	1·74	0·10 (0·09)	1·84† (0·51)		0·70†	0·64†
4	2·62	0·08 (0·08)	1·36† (0·42)		0·62†	0·55†
5	2·62	0·03 (0·08)	0·82* (0·39)		0·37*	0·25*
1	−0·16	0·30* (0·15)		−0·31 (0·95)	0·21	0·06
2	6·49	0·14 (0·11)		0·00 (0·89)	0·10	−0·07
3	1·06	0·30† (0·10)		0·29 (0·51)	0·47*	0·37*
4	2·67	0·13 (0·09)		0·83* (0·42)	0·49†	0·40†
5	1·65	0·20 (0·14)		−0·34 (0·63)	0·20	0·05
1	0·09	0·21 (0·20)	1·01 (1·53)	−0·57 (1·05)	0·23	0·03
2	6·80	0·15 (0·11)	−0·99 (1·16)	0·46 (1·05)	0·14	−0·09
3	1·67	0·11 (0·10)	1·92† (0·56)	−0·19 (0·42)	0·70†	0·63†
4	3·00	0·03 (0·08)	1·18† (0·42)	0·52 (0·37)	0·67†	0·58†
5	1·97	0·11 (0·14)	0·84* (0·40)	−0·42 (0·57)	0·39	0·22

* Indicates statistical significance at the 0·95 level.
† Indicates statistical significance at the 0·99 level.

because of the general imprecision of the cross-section regressions, no firm conclusions can be drawn.

To test for the effect of unionization on wage increases, a dummy variable was formulated which was given the value one if the union contracts covered more than 60 per cent of the workers, and zero otherwise. Significant coefficients were obtained for three out of five periods. A negative sign is found for the period 1950–51 – a period of rapid inflation when, according to Friedman (1951, pp. 204, 217–28), one might expect unionization to retard wage increases.

The results on unionization are of limited significance, however. When the usual measure, the percentage of workers organized (Douty, 1960, p. 345), is used, the results do not stand up. While we believe the dummy variable to be a sounder theoretical construct, the significance of the hypothesis should survive a minor change in conceptual definition. The failure to find consistent positive evidence for the effect of unionization in these cross sections does not mean that the effect is absent in the real world. Because of the spillovers, any wage increases caused by unionization would permeate much of the rest of the wage structure in other industries and, therefore, would not appear in cross-section comparisons.[20]

In summary, the cross-section analyses yield rather limited positive results because most of the variation in wages is associated with changes over time, not with differences among industries, and because of the prevalence of spillovers. To discover the structural properties of the time series equations, that is, to discover the explanations of the magnitude of the regression coefficients associated with time series, other research techniques must be used and, in the end, even these cannot prove wholly successful. Long-run historical analysis, covering periods in which there were substantial changes in the structure of product and factor markets in the economy, can provide significant material on this question. On the other hand, when long periods are chosen, so much of the total situation changes that it is very difficult to isolate the impact of any one structural change. A more institutional, qualitative approach may also prove useful.

20. This point was made by Slichter (1954) in commenting on the Friedman hypothesis that unions have little long-run effect on wages.

Is there a Phillips Curve for the United States?

Observers[21] have puzzled over the wide scatter of points around a Phillips curve for the United States, the curve relating wage changes to unemployment. Our findings help explain this looseness of fit. Since profits and unemployment are both important variables, and are not highly intercorrelated, one cannot expect a curve plotting wage changes against only one of the explanatory variables to fit the data well. Further, the wage round mechanism is missed by a plotting of annual data. In addition, our results suggest that the coefficients applying in different industries are not uniform and that the spillover from the key group to other industries is important; consequently, the change in average wage levels in the economy depends on the distribution of profits and unemployment among industries.

These findings imply that there is no one critical level of unemployment which is consistent with 'noninflationary' wage increases. If profits are high, a much higher level of unemployment is necessary than if profits are low.

Summary and Concluding Comment

We have presented a statistical analysis of wage changes in manufacturing from 1948 to 1960. We find that if the analysis is formulated in terms which reflect important institutional characteristics of the wage determination process, standard economic variables account for the bulk of the wage changes which have occurred. These characteristics are: first, wages are primarily determined in bargains between unions and employers; second, wages are determined in wage rounds; third, wages in a group of heavy industries, which we call the key group, move virtually identically because of the economic, political, and institutional interdependence among the companies and the unions in these industries. When these factors are incorporated into the statistical framework, wages in the key group are explained by the profit rates and the unemployment rates in the group. Wages in some

21. See Samuelson and Solow (1960) for a discussion of the Phillips curve applied to American data. Also, see Schultze (1959).

other industries outside this group are largely determined by spill-over effects of the key group wages and economic variables applicable to the industry; three industries defy explanation.

The institutional hypotheses – about bargains, the key group, and the wage rounds – were advanced to permit discovery of the relationships among the economic variables. Our statistical tests were not designed to test these hypotheses directly, but they do give some evidence. The existence of the key group is supported by the superiority of individual industry regressions with group variables over those with industry variables. Some confirmation of our choice of wage periods and the existence of the wage round mechanisms is provided by the much closer statistical relationships obtained by their use rather than by use of annual data.

Our findings can be related to the issues posed at the beginning of the paper. First, we have only weak evidence that unionization affects the long-run level of wages. But we have strong evidence that the economic variables enter into wage determination differently than they would under pure supply and demand mechanisms, with both product and factor market conditions influencing the outcome of the bargaining. We also find that both economic and political factors play a role in wage determination. Some previous attempts at synthesis stressed that economic factors set outer limits to settlements, and political and bargaining elements are determining within that range.[22] Political factors enter our theory in a different way: their importance is implicit in the hypotheses of the key group and the wage round. They also help determine the lag structure and the parameters of the economic equations, and thus influence the path of wages.

22. For one such attempt at synthesis, see Reder (1952).

References

BOWEN, W. G. (1960), *The Wage–Price Issue: A Theoretical Analysis*, Princeton University Press.

DOUTY, H. M. (1960), 'Collective bargaining coverage in factory employment, 1958', *Monthly Labor Review*, vol. 83, no. 4, pp. 345–49.

DOW, J. C. R., and DICKS-MIREAUX, L. A. (1958), 'The excess demand for labour: A study of conditions in Great Britain, 1946–56', *Oxford Economic Papers*, vol. 10, pp. 1–33.

DUNLOP, J. T. (1950), *Wage Determination under Trade Unions* (2nd edn), New York; Kelley.

FRIEDMAN, M. (1951), 'Some comments on the significance of labour unions for wage policy', in D. McCord Wright (ed.) *The Impact of the Union*, Harcourt, pp. 204–34.

KERR, C., and REYNOLDS, L. G. (1957), 'Wage relationships – the comparative impact of market and power forces', in J. T. Dunlop (ed.), *The Theory of Wage Determination*, Macmillan.

KNOWLES, J. W., and KALACHEK, E. (1961), *Higher Unemployment Rates, 1957–1960: Structural Transformation or Inadequate Demand*, Subcommittee on Economic Statistics of Joint Economic Committee, U.S. Congress.

KUH, E. (1959), 'The validity of cross-sectionally estimated behavior equations in time series application', *Econometrica*, vol. 27, pp. 197–214.

LEVINSON, H. M. (1959), *Staff Report on Employment, Growth and Price Levels*, Joint Economic Committee, U.S. Congress, pp. 150–56.

LEVINSON, H. M. (1960), 'Postwar movement of prices and wages in manufacturing industries', Study Paper No. 21, *Study of Employment, Growth and Price Levels*, Joint Economic Committee, U.S. Congress.

LEVINSON, H. M. (1962), *Collective Bargaining in the Steel Industry: Pattern Setter or Pattern Follower?*, Institute of Industrial Relations, University of Michigan.

MAHER, J. E. (1961a), 'Wages: The pattern of wage movements in the United States since 1945 – Its meaning and significance', *Review of Economics and Statistics*, vol. 43, pp. 277–82.

MAHER, J. E. (1961b), 'The wage pattern in the United States, 1946–1957', *Industrial and Labor Relations Review*, vol. 15, pp. 1–20.

PEN, J. (1952), 'A general theory of bargaining', *American Economic Review*, vol. 42, pp. 24–42.

PEN, J. (1958), 'Wage determination revisited', *Kyklos*, vol. 11, no. 1, pp. 1–28.

REDER, M. W. (1952), 'The theory of union wage policy', *Review of Economics and Statistics*, vol. 34, pp. 34–45.

REYNOLDS, L. G. (1951), *The Structure of Labor Markets*, Harper.

ROSS, A. M. (1948), *Trade Union Wage Policy*, University of California Press.

ROSS, A. M. (1957), 'The external wage structure', in G. H. Taylor and F. Pierson (eds.), *New Concepts in Wage Determination*, McGraw-Hill, pp. 173–205.

SAMUELSON, P. A., and SOLOW, R. M. (1960), 'Analytical aspects of anti-inflation policy', *American Economic Review*, vol. 50, pp. 177–94.

SCHULTZE, C. L. (1959), 'Recent inflation in the United States', Study Paper No. 1, *Study of Employment, Growth and Price Levels*, Joint Economic Committee, U.S. Congress.

SLICHTER, S. H. (1954), 'Do the wage-fixing arrangements in the American labor market have an inflationary bias?' *American Economic Review*, vol. 44, no. 2, pp. 322–46. Reprinted in S. H. Slichter, *Potentials of the American Economy*, Harvard University Press.

SOFFER, B. (1959a) 'On union rivalries and the differentiation of wage patterns', *Review of Economics and Statistics*, vol. 41, pp. 53–60.

SOFFER, B. (1959b), 'The effects of recent long-term wage agreements on general wage level movements: 1950–1957', *Quarterly Journal of Economics*, vol. 73, pp. 36–60.

Further Reading

Abbreviations:

A.E.R. – American Economic Review; *E.J.* – Economic Journal; *Ec.* – Economica; *J.P.E.* – Journal of Political Economy; *J.R.S.S.* – Journal of the Royal Statistical Society; *M.S.* – Manchester School of Economics and Social Studies; *O.E.P.* – Oxford Economic Papers; *Q.J.E.* – Quarterly Journal of Economics; *R.E. Stat.* – Review of Economics and Statistics; *R.E. Stud.* – Review of Economic Studies.

1. A. ANDO and F. MODIGLIANI, 'The relative stability of monetary velocity and the investment multiplier', *A.E.R.*, vol. 65 (1965), pp. 693–728.
2. A. ANDO and F. MODIGLIANI, 'Rejoinder', *A.E.R.*, vol. 65 (1965), pp. 786–90.
3. G. L. BACK and A. ANDO, 'The redistributional effects of inflation', *R.E. Stat.*, vol. 39 (1957), pp. 1–13.
4. M. J. BAILEY, 'The welfare cost of inflationary finance', *J.P.E.*, vol. 64 (1956), pp. 93–110.
5. M. J. BAILEY, 'Administered prices in the American economy', *The Relationship of Prices to Economic Stability and Growth*, Compendium of Papers submitted by Panelists before the Joint Economic Committee, 85th Congress, 2nd Session, Washington, 1958.
6. R. J. BALL, 'Cost inflation and the income velocity of money: A comment', *J.P.E.*, vol. 68 (1960), no. 3, pp. 288–301.
7. R. J. BALL and P. S. DRAKE, 'The impact of credit control on consumer spending in the United Kingdom, 1957–1961', *R.E. Stud.*, vol. 30 (1963), pp. 181–94.
8. R. J. BALL, *Inflation and the Theory of Money*, Allen and Unwin, 1964.
9. R. J. BHATIA, 'Profits and the rate of change in money earnings in the United States, 1935–1959', *Ec.*, vol. 29 (1962), pp. 255–62.
10. R. J. BHATIA, 'Unemployment and the rate of change in money earnings in the United States, 1900–1958', *Ec.*, vol. 28 (1961), pp. 285–96.
11. R. G. BODKIN, *The Wage–Price–Productivity Nexus*, Cowles Foundation, 1966.
12. W. G. BOWEN, *The Wage–Price Issue: A Theoretical Analysis*, Princeton University Press, 1960.
13. A. J. BROWN, *The Great Inflation, 1939–51*, Oxford University Press, 1955.
14. J. W. CONARD, 'The causes and consequences of inflation', in *Inflation, Growth and Employment*, A Series of Research Studies Prepared for the Commission on Money and Credit, Prentice-Hall, 1964.

15. J. CORINA, *The Development of Incomes Policy*, London; Institute
    Personnel Management, 1966.

16. L. A. DICKS-MIREAUX, and J. C. R. DOW, 'The determinant
    wage inflation: United Kingdom, 1946–56', *J.R.S.S.*, series A, vol
    (1959), part 2, pp. 145–84.

17. J. C. R. DOW, 'Analysis of the generation of price inflation',
    vol. 8 (1956), pp. 252–301.

18. J. C. R. DOW, and L. A. DICKS-MIREAUX, 'The excess der
    labour: A study of conditions in Great Britain, 1946–56', *O.*
    10 (1958), pp. 1–33.

19. J. C. R. DOW, *The Management of the British Econom*
    Cambridge University Press, 1964.

20. J. DUESENBERRY, 'Mechanics of inflation', *R.E. Stat.*, v
    pp. 144–9.

21. A. C. ENTHOVEN, 'Monetary disequilibria and the
    inflation', *E.J.*, vol. 60 (1950), pp. 256–70.

22. M. FRIEDMAN, 'Discussion of the inflationary gap'
    (1942), pp. 314–20.

23. M. FRIEDMAN, 'Some comments on the significanc
    for wage policy', in D. M. Wright (ed.) *Impact of th*
    1951, pp. 204–34.

24. M. FRIEDMAN, 'The quantity theory of money – A
    Friedman (ed.), *Studies in the Quantity Theory of M*
    of Chicago Press, 1956. [Reprinted in the companion vol
    Monetary Theory, edited by R. W. Clower, Penguin Book

25. M. FRIEDMAN, *A Program for Monetary Stability*, Ford
    Press, 1960.

26. M. FRIEDMAN, *Inflation: Causes and Consequences*, A
    House, 1963.

27. M. FRIEDMAN, and D. MEISELMAN, 'Reply to Ando a
    and to De Prando and Mayer', *A.E.R.*, vol. 65 (1965), p

28. M. FRIEDMAN and D. MEISELMAN, 'The relative stability of monetary
    velocity and the investment multiplier in the United States, 1897–1958'
    in Commission on Money and Credit, *Stabilisation Policies*, Prentice-
    Hall, 1963, pp. 165–268.

29. J. K. GALBRAITH, 'Market structure and stabilisation policy', *R.E.
    Stat.*, vol. 39 (1957), pp. 124–33.

30. R. M. GOODWIN, 'The multiplier' in S. E. Harris (ed.), *The New
    Economics*, New York; Knopf, 1947, pp. 482–502.

31. G. HABERLER, 'Wage policy and inflation', in P. Bradley (ed.), *The
    Public Stake in Union Power*, University of Virginia Press, 1959, pp.
    63–85.

32. A. J. HAGGER, *The Theory of Inflation: A Review*, Melbourne Univer-
    sity Press, 1964.

33. D. C. HAGUE (ed.), *Inflation*. Proceedings of the Conference of the
    International Economic Association held at Elsinore, 1959, Macmillan,
    1962.

Further Reading

34. B. HANSEN, *A Study in the Theory of Inflation*, Macmillan, 1951.

35. B. HANSEN and G. REHN, 'On wage drift: A problem of money wage dynamics', in *Economic Essays in Honour of Erik Lindahl*, Ekonomisk Tidskrift, Stockholm, 1956, pp. 87–139.

36. J. R. HICKS, 'Economic foundations of wage policy', *E.J.*, vol. 65 (1955), pp. 389–404.

37. F. D. HOLZMAN, 'Escalation and its use to mitigate the inequities of inflation', *Inflation, Growth and Employment*, Commission on Money and Credit, 1964, pp. 177–229.

8. H. G. JOHNSON, 'Monetary theory and policy', *A.E.R.*, vol. 52 (1962), pp. 335–84.

. H. G. JOHNSON, 'A survey of theories of inflation' in H. G. Johnson, *Essays in Monetary Economics*, Allen and Unwin, 1967, Chapter 3.

J. JOHNSTON, 'The price level under full employment in the United Kingdom' in D. C. Hague (ed.), *Price Formation in Various Economies*, Proceedings of a Conference held by the International Economic Association, Macmillan, 1967, Chapter 6.

N. KALDOR, 'Inflation and economic growth', *Ec.*, vol. 26 (1959), no. 3, p. 287–98.

J. KLEIN, 'German money and prices, 1932–44', in M. Friedman (ed.), *Studies in the Quantity Theory of Money*, University of Chicago Press, 56, Chapter 3.

R. KLEIN and R. BODKIN, 'Empirical aspects of trade-offs among ee goals: High-level employment, price stability and economic wth' in *Inflation, Growth and Employment*, Commission on Money Credit, Prentice-Hall, 1964, Chapter 7.

M. LERNER, 'Inflation in the Confederacy' in M. Friedman (ed.), *ies in the Quantity Theory of Money*, University of Chicago Press,

LERNER, and J. MARQUAND, 'Workshop bargaining, wage drift roductivity in the British engineering industry', *M.S.*, vol. 30 (1962), pp. 15–60.

46. R. G. LIPSEY, 'The relation between unemployment and the rate of change of money wage rates in the United Kingdom, 1862–1957: A further analysis', *Ec.*, vol. 27 (1960), pp. 1–31.

47. R. G. LIPSEY and M. D. STEUER, 'The relation between profits and wage rates', *Ec.*, vol. 28 (1961), pp. 137–55.

48. M. C. LOVELL, 'A Keynesian analysis of forced saving', Cowles Foundation manuscript CF20823, New Haven, 1962.

49. H. F. LYDALL, 'Inflation and the earnings gap', *O.I.S.*, vol. 20, no. 3 (1958), pp. 285–304. [Reprinted in the companion volume *The Labour Market*, edited by B. J. McCormick and E. Owen Smith, 1968.]

50. A. MARGET, 'Inflation: Some lessons of recent foreign experience', *A.E.R. Proc.*, vol. 50 (1960), pp. 205–11.

51. J. MARQUAND, 'Earnings drift in the United Kingdom 1948–57', *O.E.P.*, vol. 12 (1960), pp. 77–104.

52. E. V. MORGAN, 'Is inflation inevitable?' *E.J.*, vol. 76 (1966), pp. 1–15.

53. W. A. MORTON, 'Keynesianism and inflation', *J.P.E.*, vol. 59 (1951), pp. 258–65.

54. O.E.E.C., *The Problem of Rising Prices* by W. Fellner, M. Gilbert, B. Hansen, R. Kahn, F. Lutz, P. de Wolff, O.E.E.C., Paris, 1961.

55. F. W. PAISH, *Studies in an Inflationary Economy*, London; Macmillan, 1962.

56. A. W. PHILLIPS, 'Employment, inflation, growth', *Ec.*, vol. 29 (1962), pp. 1–17.

57. J. D. PITCHFORD, 'Cost and demand elements in the inflationary process', *R.E. Stud.*, vol. 24 (1957), pp. 139–48.

58. J. D. PITCHFORD, 'The inflationary effects of excess demand for goods and excessive real income claims', *O.E.P.*, vol. 13 (1961), pp. 59–71.

59. M. W. REDER, 'The theoretical problems of a national wage–price policy', *Canadian Journal of Economics and Political Science*, vol. 14 (1948), no. 1, pp. 46–61.

60. W. M. REDER, 'The theory of union wage policy', *R.E. Stat.*, vol. 34 (1952), pp. 34–45.

61. L. G. REYNOLDS, 'The impact of collective bargaining on the wage structure in the United States' in J. T. Dunlop (ed.), *The Theory of Wage Determination*, Macmillan, 1957, Chapter 13.

62. J. ROBINSON, *Essays in the Theory of Employment*, Macmillan, 1937.

63. J. ROBINSON, *Economics – An Awkward Corner*, Allen and Unwin, 1966.

64. D. J. ROBERTSON, *Growth, Wages, Money*, Cambridge University Press, 1961.

65. G. ROUTH, 'The relation between unemployment and the rate of change of money wage rates: A comment', *Ec.*, vol. 26 (1959), pp. 299–316.

66. W. SALANT, 'The inflationary gap: Meaning and significance for policy making', *A.E.R.*, vol. 32 (1942), pp. 308–13.

67. P. A. SAMUELSON and R. M. SOLOW, 'Analytical aspects of anti-inflationary policy', *A.E.R.*, vol. 50 (1960), pp. 177–94.

68. T. and A. A. SCITOVSKY, 'Inflation versus unemployment: An examination of their effects' in *Inflation, Growth and Employment*, Commission on Money and Credit, Prentice-Hall, 1964.

69. D. SEERS, 'A theory of inflation and growth in under-developed economies, based on Latin-American experience', *O.E.P.*, vol. 14 (1962), pp. 173–95.

70. R. T. SELDEN, 'Cost-push versus demand-pull inflation, 1955–57', *J.P.E.*, vol. 67 (1959), pp. 1–20.

71. R. T. SELDEN, 'Monetary velocity in the United States' in M. Friedman (ed.), *Studies in the Quantity Theory of Money*, University of Chicago Press, 1956, Chapter 5.

72. C. G. F. SIMKIN, 'Notes on the theory of inflation', *R.E. Stud.*, vol. 52 (1952–3), pp. 143–51.

73. H. W. SINGER, 'Wage policy in full employment', *E.J.*, vol. 57 (1947), pp. 438–55.

Further Reading

74. A. SMITHIES, 'Behaviour of money national income under inflationary conditions', *Q.J.E.*, vol. 56 (1942), pp. 113–29.

75. A. SMITHIES, 'The control of inflation', *R.E. Stat.*, vol. 39 (1957), pp. 272–83.

76. W. THORP and R. QUANDT, *The New Inflation*, McGraw-Hill, 1959.

77. H. A. TURNER, 'Inflation and wage differentials in Great Britain' in J. T. Dunlop (ed.), *The Theory of Wage Determination*, Macmillan, 1957. [Reprinted in the companion volume *The Labour Market*, edited by B. J. McCormick and E. Owen Smith, Penguin Books, 1968.]

78. R. TURVEY, 'Period analysis and inflation', *Ec.*, vol. 16 (1949), pp. 218–28.

79. R. TURVEY, 'Some aspects of the theory of inflation in a closed economy', *E.J.*, vol. 61 (1951), pp. 532–43.

80. L. ULMAN, 'Marshall and Friedman on union strength', *R.E. Stat.*, vol. 37 (1955), pp. 384–401.

81. S. WEINTRAUB, *A General Theory of the Price Level, Output, Income Distribution and Economic Growth*, Chilton Co., 1959.

82. S. WEINTRAUB, *Classical Keynesianism, Monetary Theory and the Price Level*, Chilton Co., 1961.

Acknowledgements

Permission to reproduce the readings in this volume is acknowledged from the following sources:

Reading 1 Macmillan & Co. Ltd, Harcourt, Brace & World, Inc. and the Trustees of the Estate of Lord Keynes.
Reading 2 *Review of Economics and Statistics*
Reading 3 Mr R. Turvey and *Economica*
Reading 4 Kansai Economic Federation
Reading 5 *Metroeconomics*
Reading 6 American Economic Association and Mr W. A. Morton
Reading 7 University of Chicago Press
Reading 9 *Review of Economics and Statistics*
Reading 10 *Kyklos*
Reading 11 Professor E. H. Phelps Brown and *Economica*
Reading 13 The Institute of Economic Affairs Ltd
Reading 14 Princeton University Press
Reading 15 Professor A. W. Phillips and *Economica*
Reading 16 The Clarendon Press
Reading 17 Royal Economic Society
Reading 18 Harvard University Press.

Author Index

387

Author Index

Subject Index